SCOTT FORESMAN

Art

TEACHER'S EDITION
Grade 2

Robyn Montana Turner, Ph.D.
Program Author

PEARSON

Scott
Foresman

Editorial Offices: Glenview, Illinois • Parsippany, New Jersey • New York, New York

Sales Offices: Needham, Massachusetts • Duluth, Georgia • Glenview, Illinois • Coppell, Texas • Sacramento, California • Mesa, Arizona

ISBN: 0-328-08041-1

4 5 6 7 8 9 10 V064 13 12 11 10 09 08 07 06

Authors

PROGRAM AUTHORS

Robyn Montana Turner, Ph.D.

Kindergarten through Grade 6, Austin, Texas An acclaimed elementary visual arts textbook author, Dr. Turner's visual arts teaching experience spans from pre-kindergarten through graduate school. Most recently, she directed the Visual Arts Student Teacher Program at the University of Texas at Austin. Dr. Turner also conceptualizes and writes trade books for children and young adults. Her award-winning artist biographies, *Portraits of Women Artists for Children*, are featured in libraries and classrooms nationally. Her visual account of the history and culture of Texas, *Texas Traditions: The Culture of the Lone Star State*, received the Teddy Award, the state's highest honor for a children's book. Her academic publications include a chapter in the National Art Education Association anthology *Gender Issues in Art Education*, as well as contributions to the NAEA Journal *Studies in Art Education*.

Rebecca Brooks, Ph.D.

Grades 7 and 8, Austin, Texas A visual arts and art education professor and graduate advisor in the Department of Art and Art History at the University of Texas at Austin, Dr. Brooks is a nationally successful textbook author, lecturer, and researcher, focusing on the development and implementation of interdisciplinary curricula at the elementary, secondary, and college levels. The recipient of two prestigious Foxworth Fellowships from the College of Fine Arts, she received the Texas Art Education Association's Art Educator of the Year for Higher Education (1990) and the National Art Education Association's Art Educator of the Year, Western Division (1991). Currently, the former middle school art teacher remains an active liaison between the public schools and the university as Coordinator of Student Field Experiences in Art.

CONTRIBUTING AUTHORS

James Clarke, M.Ed.
Grades 6 through 8, Houston, Texas

Executive Director of the Texas Coalition for Quality Arts Education, Mr. Clarke is a successful arts educator, author, consultant, editor, and speaker. The former National Art Education Association and Texas Art Education Association President has won many NAEA honors, including the Marion Quinn Dix Award for Outstanding Leadership. He was on the National Coordinating Board for America's National Standards for Arts Education and a spokesman at the National Education Goals hearings in the 1990s.

Sara A. Chapman, Ed.D.
Grades 6 through 8, Houston, Texas

Coordinator of the Visual Arts Program for Alief Independent School District in Houston, Ms. Chapman is a successful middle school textbook author who has taught all levels of art education, including university course work. Currently Western Region Vice President of the National Art Education Association, she also served as President of the Texas Art Education Association and NAEA. She chaired the Texas Fine Arts Standards Visual Arts team and is a cadre member of the state's Center for Educator Development in the Fine Arts.

PROGRAM CONSULTANTS

Christopher Adejumo, Ph.D.
Associate Professor, Visual Art Studies
University of Texas, Austin, TX

Doug Blandy, Ph.D.
Professor and Director, Arts and Administration
Program, Institute for Community Arts and Studies
University of Oregon, Eugene, OR

Rebecca Brooks, Ph.D.
Professor, Department of Art and Art History
University of Texas, Austin, TX

Sara A. Chapman, Ed.D.
Coordinator, Visual Arts Program
Alief Independent School District, Houston, TX

James Clarke, M.Ed.
Executive Director, Texas Coalition for Quality Arts
Education, Houston, TX

Georgia Collins, Ph.D.
Professor Emeritus, College of Fine Arts
University of Kentucky, Lexington, KY

Deborah Cooper, M.Ed.
Coordinating Director of Arts Education,
Curriculum and Instruction
Charlotte-Mecklenburg Schools, Charlotte, NC

Sandra M. Epps, Ph.D.
Multicultural Art Education Consultant
New York, NY

Mary Jo Gardere, B.S.
Multi-Arts Specialist, Eladio Martinez Learning Center
Dallas, TX

Carlos G. Gómez, MFA
Professor of Fine Art, University of Texas at Brownsville
and Texas Southmost College, Brownsville, TX

Kristina Lamour, MFA
Assistant Professor, The Art Institute of Boston
at Lesley University, Boston, MA

Melinda M. Mayer, Ph.D.
Assistant Professor, School of Visual Arts
University of North Texas, Denton, TX

Robyn Montana Turner, Ph.D.
Author, Austin, TX

CRITIC READERS

Celeste Anderson
Roosevelt Elementary School, Nampa, ID

Mary Jo Birkholz
Wilson Elementary School, Janesville, WI

Mary Jane Cahalan
Mitzi Bond Elementary School, El Paso, TX

Cindy Collar
Cloverleaf Elementary School, Cartersville, GA

Yvonne Days
St. Louis Public Schools, St. Louis, MO

Shirley Dickey
Creative Art Magnet School, Houston, TX

Ray Durkee
Charlotte Performing Arts Center, Punta Gorda, FL

Sue Flores-Minick
Bryker Woods Elementary School, Austin, TX

Denise Jennings
Fulton County Schools, Atlanta, GA

Alicia Lewis
Stevens Elementary School, Houston, TX

James Miller
Margo Elementary School, Weslaco, TX

Marta Olson
Seattle Public Schools, Seattle, WA

Judy Preble
Florence Avenue School, Irvington, NJ

Tonya Roberson
Oleson Elementary School, Houston, TX

Andrew Southwick
Edgewood Independent School District, San Antonio, TX

Nita Ulaszek
Audelia Creek Elementary School, Dallas, TX

Tessie Varthas
Office of Creative and Public Art, Philadelphia, PA

Penelope Venola
Spurgeon Intermediate School, Santa Ana, CA

Elizabeth Willett
Art Specialist, Fort Worth, TX

STUDIO REVIEWERS

Judy Abbott
Art Educator, Allison Elementary School
Austin Independent School District, Austin, TX

Lin Altman
Art Educator, Cedar Creek Elementary School
Eanes Independent School District, Austin, TX

Geral T. Butler
Retired Art Educator, Heritage High School
Lynchburg City Schools, Lynchburg, VA

Dale Case
Elementary Principal, Fox Meadow Elementary School
Nettleton School District, Jonesboro, AR

Deborah McLouth
Art Educator, Zavala Elementary School
Austin Independent School District, Austin, TX

Patricia Newman
Art Educator, Saint Francis Xavier School
Archdiocese of Chicago, La Grange, IL

Nancy Sass
Art Educator, Cambridge Elementary School, Alamo
Heights Independent School District, San Antonio, TX

Sue Spiva Telle
Art Educator, Woodridge Elementary School, Alamo
Heights Independent School District, San Antonio, TX

Cari Washburn
Art Educator, Great Oaks Elementary School, Round
Rock Independent School District, Round Rock, TX

Materials that inspire!

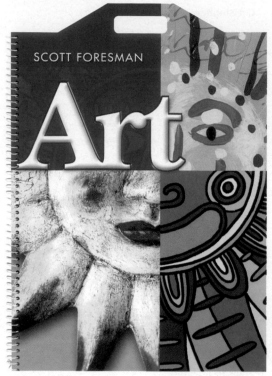

Teacher's Edition: Grade 3

STUDENT EDITION
Grades 1 through 8

- Places fine art and engaging text in students' hands

- Explores wide range of styles and media

- Exposes students to art and artists in every lesson

BIG BOOK
Kindergarten through Grade 5

- Student book pages on a larger scale

- Suitable for whole-class instruction

- Great display for center or small-group activities

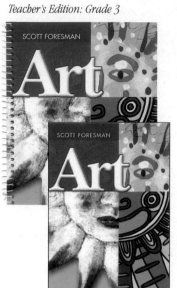

Student Edition: Grade 3   *Big Book: Grade 3*

TEACHER'S EDITION
Kindergarten through Grade 8

- Detailed overviews for flexible and easy planning

- Cross-curricular links to core disciplines

- Varied assessment options

FINE ART TRANSPARENCIES
Grades 1 through 8

- More than 1,000 images; most of the fine artworks in the program

- Ideal for Feldman Model and compare/contrast discussions

FINE ART PRINTS*
Kindergarten through Grade 8

- Laminated 18″ × 24″ prints

- Instruction and activities in English and in Spanish on the back

- Set A features artworks for Unit Openers and Unit Reviews

- Set B includes artworks for the Look and Compare activity

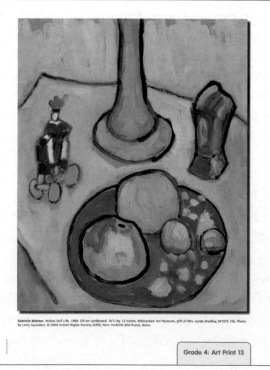

Fine Art Print: Grade 4

INSTRUCTIONAL PRINTS*
Kindergarten through Grade 8

• Fourteen colorful classroom posters with English and Spanish instruction on the back. Includes one poster for each element of art and principle of design and one classroom safety poster, available in English and in Spanish

• Grade-level sets: Kindergarten through Grade 2, Grade 3 through Grade 5, and Grade 6 through Grade 8

UNIT-BY-UNIT RESOURCES*
Kindergarten through Grade 8

• Blackline masters in English and Spanish for family letters, vocabulary, activities, games

• Unit tests and assessments in English and Spanish

TIME LINE OF ART HISTORY

• A large format, full-color time line that spans Old Stone Age through the Modern World

• Features a wide variety of media and genres

MASTER INDEX

• Comprehensive reference to simplify planning

• Cross references all fine art, artists, techniques, media, themes, and more for Grades K–8

INTEGRATED READING AND WRITING WORKBOOK AND ANSWER KEY*
Grades 1 through 8

• Integrated reading and writing activities for each unit to strengthen language arts skills

• Fiction and non-fiction passages with multiple-choice questions

• Writing exercises include writing prompts and graphic organizers

• Workbook and Answer Key available in English and in Spanish

Turn on the power of visual literacy!

Art is a powerful language that ignites imaginations and helps students to acquire critical thinking and communication skills.

Scott Foresman Art *integrates classroom instruction, hands-on activities, and literacy-building experiences to turn on the power of art for all students.* **Scott Foresman Art** *focuses on the Elements of Art and the Principles of Design, the basic tools artists use to communicate their ideas.*

Teach the basics of art

LESSONS Teach students how to explore, appreciate, and analyze the visual world and develop their artistic perception by introducing:

The Elements of Art

Line, Color, Value, Shape, Texture, Form, and Space

The Principles of Design

Balance, Rhythm, Pattern, Variety, Proportion, Emphasis, and Unity

Create art experiences

STUDIOS Involve students in the creative art process and give them an opportunity to practice the **Elements of Art** and the **Principles of Design** with age-appropriate art media and techniques. Use the Quick Studio shortcuts when time or resources are limited.

Build literacy through art

ENRICHMENT FEATURES Develop students' higher order thinking skills using the **Unit Opener, Look and Compare,** and **Artist at Work** or **Meet the Artist** features.

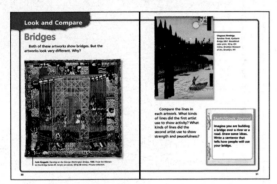

Grade 3: Look and Compare

Grade 3: Artist at Work

Assess what students learn

ASSESSMENT FEATURES

Monitor students' understanding and their development of visual literacy through hands-on **Portfolio Project** activities and written and oral responses in the **Unit Review**.

Flexible Organization

Each unit offers at least 6 Lessons, 6 Studios, Enrichment Features, and Assessment Features so you can customize curriculum.

Introduce *and motivate with engaging Fine Art in the* **Unit Opener**

> **Teach Lesson 1**
> **Create** *in* **Studio 1**
>
> **Teach Lesson 2**
> **Create** *in* **Studio 2**
>
> **Teach Lesson 3**
> **Create** *in* **Studio 3**

Enrich *with features like* **Look and Compare** *and* **Artist at Work** *or* **Meet the Artist**

> **Teach Lesson 4**
> **Create** *in* **Studio 4**
>
> **Teach Lesson 5**
> **Create** *in* **Studio 5**
>
> **Teach Lesson 6**
> **Create** *in* **Studio 6**

Enrich *with features like* **Look and Compare** *and* **Artist at Work** *or* **Meet the Artist**

Assess *with the* **Portfolio Project** *to artistically demonstrate understanding*

Assess *with the* **Unit Review** *through written and oral responses*

Teach the basics of art

Lesson 1

At a Glance

Objectives

- Identify and describe lines in artworks.
- Describe, analyze, interpret, and judge artworks.

Materials

- **Fine Art Transparency**
- jump rope
- Sketchbook Journal

Vocabulary

line, media

NVAS (K–4) #1 Understanding and applying media, techniques, and processes
NVAS (K–4) #2 Using knowledge of structures and functions
NVAS (K–4) #4 Understanding the visual arts in relation to history and cultures

National Visual Arts Standards

Discover at a glance how lesson skills correlate to national standards.

3-Step Lesson Plan

Get students thinking like artists with easy-to-follow, structured instruction.

1 Introduce

Place a jump rope on the floor. Stretch it tight so that it creates a straight line. Then let students use the rope to demonstrate lines that curve, bend, wave, zigzag, or spiral.

Next, have students look for lines in objects and artworks found in the classroom. Point out broad, straight lines in an artwork or on a student's shirt. Compare those to fine, straight lines found on a sheet of notebook paper. Then have students identify other types of lines in natural and human-made objects that they see in the classroom.

Lesson 1

Line

A **line** is a continuous mark on a surface. Most lines are created by a pen, a pencil, or a brush. Find thick, thin, and wavy lines in this painting.

Vincent van Gogh.
The Café Terrace on the Place du Forum Arles, at Night, 1888. Oil on canvas, 31½ by 25⅜ inches. Rijksmuseum Kröller-Müller, Otterlo, Netherlands.

18

 Art Background

Art History During the Impressionist era, artists attempted to show light as we see it outdoors. They used thick brushstrokes and vivid colors. Although his brushwork shows the influence of the Impressionists, Vincent van Gogh developed his own style that emphasized swirling brushstrokes and intense colors.

ESL Notes

Have students take turns drawing each kind of line on the board. Ask them yes and no questions about each line. Or give them directives that call for a nonverbal response. For example, **Is this a straight line?** or **This is a wavy line. Draw another wavy line.**

Transparency 3-18a

Vincent van Gogh. *The Café Terrace on the Place du Forum Arles, at Night*, 1888. Oil on canvas, 31½ by 25⅜ inches. Rijksmuseum Kröller-Müller, Otterlo, Netherlands.

© Pearson Scott Foresman

Fine Art Transparencies

Provide large visual models for class discussions. Transparency size is 5.5" × 8.5".

18

Grade 3: Teacher's Edition

Types of Lines

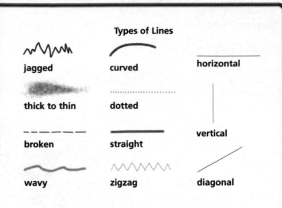

jagged   curved   horizontal

thick to thin   dotted

broken   straight   vertical

wavy   zigzag   diagonal

Horizontal lines show a peaceful scene. Vertical lines suggest strength. Diagonal lines bring motion and energy to an artwork. Find these three kinds of lines in Van Gogh's painting.

Artists use different **media** to create artworks. Van Gogh chose oil paints as his medium. Other media are pencils, paints, chalk, clay, and crayons.

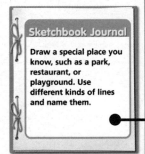

Sketchbook Journal

Draw a special place you know, such as a park, restaurant, or playground. Use different kinds of lines and name them.

19

Curriculum Connection

Science Have students look for lines on animals. Explain that lines and colors on animals can help protect them from predators and disguise them from prey. The brightly colored stripes on a snake warn others to stay away because the snake might be venomous. The lines on a tiger make it more difficult to detect in the wild. Have students use reference sources to find pictures of animals whose markings show examples of curved, dotted, straight, wavy, or zigzag lines.

---

❷ Teach

Have students read page 18 and the credit line. Tell students that one way to identify the main idea in an artwork is to describe the setting. Ask:

- **What do you see in this painting?** (people eating at an outside café) DESCRIBE
- **What art tools and media did Van Gogh use?** (paintbrushes, oil paints) ANALYZE

After students read page 19, demonstrate how a line can be made by moving an art tool across a surface. Review different kinds of lines, then ask:

- **What kinds of lines did the artist use to make objects appear rough and bumpy?** (curved, broken) ANALYZE
- **How would the painting be different if the artist had shown the café during the day instead of at night?** (Possible response: It would have had brighter colors and more people.) INTERPRET
- **Which lines are the most interesting to you? Why?** (Possible response: curved lines in the sidewalk; because Van Gogh used a simple curved line to show a rocky surface) JUDGE

Sketchbook Journal Tell students to experiment with different media to see which ones work best for creating each kind of line.

❸ Close

After students complete their sketches, have them label the different types of lines they used.

Assessment Play a game of Eye Spy. Have students take turns giving clues about lines in objects to help classmates guess the objects.

The Feldman Model

Use an easy four-step process
DESCRIBE, ANALYZE, INTERPRET, JUDGE
to guide students' responses to visual art and develop higher order thinking skills.

Sketchbook Journal

Provide an opportunity for students to record ideas and demonstrate understanding of art concepts.

Curriculum Connection

Introduce activities that help students relate art to other disciplines.

Assessment Opportunity

Evaluate student understanding of content and correlate to national standards.

Studio 1

At a Glance

Objectives

- Express ideas by drawing favorite foods.
- Demonstrate different techniques for drawing.
- Evaluate original artworks by self and peers.

Materials

- pencils, pens, crayons, water-based markers, drawing paper
- Rubric 1 from **Unit-by-Unit Resources**

NVAS (K–4) #1 Understanding and applying media, techniques, and processes
NVAS (K–4) #2 Using knowledge of structures and functions
NVAS (K–4) #6 Making connections between visual arts and other disciplines

Technique Tip

Offer easy ideas for using art tools so students can connect the process with their results.

3-Step Studio

Empower students to think and act like artists by presenting the creative process in simple terms.

Meeting Individual Needs

Include all students in studio experiences by adapting to individual needs.

① Introduce

Review types of lines. Have students use their own experiences to describe types of lines and give examples.

Then have students brainstorm a list of favorite foods. Tell them they can use their experiences with food to create an artwork. Ask:

- **What favorite foods are part of a well-balanced meal?**
- **What do these foods look like?**
- **What kinds of lines will you use to show each food item?**

Quick Studio

Offer a quick alternative to the full studio using easy-to-find materials.

Quick Studio

Have students draw two food items on a white, paper plate. Remind them to use a variety of lines in their drawings.

Studio 1

Draw Lines

What are your favorite foods? Do you like tacos best or colorful salads? Follow these steps to draw them.

1 Draw a large plate shape. Decorate the edge with many kinds of lines.

2 Draw a glass and a drink. Add your favorite foods to the plate.

Technique Tip

Use the tip of the marker to make thin lines and dots. Use the side of the marker to make thick lines.

20

🏃 Meeting Individual Needs

Inclusion Some students with physical disabilities may not be able to draw the pictures as shown. Provide a drawn plate where students can add lines to the edge. Allow students to look through magazines to find foods for their plates. You may want to assign partners who can help cut and paste pictures.

20

Grade 3: Teacher's Edition

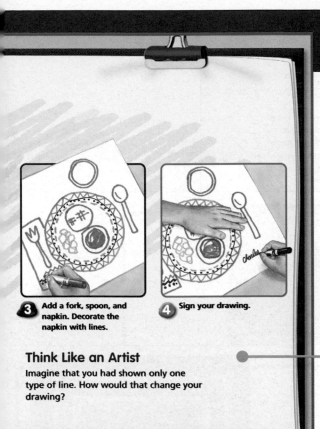

3 Add a fork, spoon, and napkin. Decorate the napkin with lines.

4 Sign your drawing.

Think Like an Artist

Imagine that you had shown only one type of line. How would that change your drawing?

Fine Arts Connection

Music There are many kinds of lines in music. Sing together "Row, Row, Row Your Boat." Point out the place in the song in which the notes form a diagonal line as they go down the scale. (Life is but a dream) Draw these notes on the board, pointing out the line. Then sing the notes again.

Life is but a dream.

Sing other familiar songs, such as "Make New Friends" or "This Old Man." Listen for notes that form a diagonal or horizontal line. If possible, let students play the notes on a piano, xylophone, or with bells.

---

② Create

Have students read the directions on pages 20–21. Then distribute materials.

- Have students draw a circle inside the plate to indicate the inside edge of the border.
- Remind students to think about the shapes of their favorite foods. Help them name the kinds of lines they should use.
- As they add details to their drawings, remind them that the fork goes on the left and the spoon goes to the right of the plate.
- Encourage students to use their best handwriting.

Technique Tip Show students ways to hold a marker to draw thick or thin lines. If using a crayon, students can remove the paper and draw with the side to make broad lines.

③ Close

Have students identify their general intent and then reflect on their work by answering the *Think Like an Artist* question. (Possible response: Using only one type of line would make my drawing boring.)

Encourage students to share their work with classmates. Have them name the different kinds of lines they see in each other's drawings.

Ongoing Assessment

If . . . students have difficulty drawing light and thin lines,

then . . . suggest that they decrease the pressure applied to the art tool as they draw.

See page 18 from **Unit-by-Unit Resources** for a rubric to assess this studio.

Studio Instruction
Engage students in the creative process using detailed, step-by-step instructions that are right on the student page.

Ongoing Assessment
Use exclusive "If . . . then" tip to intervene instantly and help students if they experience difficulty.

Rubric
Use specific criteria to analyze and evaluate student artworks.

Unit 1 *Art All Around You* **21**

Build literacy through art

Unit 1

Art All Around You

Artists find ideas for art everywhere. They use **elements of art,** or line, color, shape, value, texture, form, and space, to turn ideas into an artwork. These elements are organized in special ways by using the **principles of design,** or unity, variety,

Faith Ringgold. *Tar Beach*, 19... pieced fabric border, 74 by 69...

16

Look and Compare

Bridges

Both of these artworks show bridges. But the artworks look very different. Why?

Utagawa Hiroshige. *Bamboo Yards, Kyobashi Bridge,* 1857. Woodblock color print, 36 by 23⅜ inches. Brooklyn Museum of Art, Brooklyn, NY.

Faith Ringgold. *Dancing on the Bridge Series #5.* ...

30

Artist at Work

Story Cloths

Yang Fang Nhu is an artist with many stories to tell. She uses fabrics, or cloths, and fibers, such as thread and yarn. Look at the story cloth she made to tell about a long journey from China to Laos.

To make her artwork, Fang Nhu sewed pictures and symbols onto a large piece of cotton cloth. This story cloth shows her people, the Hmong (mung), walking to their new homeland. Follow the path they take with your finger.

Some artists, like Fang Nhu, use fabric and fibers in their work. Can you think of another career in which people work with fabric and fibers? Hint: Look at the clothes you are wearing!

Yang Fang Nhu makes story cloths.

Yang Fang Nhu. *Story Cloth,* 1978 (Hmong). Embroidered on cotton, 55 by 38 inches. Photograph by Michael Monteaux. International Folk Art Foundation Collections at the Museum of International Folk Art, Santa Fe, NM.

44

45

Unit Opener

Use motivating and engaging fine art as a springboard for discussions and language-building activities.

Look and Compare

Develop appreciation for history and cultures, as well as diverse art styles, and build higher order thinking skills with thought-provoking discussions.

Artist at Work

Help students relate art to the real world by sharing the experiences of artists and their careers.

Grade 3: Student Editio

Kindergarten through Grade 8:
Unit Opener, Look and Compare, Artist at Work or **Meet the Artist, Portfolio Project, Unit Review**

Portfolio Project

Create Scratch Art

Make a scratch art picture of a neighborhood scene. Before you begin, decide whether your picture will be symmetrical or asymmetrical.

1 Use crayons to cover a piece of tag board with lines and shapes. Use many colors.

2 Paint over the lines and shapes with black tempera paint.

3

4

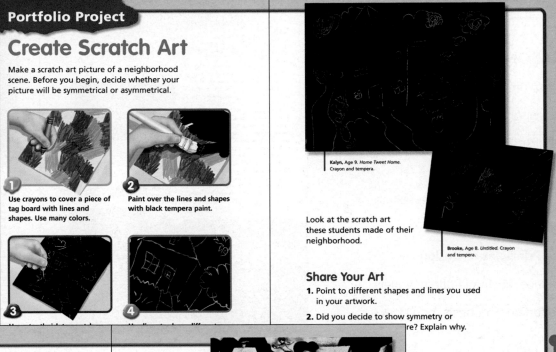

Kalyn, Age 9. *Home Tweet Home.* Crayon and tempera.

Look at the scratch art these students made of their neighborhood.

Brooke, Age 8. *Untitled.* Crayon and tempera.

Share Your Art

1. Point to different shapes and lines you used in your artwork.

2. Did you decide to show symmetry or ...re? Explain why.

47

Unit Review

Think About Art

Read the art words. Then point to a picture that matches each word.

shape	texture	negative space
asymmetry	detail	radial balance

Write About Art

Choose an artwork from one of the lessons in Unit 1. What lines, shapes, and textures do you like in it? Write about them.

Talk About Art

- Choose an artwork from your portfolio. Maybe it was the most fun or the hardest to do.
- Tell a partner how you feel about it, and why. Use words and ideas from this unit.

48

Marc Chagall. *The Musician,* 1912–1913. Oil on canvas, 74 by 62½ inches. Stedelijk Museum, Amsterdam, Netherlands.

Put It All Together

1. What lines and shapes did the artist use?

2. Is the painting balanced? Explain your answer.

3. What does the painting make you think about?

4. Do you like the way the artist expressed his ideas and feelings? Tell why.

49

Portfolio Project

Provide an opportunity for creative expression, problem solving, and demonstration of skills and concepts.

Grade 3: Student Edition

Unit Review

Monitor students' development of visual literacy with a variety of written and oral assessments. **Think, Write,** *and* **Talk About Art** *activities and* **Put It All Together** *give all students an opportunity to demonstrate what they've learned.*

Teach the basics of art

LESSONS Teach students how to explore, appreciate, and analyze the visual world and develop their artistic perception by introducing:

The Elements of Art

Line, Color, Value, Shape, Texture, Form, and Space

The Principles of Design

Balance, Rhythm, Pattern, Variety, Proportion, Emphasis, and Unity

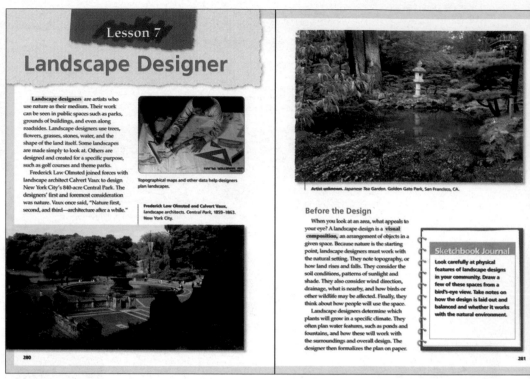

Grade 7: Student Edition, Careers in Art Unit

Create art experiences

STUDIOS Involve students in the creative art process and give them an opportunity to practice the Elements of Art and the Principles of Design with age-appropriate art media and techniques. Use the Quick Studio shortcuts when time or resources are limited.

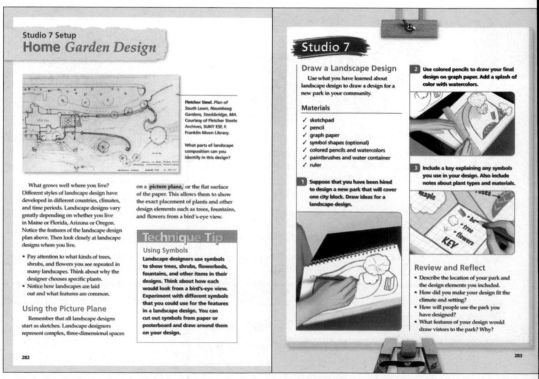

Grade 7: Student Edition, Careers in Art Unit

Build literacy through art

ENRICHMENT FEATURES

Develop students' higher order thinking skills using the **Unit Opener, Look and Compare,** and **Artist at Work** or **Meet the Artist** features.

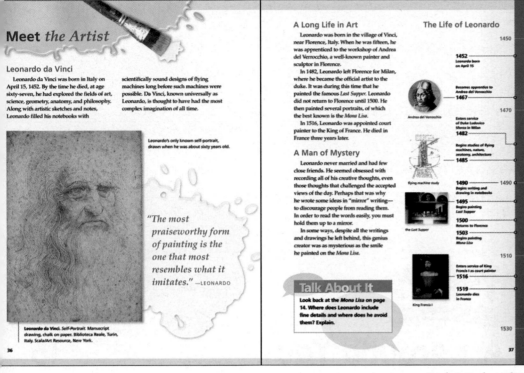

Grade 7: Student Edition

Assess what students learn

ASSESSMENT FEATURES

Monitor students' understanding and their development of visual literacy through hands-on **Portfolio Project** activities and written and oral responses in the **Unit Review.**

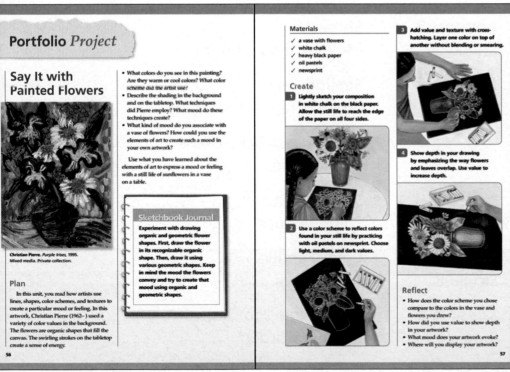

Grade 8: Student Edition

Contents

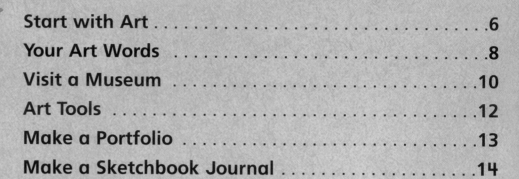

Unit 1

Art Around You 16

André Derain.
London Bridge,
1906.

Unit 2

Art Is Everywhere **50**

Kenojuak Ashevak.
The Return of the Sun, 1961.

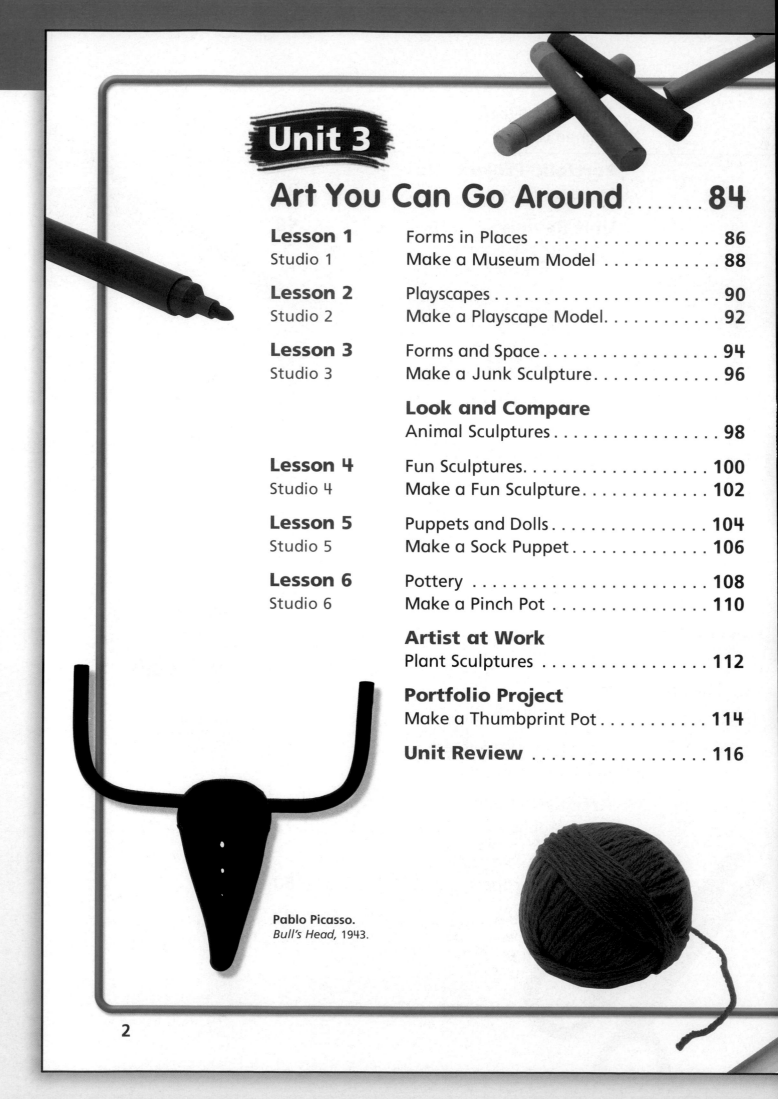

Unit 3

Art You Can Go Around 84

Pablo Picasso.
Bull's Head, 1943.

Unit 4

Creative Expression............118

Winslow Homer.
Breezing Up,
1873–1876.

3

Unit 5

Art of All Sizes 152

Artist unknown.
Firehouse Door.

Unit 6

Types of Artworks 186

Katherine Westphal.
*Unveiling of the
Statue of Liberty,
1964.*

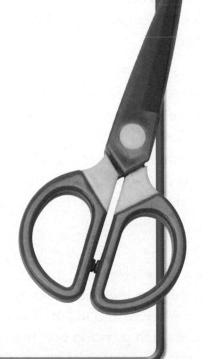

Start with Art

At a Glance

Objectives

- Identify art as a form of expression.
- Understand that art is everywhere in the environment.
- Generate ideas for art.

Vocabulary

artworks

NVAS (K–4) #3 Choosing and evaluating a range of subject matter, symbols, and ideas

Introduce

Tell children that all they have to do to see art is to look around them. Art is not just drawings, paintings, and sculptures. Buildings or chairs can be artworks. So can photographs and comic books. Ask: **What artworks do you see in the classroom? What have you seen at home? What types have you created?**

Lead children in a discussion about the child-made artwork on page 6. Identify the objects and subjects from the environment used by the child in this artwork. (objects: flowers, trees, clouds; subject: nature) Ask volunteers to draw similar objects on the chalkboard. Ask others to draw different objects. Talk about how each child's drawing varies from everyone else's.

Refer to the artworks on page 7 and ask children to identify what seems to be happening in each artwork. Point out to children that artists use their artworks to express themselves and to tell stories. Say, for example, **The Hayden painting tells the story of a man who paints a portrait of his family.** Ask children to tell the story of the other artworks.

"A picture is worth a thousand words." You may have heard someone say this. It is a reminder of the power of art. Some art communicates beyond words.

Is it any wonder that the meaning of art is hard to explain?

Most people agree that:

- artists make art
- their works are called **artworks**
- artworks show ideas and feelings

6

 Notes

Tell children that artists often use their artworks to tell stories about individuals and families. Provide several examples of both. Use photographs from magazines or child-made artworks. Help children understand the differences between *individuals* and *families*. As you show each example, say either *individual* or *family* to describe it. Ask children to name which they prefer to create artworks about individuals or families.

Artists find inspiration for artworks in many places. Some artists show families in their artworks.

You are an artist. What ideas or feelings would you show in a drawing of a family?

7

👫👫 Meeting Individual Needs

Reteach Children may use their senses to physically explore objects or artworks in the classroom. Allow children to handle objects and artworks and describe how they look, feel, sound, or smell. Lead children in describing how artworks they have seen in the past looked, felt, sounded, or smelled. Ask: **In an artwork that you are making, how might you express what your senses tell you?**

Explore

Direct children's attention to Henry Moore's sculpture on page 7. Ask them to describe what they see. (Possible responses: a family group; two parents and two children) Ask: **If you made a sculpture of a family group, what would the family members be doing? How would they look?**

Ask children to identify what the painter is painting in Palmer Hayden's artwork. (a portrait of a woman and child, probably the painter's wife and child) Ask: **Who would you like to paint a portrait of?** Encourage children to elaborate on their responses, describing how the subject of the portrait would be posed, what the person would be doing, and how the person would look.

Now ask children to describe what they see in Malcah Zeldis's painting. (Possible responses: Nine people around a large table; a family at Thanksgiving dinner.) Ask: **How is this scene different than the other family scenes on this page?** (Possible responses: It is more colorful. The people seem happier.) Brainstorm with children about other ways to show families. What stories would the artworks tell?

Develop Ideas for Artworks Artists rely on *all* of their senses when exploring their environment. Demonstrate this by holding up a piece of fruit, such as an orange. Lead children in describing how it looks, feels, smells, tastes, and sounds. Point out that artists ask these questions as they think about and plan artworks.

Close

Have children tell what kind of story they would like to show in an artwork. What ideas or feelings would the artwork include?

Your Art Words

At a Glance

Objectives

- Identify elements of art and principles of design.

Vocabulary

line, space, form, texture, shape, value, color, emphasis, proportion, variety, pattern, rhythm, balance, unity

NVAS (K–4) #1 Understanding and applying media, techniques, and processes

NVAS (K–4) #2 Using knowledge of structures and functions

NVAS (K–4) #5 Reflecting upon and assessing the characteristics and merits of their work and the work of others

Introduce

After children read pages 8–9, help them access prior knowledge by offering their ideas about what each word means. Explain to them that each word also has a meaning that applies specifically to art.

Point out that the words on pages 8 and 9 will help them better understand and talk about artworks. Model for children how vocabulary helps them talk about art by writing the word *space* on the chalkboard. Ask children what they think the word means. (Possible responses: room to move around or the area beyond Earth's atmosphere) Then tell children the art definition of *space* and write it on the chalkboard. (the empty area surrounding an object) Walk around your desk or some other central object in the room. Explain that you have been in the space around the object. Shapes and forms are defined by the space around them.

There are many words artists use to talk about art. You will see some of these art words in your book. They are shown in **yellow.** It is helpful to know these art words when you talk about art.

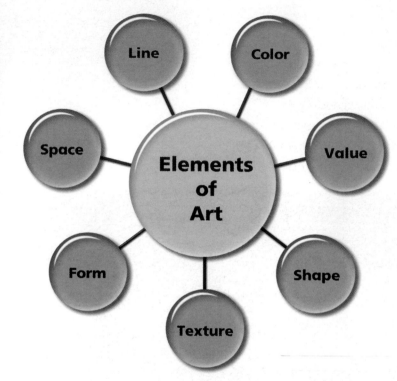

These art words name parts of an artwork.

8

 Notes

Help children understand that many of the art words on pages 8–9 may have different meanings than what they know. Say, for example, **a form in art is a three-dimensional object.** Show children an example of a form and let them explore it. Say the name of the form, such as cube, several times and ask children to repeat after you. Continue by discussing other multiple meaning art words.

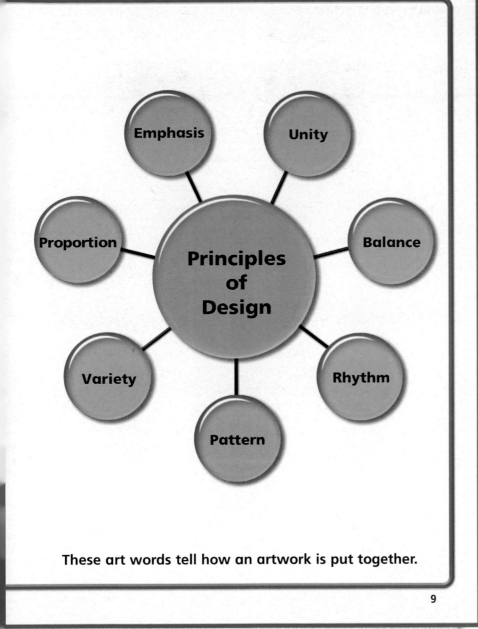

These art words tell how an artwork is put together.

Explore

Display an **Art Print** or direct children's attention to an artwork in the Student Edition. Point out each of the elements of art and principles of design that you can find in the chosen artwork.

If children have trouble with an individual element or principle, point out examples in other artworks. For example, refer children to Zeldis's painting on page 7 to talk about color. Or refer to Hayden's painting on page 7 to show examples of texture.

Identify Elements in Peer Art Model how to identify ideas in a peer's artwork by discussing the child-made artwork on page 6. First make comments on the subject. Then identify as many elements of art and principles of design that are evident in the artwork.

Extend the lesson by providing partners with a child-made artwork from a previous class. Have them identify ideas about the artwork. Remind children to treat their peers' artworks with respect.

Close

Ask children to name or point out objects in the classroom that show or relate to each element of art and principle of design.

🚶🚶🚶 Meeting Individual Needs

Extend Tactile learners might benefit from a more hands-on approach to understanding some of the art words. Cut a variety of shapes of different sizes from wrapping paper and fabric. Choose wrapping paper with bold, colorful patterns and fabrics with interesting textures, such as corduroy and velour. Model the activity by pointing out the color, shape, texture, pattern, and lines of one or two examples of paper or fabric. Then ask children to identify any of the art words that apply to the other samples.

Visit a Museum

At a Glance

Objectives

• Explore the role of art museums.

NVAS (K–4) #2 Using knowledge of structures and functions

NVAS (K–4) #3 Choosing and evaluating a range of subject matter, symbols, and ideas

NVAS (K–4) #5 Reflecting upon and assessing the characteristics and merits of their work and the work of others

Introduce

After children read page 11, talk about art museums. Let them share whatever they know or have experienced. Ask: **What was different about seeing artworks in person, compared with seeing them in a book or on a poster?** (Possible responses: artworks viewed in person seem more bright or colorful; texture is easier to identify in person; books show artwork in different sizes than the original; and so on.)

Summarize for children: **Art museums are places where people can view art exhibitions. An art exhibition is a display of several or many artworks in one location.** Point out that exhibitions can take place in many different spaces, including art museums, galleries, office buildings, or classrooms. Remind children that art exhibitions can include artworks by any artist, whether they are children in a classroom or professional artists.

Rosa Bonheur. (Detail) *Rabbits Nibbling Carrots,* 1840. Oil on canvas, 21¼ by 25½ inches. Photograph by Lysiane Gauthier/©Musee des Beaux-Arts de Bordeaux.

10

 Career Research

Guest Speaker Ask a museum curator or docent to speak in your classroom about what he or she does each day and what training or education the job requires. Have children prepare questions for the speaker ahead of time.

Field Trip Take children on a field trip to see an art exhibition. If there is not a local museum, you could take children to an alternative exhibition space, such as a community building or office building. Be sure to provide opportunity for children to identify ideas in the exhibition. Model identifying ideas first. Say, for example, **The artworks in this exhibition were made of many different media. It was interesting to see the variety of sizes of the artworks, too.**

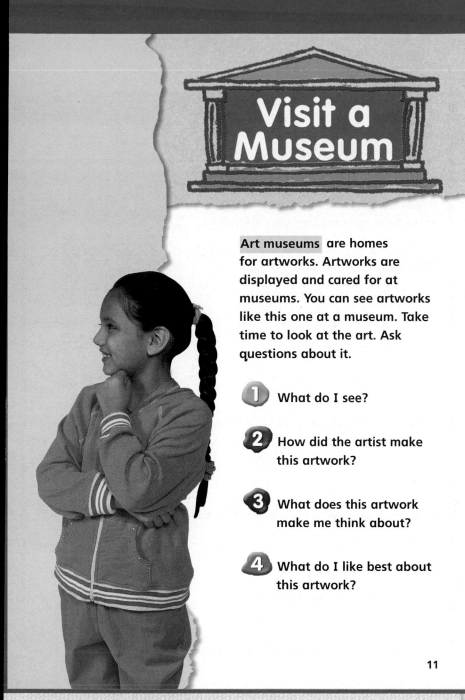

Art museums are homes for artworks. Artworks are displayed and cared for at museums. You can see artworks like this one at a museum. Take time to look at the art. Ask questions about it.

1 What do I see?

2 How did the artist make this artwork?

3 What does this artwork make me think about?

4 What do I like best about this artwork?

11

 Gallery Options

Classroom Exhibition Create an art museum space right in the classroom. Choose a theme for the exhibition, or allow children to choose an artwork of which they are proud. Have children help you arrange the display space and mount and/or hang the artworks. Each artwork should have a label that includes the artist's name, title of work, and the medium or media. When children are in the "art museum," they should observe the rules of museum etiquette. Give children an opportunity to identify ideas in their peers' exhibition. Remind children to ask themselves questions (see page 11) as they view the artworks. Then summarize their ideas about the entire exhibition.

Explore

Use the artwork on page 10 to model for children how to identify ideas in original artworks. Tell children that they can better understand artworks by looking closely and by silently asking questions like those on page 11. Here are some additional questions:

- Who made this artwork? What is the title?
- Which part of the artwork first catches my attention?
- Does the artwork tell a story? If so, what is it?
- How does the artwork make me feel?

Point out that these types of questions can also help them define reasons for preferences in personal artwork as well as in artworks by peers and professionals.

Museum Etiquette

Tell children that they should follow certain rules when they visit a museum.

- Talk softly so you do not disturb others.
- Never touch an artwork.
- Do not walk in front of someone who is viewing an artwork.
- Do not take food or drinks into a museum.
- Do not photograph artworks; flash photography can damage artworks.
- Leave backpacks and book bags elsewhere. Bulky objects can swing into artworks and damage them.

Close

Have children view an artwork and share with the class one question they would ask themselves about it.

Art Tools

At a Glance

Objectives

- Understand how to use a variety of art tools.
- Assemble a portfolio.

Materials

- Various art materials as shown on Student Edition page 12
- poster board
- markers and crayons
- tape

NVAS (K–4) #1 Understanding and applying media, techniques, and processes

NVAS (K–4) #3 Choosing and evaluating a range of subject matter, symbols, and ideas

NVAS (K–4) #5 Reflecting upon and assessing the characteristics and merits of their work and the work of others

Introduce

After reading page 12, ask volunteers to name the tools shown. Ask children if they have ever used any of these tools. Encourage them to model how they used the tools. Let children handle the art tools you have on display.

Explain to children that art tools can produce drawings, paintings, prints, constructions, and modeled forms with a variety of art materials. Describe some of the types of artworks that can be created with the tools on display or pictured on page 12. Discuss other tools, as well, such as oil pastels for drawing or stamps for making prints.

Model how some of the tools work. For example, show how different types of pencils make different line widths. Or show children how to look through the viewfinder of a camera to "frame" a photograph or focus on a detail.

Art Tools

Artists use different art tools to make different types of art. You will use some of these tools as you make your artworks.

These tools are used for drawing.

These tools are used for painting.

These tools are used for cutting, taping, and pasting.

These tools are used for working with clay.

This tool is used for taking photographs.

 Home Connection

Tell children that they do not have to go to a store to get art tools. Have them look around their homes for art tools they might already have, such as paintbrushes, plastic forks and knives, paper or fabric scraps. Encourage children to share artworks they make at home with the class.

Make a Portfolio

Artists often keep samples of their artworks in a portfolio. Follow these steps to make your own portfolio.

1

Use two sheets of poster board. Write your name across the top of one sheet.

2

Place one sheet over the other. Be sure your name is on the front.

3

Tape the bottom and sides together.

4

Use crayons and markers to decorate your portfolio.

13

🏃 Meeting Individual Needs

Inclusion Some children may have difficulty holding thin-handled tools. Bulk up any thin handles by cutting foam pipe insulation into four-inch lengths and sliding them over the handles. Work with an occupational therapist or a physical therapist to adapt art tools for children with physical challenges.

Explore

Make a Portfolio After children read the steps on page 13, brainstorm ideas for applying personal designs to their portfolios. You might write the elements of art on the board and talk about how children could use or show some or all of the elements on their portfolios.

Analyze Portfolios Tell children that their portfolios can be used for more than just holding and protecting artworks. They can study the artworks in their portfolio to help them define reasons for preferences in their personal artwork. For example, a child might find that she prefers artworks with certain colors or subjects. Another child might discover that he prefers mixed-media artworks to single-medium artworks.

Point out that monitoring their progress can help children identify and practice skills necessary for producing a variety of artworks and then apply these improved skills to future artworks. In addition, studying their own artwork can help children learn to identify ideas in original artworks, portfolios, and exhibitions by peers and professional artists.

Encourage children to share the artworks in their portfolios with classmates, friends, and family. Remind them to be respectful when discussing ideas about artworks.

Close

Have children demonstrate the use of an art tool of their choosing.

Sketchbook Journal

At a Glance

Objectives

- Create a personal Sketchbook Journal.
- Express ideas and feelings in artworks.

Materials

- drawing paper
- construction paper
- markers or other art tools and materials
- stapler

NVAS (K–4) #1 Understanding and applying media, techniques, and processes

NVAS (K–4) #3 Choosing and evaluating a range of subject matter, symbols, and ideas

Introduce

Explain that artists use Sketchbook Journals to record what their senses tell them about the objects and subjects in their environment. Tell children that a Sketchbook Journal will be a place to sketch ideas and write down their thoughts about their environment. After children read page 14, ask: **Where do you think the artist might have been when he made these sketches? Why do you think he made several sketches of the animal's head?** Point out that Sketchbook Journals are good places to practice and try new ideas.

Ask a volunteer to read the steps on page 15 aloud. Brainstorm ideas for different ways to express themselves. Model for children by discussing your favorite colors, shapes, and lines and how you might show them on your own Sketchbook Journal. Help children brainstorm about objects or subjects in their environment that they find appealing or interesting. Talk about how the objects and subjects vary from child to child. Then remind them to use this information to decide what personal designs to add to their Sketchbook Journals.

Make a Sketchbook Journal

Artists often use sketchbooks to draw pictures or to write words about their ideas. A sketchbook is an art tool. A small sketchbook idea can lead to a much larger artwork.

Georges Seurat. *Seven Monkeys,* 1884. Conté crayon on white paper, 11³⁄₄ by 9¹⁄₁₆ inches. Musée du Louvre, Paris.

14

 ESL Notes

English language learners can use their Sketchbook Journals to reinforce new art vocabulary. Whenever they come across a new art term, they can write the word, its pronunciation, and its definition in their Sketchbook Journals. Tell them to provide an example beside each word and definition. For instance, children could draw different types of lines beside the word *line*.

Follow these steps to make your own Sketchbook Journal.

Fold eight sheets of drawing paper in half.

Staple the sheets together along the fold.

Fold and staple a construction paper cover.

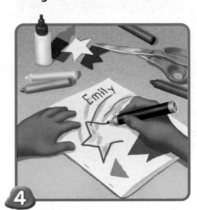

Decorate the cover. Write your name on it.

15

👫👫 Meeting Individual Needs

Extend Offer children alternative approaches to creating their Sketchbook Journals. For example, they could bind their journals with yarn woven through holes, or they could use cardboard instead of construction paper for the cover.

Explore

Tell children that it is important to both draw and write in their Sketchbook Journals. For example, an artist might quickly draw a picture of a girl playing soccer in the rain. Next to the sketch, the artist might take notes about the color of the girl's uniform, the shape of her face, or the feel of wet grass against the skin. Sketches and notes like these can help artists figure out how to express their ideas and feelings in their artworks.

Stress to children that they should be aware of all their senses, not just their sense of sight. Explain that notes about how things smell, taste, sound, or feel can help them express ideas and feelings in their artworks.

Model this by recalling a community event that you attended, such as a concert or festival. Describe to children all the sensory details that you can recall about the event. With the class, brainstorm different ways to show these details in an artwork.

Ask children to think about a recent special occasion, such as a birthday or holiday celebration. What things did they see? What sounds did they hear? What aromas did they smell? What did the food taste like? What did the clothes they were wearing feel like? Tell children that paying attention to all of their senses will help them get ideas to use in their artworks.

Close

Have children display their Sketchbook Journals for their classmates. Remind them to be respectful of other people's artworks, both in terms of handling it and in terms of commenting on its qualities.

Unit 1 Overview

Our world is full of objects that provide inspiration to artists. Artists use ideas from the people, places, and things around them to create artworks. In this unit, children will explore how artists get their ideas. They will also lines, shapes, and colors to create their own artworks.

	Unit Opener, p. 16	Lesson 1, p. 18 Line Studio 1, p. 20 Draw Different Lines	Lesson 2, p. 22 Shape Studio 2, p. 24 Make Animal Shapes	Lesson 3, p. 26 Feeling Texture Studio 3, p. 28 Make a Texture Rubbing	Look and Compare, p. 30 River Scenes
Artworks	 **Mary Cassatt.** *Children Playing on the Beach*, 1884.	 **Katsushika Hokusai.** *The Great Wave Off Kanagawa*, 1823–1829.	 **Paul Klee.** *Cat and Bird*, 1928.	 **Albrecht Dürer.** *Rhinoceros*, 1515.	 **André Derain.** *London Bridge*, 1906. **Mary Cassatt.** *The Boating Party*, 1893–1894.
Vocabulary	artwork	line	shapes, collage	texture, tactile textures	
Materials	• **Art Print 1** • **Fine Art Transparency** • **Instructional Prints**	• **Fine Art Transparency** • long pieces of yarn • Sketchbook Journal • drawing paper • crayons, pencils, pens, water-based markers	• **Fine Art Transparency** • pipe cleaners ⚠ • Sketchbook Journal • manila paper cut into 3-by-3-inch squares • scissors ⚠, glue, crayons, colored construction paper	• **Fine Art Transparency** • textured objects • Sketchbook Journal • drawing paper • crayons without wrappers • a variety of textured materials (sandpaper, wire screening, wrinkled and flattened aluminum foil, plastic mesh, produce bags, lace, corrugated cardboard) ⚠	• **Art Prints 1, 2, 3** • **Fine Art Transparency** • Sketchbook Journal
Connections	**Home Connection** family activities **Bookshelf** *Come Look with Me: Enjoying Art with Children* by Gladys S. Blizzard, Lickle Publishing Inc., 1991	**Curriculum Connection** Physical Education: lines in hopscotch **ESL Notes** **Fine Arts Connection** Dance: lines in movements **Meeting Individual Needs** Reteach, Extend	**Curriculum Connection** Math: geometric and organic shapes **ESL Notes** **Fine Arts Connection** Theatre: animal scripts **Meeting Individual Needs** Inclusion	**Curriculum Connection** Science: textures in nature **ESL Notes** **Fine Arts Connection** Music: texture in instruments **Meeting Individual Needs** Reteach, Extend	**Reading Strategy** Identify detail
Assessment Opportunities		Visual Culture Rubric 1 from **Unit-by-Unit Resources** Ongoing Assessment	Informal Assessment Rubric 1 from **Unit-by-Unit Resources** Ongoing Assessment	Informal Assessment Rubric 1 from **Unit-by-Unit Resources** Ongoing Assessment	

Lesson 4, p. 32 **Seeing Texture** **Studio 4, p. 34** Paint Texture	Lesson 5 p. 36 **Color Families** **Studio 5, p. 38** Mix Colors	Lesson 6, p. 40 **Warm and Cool Colors** **Studio 6, p. 42** Make a Garden	Artist at Work, p. 44 **Stained Glass**	Portfolio Project, p. 46 **Make a Diorama**	Unit Review, p. 48
Rosa Bonheur. *The King of the Desert,* 19th century.	**Stanton Macdonald-Wright.** *Conception Synchromy,* 1914.	**Janet Fish.** *Jonathan and Lorraine,* 1988.	**Sarah Hightower.** *Mr. Bubbles.*		**Joan Miró.** *Woman with Three Hairs Surrounded by Birds in the Night,* 1972.
visual texture	colors, primary colors, secondary colors, intermediate colors	mood, warm colors, cool colors			
• Fine Art Transparency • animal magazines • paintbrushes, muffin tins or palettes • liquid tempera paints, white paper, paper towels	• Fine Art Transparency • Sketchbook Journal • red, blue, and yellow liquid tempera paints • muffin tins or palettes • paintbrushes	• Fine Art Transparency • Sketchbook Journal • warm and cool colors of oil pastels • heavy white paper • cotton swabs or tissues • warm and cool colors of tempera wash (thin, diluted paint) • paintbrushes, muffin tins	• Fine Art Transparency • photographs of stained-glass windows (optional) • Sketchbook Journal	• shoeboxes, tagboard, scissors ⚠ • tempera paints in warm colors (red, orange, yellow) and cool colors (blue, green, violet) • paintbrushes, clear tape • Sketchbook Journal	• Art Print 4 • Fine Art Transparency
Curriculum Connection Social Studies: visual texture in community objects **ESL Notes** **Fine Arts Connection** Theatre: visual texture in theatre backdrops **Meeting Individual Needs** Extend	**Technology** Computerized colors **ESL Notes** **Fine Arts Connection** Music: sing color songs **Meeting Individual Needs** Inclusion	**Curriculum Connection** Social Studies: neighborhood place mural **ESL Notes** **Fine Arts Connection** Theatre: flower role play **Meeting Individual Needs** Inclusion	**Career Research** Stained-glass artists **Reading Strategy** Identify details	**Gallery Options** Art exhibition **Meeting Individual Needs** Reteach, Extend	
Informal Assessment Rubric 1 from **Unit-by-Unit Resources** Ongoing Assessment	Visual Culture Rubric 1 from **Unit-by-Unit Resources** Ongoing Assessment	Informal Assessment Rubric 1from **Unit-by-Unit Resources** Ongoing Assessment		Rubric 1 from **Unit-by-Unit Resources**	**Unit-by-Unit Resources** Vocabulary Worksheets, pp. 11–14 Unit 1 Test, pp. 19–22

Unit 1

Introduce the Unit

Ask children to name different artworks they have seen at school or in their neighborhood, including paintings, drawings, sculptures, murals, crafts, and mosaics. Have them talk about what they see in each artwork. Explain that artists sometimes get their ideas from their community, the places they visit, or the people in their lives.

Encourage children to visualize favorite people and places in their lives. Ask: **What person or place would you like to show in an artwork?**

Mary Cassatt. *Children Playing on the Beach*, 1884. Oil on canvas, 38³/₈ by 29¼ inches. National Gallery of Art, Washington, D.C., Ailsa Mellon Bruce Collection. Photograph ©1997 Board of Trustees, National Gallery of Art.

16

 Art Background

Children Playing on the Beach In this nineteenth-century painting, Mary Cassatt captures the natural positions of two self-absorbed toddlers playing in sand. Typical of her work after 1883, the figures are clearly defined by sharp contours and solid areas of color. The painting clearly demonstrates Cassatt's talent for capturing natural poses of children in serene, informal settings.

 Home Connection

Have children discuss with family members activities they like to do at the beach, park, or pool. Have them draw or take pictures of themselves doing those activities. Invite children to share their pictures with classmates.

Art Around You

Some artists paint people they know or places they like to visit. They use line, shape, and color in their art. What does this artwork show?

Meet the Artist

Mary Cassatt was born in the United States in 1844. She spent much of her life painting in France. She is best known for her paintings of women and children. You can find another painting by Cassatt in this unit. What is that painting about?

Mary Cassatt. *Self-Portrait,* ca. 1880.

17

Bookshelf

Come Look with Me: Enjoying Art with Children
by Gladys S. Blizzard
Lickle Publishing, Inc., 1991

This book will introduce children to the world of art. It features twelve paintings, all with children as their subjects. Each painting will give children background information about the artist and the artwork itself. Use this book to help children begin to notice art around them.

Discuss Unit Concepts

Tell children that in this unit they will be exploring how artists get their ideas from the people and places around them. Explain that artists use those ideas to create *artwork*—a creative object such as a painting, drawing, sculpture, or other craft.

Have children look at page 16 and invite them to tell what they see. Point out the *credit line*—the information that accompanies a reproduction of an artwork. Then have children read the top of page 17 and answer the question. (The artwork shows two children playing on the beach.)

Point out the different colors and shapes used in the painting. Invite children to use their finger "like a paintbrush" and follow the lines of the artwork.

As you introduce each element of art and principle of design in Unit 1, you may wish to display the **Instructional Prints.** A print is provided for each element and principle.

In addition, **Art Prints 1–4** and **Transparencies** are available for fine art in the unit.

Meet the Artist

Mary Cassatt (1844–1926) Mary Cassatt was an American-born painter who was part of the French Impressionist movement in the nineteenth century. She most enjoyed painting portraits of mothers and children in intimate relationships and domestic settings. She used members of her own family as subjects. Later in life she lost her sight and was no longer able to paint.

Lesson 1

Lesson 1

At a Glance

Objectives
- Identify and describe types of lines.
- Describe, analyze, interpret, and judge artworks.

Materials
- **Fine Art Transparency**
- long pieces of yarn
- Sketchbook Journal

Vocabulary
line

NVAS (K–4) #2 Using knowledge of structures and functions

NVAS (K–4) #5 Reflecting upon and assessing the characteristics and merits of their work and the work of others

NVAS (K–4) #6 Making connections between visual arts and other disciplines

① Introduce

Distribute yarn pieces to children. Demonstrate how to extend the yarn to make straight, horizontal, vertical, and diagonal lines. Let the children use their yarn to show lines that are curved, bent, spiral, wavy, and zigzag.

Invite children to look for lines in objects that surround them, such as the broken and straight lines of writing paper, the broad lines of a flag, the thin lines of a calendar, and the continuous line of a frame.

Line

A **line** is a mark that goes from one point to another. Lines can make waters look stormy. Follow the waves with your finger. Do you feel motion? How do these lines show action?

Katsushika Hokusai. *The Great Wave Off Kanagawa,* 1823–1829. Colored woodcut, 10⅛ by 15 inches. Metropolitan Museum of Art, New York.

18

 Art Background

Art and Culture Artist Katsushika Hokusai used a Japanese printmaking technique called *ukiyo*-e ("pictures of the floating world") to make *The Great Wave Off Kanagawa.* The *ukiyo-e* prints were made from woodcut designs and typically portrayed nature scenes, historical events, or aspects of contemporary urban life.

 Notes

Have children draw and label each type of line on separate index cards, or have them glue and label yarn pieces to show the lines. Then draw one of the lines on the board. Say its name and have children repeat after you. Then have children hold up their matching card. Repeat the process for the other lines.

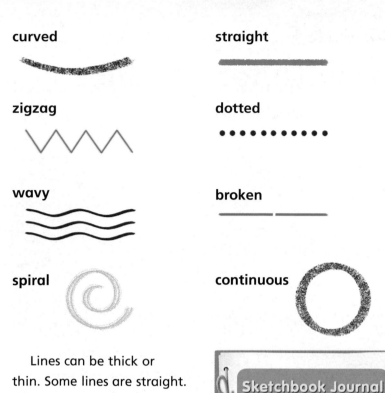

curved

straight

zigzag

dotted

• • • • • • • • • •

wavy

broken

spiral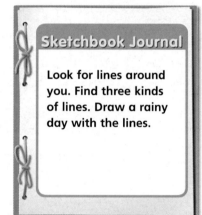

continuous

Lines can be thick or thin. Some lines are straight. Curved lines go around. Zigzag and wavy lines go up and down. Find lines that are straight, curved, dotted, broken, and wavy.

What kinds of lines show waves in the storm?

> **Sketchbook Journal**
>
> **Look for lines around you. Find three kinds of lines. Draw a rainy day with the lines.**

19

 Curriculum Connection

Physical Education Use chalk to draw hopscotch patterns on a paved area outdoors. Have children identify the kinds of lines used to draw the shapes and numbers. Then have them play hopscotch.

Review the rules of the game: take turns tossing a marker (rock, button) into each numbered box, in sequence, and then hopping through the grid without stepping on the grid lines. The first player to finish the course wins.

---

❷ Teach

Read page 18 together. Ask:

- **What kinds of lines did the artist use to show *The Great Wave Off Kanagawa*?** (wavy, zigzag, dotted, broken, continuous, straight) DESCRIBE
- **How did the artist use boats to show the size of the waves?** (He drew small boats in the large waves.) ANALYZE
- **What do you think the artist wanted people to know by looking at this artwork?** (Possible response: He wanted people to know the size, shape, movement, and power of a giant wave in the ocean.) INTERPRET
- **What thoughts come to mind as you look at this artwork?** (Possible response: The giant wave looks scary.) JUDGE

Have children look at page 19. Have volunteers point to each type of line as you say the name. Read aloud the rest of the page, and invite children to answer the question. (Possible response: The curved lines show waves in the storm.)

Sketchbook Journal Encourage children to visualize the motion of raindrops before they begin to draw their picture.

❸ Close

Have partners share and compare their drawings. Work with a volunteer to model identifying ideas in artworks by peers. Then ask children to name the kinds of lines used in their partner's drawing. Remind them to give positive, thoughtful feedback.

Visual Culture Have children find and name types of lines in their clothing, or take them outdoors to identify lines in their school.

Studio 1

At a Glance

Objectives

- Express ideas by drawing a picture of a school.
- Demonstrate how to draw a variety of lines to create artworks.
- Evaluate original artworks by self and peers.

Materials

- drawing paper
- crayons, pencils, pens, water-based markers
- Rubric 1 from **Unit-by-Unit Resources**

NVAS (K–4) #1 Understanding and applying media, techniques, and processes

NVAS (K–4) #3 Choosing and evaluating a range of subject matter, symbols, and ideas

NVAS (K–4) #5 Reflecting upon and assessing the characteristics and merits of their work and the work of others

❶ Introduce

Review types of lines with children. Invite volunteers to share examples. Then have children brainstorm ideas for drawing a school. Ask:

- **What are the parts of a school?**
- **How will you describe this school to someone who has never seen it?**
- **What kinds of lines will you use to draw this school?**

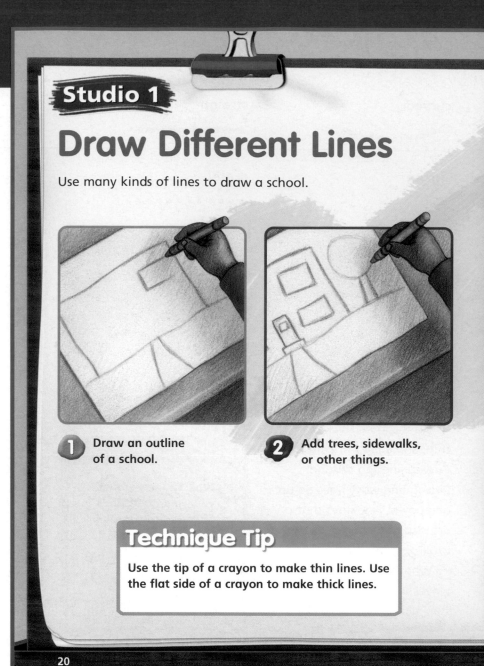

Draw Different Lines

Use many kinds of lines to draw a school.

1. Draw an outline of a school.
2. Add trees, sidewalks, or other things.

Technique Tip

Use the tip of a crayon to make thin lines. Use the flat side of a crayon to make thick lines.

20

Quick Studio

Provide children with an outline of a school and have them draw different types of lines to complete the picture.

🚶 Meeting Individual Needs

Reteach Children who have difficulty seeing and drawing many different lines may benefit from narrowing their focus. Have them use just one tool, such as a crayon or marker, and have them illustrate just one feature of the school, such as a window or door.

Extend Encourage children to show greater detail in their drawing of the school. Challenge them to include four or more kinds of lines in their drawing. You may want to take a small group of children to the front of the school and point out the variety of lines in the building and landscape.

3 Use different kinds of lines in your drawing.

4 Show motion by adding curved and zigzag lines.

Think Like an Artist

Tell about the lines in your drawing.
What feeling of motion did you show?

21

 Fine Arts Connection

Dance Use chalk to draw different types of lines on a paved area outdoors, or use masking tape to show the lines on the floor of a large room. Have children identify each line. Then organize the class into small groups and have each group create a dance routine along one of the lines. Children can use dance movements that you teach them, or they can think of their own. Invite each group to perform their routine to music in front of the class.

② Create

Read aloud pages 20–21 and distribute the materials.

- Explain that an *outline* is the main shape of the school.
- Encourage children to use their brainstorming ideas.
- Remind children to look at page 19 as a reference for different types of lines.
- Tell children that plants and trees should show movement, as if the wind is blowing the leaves and grass.

Technique Tip Demonstrate how to use the tip of a crayon to make thin lines and the side of a crayon to make thick lines.

③ Close

After children finish the activity, have them reflect on their work by answering the *Think Like an Artist* question on page 21. (Possible response: I made the tree look like wind was blowing through it.)

Ongoing Assessment

If . . . children have difficulty drawing thick lines,

then . . . suggest that they apply less pressure and use a smaller piece of crayon.

See page 18 from **Unit-by-Unit Resources** for a rubric to assess this studio.

Lesson 2

At a Glance

Objectives

- Identify, describe, and compare shapes in an original artwork.
- Describe, analyze, interpret, and judge artworks.

Materials

- **Fine Art Transparency**
- pipe cleaners
- Sketchbook Journal

Vocabulary

shapes, collage

NVAS (K–4) #5 Reflecting upon and assessing the characteristics and merits of their work and the work of others

NVAS (K–4) #6 Making connections between visual arts and other disciplines

①Introduce

Distribute pipe cleaners to children. Explain that each stick is a straight line. Model how to use the pipe cleaners to make a shape, such as a triangle. Then have children use their pipe cleaners to make other geometric shapes and organic (free-form) shapes.

Invite children to describe and compare their shapes. Have children match their shapes to similar ones in the classroom.

Shape

Sometimes artists use lines to make **shapes.** What shapes are in this artwork? Name the animals you see.

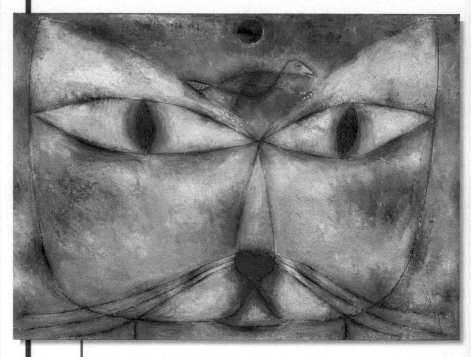

Paul Klee. *Cat and Bird*, 1928. Oil, ink, and gesso on canvas, mounted on wood, 15 by 21 inches. Museum of Modern Art, NY.

22

Art Background

About the Artist Swiss artist Paul Klee (1879–1940) was an Expressionist who often used fantasy-like images to express his thoughts and feelings about the world around him.

About the Artist Roberta Arenson, an illustrator for children's books, uses brightly colored collages in her artworks. Most of her books show interpretations of folk tales, myths, and poetry.

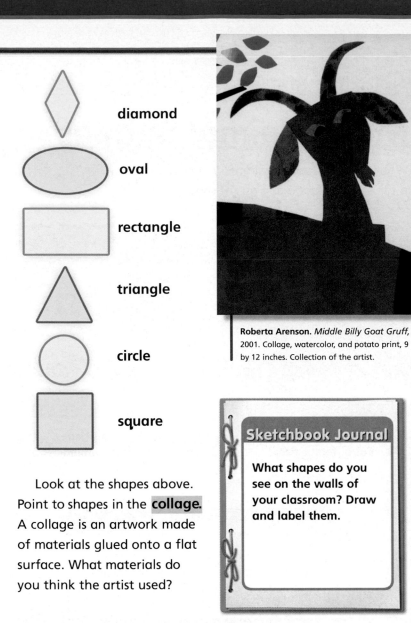

diamond

oval

rectangle

triangle

circle

square

Look at the shapes above. Point to shapes in the **collage.** A collage is an artwork made of materials glued onto a flat surface. What materials do you think the artist used?

Roberta Arenson. *Middle Billy Goat Gruff,* 2001. Collage, watercolor, and potato print, 9 by 12 inches. Collection of the artist.

Sketchbook Journal

What shapes do you see on the walls of your classroom? Draw and label them.

23

2 Teach

Read page 22 with children. Ask:

- **What shapes do you see in this artwork?** (triangles, circles, ovals) DESCRIBE
- **Which animal is the largest? Which animal is the smallest? Why?** (the cat; the bird; the bird is smallest because the artist wanted to show that the cat wants to eat it.) ANALYZE
- **What is this artwork about?** (a cat who sees a bird and wants to eat it) INTERPRET
- **What do you like best about this artwork?** (Possible response: the cat's eyes; they are looking right at the bird.) JUDGE

Then read page 23 with children. Have them point to the shapes as you name and describe each one. Encourage them to look at *Middle Billy Goat Gruff* to see which shapes were used. Ask similar questions as above.

Sketchbook Journal Encourage children to refer to the labeled shapes on page 23 as they identify the shapes in their classroom.

3 Close

Organize children into pairs. Have children share the shapes they drew with their partners. Prompt children to describe what they see in their partner's drawing.

Assessment Have children follow directions to draw an imaginary animal. For example, say: **Draw a circle for the head. Use triangles for the ears. Draw an oval body.** Then invite children to share their results and name the shapes that they used.

Curriculum Connection

Math Make a two-column chart and write *Geometric Shapes* at the top of one column and *Organic Shapes* at the top of the other. Have children draw a variety of shapes on the paper. Then invite them to describe and compare the shapes.

 Notes

On the board draw a circle, rectangle, square, and triangle. Point to each shape and name it. Have children repeat after you.

Studio 2

At a Glance

Objectives

• Express ideas by using shapes in an original artwork.
• Evaluate original artworks by self and peers.

Materials

• manila paper cut into 3" × 3" squares
• scissors ⚠, glue, crayons, colored construction paper
• Rubric 1 from **Unit-by-Unit Resources**

NVAS (K–4) #1 Understanding and applying media, techniques, and processes

NVAS (K–4) #3 Choosing and evaluating a range of subject matter, symbols, and ideas

NVAS (K–4) #5 Reflecting upon and assessing the characteristics and merits of their work and the work of others

① Introduce

Review geometric and organic (free-form) shapes with children. Then help children brainstorm ideas for their animal collage. Ask:

• **What animal will you make?**
• **What does your animal look like?**
• **What shapes will you need to make that animal?**

Quick Studio

Have children create an animal or creature collage using a variety of precut shapes.

Studio 2

Make Animal Shapes

What are your favorite animals? Follow these steps to make one out of shapes.

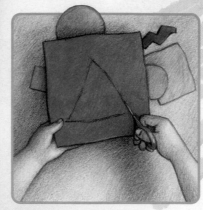

1 Cut out paper shapes. Cut different sizes.

2 Arrange the shapes to make an animal.

Technique Tip

Squeeze a little bit of glue in the center of the shape. Dab a thin line around the edges. Spread the glue with your fingers.

24

🚶🚶🚶 Meeting Individual Needs

Inclusion For children who are visually impaired, provide large, high-contrast paper or precut shapes for them to use. Then pair each child with a child who is sighted to help them arrange the shapes onto the page.

3 Glue them down.

4 Use crayons to finish your picture.

Think Like an Artist

Describe your animal collage to a friend. Tell what shapes you used. Have your friend guess what animal you made.

25

 Fine Arts Connection

Theatre Have children perform an imaginative story about their animals. Work with the class to write a script, or have groups make up stories on their own. Children can hold up their collages as they say their lines, or they can cut out the animals and glue them onto craft sticks to make puppets.

② Create

Have children follow along as you read the directions on pages 24–25. Then distribute the materials.

- Remind children how to use scissors safely.
- Encourage them to think about the shapes that they need to make their animal.
- Remind children to make a thin line of glue around the outline of the shape. Identify this as an important skill to know when producing this type of artwork.
- Tell children to let the glued shapes dry completely before drawing on them.

Technique Tip Show children how to apply glue. If they have difficulty using glue bottles, consider providing glue sticks or paste for them to use.

③ Close

Have each child discuss his or her collage with a friend using the ideas presented in *Think Like an Artist.* (Possible response: I made a cat. I used circles and triangles.)

Ongoing Assessment

If . . . children use too much glue,

then . . . tell them to add more shapes to their collage.

See page 18 from **Unit-by-Unit Resources** for a rubric to assess this studio.

Lesson 3

At a Glance

Objectives

- Identify and describe tactile textures.
- Describe, analyze, interpret, and judge artworks.

Materials

- **Fine Art Transparency**
- textured objects
- Sketchbook Journal

Vocabulary

texture, tactile textures

NVAS (K–4) #2 Using knowledge of structures and functions

NVAS (K–4) #5 Reflecting upon and assessing the characteristics and merits of their work and the work of others

NVAS (K–4) #6 Making connections between visual arts and other disciplines

❶ Introduce

Give each pair of children a textured object. Write the following words on the board and read them aloud to children: *soft, hard, smooth, rough, pebbly, bumpy, scratchy, silky.* As you say each word, ask children to raise their hands if their object shares the same texture that you name.

Then invite children to explore and discover other textured objects in the classroom. Encourage them to describe how the objects look and feel.

Feeling Texture

Texture is the way a surface looks and feels. Texture can feel soft or hard. It can look rough or scratchy.

Albrecht Dürer. *Rhinoceros,* 1515. Woodcut, 9¼ by 11¾ inches. Prints Collection Miriam and Ira D. Wallach Division of Art, Prints and Photography, New York Public Library, Astor, Lenox and Tilden Foundation.

26

 Art Background

Art and Culture Albrecht Dürer (1471–1528), a German painter and engraver, lived during a time of European expansion. In 1515, Portuguese merchants brought to Lisbon the first Indian rhinoceros and Indian elephant ever seen in Europe. Dürer enjoyed using these exotic animals as subjects.

 Notes

Place several objects in a large bag. Have a volunteer choose one object and show it to the rest of the group. Ask questions about the texture of the object that require a yes or no answer: **Is it soft? Is it bumpy? Is it scratchy?** After asking several questions, let another child choose an object. Continue until each child has a turn.

If you touch a rock, it feels hard. Other objects may have silky, soft, or bumpy textures. These are **tactile textures,** or textures you can feel.

Look at *Rhinoceros*. The artist used carving tools to show texture. What textures did he want you to imagine?

Art in My World

Look outside. Draw a plant or an animal you see. Show textures with lines and shapes.

27

 Curriculum Connection

Science Take children outdoors to collect a variety of textured objects from nature, or have them bring textured objects from home. Have them identify, describe, and sort the objects by texture. Then work with children to make a "nature collage" on thick cardboard or foamboard. Have children arrange the objects on the board while you glue the objects down with a glue gun.

② Teach

Read page 26 with children. Ask:

- **Does this rhinoceros look soft or hard? Smooth or rough?** (hard; rough) DESCRIBE
- **How did the artist make the rhinoceros appear hard and rough?** (Possible response: The artist used thin, straight, and curved lines.) ANALYZE
- **What textures did the artist want you to imagine?** (rough skin; hard horns; scratchy, bristly hairs; soft ears; smooth hooves) INTERPRET
- **What part of this artwork is the most interesting to you? Why?** (Answers will vary.) JUDGE

Then read aloud page 27. Talk about different textured objects shown on the page. As you name each object, ask children to raise their hands if they have ever touched something like it. If they have, ask them to describe it.

Art in My World Point out simple plants and animals for children to draw, such as a tree, an acorn, a rabbit, a bird, or a lizard. Encourage them to refer back to pages 19 and 23 to choose the lines and shapes they will use to show textures.

③ Close

Invite children to show their drawings and describe the textures of the plant or animal. Encourage them to point to objects on page 27 that share the same texture.

Assessment Put different textured objects inside lunch bags. Have children reach inside the bag and feel the object without looking. Have them describe the texture and shape.

Studio 3

At a Glance

Objectives

- Express ideas by using texture to create an original artwork.
- Demonstrate how to create texture rubbings.
- Evaluate original artworks by self and peers.

Materials

- drawing paper
- crayons without wrappers
- a variety of textured materials (sandpaper, wire screening, wrinkled and flattened aluminum foil, plastic mesh, produce bags, lace, corrugated cardboard) ⚠
- Rubric 1 from **Unit-by-Unit Resources**

NVAS (K–4) #1 Understanding and applying media, techniques, and processes

NVAS (K–4) #3 Choosing and evaluating a range of subject matter, symbols, and ideas

NVAS (K–4) #5 Reflecting upon and assessing the characteristics and merits of their work and the work of others

Make a Texture Rubbing

Look around. Describe the textures you see.

1 Draw the outline of an object with large shapes.

2 Find objects with textures you like.

Technique Tip

To make a rubbing, place paper over a textured surface. Hold the side of a peeled crayon and gently rub the crayon back and forth.

28

❶ Introduce

Display the textured materials that will be used for the studio, and have children describe each one. Then help children brainstorm ideas for their texture rubbings. Ask:

- **What picture will you draw to show textures? Why?**
- **What other objects have the same texture as this one?**
- **What textures will you show in a drawing of some clothes?**

Quick Studio

Have children draw a shape. Then have them fill it with a texture rubbing.

🚶🚶🚶🚶 Meeting Individual Needs

Reteach If children have difficulty choosing textures, focus on one texture at a time. Prepare by gathering objects that can be used to show soft textures. Then ask children to use crayons to draw an animal with a soft texture, such as a dog or cat.

Extend Display textured materials and teacher-made sample rubbings in random order. Invite early finishers to match the rubbings with the correct materials used to make them. For a greater challenge, use overlapping textures for each sample.

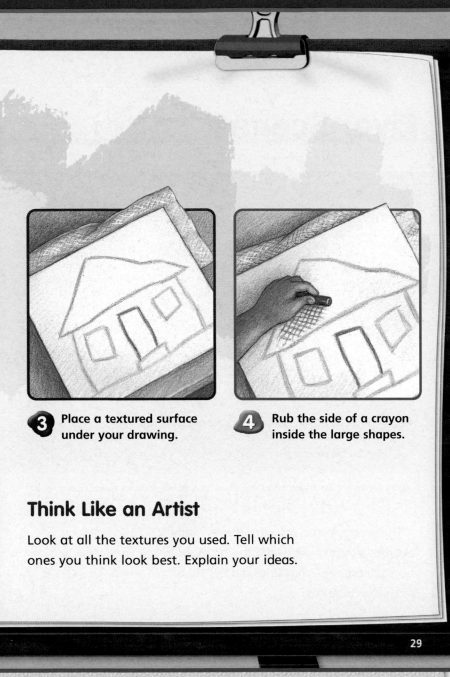

③ Place a textured surface under your drawing.

④ Rub the side of a crayon inside the large shapes.

Think Like an Artist

Look at all the textures you used. Tell which ones you think look best. Explain your ideas.

29

Fine Arts Connection

Music Have children create simulated textured paper by using texture rubbing techniques. Then have them use that paper to make a shoebox guitar or a maraca. To make a guitar, have them glue the paper onto the sides of a shoebox and then wrap rubber bands around the box for the strings. To make a maraca, have them roll and tape the paper into a tube (or on a cardboard tube), fill it with uncooked rice, and then cover the ends with paper. Invite children to play their instruments together.

② Create

Read aloud pages 28–29 and distribute materials.

- Encourage children to draw a real or imaginary object that has large shapes.
- Place a set of materials at each workstation for easier management. Remind children to be careful with objects that can poke or scratch.
- Model how to position a textured surface under drawing paper. Help children identify this as a necessary skill when making texture rubbings.
- Demonstrate how to use more than one color or textured surface in the same area to show overlapping textures.

Technique Tip Encourage children to practice rubbing techniques on scratch paper. Ask: **What skills does an artist need to make a texture rubbing?** (positioning materials under paper, using a peeled crayon)

③ Close

Have children read and discuss *Think Like an Artist* on page 29. (Possible response: I like the texture of the ball because it is bumpy.)

Ongoing Assessment

If . . . children tear their paper while making texture rubbings,

then . . . remind them to rub the crayon lightly and to use repetitive strokes.

See page 18 from **Unit-by-Unit Resources** for a rubric to assess this studio.

Look and Compare

Look and Compare

At a Glance

Objectives

- Compare and contrast two artworks with similar themes.
- Respond to and make judgments about artworks.

Materials

- **Art Prints 1, 2, 3**
- **Fine Art Transparency**
- **Sketchbook Journal**

NVAS (K–4) #5 Reflecting upon and assessing the characteristics and merits of their work and the work of others

Explore

Display **Art Print 1,** *Children Playing on the Beach.* Help children recall this artwork by Mary Cassatt from page 16. As children look at the two artworks on pages 30–31, ask them to predict which one was also created by Cassatt, and give reasons for their answers. (Possible response: *The Boating Party;* the people look similar.)

Discuss

After children read pages 30–31, have them focus on the lines and textures used in each artwork. Help them identify the curved, thick, and thin lines in Derain's *London Bridge.*

Explain that these lines are used to make the water look like it is moving. Children can contrast this with the wavy lines in Cassatt's *The Boating Party,* which show calmness in the water.

River Scenes

André Derain. *London Bridge,* 1906. Oil on canvas, 26 by 39 inches. The Museum of Modern Art, NY.

The water in this artwork shows many textures. What textures did the artist want you to imagine? What lines did he use to create the textures?

30

 Art Background

London Bridge This portrait of a famous bridge that used to cross the Thames River in England was created by French artist André Derain (1880–1954). Painted in the Fauve style, the perspective is unusual, the figures are less natural, and the colors are bright and choppy.

The Boating Party Mary Cassatt began painting *The Boating Party* in 1893 while vacationing on the Riviera. It was one of her largest and most impressive paintings. Her inspiration may have come from a similar painting, *Boating,* created by Édouard Manet in 1874.

Mary Cassatt. *The Boating Party,* 1893–1894. Oil on canvas, 35 ⁷/₁₆ by 46 ⅛ inches. National Gallery of Art, Washington, D.C.

What do you notice about the texture of the water in this painting? How is this artwork like *London Bridge?* How is it different?

Sketchbook Journal

How can you show textures in your own artwork? Draw and write your ideas.

31

Identify Detail Remind children that details help tell about the main idea. Ask: **What is the main idea of Derain's painting?** (London Bridge) Have children reread the first sentence on page 30. Ask: **What detail does this sentence tell you?** (The water shows many textures.) Then invite children to share other details about *London Bridge.* (A boat is under the bridge; there are lots of buildings near the bridge; the bridge is big.) Repeat for Cassatt's painting.

Apply

Work with children to complete a Venn diagram like the one below. Tell children that this graphic organizer is a good way to show how two artworks are the same and different.

To fill in the diagram, suggest that children first compare the artworks, looking for ways they are alike. Fill in the middle section with common ideas.

Guide children to look for differences by suggesting that they focus on lines, shapes, and textures in the two artworks. Possible responses are shown in blue:

River Scenes

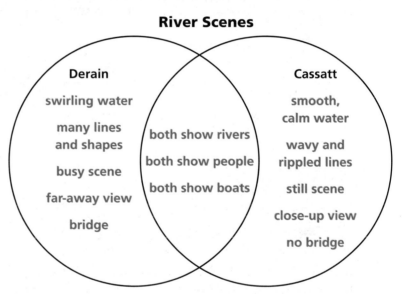

Derain

swirling water

many lines and shapes

busy scene

far-away view

bridge

both show rivers

both show people

both show boats

Cassatt

smooth, calm water

wavy and rippled lines

still scene

close-up view

no bridge

Close

Ask children what they learned about rivers and boats from these artists. (Possible response: Some rivers are busy and some rivers are calm.)

Sketchbook Journal Encourage children to refer back to the paintings on pages 30–31 as they draw and tell about textures in their own artwork.

Lesson 4

At a Glance

Objectives

- Identify and describe visual textures.
- Describe, analyze, interpret, and judge artworks.

Materials

- **Fine Art Transparency**
- animal magazines

Vocabulary

visual texture

NVAS (K–4) #2 Using knowledge of structures and functions

NVAS (K–4) #5 Reflecting upon and assessing the characteristics and merits of their work and the work of others

NVAS (K–4) #6 Making connections between visual arts and other disciplines

Introduce

Play a game of Eye Spy using natural and human-made objects that show visual textures. Include objects that are dull, shiny, silky, smooth, rough, and pebbly. For example: **I spy a smooth, shiny object that shows the time.** (a clock)

Continue by asking the child who guesses the correct answer to give the next clue. End the activity by explaining to children that they will be learning more about visual textures—textures they can see.

Lesson 4

Seeing Texture

How would touching a real lion feel to your fingers? Your eyes can help you understand the texture of the lion. You can see **visual texture,** or how something seems to feel.

Rosa Bonheur. *The King of the Desert,* 19th century. Oil on canvas, 39³/₈ by 37⁵/₈ inches. Courtesy of Southeby's, Inc., New York.

32

Art Background

About the Artist French artist Rosa Bonheur (1822–1899) had a passion for animals. At one point, her household included a wild sheep, a gazelle, a lion, and a lioness. As a young girl, she dressed as a boy to visit fairs so she could study the anatomy of animals.

ESL Notes

Display smooth and rough objects. Have children touch each smooth object as they say the word *smooth*. Repeat with the rough objects. Then have children look at smooth and rough objects in the classroom.

Look at the objects in the photograph. Let your eyes tell about their textures. What are some words that describe the wall's texture? How could you describe the leaves?

Research

Find pictures of animals. Notice the visual texture. Tell how each animal might feel.

33

 Curriculum Connection

Social Studies Display photographs of large objects from different communities. Point to and identify constructions, or architecture, in each photograph. For example, show and identify a barn from a rural area, a skyscraper from an urban area, and a house from a suburban area. Invite children to name and describe the visual textures they see in each construction. Then have them look for visual textures in other photographs they find in magazines or newspapers. Invite them to show and tell what they discover. Extend the lesson by having them look for visual textures at home.

❷ Teach

Read aloud the first sentence on page 32 as children look at *The King of the Desert*. Have volunteers describe how a real lion might feel. (soft, fluffy, silky) Then read aloud the rest of the page. Ask:

- **What textures do you see?** (soft, dull fur; smooth, shiny eyes; hard, pointy teeth; soft, fluffy clouds) DESCRIBE
- **How does the artist show visual texture?** (by using lines and shapes) ANALYZE
- **Why did the artist show fluffy clouds and small mountains in the background?** (Possible response: to make the lion look bigger, stronger, and more dangerous) INTERPRET
- **What are your thoughts about this artwork?** (Answers will vary.) JUDGE

Then read page 33 together. Have children describe the visual textures of the wall and the leaves. (rough, dull, bumpy; smooth and shiny)

Research Have children work with a partner to find magazine pictures of animals that show texture. Have partners discuss how each animal might feel when touched. Then have them cut out each picture, glue it onto paper, and write descriptive words below it.

❸ Close

Invite partners to share their animal pictures with the rest of the class. Have classmates describe the visual textures they see in the photographs.

Assessment Provide pictures of various animals. Have children describe the texture.

Studio 4

At a Glance

Objectives

- Express ideas by painting texture in an artwork.
- Demonstrate how to paint texture.
- Evaluate original artworks by self and peers.

Materials

- paintbrushes, muffin tins or palettes
- liquid tempera paints, white paper, paper towels
- Rubric 1 from **Unit-by-Unit Resources**

NVAS (K–4) #1 Understanding and applying media, techniques, and processes

NVAS (K–4) #3 Choosing and evaluating a range of subject matter, symbols, and ideas

NVAS (K–4) #5 Reflecting upon and assessing the characteristics and merits of their work and the work of others

① Introduce

Set up workstations before beginning the studio.

Use classroom artwork to review visual textures with children. Tell them that they will be painting texture. Hold up a paintbrush and ask:

- **What texture do you think a paintbrush and paint will make?**
- **What types of lines will you paint?**
- **What textures will you show?**

Studio 4

Paint Texture

Paint a picture. Use your brush to show texture.

1 Paint brushstrokes in one direction.

2 Wash your brush. Wipe it.

Technique Tip

Dip the paintbrush into the paint. Push down on the paintbrush for thick lines. Use the tip for thin lines.

34

🏃🏃🏃🏃 Meeting Individual Needs

Extend Have children paint different textures using a variety of tools, such as wide and thin paintbrushes, foam brushes, sponge pieces, cotton swabs, strips of corrugated cardboard, and feathers.

Quick Studio

Suggest that children paint texture using one color of paint.

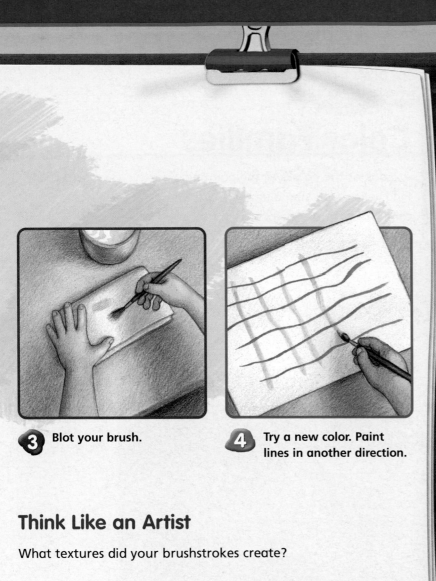

③ Blot your brush.

④ Try a new color. Paint lines in another direction.

Think Like an Artist

What textures did your brushstrokes create?

 Fine Arts Connection

Theatre Have the class paint a backdrop for a favorite children's story, such as "Little Red Riding Hood" or "The Three Little Pigs." Have them use tempera paint on butcher paper or an old white sheet. Remind children to paint visual textures for trees, bushes, huts, dirt roads, and other parts of the scenery. After the backdrop dries, invite groups of children to act out the story.

② Create

Read aloud pages 34–35 as children follow along. Distribute the materials for the studio.

- Model Step 1 using a clean paintbrush on the chalkboard. Show children how to hold the paintbrush and make the brushstrokes.
- Remind children to wash the paintbrush thoroughly to avoid mixing colors.
- Tell children to blot the paintbrush to remove excess water.
- Remind children that horizontal, vertical, and diagonal lines can all be used to show texture.

Technique Tip Model for children how to reshape a wet paintbrush to form a pointed tip. Explain that the pointed tip will make thin lines.

③ Close

After children finish the studio, have them reflect on ideas expressed in their work by answering the *Think Like an Artist* question on page 35. (I made soft textures with curved lines.)

Ongoing Assessment

If . . . children mix colors in their artwork,

then . . . remind them to rinse their paintbrush thoroughly and blot to remove excess water.

See page 18 from **Unit-by-Unit Resources** for a rubric to assess this studio.

Lesson 5

At a Glance

Objectives

- Identify and compare color families (primary, secondary, intermediate).
- Describe, analyze, interpret, and judge artworks.

Materials

- **Fine Art Transparency**
- Sketchbook Journal

Vocabulary

colors, primary colors, secondary colors, intermediate colors

NVAS (K–4) #2 Using knowledge of structures and functions

NVAS (K–4) #5 Reflecting upon and assessing the characteristics and merits of their work and the work of others

1 Introduce

Name several colors, such as red, blue, yellow, and orange. After you say each color word, ask children who are wearing that color to stand and point to it on their clothing.

Then have children name colors in the classroom. Explain that each color belongs in its own color family. Tell children that red, yellow, and blue are the primary colors because they are used to make other colors. The secondary colors (orange, green, violet) are created when primary colors are mixed together. Red and blue make violet. Yellow and blue make green. Red and yellow make orange. Intermediate colors are created when the secondary colors are mixed with a primary color. For instance, blue and violet create a blue-violet color. Finally, tell children that neutral colors are black, white, and gray. When mixed with other colors, they make them lighter or darker.

Lesson 5

Color Families

Look at the **colors** in the painting. Find yellow, red, and blue. They are the family of **primary colors.**

Stanton Macdonald-Wright. *Conception Synchromy,* 1914. Oil on canvas, 36 by 30⅛ inches. Hirshhorn Museum and Sculpture Garden, Smithsonian Institution, Washington, D.C.

 Art Background

Art History Stanton Macdonald-Wright (1890–1973) created "Synchromism" in the early 1900s. He explained that "Synchromism simply means 'with color' as a symphony means 'with sound.'" Followers of the movement believed that color had musical qualities. In fact, they believed that if they painted in color scales, their paintings would produce musical sensations.

 Notes

Have children point to each color on the color wheel and say the name after you. Then give each child an outline of twelve identical shapes in a row (e.g., circles, hearts, flowers). Have them color the shapes to match the color wheel.

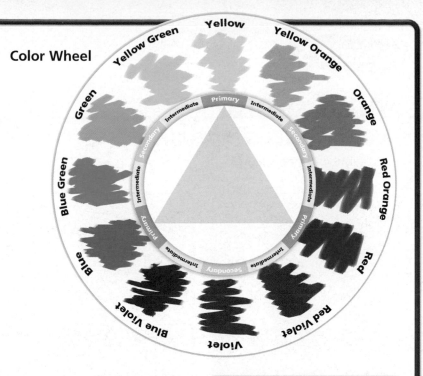

Color Wheel

Green, orange, and violet are a family of **secondary colors.** You can make a secondary color by mixing primary colors. What two primary colors make green? orange? violet?

Look at the color wheel. Name the colors that form the **intermediate colors.**

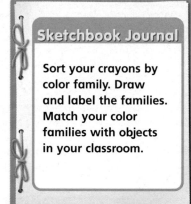

Sketchbook Journal

Sort your crayons by color family. Draw and label the families. Match your color families with objects in your classroom.

37

② Teach

Read page 36 with children, and discuss the artwork. Ask:

- **What primary colors do you see in this painting? Point to each color and name it.** (Children should point to and name yellow, red, and blue colors in the painting.) DESCRIBE
- **What color in the painting do you notice the most? Why?** (Possible response: Yellow, because it is the brightest.) ANALYZE
- **What do you think the artist wanted people to know by looking at this picture?** (Possible response: I think the artist wanted people to know that he loved colors.) INTERPRET
- **Do you like this painting? Why?** (Answers will vary.) JUDGE

Then read page 37 with children. Have children name the colors as you tell them in which color family they belong.

Sketchbook Journal Distribute sets of crayons that include primary, secondary, and intermediate colors. Check that children have sorted their crayons correctly before they draw and label the color families. Invite them to draw or list classroom objects that match those colors.

③ Close

Have partners compare the colors and objects they drew in their journals. Then gather the class together and invite them to share their results.

Visual Culture Extend the lesson by having children search for primary, secondary, and intermediate colors in nature. Take them outdoors or show them documentary videos of colorful plants and animals from around the world.

Studio 5

At a Glance

Objectives

- Express ideas by using a variety of colors to paint a picture.
- Demonstrate mixing colors of paint.
- Evaluate original artworks by self and peers.

Materials

- red, blue, and yellow liquid tempera paints
- muffin tins or palettes
- paintbrushes
- Rubric 1 from **Unit-by-Unit Resources**

NVAS (K–4) #1 Understanding and applying media, techniques, and processes

NVAS (K–4) #3 Choosing and evaluating a range of subject matter, symbols, and ideas

NVAS (K–4) #5 Reflecting upon and assessing the characteristics and merits of their work and the work of others

① Introduce

Review primary colors with children by using jars of paint. Then have children brainstorm ways to mix and use colors of paint. Ask:

- **How will you use red, blue, and yellow paint to make new colors?**
- **How will you make green paint? Violet paint? Yellow-orange paint?**
- **What picture will you paint?**
- **What colors will you need to paint it?**

Mix Colors

Mix primary colors to make new colors.
Paint with your new colors.

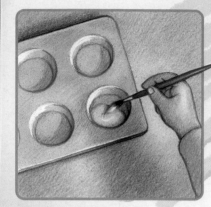

① **Put yellow paint on your palette.**

② **Mix in a small dab of red to make orange.**

Technique Tip

Choose colors you want to make. Use the color wheel to help you.

👪 **Meeting Individual Needs**

Inclusion For children who are developing fine motor skills, have them use larger paintbrushes with wider handles and brush tips. These brushes will be easier to hold and manipulate.

Quick Studio

Have children mix red and yellow to make orange. Then have them paint a picture.

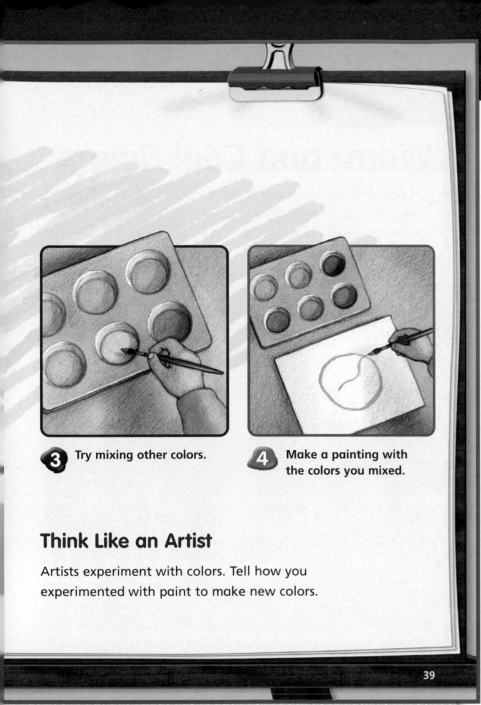

③ Try mixing other colors.

④ Make a painting with the colors you mixed.

Think Like an Artist

Artists experiment with colors. Tell how you experimented with paint to make new colors.

39

② Create

② Create

Read pages 38–39 with children. Distribute the materials.

- Suggest that children cover the bottom of the muffin tin or palette with yellow paint.
- For Step 2, tell children to mix one brush tip full of red into the yellow.
- Tell children that understanding how to make intermediate colors by mixing primary and secondary colors is an important skill for a painter to know.
- Remind children to wash their paintbrushes and blot them before using or mixing a new color.

Technique Tip Review with children the color wheel on page 37. Suggest that they write equations to help them remember different color combinations, such as blue + yellow = green.

③ Close

Have the class read and respond to *Think Like an Artist.* (Possible response: I mixed green and blue to make a blue-green color.) Encourage children to discuss skills a good painter should know.

Fine Arts Connection

Music Provide each child with three strips of construction paper: one red strip, one yellow strip, and one blue strip. Have children show which two primary colors create secondary colors, such as red and yellow make orange.

Sing the familiar song "Mary Wore Her Red Dress" with children. Invite them to hold up the appropriate color strips as you name each new color. Be sure to include secondary colors, which would require children to hold up two color strips.

Ongoing Assessment

If . . . children make too many browns and blacks,

then . . . remind them to mix only two or three colors at a time and to wash and blot their paintbrushes frequently.

See page 18 from **Unit-by-Unit Resources** for a rubric to assess this studio.

Lesson 6

At a Glance

Objectives

- Identify and describe warm and cool colors in artworks.
- Describe, analyze, interpret, and judge artworks.

Materials

- **Fine Art Transparency**
- Sketchbook Journal

Vocabulary

mood, warm colors, cool colors

NVAS (K–4) #2 Using knowledge of structures and functions

NVAS (K–4) #5 Reflecting upon and assessing the characteristics and merits of their work and the work of others

NVAS (K–4) #6 Making connections between visual arts and other disciplines

① Introduce

Have children color a happy face, a sad face, and a mad face. Encourage them to use colors that help show each feeling. Then invite children to tell which colors they used.

Explain that artists use certain colors because they want people to feel a certain emotion. The artist, Janet Fish, expressed a happy emotion with her painting *Jonathan and Lorraine*. She used warm colors, which include many yellows, oranges, and reds. Violet, blue, and green are cool colors. These colors generally bring about a calm or sometimes sad feeling.

Warm and Cool Colors

Some artworks tell about feelings. Colors help show a feeling, or **mood.** What do you think the artist wanted you to feel about this painting?

Janet Fish. *Jonathan and Lorraine,* 1988. Oil on canvas, 64 by 72¾ inches. Abudefduf, Inc., New York.

40

 Art Background

About the Artist Janet Fish (1938–) grew up surrounded by artists. Her grandfather was an American Impressionist, her father is an art history teacher, and her mother is a sculptor and a potter. She knew she wanted to be an artist too. She attended Smith College and Yale, where she learned to paint in the Abstract Expressionist style. Later, however, she began to paint realistic images.

 Notes

Use warm-colored crayons to draw a sun, and use cool-colored crayons to draw a glass of ice water. Show children your pictures and ask them to find the crayons you used to draw each one. Have them say *warm color* or *cool color* as they hold up each crayon.

Yellow, red, and orange are **warm colors.** Name some objects that have warm colors. What mood do the objects show?

Violet, blue, and green are **cool colors.** Describe a mood that cool colors show.

Sketchbook Journal

Use colored pencils. Draw two objects using cool colors and two objects using warm colors.

41

 Curriculum Connection

Social Studies Discuss types of places that can be found in a neighborhood, such as homes, schools, offices, stores, and restaurants. Then work with children to create a class mural or model of a neighborhood. Encourage children to use a variety of media, such as crayons, water-based markers, paint, construction paper, fabric scraps, milk cartons, and cardboard boxes. Remind them to use warm colors and cool colors to show mood. Have children discuss how their finished artworks compare to their actual neighborhoods.

② Teach

Read page 40 with children. Ask:

- **What does this painting show?** (Possible responses: a boy and girl reading a magazine at their kitchen table, a big vase of colorful flowers on the table) DESCRIBE
- **What was the first object or person you noticed in the artwork?** (Possible response: I noticed the vase of flowers first because the flowers are so bright and cheerful.) ANALYZE
- **Why do you think the artist used warm colors in this artwork?** (Possible response: She wanted the artwork to express a very happy mood.) INTERPRET
- **What do you like best about this artwork?** (Answers will vary.) JUDGE

Then read page 41. Have children talk about the cool colors used in this photograph.

Sketchbook Journal Help children brainstorm a list of warm-colored and cool-colored objects that they can draw.

③ Close

Invite children to share their artworks and discuss the colors they used.

Assessment Have children write *warm color* and *cool color* on opposite sides of a sheet of paper. Hold up a warm-colored object or a cool-colored object and have children show you the correct label. Repeat with other objects.

Studio 6

Studio 6

Make a Garden

Show a mood using warm or cool colors.

At a Glance

Objectives

- Express ideas by using warm and cool colors in artworks.
- Demonstrate drawing and painting to create mood.
- Evaluate original artworks by self and peers.

Materials

- warm and cool colors of oil pastels
- heavy white paper
- cotton swabs or tissues
- warm and cool colors of tempera wash (thin, diluted paint)
- paintbrushes, muffin tins
- Rubric 1 from **Unit-by-Unit Resources**

NVAS (K–4) #1 Understanding and applying media, techniques, and processes

NVAS (K–4) #3 Choosing and evaluating a range of subject matter, symbols, and ideas

NVAS (K–4) #5 Reflecting upon and assessing the characteristics and merits of their work and the work of others

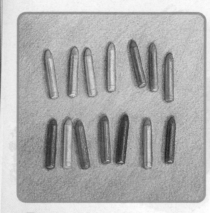 

1 Choose warm or cool colors.

2 Draw a garden with oil pastels.

Technique Tip

Oil pastels have lots of color. Press lightly. Dab on a little color. Then smooth the color with a cotton swab or tissue.

❶ Introduce

Use classroom objects to review warm and cool colors. Remind children that artists can use colors to show feelings in artworks. Then help them brainstorm ideas for drawing a garden. Ask:

- **What type of garden will you show?**
- **Will your garden be sunny or cloudy?**
- **What colors will you use for a sunny day? A cloudy day?**
- **What feelings will your artwork show?**

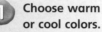

Quick Studio

Have children use warm or cool colors to draw a vase of flowers.

🚶🚶🚶 Meeting Individual Needs

Inclusion For children who are visually impaired, have them use felt cutouts to create a tactile garden. Have them assemble the parts on felt board or glue the pieces down on cardboard. Then invite children to share their feelings about what they included in their garden.

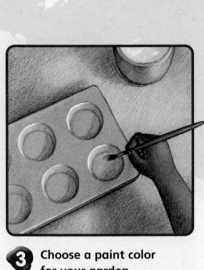

③ Choose a paint color for your garden.

④ Brush a thin coat of paint over your drawing.

Think Like an Artist

Think about the warm or cool colors that you used. Tell the mood the colors help show.

43

 Fine Arts Connection

Theatre Have children pretend they are flowers in an imaginary garden. Encourage them to use body movements and facial expressions to show their actions and feelings. Have them act out these scenarios:

• growing from seed to flower
• getting blown during a windstorm
• enjoying a visit from a bee or butterfly
• withering on a hot summer day
• getting watered

Ask: **How is your role play similar to your drawing?** (They are both about flowers.) **How are they different?** (I did the role play with my body. I made the drawing with pastels and paper.)

② Create

Read pages 42–43 with children. Then distribute the materials.

• Remind children that the warm colors are *red, yellow, orange* and the cool colors are *blue, green, violet.*
• Have children choose whether they would like to show a flower or vegetable garden.
• Have children choose the color of paint from the same color family they used for their drawing.
• For Step 4, model how to apply a thin coat of paint over the drawing. Discuss the effects.

Technique Tip Point out that applying more pressure to the pastels will make darker colors.

③ Close

After children finish the activity, have them read and respond to *Think Like an Artist.* (Possible response: I used warm colors to make my garden sunny and happy.)

Ongoing Assessment

If . . . children have difficulty using pastels without smudging their work,

then . . . suggest that they apply less pressure on the pastels.

See page 18 from **Unit-by-Unit Resources** for a rubric to assess this studio.

Artist at Work

At a Glance

Objectives

- Read about a career in art.
- Identify the use of art in everyday life.
- Relate art to personal experiences.

Materials

- **Fine Art Transparency**
- photographs of stained-glass windows (optional)
- Sketchbook Journal

NVAS (K–4) #5 Reflecting upon and assessing the characteristics and merits of their work and the work of others

Explore

Display a photograph of a stained glass window. Ask children to discuss how they think it might have been made. Explain that stained glass is made by cutting glass into pieces and then joining the pieces together in an artful or interesting way. Then have children talk about any experiences with stained glass they have had.

Discuss

Help children read pages 44–45. Ask:

- **Why do you think Sarah Hightower named her artwork *Mr. Bubbles*?** (Possible response: Because she used cool colors that reminded her of water and soap bubbles.)
- **What skills does Hightower need to create stained glass artworks?** (Possible responses: She needs to know how to cut glass and to shape lead.)
- **What do you find most interesting about a job as a stained glass artist?** (Possible answer: using my creativity and hands to make something.)

Stained Glass

Sarah Hightower creates artworks from stained glass. She makes windows, lampshades, and other pieces.

Stained glass artists cut glass into shapes. Then they arrange the shapes and put them together.

Look at page 45. What colors do you see? What do the shapes remind you of?

Hightower says, "I feel that the glass reflects the way I feel about myself. I am strong, yet weak." What do you think she means?

Sarah Hightower cuts stained glass.

44

 Career Research

Have children identify different kinds of jobs in art as they research information about a career as a stained glass artist and the specific skills required. You may want to share these facts with children to get them started:

- Some stained glass artists design and make original artworks while others restore or repair existing artworks.
- Many stained glass artists are self-employed. Therefore, in addition to being good artists, they also need to know how to run their own businesses.
- Working with stained glass can be dangerous. Stained glass artists often wear protective clothing, boots, and safety glasses. They also wear face masks that protect them from chemical fumes.

Sarah Hightower. *Mr. Bubbles.*
Stained glass and lead, 11 by 8 by 13 inches.

Sarah Hightower. *Fire and Ice.*
Stained glass and lead, 15 by 12 by 14 inches.

45

Reading Strategy

Identify Details Remind children that there are often many details in a story or passage. These details add important and interesting information to the passage; however, they do not express the main idea of the passage. As an example, point out that on page 44, there is a quote by Sarah Hightower, the stained glass artist. This detail is interesting because it shows how important her work is to her; however, it does not help determine the main idea of the passage. Have children list other details they feel make the passage more interesting and list their responses on the board.

Apply

Tell children that they are going to design their own stained glass artwork. Ask them to think about the details in the story that would help them make their own stained glass artwork, such as what they would like to make, the materials they need, and the procedure. Display a list such as the following. Invite children to fill it in with how they will plan the details of their stained glass artwork. Possible responses are shown below.

How to Make a Stained Glass Artwork

1. Plan our design.

2. Gather materials.

3. Cut glass into shapes.

4. Arrange the shapes and mold them together.

SAMPLE

Have children sketch possible stained glass artworks in their Sketchbook Journals. Encourage them to use various lines, shapes, and colors.

Close

Have volunteers share their stained glass artworks with the class. As children discuss the sketches, have them name other possible uses for stained glass art. (Answers will vary.)

Portfolio Project

At a Glance

Objectives

• Develop and organize ideas from the environment.
• Demonstrate an understanding of line, shape, texture, and color.
• Evaluate original artworks by self and peers.

Materials

• shoeboxes, tagboard, scissors ⚠
• tempera paints in warm colors (red, orange, yellow) and cool colors (blue, green, violet)
• paintbrushes, clear tape
• Sketchbook Journal
• Rubric 1 from **Unit-by-Unit Resources**

NVAS (K–4) #1 Understanding and applying media, techniques, and processes
NVAS (K–4) #3 Choosing and evaluating a range of subject matter, symbols, and ideas

Make a Diorama

Make a diorama of your neighborhood.
Show people and places you find there.

1 Cut away a side from a box.

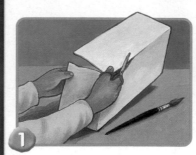

2 Use cool colors. Paint buildings and plants.

3 Use warm colors. Paint and cut out people.

4 Make the people stand up.

Plan

Read page 46 together. Ask:

• **What is special about your neighborhood?**
• **What buildings do you see there?**
• **What people do you see?**
• **What do these people do?**

Have children brainstorm what they will show in their diorama. Prompt them to think about the lines, shapes, textures, and colors they have seen in their neighborhood.

Quick Project

Have children use magazine cutouts of people, buildings, and plants to make a diorama of their neighborhood.

🧍🧍🧍🧍 Meeting Individual Needs

Reteach Have children make a diorama of only one favorite place in their neighborhood, such as their home, favorite park, or their school.

Extend Invite children to write a real or imaginative story about their neighborhood. Have them tape the story to the back of the diorama.

Look at how these children showed their neighborhoods.

Cori, Age 7. *Spring Creek.* Tempera on paper and cardboard.

Lilly, Age 7. *Lion Sun.* Tempera on paper and cardboard.

Share Your Art

1. Point out some lines, shapes, textures, and colors you used.
2. Tell how you decided what things from your neighborhood to show.

 Gallery Options

Art Exhibition Have children write information cards to display along with their dioramas. Cards should include their name, age, title of the artwork, and a short description of what the diorama shows.

Display the dioramas in a class "exhibition," or contact places in your neighborhood that might display children's artwork, such as a library or community center.

When viewing the exhibition, model for children how to identify ideas in an artwork. Then ask volunteers to choose an artwork and tell the main idea.

Create

Read page 46 and distribute the materials for the project.

- Make sure children hold the box with one hand as they cut with the other hand.
- Have children use cool colors to paint grass, sidewalks, streets, and so forth, on the bottom of the inside of the box.
- Provide tagboard for the figures children want to create for Step 3. These figures should be about four inches tall.
- Show children how to fold and tape tagboard tabs onto their figures to stand them upright. Give them 1-by-2-inch tagboard strips to use.

Monitor children's progress as they complete their dioramas. Warn them several minutes before cleanup time so they can prepare to finish.

Close

Point out children's art on page 47. Explain that these dioramas are from other second graders' portfolios. Ask:

- **What lines, shapes, colors, and textures do you see in these dioramas?** (Possible response: I see curved lines, circles and squares, warm colors, and fluffy textures.)
- **How are these dioramas similar to your own? How are they different?** (Answers will vary.)

Then use *Share Your Art* to help children define reasons for preferences in their own artwork. (Possible response: I used straight, thick lines; squares and rectangles; soft textures; and cool colors. I chose my favorite place to go in my neighborhood.)

See page 18 from **Unit-by-Unit Resources** for a rubric to assess this project.

Unit 1 Review

At a Glance

Objectives

- Relate art terms to the environment.
- Identify line, shape, texture, and color in artworks.
- Describe, analyze, interpret, and judge an artwork.

Materials

- Art Print 4
- Fine Art Transparency

NVAS (K–4) #1 Understanding and applying media, techniques, and processes

NVAS (K–4) #2 Using knowledge of structures and functions

NVAS (K–4) #5 Reflecting upon and assessing the characteristics and merits of their work and the work of others

Think About Art

Possible responses include:

line (Point to lines in the mosaic.)

tactile texture (Point to the scales on the goldfish.)

warm colors (Point to red, yellow, and orange colors in the goldfish.)

shape (Point to the mosaic.)

visual texture (Point to the smooth, flat surface on the mosaic.)

cool colors (Point to the colors of the grapes and leaves.)

Write About Art

Before children write, ask:

- **Who saw an object with interesting lines (shapes, colors, textures)? What was it?**
- **What would you like to draw or paint using similar lines (shapes, colors, textures)?**

Unit Review

Think About Art

Match the art words with the pictures.

line	tactile texture	warm colors
shape	visual texture	cool colors

Write About Art

Look at what a friend is wearing. Write about the textures and colors. Read your description aloud. Let the class guess who you wrote about.

Talk About Art

- Choose an artwork from your portfolio.
- Describe the mood in the artwork.

 Assessment Options

Options for assessing children appear in the **Unit-by-Unit Resources.**

- Use the **Vocabulary Worksheets** on pages 11–14 for an informal assessment of Unit 1 vocabulary.
- Use the **Unit 1 Test** on pages 19–22 to assess children's mastery of unit vocabulary and concepts.

Put It All Together

1. What colors do you see in this artwork?
2. What do you notice about the woman's hair?
3. Read the title. What is Miró's artwork about?
4. What would you name this artwork? Why?

49

Talk About Art

Have children define reasons for preferences in personal artworks. Ask: **Why did you choose this artwork to share?** (Answers will vary.)

Then ask children to tell why they created the artwork as they did. Prompt children to use words such as *line, shape, tactile texture, visual texture, warm colors,* and *cool colors* to describe their artwork.

Put It All Together

Use the questions on page 49 to help children evaluate the artwork. Possible responses:

1. red, yellow, blue, green, orange, and black
   DESCRIBE
2. Her hair is made with curved, thin lines. ANALYZE
3. Miró's artwork is about a woman who has only a few strands of hair. INTERPRET
4. Answers will vary. JUDGE

 Art Background

About the Artist Joan Miró (1893–1983) was a Spanish painter who provided some of the most original surrealist works in the twentieth century. Miró's artworks became popular because of their underlying humorous tone. He used neutral colors for his backgrounds in combination with brightly colored organic and geometric shapes.

Unit 2 Overview

In this unit, children will learn that art can be found in both natural and human-made objects. Often, the lines, shapes, and colors of everyday subjects work together to make them "artful." Children will learn how artists create still lifes, landscapes, and portraits using patterns, prints, and overlapping. They will also use their thoughts, feelings, and imaginations to create their own artworks.

	Unit Opener, p. 50	Lesson 1, p. 52 **Patterns and Prints** Studio 1, p. 54 **Make Creature Prints**	Lesson 2, p. 56 **Another Way to Print** Studio 2, p. 58 **Make Leaf Stencil Prints**	Lesson 3, p. 60 **Realistic and Abstract** Studio 3, p. 62 **Make an Abstract Collage**	Look and Compare, p. 64 **Musicians in Artworks**
Artworks	 **Fernand Léger.** *The Construction Workers,* 1950.	 **Kenojuak Ashevak.** *The Return of the Sun,* 1961.	 **Kenojuak Ashevak.** *Young Owl Takes a Ride,* 1984.	 **Hans Hoffmann.** *Red Squirrel,* 1578.	 **Fernand Léger.** *Three Musicians,* 1944. **Pablo Picasso.** *Three Musicians,* 1921.
Vocabulary		pattern, print	style, stencil print	subject, realistic, abstract	
Materials	• Art Print 5 • Fine Art Transparency • Instructional Prints	• **Fine Art Transparency** • Sketchbook Journal • tempera paint, water-based markers, crayons, paintbrushes, water containers, paper towels, newsprint • muffin tins or palettes for mixing paint (optional)	• **Fine Art Transparency** • pictures from a magazine or book of stencil prints (optional) • Sketchbook Journal • 3" x 5" heavy paper for stencils, drawing paper, scissors ⚠, colored chalk • transparent tape (optional)	• **Fine Art Transparency** • pencils, crayons, water-based markers • Sketchbook Journal • various colors of construction paper, scissors ⚠, glue	• Art Prints 5, 6, 7 • **Fine Art Transparency** • Sketchbook Journal
Connections	**Home Connection** neighborhood workers **Bookshelf** *Those Building Men* by Angela Johnson, Blue Sky Press, 2001	**Curriculum Connection** Math: patterns in math **ESL Notes** **Fine Arts Connection** Dance: patterns in dance **Meeting Individual Needs** Reteach, Extend	**Curriculum Connection** Science: lines, shapes, and patterns in nature **ESL Notes** **Fine Arts Connection** Music: nature sounds **Meeting Individual Needs** Reteach, Extend	**Curriculum Connection** Science: research tigers **ESL Notes** **Fine Arts Connection** Dance: realistic and abstract movement **Meeting Individual Needs** Reteach, Extend	**Reading Strategy** Relate to personal experience
Assessment Opportunities		Informal Assessment Rubric 2 from **Unit-by-Unit Resources** Ongoing Assessment	Visual Culture Rubric 2 from **Unit-by-Unit Resources** Ongoing Assessment	Informal Assessment Rubric 2 from **Unit-by-Unit Resources** Ongoing Assessment	

Lesson 4, p. 66 **Portraits** Studio 4, p. 68 **Draw a Self-Portrait**	Lesson 5 p. 70 **Still Life** Studio 5, p. 72 **Paint a Still Life**	Lesson 6, p. 74 **Landscape as a Subject** Studio 6, p. 76 **Build a Landscape**	Artist at Work, p. 78 **Photographs**	Portfolio Project, p. 80 **Print a Seascape**	Unit Review, p. 82
George Catlin. *Big Elk, a Famous Warrior,* 1832.	**Paul Cezanne.** *Still Life with Basket,* ca. 1888–1900.	**Henri Rousseau.** *Virgin Forest,* ca. 1910.	**Keba Armand Konte.** *Vanishing Point,* 1999.		**Franz Marc.** *Yellow Cow,* 1911.
portrait, expression, self-portrait	still life, shade, tint	landscapes, overlap			
• **Fine Art Transparency** • portrait-style photograph (optional) • Sketchbook Journal • safety-glass mirrors, pencils, oil pastels, construction paper, black glue in small squeeze bottles	• **Fine Art Transparency** • Sketchbook Journal • drawing paper, tempera paint, water containers, palettes, paintbrushes	• **Fine Art Transparency** • magazines featuring landscapes, such as *National Geographic* • Sketchbook Journal • tagboard, scissors ⚠, glue, craft sticks, tempera paints, paintbrushes, water containers, palettes, clothespins • paper clips (optional)	• **Fine Art Transparency** • photograph (optional)	• 1" x 3" rectangles and 3" x 5" rectangles cut from meat trays • pencils, tempera paint, blue watercolor paint, crayons, masking tape, paintbrushes, water containers, palettes, white construction paper	• **Art Print 8** • **Fine Art Transparency**
Technology Writing stories **ESL Notes** **Fine Arts Connection** Theatre: variety in expressions **Meeting Individual Needs** Reteach, Extend	**Curriculum Connection** Health: favorite fruits and vegetables **ESL Notes** **Fine Arts Connection** Music: variation in music **Meeting Individual Needs** Inclusion	**Curriculum Connection** Social Studies: state maps of natural areas **ESL Notes** **Fine Arts Connection** Theatre: stage directions **Meeting Individual Needs** Reteach, Extend	**Career Research** Photographer **Reading Strategy** Activate prior knowledge	**Gallery Options** Make your own frame **Meeting Individual Needs** Inclusion	
Visual Culture Rubric 2 from **Unit-by-Unit Resources** Ongoing Assessment	Visual Culture Rubric 2 from **Unit-by-Unit Resources** Ongoing Assessment	Visual Culture Rubric 2 from **Unit-by-Unit Resources** Ongoing Assessment		Rubric 2 from **Unit-by-Unit Resources**	**Unit-by-Unit Resources** Vocabulary Worksheets, pp. 29–32 Unit 2 Test, pp. 37–40

Unit 2

At a Glance

Objectives
- Identify the elements of art in artworks.
- Relate art to personal experiences.
- Respond to and make judgments about artworks.

Materials
- **Art Print 5**
- **Fine Art Transparency**

NVAS (K–4) #4 Understanding the visual arts in relation to history and cultures

NVAS (K–4) #5 Reflecting upon and assessing the characteristics and merits of their work and the work of others

Introduce the Unit

Ask a volunteer to read the title of Unit 2. Tell children that they will learn that art can be found all around. Art is in the patterns we see on the streets, in a field of flowers, or in a fruit arrangement. Often, the lines, shapes, and colors work together to make an everyday subject "artful." Ask:

- **Where can you find art?** (pictures at a museum, colors in a rainbow, shapes on a T-shirt)
- **What do you see that you think is art?** (posters, book covers, playground equipment, clouds)

Tell children that in this unit they will explore art that exists in nature as well as in human-made objects. They will learn how artists create still lifes, landscapes, and portraits using patterns, prints, and overlapping. They will use their thoughts, feelings, and imaginations to create their own artworks.

Fernand Léger. *The Construction Workers*, 1950. Oil on canvas, 118⅛ by 89 inches. Musée National Fernand Léger, Biot, France.

50

 Art Background

The Construction Workers Fernand Léger created this painting in 1950, several years after his return to France from exile in the United States. *The Construction Workers* represents Léger's later style, a period in which he painted workers, musicians, acrobats, and circus performers.

 Home Connection

Invite children to walk with a family member and observe people working in their neighborhood. For instance, they may watch a postal carrier delivering mail or a construction worker working on a building. Ask them to spend a few moments observing and taking notes on what they see. Then invite volunteers to discuss what they observed with the class.

Art is Everywhere

Where can you find art? It is in many places. Look for art at home, at school, and as you play. Art is everywhere! Find line, shape, color, and texture in the things around you. What do you see that you think is art?

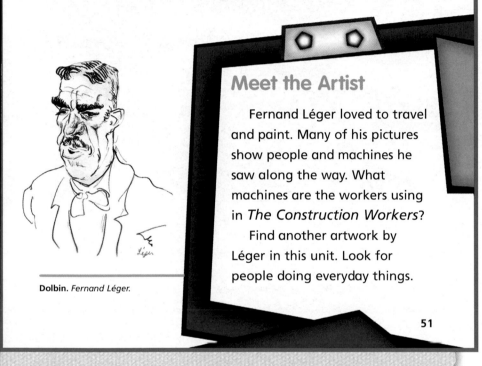

Dolbin. *Fernand Léger.*

Meet the Artist

Fernand Léger loved to travel and paint. Many of his pictures show people and machines he saw along the way. What machines are the workers using in *The Construction Workers*?

Find another artwork by Léger in this unit. Look for people doing everyday things.

51

Bookshelf

Those Building Men
by Angela Johnson
Blue Sky Press, 2001

Children who like *The Construction Workers* may also enjoy reading this selection to learn about the people who built the railroads, bridges, buildings, and roads in the United States a long time ago.

Discuss Unit Concepts

Have children read page 51. Share ideas about the artwork. For instance, say: **Some artworks like to show a construction. This is a construction. The builders are still working on it. I like this painting because of the thick lines and the bright colors.** Provide photographs or other artworks that contain constructions. Ask children to identify the construction in each.

Then initiate a discussion of the lines, shapes, and colors in *The Construction Workers*. Encourage children to offer responses based on what they learned in the previous unit. Then explain that in this unit they will learn additional terms and concepts that will help them create their own artworks.

As you introduce each element of art and principle of design in Unit 2, you may also wish to display the **Instructional Prints.** A print is provided for each element and principle.

In addition, **Art Prints 5–8** and **Transparencies** are available for fine art in the unit.

Meet the Artist

Fernand Léger (1881–1955) French artist Fernand Léger's early paintings were in the Impressionist and Fauvist styles. However, in 1907, Léger changed his style dramatically. He became interested in Cubism. In 1917, he began painting machines and mechanical objects, a style for which he is known. Léger also tried his hand at stained glass, ceramics, mosaics, and set and costume design.

Lesson 1

At a Glance

Objectives

• Identify and describe patterns.
• Describe, analyze, interpret, and judge artworks.

Materials

• **Fine Art Transparency**
• Sketchbook Journal

Vocabulary

pattern, print

NVAS (K–4) #2 Using knowledge of structures and functions

NVAS (K–4) #4 Understanding the visual arts in relation to history and cultures

NVAS (K–4) #5 Reflecting upon and assessing the characteristics and merits of their work and the work of others

Introduce

Have children focus on a bookshelf or windowpane that has repeating horizontal lines. Explain that the lines create a *pattern.* Have children look for other patterns in the classroom.

Explain that some artists make patterns in stone or in wood. They add ink to the pattern and place it onto paper to make a *print.* The girl on page 53 is making a print using a sponge covered with paint. Artists make prints so they can have copies of their artworks.

Patterns and Prints

A **pattern** is repeated shapes, lines, or colors. You can find patterns in nature, in things people make, and in artworks. Which patterns are in this artwork?

Kenojuak Ashevak. *The Return of the Sun,* 1961. Stonecut, 24 by 36 inches. ©West Baffin Eskimo Co-operative Ltd.

52

 Art Background

Art and Culture While growing up in the Canadian North, Kenojuak Ashevak (1927–) learned traditional Inuit handicrafts from her grandmother. Today, her artworks reflect the animals and people of the region as well as the Inuit lifestyle.

ESL **Notes**

Point to an object in the classroom that has a simple pattern, such as the stripes in the U.S. flag. Name the colors in order. Say: **This is a pattern.** Have children repeat after you. Continue choosing objects that contain patterns.

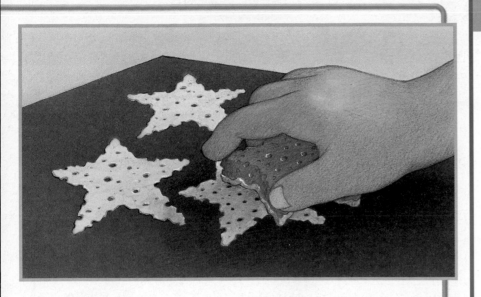

An Inuit woman drew the birds on page 52. To make a **print,** the bird patterns were cut in stone. Ink was placed on the stone and then the stone was pressed on paper.

There are other ways to make prints. How is the girl in the picture making a stamp print?

Sketchbook Journal

Dip your pencil eraser in paint, or tap it against an inkpad. Use the eraser to stamp a pattern.

53

② Teach

Have children read pages 52–53 and discuss *The Return of the Sun*. Point out that this artwork is an example of a stonecut print of a patterned design. Ask:

- **What do you see in this print?** (a sun, birds, animals) DESCRIBE
- **What patterns are in this artwork?** (the curved, pointed shapes of the birds' wings and tails and the animals' bodies; the petal-like shapes of the sun's rays; the wavy lines of the animals' paws) ANALYZE
- **Why do you think the artist used so many curvy lines that point up?** (to make the animals look happy.) INTERPRET
- **What do you like best about this artwork?** (Possible response: I like the sun's rays because they add a bright color to the print.) JUDGE

Sketchbook Journal Have children draw the patterns they will make in their eraser prints on drawing paper.

③ Close

Have children share their prints with the class. Encourage them to talk about their patterns and prints.

Assessment Organize children into pairs and ask them to tell what they learned in this lesson. Listen as they talk about patterns and printmaking.

Curriculum Connection

Math On the chalkboard, draw a pattern using shapes. Ask children what shape comes next. Make the patterns increasingly more complicated and invite children to complete the patterns by drawing the next shapes on the board.

Have children use drawing paper to make repeating patterns of their own with lines or shapes. Then have them exchange papers with a partner and draw what would come next in their partner's pattern.

Studio 1

At a Glance

Objectives

- Express ideas using patterns to make a print.
- Demonstrate how to make prints with paint.
- Evaluate original artworks by self and peers.

Materials

- tempera paint, water-based markers, crayons, paintbrushes, water containers, paper towels, newsprint
- muffin tins or palettes for mixing paint (optional)
- Rubric 2 from **Unit-by-Unit Resources**

NVAS (K–4) #1 Understanding and applying media, techniques, and processes

NVAS (K–4) #3 Choosing and evaluating a range of subject matter, symbols, and ideas

① Introduce

Review patterns with children. Have them brainstorm ideas for their artwork. Ask:

- **What kind of creature will you make? What will it look like?**
- **What patterns (using colors, shapes, and lines) will you make?**
- **What interesting details will you add to your picture?**

Quick Studio

Have children make one fingerprint on a sheet of paper. Have them use crayons or markers to make it look like an animal.

Studio 1

Make Creature Prints

You can make a print with almost anything.
Follow these steps to make prints with your hand.

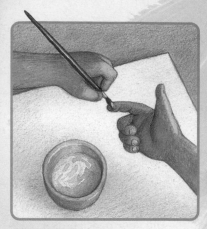
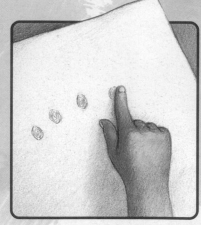

1. **Paint your fingertip with a light coat of paint.**

2. **Press your fingertip against the paper.**

Technique Tip

Press lightly when you print so the lines in your hand will show.

👥 Meeting Individual Needs

Reteach Encourage children to take a few moments to think about their patterns and then have them draw a pattern on drawing paper with pencil before painting the pattern on the newsprint.

Extend Invite children to explore more complex patterns in their artwork, incorporating different lines, shapes, and colors.

3 Paint a different part of your hand. Make new prints.

4 Add details to make creatures.

Think Like an Artist

Which print do you find most interesting? Why?

 Fine Arts Connection

Dance Play a song or music with a steady rhythm. Demonstrate the following: clap your hands, snap your fingers, clap your hands, snap your fingers. Tell children that you are making a pattern through movement. Invite children to follow along with you. Then challenge them to make patterns of their own.

❷ Create

Have children look at the pictures and read the directions on pages 54–55. Then distribute materials.

• Instruct children to coat their fingertips evenly with paint. They should use one fingertip for each paint color.
• Make sure children press their fingertips evenly but gently. Identify this as a necessary skill for producing prints.
• Suggest that children first wash their fingertips. Then encourage them to make prints of their palms.
• Have them use a crayon or water-based marker to add details to complete their imaginary creatures.

Technique Tip Tell children to blot their fingertips first and then use a rolling motion as they place their finger on the construction paper.

❸ Close

Have children define reasons for preferences in personal artworks by answering the *Think Like an Artist* questions. (Possible response: the one I made with my index finger; because I can see the tiny lines in my fingerprint)

Ongoing Assessment

If . . . children's prints do not show the fingerprint details,

then . . . remind them to lift their fingertips or hands straight up from the paper after making their print.

See page 36 from **Unit-by-Unit Resources** for a rubric to assess this studio.

Lesson 2

At a Glance

Objectives

- Identify and describe style.
- Identify and describe stencil print.
- Describe, analyze, interpret, and judge artworks.

Materials

- **Fine Art Transparency**
- pictures from a magazine or book of stencil prints (optional)
- Sketchbook Journal

Vocabulary

style, stencil print

NVAS (K–4) #4 Understanding the visual arts in relation to history and cultures

NVAS (K–4) #5 Reflecting upon and assessing the characteristics and merits of their work and the work of others

NVAS (K–4) #6 Making connections between visual arts and other disciplines

①Introduce

Show children examples of objects that were printed with stencils. Point out stencils in the classroom, such as on children's clothing, a poster, or on wallpaper samples. Discuss how the designs vary from subject to subject.

Explain that a *stencil print* is made by using a stencil, which is most often a piece of paper, cardboard, or plastic with a cutout design. Paint is then applied through the cutout, or stencil, to a surface underneath.

Explain that artists each have their own *style,* or special way of creating artworks. An artwork's style makes it different from or similar to other artworks.

Lesson 2

Another Way to Print

Look at this print. The same artist made the print on page 52. Did you notice how she used the same colors in both prints? What else can you say about this artist's **style?**

Kenojuak Ashevak. *Young Owl Takes a Ride,* 1984. Stonecut and stencil, 19½ by 25½ inches. ©West Baffin Eskimo Co-operative Ltd.

56

 **Art Background**

Art History Stencil printing dates back as early as prehistoric times. The first evidence was found in cave paintings in France and Spain. Prehistoric man placed his hand on the wall of the cave. Then he blew pulverized pigment, similar to chalk, all around it.

The Japanese, however, are the people credited with perfecting the printmaking technique most similar to how it is done today.

About the Artist Amado Peña (1943–) was raised in Laredo, Texas. He was an art teacher for sixteen years before deciding to make his living as an artist. A master serigrapher, Peña is well known for his colorful silk-screen prints that feature bold outlines and strong patterns.

Amado Peña. *Los Pescados Peña (The Peña Fish)*, 1978.
Serigraph, 22 by 32 inches. Courtesy of the artist.

The artwork above shows patterns with bright colors. The artist cut out stencils for the patterns. He put ink over his stencils. The ink printed onto the paper below to make a **stencil print.** Which parts do you think were made with a stencil?

Art in My World

Look for patterns in curtains, rugs, and clothes. Which patterns might have been made with a stencil?

57

② Teach

Have children read page 56. Ask:

- **What do you see?** (an owl having a piggyback ride on another owl) DESCRIBE
- **What does the artwork tell you about the artist?** (Possible response: It shows her love of animals or it shows that she had observed owls.) ANALYZE
- **What do you think this artwork is about?** (Possible response: The artist may want to express the freedom of an owl taking flight.) INTERPRET
- **What impact does this artwork have on you? Explain.** (Possible response: This artwork has a big impact on me; I like how the owls are shown as strong and loving.) JUDGE

Have children read page 57. Ask similar questions as children look at Amado Peña's artwork.

Art in My World Remind children that artists often stencil a shape that they want to use many times. Then they add details to each stencil print to make it special.

③ Close

Have children discuss the various stencil prints they found in the classroom and what they like about them.

Visual Culture Bring in photographs to generate discussion of clothing with stencil patterns. Have children describe the prints and consider what inspired these patterns.

Curriculum Connection

Science Explain that artists often get ideas from the natural world. Have children discuss items such as leaves, acorns, fruits, and vegetables that they could use in their own stencil prints. Have each child use a hand lens to look at various objects and discuss the lines, shapes, and patterns they may see.

 Notes

Prior to the activity, find several examples of a stencil print. Show each example and say, **This is a stencil print.** Have children repeat after you.

Studio 2

Studio 2

Make Leaf Stencil Prints

Follow these steps to make stencil prints.

At a Glance

Objectives

• Express ideas using pattern to make a stencil print.

• Demonstrate how to use a variety of art materials to make a stencil print.

• Evaluate original artworks by self and peers.

Materials

• 3" × 5" heavy paper for stencils, drawing paper, scissors ⚠, colored chalk

• transparent tape (optional)

• Rubric 2 from **Unit-by-Unit Resources**

NVAS (K–4) #1 Understanding and applying media, techniques, and processes

NVAS (K–4) #5 Reflecting upon and assessing the characteristics and merits of their work and the work of others

1 Fold a paper in half. Draw a leaf shape on the fold.

2 Cut out the leaf shape and set it aside.

Technique Tip

To cut out the leaf, gently fold it and cut into the fold. Carefully cut out the leaf shape to create your stencil.

❶ Introduce

Review stencil patterns with children and have them describe stencil patterns they have seen. Ask:

• **What kind of leaf will you make?**

• **Where have you seen this leaf before?**

• **What shape and lines will it have? For example, will it be long and narrow or wide with curved lines?**

👫👫 Meeting Individual Needs

Reteach You may want to instruct children who are having difficulty using scissors to cut out a simpler geometric shape, such as a circle or a rectangle.

Extend Encourage children to share stencils to provide variety in their artworks. Have them experiment with new leaf shapes by placing the edges of their stencils on top of one another.

Quick Studio

Have children create a stencil by using a hole punch and a sheet of paper. Have them color over the holes to make prints.

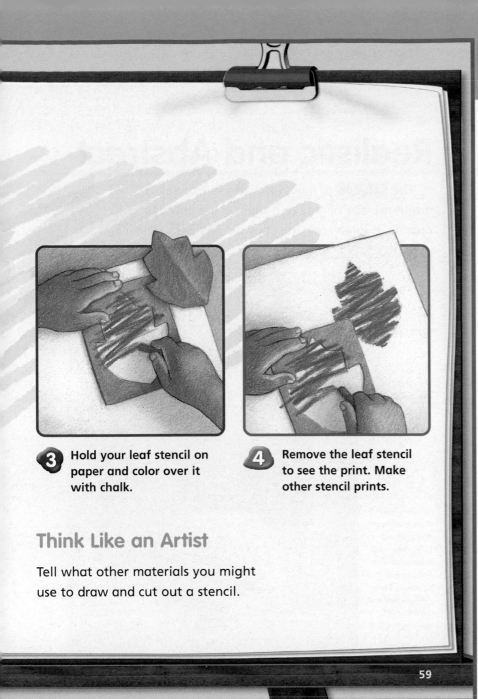

3 Hold your leaf stencil on paper and color over it with chalk.

4 Remove the leaf stencil to see the print. Make other stencil prints.

Think Like an Artist

Tell what other materials you might use to draw and cut out a stencil.

59

 Fine Arts Connection

Music Have children close their eyes and imagine it is a cool autumn day. Have them think about the sounds they would hear if they were in a forest or park with leaves blowing all around them. Have them think about the sounds that the leaves and the wind and any animals such as birds and rabbits would make.

Then, while they work on their stencil prints, play CDs of nature sounds and other music that you might associate with seasons. Have children name instruments that sound like objects in nature.

② Create

Have children look at the pictures and read the directions on pages 58–59. Then distribute materials. Caution children against blowing or inhaling chalk dust as they work. Make provisions for children who may be allergic.

- Have children make sketches in their Sketchbook Journal of different leaves before they begin.
- Show children where to start cutting on the fold to make sure their stencil turns out intact. Guide them to identify this as a necessary skill for producing stencil prints.
- Children may need to tape their stencils in place as they apply chalk.
- Suggest that they try several arrangements before settling on a final design.

Technique Tip Guide children to see that a stencil with a thicker border will be easier to work with during Steps 3 and 4.

③ Close

Have children reflect on their prints as they discuss the *Think Like an Artist* feature. (Possible responses: pencil or crayon, paper punch)

Ongoing Assessment

If . . . children notice that the edges of their prints appear to bleed,

then . . . tell them to work their chalk toward the center of the stencil.

See page 36 from **Unit-by-Unit Resources** for a rubric to assess this studio.

Lesson 3

At a Glance

Objectives

- Identify and discuss realistic and abstract.
- Describe, analyze, interpret, and judge artworks.

Materials

- **Fine Art Transparency**
- pencils, crayons, water-based markers
- Sketchbook Journal

Vocabulary

subject, realistic, abstract

NVAS (K–4) #2 Using knowledge of structures and functions

NVAS (K–4) #5 Reflecting upon and assessing the characteristics and merits of their work and the work of others

NVAS (K–4) #6 Making connections between visual arts and other disciplines

❶ Introduce

Show children an illustration of a child. Then draw a stick figure on the chalkboard. Ask children to discuss how the illustration and the stick figure are different. (Possible responses: The illustration looks like a real person and the stick figure does not.)

Explain to children that some artists create artworks that are realistic. These artworks have subjects that look real to the audience.

Then explain that some artists create artworks that are abstract. Abstract artworks have subjects that cannot easily be identified. Artists use color, line, shape, and texture to emphasize or reveal certain qualities. For instance, point out that even though the stick figure was made of simple lines and a circle, they were able to determine that it was a person. Ask: **Where else have you seen realistic subjects or objects?** (in books, posters, and greeting cards) **Where else have you seen abstract subjects or objects?** (clothing designs, fabrics for furniture)

60

Realistic and Abstract

The **subject,** or main idea, of this artwork is a squirrel. You might see a squirrel like this one outside. It looks real. This shows a **realistic** style.

Hans Hoffmann. *Red Squirrel,* 1578, Watercolor, heightened with white and gold on vellum, 9⅞ by 7 inches. National Gallery of Art, Washington, D.C.

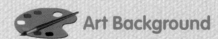

60

 Art Background

About the Artist German artist Hans Hoffmann (1880–1966) lived in Paris and was acquainted with Pablo Picasso, Henri Matisse, and Robert Delaunay. Hoffmann was an art teacher first. It was not until he resigned at the age of seventy-eight that he produced what many believe to be his best artworks.

About the Artist Franz Marc (1880–1916) was born in Munich, Germany. The majority of his artworks portray animals. In 1911, he helped found *Der Blaue Reiter* (the Blue Rider), a group of German Expressionist painters.

Franz Marc.
The Tiger, 1913.
Städtisches Galerie
im Lenbachhaus,
Munich, Germany.

What is the subject of this artwork? The style of Marc's *Tiger* is **abstract.** Most of the shapes do not show a real tiger. Yet, the painting may remind you of a tiger. Why?

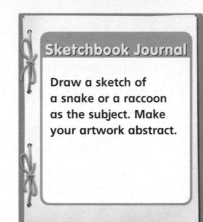

Sketchbook Journal

Draw a sketch of a snake or a raccoon as the subject. Make your artwork abstract.

61

Curriculum Connection

Science Organize the class into groups. Have each group conduct its own research on tigers using library and online sources. When completed, have them share their findings with the class.

Notes

Give children more examples of realistic versus abstract artworks to check their understanding of the words. You may want to share illustrations from books to help children understand the difference. For instance, *The Three Pigs* by David Wisener (Clarion Books, April 2001) shows realistic illustrations. *Follow That Hat!* by Pierre Pratt (Annik, 1992) provides examples of abstract illustrations.

② Teach

Have children read pages 60–61 and examine the artwork on page 61. Ask:

- **What is the subject of this artwork?** (Possible response: tiger) DESCRIBE
- **What geometric shapes and colors do you see?** (triangles; yellow, brown, orange, green, blue, purple) DESCRIBE
- **What is it about the painting that reminds you of a tiger?** (Possible response: The colors are those of a tiger.) ANALYZE
- **What mood do you think the artist was trying to express?** (He was trying to make the tiger look mysterious and fierce.) INTERPRET
- **What do you like best about this artwork?** (Answers will vary.) JUDGE

Ask children similar questions as they examine *Red Squirrel* on page 60.

Sketchbook Journal Remind children that abstract artists use colors, shapes, and lines in interesting ways. Tell them to use colors, shapes, or lines that remind them of a snake or raccoon to create their artwork.

③ Close

Invite children to talk about the shapes and colors they used in their sketches and what details they find most interesting.

Assessment Let each child select a picture book. Then have all children who have books with realistic illustrations stand. Next, have all children who have books with abstract illustrations stand. Pair children and listen as they discuss the illustrations of each other's books.

Studio 3

Make an Abstract Collage

Think of an animal. Follow these steps to show it in an abstract artwork.

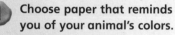
1 Choose paper that reminds you of your animal's colors.

2 Tear some shapes. Glue them down.

Technique Tip

You may want to cut 2 or 3 shapes at once. To do so, stack or fold the paper before cutting.

62

At a Glance

Objectives

- Express ideas about abstract art by making an original artwork.
- Demonstrate how to make a collage.
- Evaluate original artworks by self and peers.

Materials

- various colors of construction paper, scissors ⚠, glue
- Rubric 2 from **Unit-by-Unit Resources**

NVAS (K–4) #1 Understanding and applying media, techniques, and processes

NVAS (K–4) #3 Choosing and evaluating a range of subject matter, symbols, and ideas

NVAS (K–4) #5 Reflecting upon and assessing the characteristics and merits of their work and the work of others

❶ Introduce

Have children discuss what makes an artwork abstract. Ask:

- **Will you create a real or imaginary animal? What will it look like?**
- **What kinds of colors, shapes, and lines will you use to remind someone of your animal?**
- **What abstract details will you add to the background?**

Quick Studio

Have children make an animal or creature using only three geometric or organic shapes.

👨‍👧‍👦 Meeting Individual Needs

Reteach Some children may benefit from thinking about the shapes that they will use. Ask them to reflect and draw these shapes before beginning the project.

Extend Have children create an abstract collage of a different subject, such as a person or an object. Challenge them to use shapes such as ovals, rectangles, diamonds, and hearts. Furthermore, have children determine the mood they want to create in the artwork, and choose their colors accordingly.

3 Cut a shape that looks like part of your animal. Glue it down.

4 Tear shapes from other colors to glue around your animal.

Think Like an Artist

Ask a friend to guess your animal. Talk about what reminds you of the real animal.

 Fine Arts Connection

Dance Explain to children that movement can also be expressed in realistic and abstract ways. First model a realistic portrayal of an animal such as a cat. (For instance, pretend to lick your paws.) Then put on some music and "dance" like a cat. Ask children to explain the difference in your cat-like movements. Explain that the first one was realistic, but the second one was abstract. You conveyed a cat's mood or feelings. Have children join in as they create their own realistic and abstract movements for snakes, chickens, and other animals.

2 Create

Have children look at the pictures and read the directions on pages 62–63. Then distribute materials.

- Have children take time to select the colors that best represent their animals.
- Suggest to children that they arrange their shapes on paper before they begin to glue.
- Have children experiment with different geometric shapes before adding one to their collages.
- As children add details, encourage them to think about the colors of their animal's environment or home.

Technique Tip Have children experiment with both torn and cut shapes to vary the texture of their collages.

3 Close

Have children examine their artworks as they discuss the *Think Like an Artist* feature. (Possible response: The round spots that I put on my dog remind me of my real dog.)

Ongoing Assessment

If . . . children have difficulty thinking of abstract details,

then . . . suggest they look around the classroom for ideas in clothing, posters, or floor coverings.

See page 36 from **Unit-by-Unit Resources** for a rubric to assess this studio.

Look and Compare

Look and Compare

At a Glance

Objectives

- Compare and contrast two artworks that show three musicians.
- Respond to and make judgments about artworks.

Materials

- **Art Prints 5, 6, 7**
- **Fine Art Transparency**
- Sketchbook Journal

NVAS (K–4) #5 Reflecting upon and assessing the characteristics and merits of their work and the work of others

Explore

Display **Art Print 5,** *The Construction Workers.* Help children recall the artwork by Fernand Léger from page 50. As children look at the two artworks on pages 64–65, ask them to predict which one was created by Léger and give reasons for their answer. (Possible response: The men have similar looks on their faces and the figures are rounded.)

Discuss

After children read pages 64–65, identify a story in Léger's *Three Musicians.* Say: **Léger's artwork is about three musicians. They each have different instruments and they look like they are playing for an audience.** Then have children tell a story about Picasso's *Three Musicians.* (Possible response: This is about three musicians who work in a circus.)

Musicians in Artworks

Artists may paint the same subject. These two artists painted pictures of musicians. How are their styles alike?

Fernand Léger.
Three Musicians,
1944. Oil on canvas,
68½ by 57¼ inches.
Museum of Modern
Art, New York.

 Art Background

Three Musicians Fernand Léger created this painting in 1944 after a drawing he made in 1924–1925. He painted *Three Musicians* while he was living in the United States. Several years earlier, he had developed a style of painting figures that appear thick, robust, and cylindrical.

Three Musicians Pablo Picasso (1881–1973) created this painting in the Cubist style, which is characterized by flat, geometric shapes. Picasso's three characters (Harlequin with a guitar, Pierrot with a clarinet, and the monk with an accordion) were influenced by Italian, French, and Spanish popular theater and carnival traditions.

Pablo Picasso. *Three Musicians*, Fontainebleau, summer 1921. Oil on canvas, approximately 79 by 88 inches. The Museum of Modern Art, New York. Mrs. Simon Guggenheim Fund. Photograph ©1997 The Museum of Modern Art, New York. ©1998 Estate of Pablo Picasso/Artists Rights Society (ARS), New York.

Point out patterns in each artwork. Describe where you see them. How are the patterns different?

Sketchbook Journal

Draw two pictures of the same subject. Make one realistic. Make one abstract. Use patterns in both.

65

Apply

Draw a Venn diagram like the one below on the chalkboard. Explain to children that graphic organizers such as these can help us to see how artworks are similar and different.

To fill in the diagram, suggest that children first compare the artworks, looking for ways that they are alike. Fill in the middle section as children offer ideas.

Guide children as they look for differences by suggesting that they focus on shapes, patterns, and lines in the two artworks. Possible responses are shown in blue.

Paintings of Three Musicians

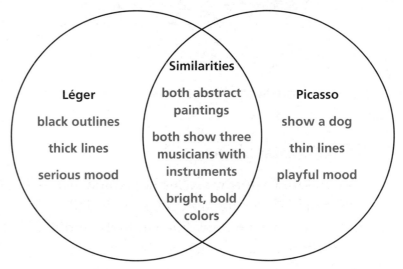

Léger

black outlines

thick lines

serious mood

Similarities

both abstract paintings

both show three musicians with instruments

bright, bold colors

Picasso

show a dog

thin lines

playful mood

Close

Ask children what they learned about musicians in artworks from these artists. (Possible response: Artists can show the same subject in different ways.)

Sketchbook Journal Before children begin drawing the subjects in their Sketchbook Journal, have them first take some time to think about the shapes and the lines they will use.

 Reading Strategy

Relate to Personal Experience Remind children that when we read or look at artworks, we use our personal experiences to help us understand them. For instance, point out to children that they knew that the subjects of Léger's and Picasso's artworks were musicians because they have seen musicians or instruments before.

Provide a portfolio, or book with a collection of artworks by Léger or Picasso. Ask children to identify ideas about the portfolio based upon what they already learned about the artist. Model by saying: **Léger's portfolio includes artworks with abstract style. He uses thick lines in many of his artworks.**

Lesson 4

At a Glance

Objectives

- Identify and describe portraits and self-portraits.
- Describe, analyze, interpret, and judge artworks.

Materials

- **Fine Art Transparency**
- portrait-style photograph (optional)
- Sketchbook Journal

Vocabulary

portrait, expression, self-portrait

NVAS (K–4) #2 Using knowledge of structures and functions

NVAS (K–4) #4 Understanding the visual arts in relation to history and cultures

NVAS (K–4) #5 Reflecting upon and assessing the characteristics and merits of their work and the work of others

Introduce

Show children a portrait-style photograph and explain that the photograph is a portrait. Tell children that portraits are different from candid pictures because the model, or person sitting for the picture, is almost always aware of the artist and often looks directly at him or her.

Explain that artists often show a model's expression as a way to reveal something unique about the model. For instance, a small boy with big round eyes may express innocence.

Last, explain that a self-portrait is a picture that the artist makes of himself or herself. Have children think about what they would want to tell about themselves in a self-portrait.

Portraits

The picture on this page is a **portrait.** The **expression,** or look on the person's face, shows thoughts and feelings. What do you think the man in this portrait might be thinking?

George Catlin. *Big Elk, a Famous Warrior,* 1832. Oil on canvas, 29 by 24 inches. Smithsonian American Art Museum, Washington, D.C.

 Art Background

About the Artist Painter George Catlin (1796–1872) was the first artist to paint Native Americans, including Blackfoot, Crow, and Sioux warriors, in their own environments. During his five trips west, he painted more than 500 artworks, including this one of an Omaha warrior, Big Elk, whom he painted in 1832. Through his artworks, Catlin hoped to bring attention to the Indian way of life that he admired so much.

About the Artist From an early age, Alice Neel (1900–1984) wanted to be an artist. She studied art at the Philadelphia School of Design for Women. After living in Havana, Cuba, for a year after graduation, Neel eventually settled in New York City. She became known for her portraits of her children, of neighbors in Spanish Harlem, and of famous artists.

Alice Neel. *Sarah Greenberg,*
1967. Oil on canvas, 46 by 32
inches. The Estate of Alice Neel,
Courtesy of Robert Miller Gallery,
New York.

A young girl posed for
this portrait. The girl was
the artist's model. Look at
the expression on her face.
What do you think she
might be feeling?

Sometimes artists use
themselves as models. A
portrait that shows the
artist who made it is a
self-portrait.

Art Fact

One artist, Frida
Kahlo, painted over
fifty self-portraits in
her lifetime.

67

Technology

Writing Stories Have children work in pairs to write a
story. Ask them to imagine that Sarah Greenberg or Big
Elk is one of their main characters. Have one child start the
story with the first sentence. Then have children take turns
adding to the story until it is finished. Have each pair print
out the story and take turns reading it to the class.

 Notes

To check children's understanding of portrait, provide
several examples of photographs. Show an example of a
portrait and say: **This is a portrait.** Have children repeat
after you. Ask children to tell whether the others are
portraits or not by answering yes or no.

② Teach

Have children read pages 66–67. Then have them
focus on the expression of the young girl. Ask:

- **What do you see in this painting?** (a young girl
  sitting in a chair) DESCRIBE
- **What lines, shapes, and patterns do you see?**
  (the wavy lines of the arms of the chair, the
  geometric shapes on the wall, the curvy lines of
  the pattern on her dress, the curved lines of the
  curls in her hair) ANALYZE
- **Why do you think the artist painted the girl
  this way?** (to show her in a natural way)
  INTERPRET
- **What do you like best about this artwork?**
  (Possible answer: I like the look on the girl's
  face.) JUDGE

Direct children to *Big Elk, a Famous Warrior* and
ask similar questions. Then ask children to
compare the two artworks, focusing on how the
individuals are depicted.

Research Create a classroom exhibit of self-portraits
made by several well known artists. Display self-
portraits shown in the Student Edition or find other
books with self-portraits that can be placed around
the classroom. Have children identify ideas about
the exhibition. Model by saying, **Many artists have
painted self-portraits of themselves. They all are
unique and have interesting expressions.**

③ Close

Invite children to share their research findings
with the class.

Visual Culture Have children think about and
discuss how clowns and other performers use
theatrical makeup to show moods, thoughts, and
feelings.

Studio 4

At a Glance

Objectives

- Express ideas by drawing a self-portrait.
- Demonstrate how to use oil pastels to create a self-portrait.
- Evaluate original artworks by self and peers.

Materials

- safety-glass mirrors, pencils, oil pastels, construction paper, black glue in small squeeze bottles
- Rubric 2 from **Unit-by-Unit Resources**

NVAS (K–4) #1 Understanding and applying media, techniques, and processes

NVAS (K–4) #5 Reflecting upon and assessing the characteristics and merits of their work and the work of others

❶ Introduce

Review and discuss self-portraits with children. Then ask:

- **Will your self-portrait be realistic or abstract?**
- **What colors, shapes, and lines will you use?**
- **Will you create patterns? If so, what will they be?**

Quick Studio

Have children bring in a photograph of themselves and then draw a self-portrait based on it.

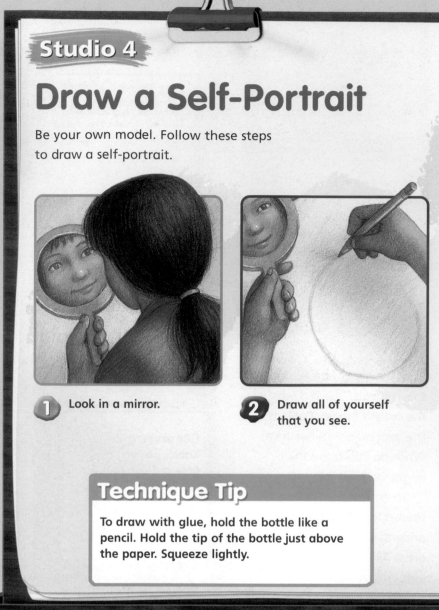

Studio 4

Draw a Self-Portrait

Be your own model. Follow these steps to draw a self-portrait.

1 Look in a mirror.

2 Draw all of yourself that you see.

Technique Tip

To draw with glue, hold the bottle like a pencil. Hold the tip of the bottle just above the paper. Squeeze lightly.

68

🚶 Meeting Individual Needs

Reteach If children have difficulty with their self-portraits, have them focus on their face first. Explain to children that each facial feature can begin with a shape. For instance, eyes are ovals and a nose is a basic triangle. Remind children that if they make an abstract drawing, then they do not have to make their artwork look exactly like themselves.

Extend Explain that some portraits include animals or objects that tell about the person in the picture. Have children list or draw objects or animals they will include in a self-portrait to show what is important to them.

3 Go over your pencil lines with black glue. Let the glue dry.

4 Fill in the spaces with oil pastels.

Think Like an Artist

What shape is your face? Tell other shapes that you used to draw your self-portrait.

 Fine Arts Connection

Theatre Remind children that their faces can show feelings and emotions no matter what words they are saying. Invite volunteers to say any silly phrase, such as "macaroni and cheese," using a variety of expressions including happy, sad, bored, excited, embarrassed, and angry.

As children take turns saying the phrase, have them notice whether their faces change with the changing emotions. Ask them to describe what they sensed about their faces. Invite others to describe the changes they observed in their classmates' faces.

2 Create

Have children read the directions and look at the pictures on pages 68–69. Prepare the black glue. Add black tempera paint to a partially used bottle of glue, so children can squeeze the glue directly from the bottle. Then distribute materials.

- Tell children with long hair to pull their hair back so they can see the shape of their face.
- Remind children that the eyes are usually halfway between the top of the head and the bottom of the chin.
- Have a designated drying area.
- Demonstrate how to hold the oil pastel like a pencil, varying the pressure to create different intensities of color.

Technique Tip Invite children to experiment with the glue on scrap paper before applying it to lines of their portraits.

3 Close

Have children think about their artworks and discuss *Think Like an Artist* on page 69. (Possible responses: oval; round shapes for the eyes and mouth) Ask children to describe why the shapes worked well or did not work well in their self-portrait.

Ongoing Assessment

If . . . children find "crumbs" of color on their papers,

then . . . they are applying the pastels too heavily. Instruct them to apply less pressure.

See page 36 from **Unit-by-Unit Resources** for a rubric to assess this studio.

Lesson 5

At a Glance

Objectives

- Identify and describe a still life.
- Describe, analyze, interpret, and judge artworks.

Materials

- **Fine Art Transparency**
- Sketchbook Journal

Vocabulary

still life, shade, tint

NVAS (K–4) #2 Using knowledge of structures and functions
NVAS (K–4) #5 Reflecting upon and assessing the characteristics and merits of their work and the work of others

❶ Introduce

Bring together a collection of objects found in the classroom, such as a book, a paintbrush, and eyeglasses. Explain to children that this composition is a still life, or a collection of objects that can't move on their own. Ask children to name other objects in the classroom that can be used as models for a still life.

Tell children that some artists like to paint still lifes. They like to collect objects that have interesting lines, shapes, and colors to make a composition. Have children identify various lines, shapes, and colors in the objects they named above.

Continue by telling children that artists who paint still lifes often use different shades and tints of color. Explain that shades are dark colors made by adding black to a color, and tints are light colors made by adding a color to white. Point out that the different shades and tints of a color are also the value of a color. *Value* is the lightness and darkness of each color.

Still Life

This artwork is a **still life.** It shows objects that cannot move on their own. What did this artist use as models for his still life?

Paul Cézanne. *Still Life with Basket,* ca. 1888-1900. Musée d'Orsay, Paris, France.

70

 Art Background

About the Artist Paul Cézanne (1839–1906) was born in Aix-en-Provence in the south of France. Many of Cézanne's artworks were still lifes of fruits, though he also painted mountains and portraits.

About the Artist Gabriele Münter (1877–1962) became one of the first students of the avant-garde Phalanx School founded by Wassily Kandinsky. This was one of the few art academies to accept women. Later, she helped organize the Blue Rider, a group of German Expressionist painters.

Gabriele Münter. *Blumen in der Nacht (Flowers at Night)*, 1941. Oil on cardboard, 20 by 26 inches. Hamburger Kunsthalle, Hamburg.

Flowers and vases can be models too. Look at the colors in this still life. Point to something blue.

Some blues are light, and some are dark. A dark color is a **shade.** A shade is made by adding black to a color. A light color is a **tint.** A tint is made by adding a color to white.

Sketchbook Journal

Plan a still life that shows your favorite foods. Make a list of foods you would paint.

71

Have children read pages 70–71. Next, have children direct their attention to *Flowers at Night*. Ask:

- **What did this artist use as models for her still life?** (vases and flowers) DESCRIBE
- **How are shapes and lines combined in this artwork?** (Possible responses: curved lines of the blue vase, rounded lines of the flower's petals, straight lines of the red vase) ANALYZE
- **How does this artwork affect you?** (Possible response: It is colorful and makes me feel happy.) INTERPRET
- **What part of this painting is the most interesting to you?** (Possible response: the bright red flower against the dark shadows) JUDGE

Then have children look at *Still Life with Basket* as you ask similar questions.

Sketchbook Journal Before children begin to plan their still life drawings, ask them to identify the colors and shapes of the foods they want to use.

③Close

Have children share their plans. Ask them to name the lines, shapes, and colors that would make up their composition.

Visual Culture Have children think about illustrations and photographs of food that are often displayed in fast-food restaurants to show which foods can be ordered. Have children draw a picture of a favorite dish on a sheet of construction paper to create a restaurant menu.

Curriculum Connection

Health Tell children that many artists who paint still lifes use fruits and vegetables as their models. Remind children that including fruits and vegetables in their diet will keep them healthy and help protect their body from getting sick. Have children create a class list of their favorite fruits and vegetables.

ESL Notes

Have children look at the artworks on pages 70–71. Remind children that still lifes show objects that do not move. Have children name several objects, such as toys, fruit, flowers, and vases, that can be used in a still life.

Studio 5

At a Glance

Objectives

• Demonstrate how to make tints and shades in a painting.
• Evaluate original artworks by self and peers.

Materials

• drawing paper, tempera paint, water containers, palettes, paintbrushes
• Rubric 2 from **Unit-by-Unit Resources**

NVAS (K–4) #1 Understanding and applying media, techniques, and processes

NVAS (K–4) #3 Choosing and evaluating a range of subject matter, symbols, and ideas

❶ Introduce

Review still life with children. Then ask:

• **What will you include in your still life?**
• **What colors will you use? What shades and tints will you use?**
• **What shapes and lines will you use in your artwork?**

Studio 5

Paint a Still Life

Think of subjects for a still life. Then follow these steps to paint them.

 1 Mix tints of one color of paint.

2 Mix shades of the same color.

Technique Tip

When you make shades, add tiny amounts of black at first. A little black goes a long way.

72

🧍🧍🧍 Meeting Individual Needs

Inclusion For children who are visually challenged, help them create a still life composition with objects that have different textures. Provide a variety of fruits and vegetables. Let children choose those that have textures they like for their composition. Have children arrange their fruits and vegetables in a plastic bowl or plate you have provided.

Quick Studio

Have children divide a sheet of paper into four panels and paint two with tints and two with shades of one color.

③ With shades, paint the outlines of the subjects.

④ Use shades and tints to fill in your still life.

Think Like an Artist

How do you think the colors work together?
Tell which shades and tints you think work best.

 Fine Arts Connection

Music Music can show variation just like shades and tints of colors do in an artwork. In music, loudness and softness are known as *dynamics*. As a class, sing "Heigh-ho" from the animated movie *Snow White and the Seven Dwarfs.* Listen to the loud and soft parts of the song. If possible, have children choose a percussive instrument and let them practice accompanying the song's loud and soft dynamics.

② Create

Have children read pages 72–73. Encourage them to practice mixing tints and shades before painting. Explain that this is an important skill to know when producing paintings.

- To mix tints, children need to paint a small dot of white on the palette. Then add a small amount of blue, or other paint color, to the white and mix them together.
- To mix shades, children need to paint a small circle of blue, or some other color, on their palette. Add a small amount of black paint to the blue paint and mix.
- Have them plan their paintings by making a pencil sketch on their drawing paper.
- Remind children to clean their brushes each time they use a new color.

Technique Tip Explain to children that when they are mixing the shade, cover only the tip of the paintbrush with black.

③ Close

Have children define reasons for preferences in their artworks as they answer the *Think Like an Artist* questions. (Possible response: The dark and light blues make the painting more interesting.)

Ongoing Assessment

If . . . children's still lifes have too many dark colors,

then . . . remind them to make sure their brushes are clean.

See page 36 from **Unit-by-Unit Resources** for a rubric to assess this studio.

Lesson 6

At a Glance

Objectives

- Identify and describe landscapes.
- Describe, analyze, interpret, and judge artworks.

Materials

- **Fine Art Transparency**
- magazines featuring landscapes, such as *National Geographic*
- Sketchbook Journal

Vocabulary

landscapes, overlap

NVAS (K–4) #2 Using knowledge of structures and functions

NVAS (K–4) #4 Understanding the visual arts in relation to history and cultures

NVAS (K–4) #6 Making connections between visual arts and other disciplines

Introduce

Show children an example of an outdoor scene. Explain to children that these pictures of outdoor scenes are *landscapes.*

In a landscape, the *foreground* is the area that appears nearest the viewer, or in front. The *background* is the area that appears farthest from the viewer, or in the distance. The *middle ground* is the area between the foreground and background. Using a landscape photograph, point to and identify objects in the foreground, middle ground, and background. Then have volunteers point to and identify other objects.

Tell children that objects can also *overlap,* or partially cover another shape or form. Have children identify overlapping objects. Finally, explain that open or empty areas above, between, or below objects in an artwork or photograph are called *space.* Using a circular motion with your finger, indicate areas with open space.

Landscape as a Subject

Artworks that show an outdoor scene are called **landscapes.** A landscape could show a yard, park, forest, or a farmer's field. What does this landscape show?

Henri Rousseau. *Virgin Forest,* ca. 1910. Oil on canvas, 44 by 63²/₅ inches. Kunstmuseum, Basel, Switzerland.

 Art Background

About the Artist Henri Rousseau (1844–1910) began his career as an artist after retiring from a position with the Paris Customs office. Because he received no formal art training, he is sometimes called a Primitive painter. Rousseau's best-known artworks show exotic jungle scenes.

ESL Notes

Invite three volunteers to stand. Have them stand in a row, one in front of the other. As you point to each child, explain that Child A is in the *foreground,* Child B is in the *middle ground,* and Child C is in the *background.* Repeat several times until children demonstrate an understanding. Then ask: **Is Child B in the background?** (no) Have children change positions and repeat the process.

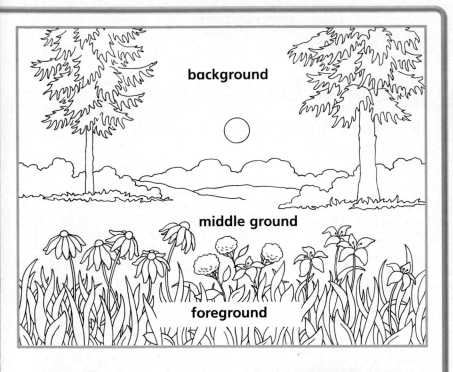

background

middle ground

foreground

In a landscape, objects in the foreground are bigger. They **overlap** parts of objects behind them. What objects are in the front, or foreground?

Point to a shape that looks farther away, in the background. Where do you see overlapping?

Research

Find landscapes in magazines. Study them. Look for open space. Look for plants that overlap other plants.

75

 Curriculum Connection

Social Studies Tell children that many forests and other natural areas exist in the United States. Have children conduct research on the forests, mountain ranges, rivers, deserts, and lakes in their state. Have them make colorful maps of their state indicating where these natural areas are. When children are finished, have them share their maps and display them around the class.

2 Teach

Have children read pages 74–75. Ask:

- **What do you see in this painting?** (trees, flowers, grass, two figures, a moon) DESCRIBE
- **What objects are in the foreground?** (grasses and plants) **Where do you see overlapping?** (The branches of the plants in front overlap the plants in the background.) ANALYZE
- **What objects fill the majority of the canvas? What colors are primarily used?** (trees and grass; shades and tints of green) ANALYZE
- **Where do you think this forest is located? How is it different from forests you know?** (It looks like it may be a rainforest. Answers will vary.) INTERPRET
- **What would you do differently in your artwork? Explain.** (I'd include a tiger and make fewer trees so everyone would be able to see the tiger's expression.) JUDGE

Sketchbook Journal After children have located the open spaces and overlapping in their magazine clippings, suggest that they draw their own landscapes.

3 Close

Have children share their landscape drawings with a partner. Have children point out the foreground, middle ground, and background.

Visual Culture Discuss what children know about landscape and garden design. Ask: **Have you ever had a garden?** If so, invite children to describe their gardens or a garden they would like to have.

Studio 6

At a Glance

Objectives

- Demonstrate how to use a variety of art materials to create a landscape.
- Evaluate original artworks by self and peers.

Materials

- tagboard, scissors ⚠, glue, craft sticks, tempera paints, paintbrushes, water containers, palettes, clothespins
- paper clips (optional)
- Rubric 2 from **Unit-by-Unit Resources**

NVAS (K–4) #1 Understanding and applying media, techniques, and processes

NVAS (K–4) #3 Choosing and evaluating a range of subject matter, symbols, and ideas

NVAS (K–4) #5 Reflecting upon and assessing the characteristics and merits of their work and the work of others

❶ Introduce

Review landscapes with children. Ask:

- **What type of landscape do you like?**
- **What plants do you see?**
- **Do you see warm or cool colors? What are they?**

Quick Studio

Have children draw a real or imaginary landscape using crayons or water-based markers.

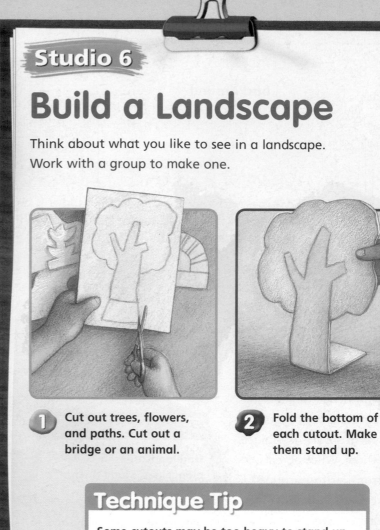

Studio 6

Build a Landscape

Think about what you like to see in a landscape. Work with a group to make one.

1 Cut out trees, flowers, and paths. Cut out a bridge or an animal.

2 Fold the bottom of each cutout. Make them stand up.

Technique Tip

Some cutouts may be too heavy to stand up. Tape craft sticks to the backs of those cutouts.

76

 Meeting Individual Needs

Reteach Help children focus on a specific environment before they begin to draw their landscape. Ask: **Do you want a landscape of a jungle? Of a farm? Would you like to draw a landscape similar to your backyard?**

After children decide which environment they would like to feature, help them generate a list of plants and animals that would be found in that environment.

Extend Challenge children to explore how plants can overlap in their landscapes. Encourage them to look at other artworks and illustrations in books for more examples. Then have them show different plants that overlap each other in their drawings.

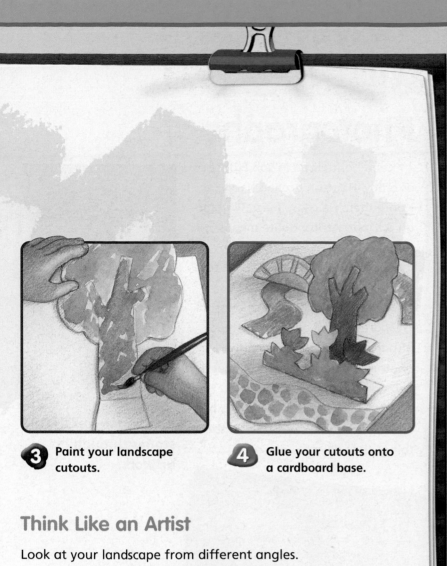

③ Paint your landscape cutouts.

④ Glue your cutouts onto a cardboard base.

Think Like an Artist

Look at your landscape from different angles. Tell which things are in the foreground, middle ground, and background.

 Fine Arts Connection

Theatre Explain to children that in a theatre, a stage is designed with different areas, just like a landscape. The names for these areas help the performers know where they need to be.

• *Upstage* is at the rear of the stage (background).
• *Downstage* is closest to the audience (foreground).
• *Center stage* is between upstage and downstage (middle ground). Take children on a field trip in your school or to another school that has a stage. Explore the different parts of the stage.

② Create

Read and discuss pages 76–77. Then distribute the materials.

• Brainstorm a list of plants, trees, or animals in their landscape.
• Tell children that they will need to make the bottoms of the cutouts one inch longer in length.
• Tell them to use a variety of shades and tints.
• Have children position the cutouts in several different places on the background before making the final arrangements.

Technique Tip Demonstrate how to glue the craft stick to the bottom of the folded tab so that it extends out from the cutout at a right angle.

③ Close

After children finish their landscapes, have them respond to the *Think Like an Artist* feature. (Possible response: I put flowers in the foreground, the path in the middle ground, and the tree in the background.) Then have children point out and discuss a favorite part of their artwork.

Ongoing Assessment

If . . . children's cutouts are not staying attached to the base,

then . . . tell them to try using paper clips or clothespins to hold the cutouts and base together while the glue dries.

See page 36 from **Unit-by-Unit Resources** for a rubric to assess this studio.

Artist at Work

Artist at Work

At a Glance

Objectives

- Read about a career in art.
- Identify the use of art in everyday life.
- Relate art to personal experiences.

Materials

- **Fine Art Transparency**
- photograph (optional)

NVAS (K–4) #5 Reflecting upon and assessing the characteristics and merits of their work and the work of others

NVAS (K-4) #6 Making connections between visual arts and other disciplines

Explore

Bring to class a photograph that will be of interest to children. Pass around the photograph and allow them to examine it. Point out that your photograph is printed on paper. Ask whether children have seen photographs printed on any other media, such as wood.

Discuss

Have children read pages 78–79 and reflect on the artwork by Keba Konte. Explain that Konte has a career as a photographer, but he is also a storyteller. Ask:

- **What do you find most interesting about this photograph?** (I like how the pictures overlap.)
- **Why do you think Konte prints his photographs on wood?** (Maybe he wants to show the beauty and texture in an everyday object, such as wood.)
- **What kind of stories would you tell if you were a photographer?** (I would tell stories about my life, family, and friends.)

Ask children to identify other jobs involving photography. (Possible responses: photojournalist, filmmaker)

78

Photographs

Keba Konte lived in San Francisco as a boy. He wasn't called Keba Konte then. He chose his new name on a trip to Africa. *Konte* means "storyteller."

Konte likes to tell stories. He tells them with photographs.

Konte's photographs are unusual. They are printed on wood instead of paper. When you look at the photograph, you can see the wood behind it.

Konte shows beauty through his artwork. He shows people and the things they do every day.

Keba Konte tells stories through his artwork.

78

Career Research

Invite a guest speaker to talk with the class about his or her career as a photographer. Encourage the speaker to bring photographs for children to view. Have children prepare by brainstorming questions they want to ask. Write their questions on the board. As children view the photograph, be sure to point out appropriate unit concepts and terms.

Keba Armand Konte.
Vanishing Point, 1999.
Photo montage on
wood, 42 by 60 inches.
© Keba Armand Konte

Konte says this artwork **"is about people, love, and struggle."**

79

Reading Strategy

Activate Prior Knowledge Remind children that good readers use and build upon their prior knowledge to help them comprehend what they are reading. As a class, fill in a K-W-L chart. Under K, list items that children know about photography. Under W, have children brainstorm questions that they would like to know more about. Then leave the third column for children to list new ideas that they learned after the discussion is over.

K	W	L
Photographers use cameras.	What type of cameras do photographers like?	I learned that there are many kinds of cameras.
Photographers take pictures of many different subjects.	What are the negatives of photographs?	

Apply

Tell children that they are going to write a letter to Keba Konte. Ask them to think about what they would like to ask him, such as what it is like to have a career making photographs (and telling stories). Display a graphic organizer such as the following to help children plan the details of their letters:

Letter to Keba Konte

What I like about your photographs	• They are colorful. • They are interesting and unusual to look at.
What I like about your technique	• I like that you print your photos on wood. • I like the lines and textures in your photos.
What I want to know about being a photographer who tells stories	• How did you become interested in telling stories? • What other stories do you want to tell?

Have children write a rough draft of their letters. Then have children proofread the letters, checking for spelling and grammar. Ask them to hand in a final draft.

Close

Have volunteers read their letters aloud. Ask them to describe how writing a letter to Keba Konte helped them to think more deeply about his artwork and what it would be like to have a career as a photographer.

Portfolio Project

Portfolio Project

Print a Seascape

A **seascape** is almost like a landscape.
One thing is different. The subject is the sea.

1 Press hard on printing plates to draw fish and other sea life.

2 Tape handles to the backs of your printing plates.

3 Press your plates into paint and make prints on paper.

4 Paint a blue tint over your sea creature print.

80

At a Glance

Objectives

• Develop and organize ideas from the environment.
• Demonstrate knowledge about patterns and designs.

Materials

• 1" × 3" rectangles and 3" × 5" rectangles cut from meat trays
• pencils, tempera paint, blue watercolor paint, crayons, masking tape, paintbrushes, water containers, palettes, white construction paper
• Rubric 2 from **Unit-by-Unit Resources**

NVAS (K–4) #1 Understanding and applying media, techniques, and processes

NVAS (K–4) #3 Choosing and evaluating a range of subject matter, symbols, and ideas

NVAS (K–4) #5 Reflecting upon and assessing the characteristics and merits of their work and the work of others

Plan

Guide children to read page 80. Ask:

• **What kinds of plants and animals would you find in the sea?**
• **What will you include in a drawing of the sea?**

Have children brainstorm all of the colors, shapes, and patterns that could be found in the sea. Ask them to think about the plants and animals they would like to include in their seascape.

Quick Project

Have children draw a seascape using markers. Then have them lightly color over their entire picture to create a water effect.

🏃🏃🏃 Meeting Individual Needs

Inclusion Allow those children who may have difficulty with the project to create a monoprint using their fingers. Have children paint an acetate sheet with tempera paint. Then have them draw a design in the paint with their fingers. Ask children to place a sheet of paper over the acetate and to gently rub the back of the paper. Then they may remove the paper and view the print. A monoprint block can be used only once.

Look at the seascapes these children made.

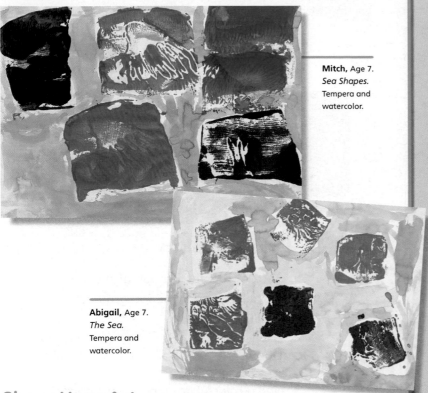

Mitch, Age 7.
Sea Shapes.
Tempera and
watercolor.

Abigail, Age 7.
The Sea.
Tempera and
watercolor.

Share Your Art

1. Tell if your seascape looks realistic or abstract.
2. Describe the hardest part of the project.

 Gallery Options

Make Your Own Frame Children may enjoy mounting their artworks for display. Have children cut "frames" from colored construction paper. Then have them glue the print to the center of the frame. Invite them to decorate their frame and write a title and their name on the paper frame. Designate a gallery area to hang the completed artworks. Encourage a discussion of the seascapes and the printmaking process.

Create

Gather your materials and guide children through the steps on page 80 to complete the project.

- For Step 1, encourage children to add lines or dots to create patterns on their fish and other sea life.
- Explain that the handles will make it easier to lift the plates from the paper.
- Instruct children to make sure that their plates are evenly coated with paint.
- Let the stamps dry completely before children use a large brush to wipe a wash of blue watercolor paint over the entire print.

Have children clean the brushes after they have completed their seascapes. They should use warm, soapy water and then rinse their brushes thoroughly. Have them blot the brushes on a towel before putting them in a jar to dry, bristles up.

Close

Point out the artworks from children's portfolios on page 81. Ask:

- **What animals or sea life do you see in these artworks?** (octupus, fish, and seaweed)
- **Which of these sea creatures looks real?** (The octopus looks real.)
- **How can you tell that these children used their imaginations to make these creatures?** (because each artwork is different)

Have children share their artworks with other children as they answer the *Share Your Art* activity.

See page 36 from **Unit-by-Unit Resources** for a rubric to assess this project.

Unit 2 Review

At a Glance

Objectives

- Relate art terms to the environment.
- Identify pattern, prints, portraits, landscapes, realism, and abstraction in artworks.
- Describe, analyze, interpret, and judge an artwork.

Materials

- Art Print 8
- Fine Art Transparency

NVAS (K–4) #1 Understanding and applying media, techniques, and processes

NVAS (K–4) #2 Using knowledge of structures and functions

NVAS (K–4) #5 Reflecting upon and assessing the characteristics and merits of their work and the work of others

Think About Art

Possible responses include:

pattern (Point to the patterns in the abstract artwork.)
abstract (Point to the abstract artwork.)
landscape (Point to the landscape.)
realistic (Point to the landscape.)
portrait (Point to the photograph of the boy.)
overlap (Point to overlapping objects in the landscape.)

Write About Art

Before children write, ask:

- **Describe the mood of this landscape.** (Possible response: peaceful, lazy day)
- **Imagine that you are walking through this landscape. What would you be thinking, seeing, and feeling?** (Possible response: I might be feeling happy and thinking about what to do. When I see the lake, I decide to go swimming.)

Think About Art

Read the art words. Then point to a picture that matches each word.

pattern   **abstract**   **landscape**
realistic   **portrait**   **overlap**

Write About Art

Look at the photograph of the landscape. What objects are in the foreground? Write about them.

Talk About Art

- Find a colorful artwork in your portfolio.
- Describe the tints and shades that you see.
- Explain why you like the artwork.

82

 Assessment Options

Options for assessing children appear in the **Unit-by-Unit Resources.**

- Use the **Vocabulary Worksheets** on pages 29–32 for an informal assessment of Unit 2 Vocabulary.
- Use the **Unit 2 Test** on pages 37–40 to assess children's mastery of unit vocabulary and concepts.

Franz Marc. *Yellow Cow*, 1911. Oil on canvas, 54¾ by 73¾ inches. Solomon R. Guggenheim Museum, New York. Photograph by David Heald. © The Solomon R. Guggenheim Foundation, New York. (FN49.1210).

Put It All Together

1. What do you notice about the colors in this artwork?
2. Where did the artist use tints and shades?
3. Do you think the cow looks happy or sad? Why?
4. What do you think of when you see this artwork?

83

 Art Background

Yellow Cow Franz Marc (1880–1916) preferred to paint animals rather than people, ". . . animals with their virginal sense of life awakened all that was good in me."

Marc also felt strongly that color provided symbolism. He used yellow for this painting because he felt this color was gentle and cheerful. He also thought yellow represented femininity.

Talk About Art

Have children define reasons for preferences in personal artworks. Ask: **Why did you choose this artwork to share?** (Answers will vary.) Prompt children to use words such as *pattern, abstract, landscape, portrait,* and *overlap* to describe their artwork.

Then pair children to look at each other's portfolios. Ask children to identify ideas in their partner's portfolios. Model by sitting beside a volunteer, paging through their portfolio, and then identifying ideas about their artworks.

Put It All Together

Use the questions on page 83 to evaluate the artwork. Possible responses follow.

1. Cows are not really yellow with blue spots. The colors in the landscape are unusual too. DESCRIBE
2. There are yellow tints on the cow's back and in the light yellows and light purples of the sky. There are dark blue shades on the sides of the hills and dark green shades in the leaves on the plants. ANALYZE
3. The cow looks happy and seems to be kicking up its heels as if it is playing. Its face has a happy expression. INTERPRET
4. This reminds me of the cow jumping over the moon. JUDGE

Unit 3 Overview

In this unit children will learn about artworks they can see from all sides. These three-dimensional artworks will include sculptures, models, puppets, and pottery. Children will also create their own 3-D art.

	Unit Opener, p. 84	Lesson 1, p. 86 Forms in Places Studio 1, p. 88 Make a Museum Model	Lesson 2, p. 90 Playscapes Studio 2, p. 92 Make a Playscape Model	Lesson 3, p. 94 Forms and Space Studio 3, p. 96 Make a Junk Sculpture	Look and Compare, p. 98 Animal Sculptures
Artworks	 **Felipe Benito Archuleta.** *Baboon,* 1978.	 **Venturi, Scott Brown, and Associates.** *Children's Museum of Houston,* 1992.		 **Pablo Picasso.** *Bull's Head,* 1943.	 **Felipe Archuleta.** *Tiger,* 1977. **Isaac Smith.** *Polar Bear,* 1994.
Vocabulary	sculpture, sculptor	architecture, forms	playscape, design	space, positive space, negative space assemblage	
Materials	• Art Print 9 • Fine Art Transparency • Instructional Prints	• **Fine Art Transparency** • Sketchbook Journal • recycled cardboard forms, cardboard squares for bases • tacky glue or craft glue, transparent tape (optional) • tempera paints, paintbrushes, palettes	Sketchbook Journal • construction paper in various colors, cardboard • tacky glue or craft glue, scissors ⚠, tape • bendable materials such as pipe cleaners, aluminum foil, or chenille sticks • clothespins or paper clips (optional)	• **Fine Art Transparency** • Sketchbook Journal • small, lightweight found metal objects ⚠ • tempera paints, paintbrushes, palettes • white glue, modeling clay, rolling pin (optional)	• Art Prints 9, 10, 11 • **Fine Art Transparency** • Sketchbook Journal
Connections	**Home Connection** three-dimensional artworks at home **Bookshelf** *When Clay Sings* by Byrd Baylor, Aladdin Library, 1987	**Curriculum Connection** Math: forms chart **ESL Notes** **Fine Arts Connection** Theatre: commercials **Meeting Individual Needs** Extend	**Curriculum Connection** Physical Education: pantomime physical activities **ESL Notes** **Fine Arts Connection** Music: instrument forms **Meeting Individual Needs** Reteach, Extend	**Curriculum Connection** Science: air and space experiment **ESL Notes** **Fine Arts Connection** Dance: dance assemblages **Meeting Individual Needs** Reteach, Extend	**Reading Strategy** Compare and contrast
Assessment Opportunities		Visual Culture Rubric 3 from **Unit-by-Unit Resources** Ongoing Assessment	Informal Assessment Rubric 3 from **Unit-by-Unit Resources** Ongoing Assessment	Informal Assessment Rubric 3 from **Unit-by-Unit Resources** Ongoing Assessment	

Lesson 4, p. 100 **Fun Sculptures** Studio 4, p. 102 Make a Fun Sculpture	Lesson 5 p. 104 **Puppets and Dolls** Studio 5, p. 106 Make a Sock Puppet	Lesson 6, p. 108 **Pottery** Studio 6, p. 110 Make a Pinch Pot	Artist at Work, p. 112 **Plant Sculptures**	Portfolio Project, p. 114 **Make a Thumbprint Pot**	Unit Review, p. 116
Saarenald T. S. Yaawaisan. *Toy Helicopter.*	**Artist unknown.** *Marionettes: Sword Fighter and Dancer,* ca. 1900.	**María and Julian Martínez, San Ildefonso Pueblo.** *Jar,* ca. 1937.	A plant sculpture by James Mason.		**George Segal.** *Walk, Don't Walk,* 1976.
carved	puppets, puppeteer, folk art	pottery, clay, kiln			
• **Fine Art Transparency** • wooden toy or sculpture • Sketchbook Journal • meat trays ⚠ • pencils, scissors ⚠, glue, tape, pipe cleaners ⚠ • found art objects, such as string, paper clips, toothpicks ⚠, and foam packing peanuts	• **Fine Art Transparency** • puppets • Sketchbook Journal • long socks, newspaper, rubber bands, fabric glue, colored paper, yarn, bird seed, fabric pieces • stapler (optional) ⚠	• **Fine Art Transparency** • Sketchbook Journal • self-hardening clay • plastic forks ⚠, pencils, acrylic paint, paintbrushes	topiary (optional)	• aluminum cans with smooth tops • self-hardening clay, dampened paper towels • acrylic paints, paintbrushes	• **Art Print 12** • **Fine Art Transparency**
Curriculum Connection Social Studies: toys made from natural objects **ESL Notes** **Fine Arts Connection** Dance: positive and negative space in dance **Meeting Individual Needs** Inclusion	**Technology** Make puppets **ESL Notes** **Fine Arts Connection** Music: sing with a puppet **Meeting Individual Needs** Reteach, Extend	**Curriculum Connection** Social Studies: community symbols **ESL Notes** **Fine Arts Connection** Theatre: pinch pot skit **Meeting Individual Needs** Reteach, Extend	**Career Research** Careers with flowers and plants **Reading Strategy** Summarize and paraphrase information	**Gallery Options** School display **Meeting Individual Needs** Inclusion	
Visual Culture Rubric 3 from **Unit-by-Unit Resources** Ongoing Assessment	Informal Assessment Rubric 3 from **Unit-by-Unit Resources** Ongoing Assessment	Visual Culture Rubric 3 from **Unit-by-Unit Resources** Ongoing Assessment		Rubric 3 from **Unit-by-Unit Resources**	**Unit-by-Unit Resources** Vocabulary Worksheets, pp. 47–50 Unit 3 Test, pp. 55–58

Unit 3

Objectives

• Identify elements of art and principles of design in artworks.

• Respond to and make judgments about artworks.

• Relate art to personal experiences.

Materials

• Art Print 9

• Fine Art Transparency

Vocabulary

sculpture, sculptor

NVAS (K–4) #4 Understanding the visual arts in relation to history and cultures

NVAS (K–4) #5 Reflecting upon and assessing the characteristics and merits of their work and the work of others

Introduce the Unit

Ask children to name different types of artwork they have learned about so far, such as still life, portraits, stencils, and collages. Invite volunteers to share their favorite artwork. Tell them to identify the colors, lines, and texture in their artwork. Explain that in this unit they will learn about artworks that they can go around. Ask:

• **How do you think creating an artwork that you can go around is different from creating a painting?** (Possible response: The artist needs to be able to see and create the artwork from all angles.)

Ask a volunteer to read the title of Unit 3. Have children look through the artworks in this unit and choose a favorite. Ask them to explain what aspects of the artwork they liked the most and tell them that they will create their own artworks using similar elements of art and principles of design.

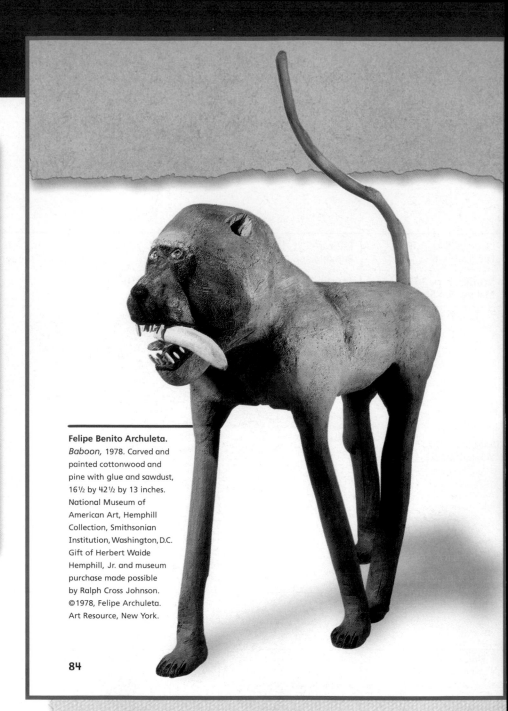

Felipe Benito Archuleta. *Baboon,* 1978. Carved and painted cottonwood and pine with glue and sawdust, 16½ by 42½ by 13 inches. National Museum of American Art, Hemphill Collection, Smithsonian Institution, Washington, D.C. Gift of Herbert Waide Hemphill, Jr. and museum purchase made possible by Ralph Cross Johnson. ©1978, Felipe Archuleta. Art Resource, New York.

84

 Art Background

Baboon As is typical of other animal carvings by Felipe Archuleta, *Baboon* looks like a real baboon. Yet the viewer can only guess the animal's intent. Archuleta chose to portray the baboon with ferocious teeth but with a soft banana in its mouth as a humorous contrast.

 Home Connection

Have children look for three-dimensional artworks in their home. Ask them to find out the story behind the artwork from family members. Encourage children to ask permission to bring these artworks to share with classmates.

Art You Can Go Around

You have made drawings, paintings, and prints. Each has a front and a back. But you can go all the way around this baboon sculpture. Just don't get too close to the big teeth!

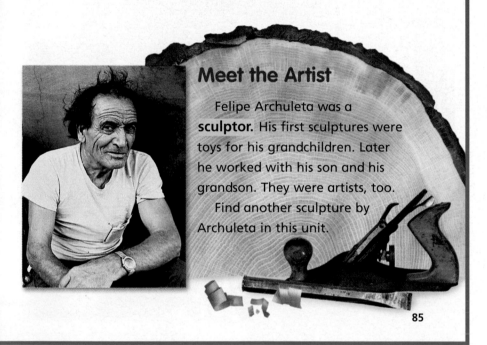

Meet the Artist

Felipe Archuleta was a **sculptor.** His first sculptures were toys for his grandchildren. Later he worked with his son and his grandson. They were artists, too.

Find another sculpture by Archuleta in this unit.

85

Bookshelf

When Clay Sings
by Byrd Baylor
Aladdin Library, 1987

Children will enjoy reading this story about the symbolic clay pots of the Southwest Native Americans. These Native Americans hold the clay in such high esteem, they claim each "piece of clay is a piece of someone's life."

Discuss Unit Concepts

Have children read page 85. Explain to them that *Baboon* is a *sculpture*, an artwork that has three dimensions. Artists called *sculptors* make sculptures from a variety of media. Tell children that this sculpture was carved from wood.

Have children describe their initial responses to *Baboon*. Ask: **What do you think about this sculpture?** (Possible response: It looks just like a real baboon.)

As you introduce each element of art and principle of design in Unit 3, you may wish to display the **Instructional Prints.** A print is provided for each element and principle.

In addition, **Art Prints 9–12** and **Transparencies** are available for fine art in the unit.

Meet the Artist

Felipe Archuleta (1910–1991) Felipe Archuleta was born in New Mexico. When he was young, he worked as a laborer and a carpenter. Archuleta eventually became discouraged because there was little or no work for him. At age fifty-seven he taught himself the art of sculpting. Archuleta is known for his extraordinary sense of form, color, and materials and for his love of nature.

Lesson 1

Lesson 1

At a Glance

Objectives

- Identify and describe forms in architecture.
- Respond to and make judgments about artworks.

Materials

- **Fine Art Transparency**
- Sketchbook Journal

Vocabulary

architecture, forms

NVAS (K–4) #2 Using knowledge of structures and functions

NVAS (K–4) #5 Reflecting upon and assessing the characteristics and merits of their work and the work of others

NVAS (K–4) #6 Making connections between visual arts and other disciplines

①Introduce

Have children name types of buildings, such as a library or museum. Remind them that a school is also a type of building.

Explain that buildings are made up of forms. Draw the following forms on the chalkboard: sphere, cone, cylinder, and cube. Point to each as you say its name. Guide children to identify objects that each form resembles. (a ball, an ice cream cone, a cardboard tube, a block) Talk with children about the forms that make up their homes or other buildings in their neighborhoods.

Discuss that there are many people who work together to make a building or a house. Explain that architects begin the process by creating the plans and models. Ask children to identify different workers needed to create a building. (Possible responses: builders, designers, landscapers) Say: **These people all have different kinds of jobs that involve art.**

Forms in Places

A building is an artwork people use. It is an example of **architecture.**

Venturi, Scott Brown, and Associates. *Children's Museum of Houston,* 1992. Houston, TX.

86

Art Background

Children's Museum of Houston This museum is located in Houston, Texas. While it looks like a traditional adult museum, the details are playful, friendly, and colorful. For instance, the children representing columns on the side of the structure resemble, in a fun way, traditional classical architecture.

ESL Notes

Point to an object that is a form, such as a block. With your finger outline its form and say: **This is a block.** Pass the object around, have children look at the details and repeat the sentence after you. Continue with the other forms.

Builders and architects work together to make a building. Architects draw plans. Then they make a model. The model is a small version of the real thing.

The architect uses **forms** to make a model. Name the forms above.

Art Fact

Most columns are tall cylinders. But look at the building on page 86. Architects made some of the columns look like children!

87

Have children read pages 86–87. Identify the forms on page 87 (spheres, cones, cylinders, cubes, arch, organic forms). Then have them name forms they see in the museum on page 86. Ask:

- **What do you like about this museum?** (Possible response: I like the columns.)
- **Why do you think the architect placed images of children on the columns?** (It is a children's museum.)
- **If you designed this building, what would you change or do differently?** (Possible response: I would make tunnels and caves that children can crawl into and explore.)

Art Fact Encourage children to draw a real or imaginary building that has columns. Have them draw it in their Sketchbook Journals.

③ Close

After children have completed their sketches, pair them with a partner. Have children name the forms their peers used, as well as identify any ideas about their drawing.

Visual Culture Take a walk around your school and point out the variety of shapes and forms. Encourage children to point to and name any forms they see.

 Curriculum Connection

Math Make a chart with four columns and three rows. Label each column with one of the following forms: cone, sphere, cylinder, and cube. Remind children that some forms can be very large (a building, for example) and others are very small (such as a marble or pencil).

Have children brainstorm different objects or buildings that have similar shapes. Ask children to draw the object or write its name in the appropriate column on the chart.

Studio 1

At a Glance

Objectives

- Demonstrate how to create a model of a building using a variety of art materials.
- Evaluate original artworks by self and peers.

Materials

- recycled cardboard forms, cardboard squares for bases
- tacky glue or craft glue, transparent tape (optional)
- tempera paints, paintbrushes, palettes
- Rubric 3 from **Unit-by-Unit Resources**

NVAS (K–4) #1 Understanding and applying media, techniques, and processes

NVAS (K–4) #3 Choosing and evaluating a range of subject matter, symbols, and ideas

NVAS (K–4) #5 Reflecting upon and assessing the characteristics and merits of their work and the work of others

Studio 1

Make a Museum Model

Think like an architect. Make a model of a museum.

1 Choose some cardboard forms.

2 Arrange the forms on a cardboard base.

Technique Tip

Secure each form with glue before adding the next one. When you add one, hold the shapes together and count to fifteen.

① Introduce

Review forms with children. Remind them that architects use forms to create models of buildings they are planning. Point out how the forms used in the museum on page 86 make it seem like a fun and exciting place to visit. Then have children recall any experiences that they have had with models. Ask:

- **What type of museum will you make?**
- **What forms will you use?**
- **What colors will you use to paint your model?**
- **How will the colors and forms you use reflect the feelings of your building?**

👫👫 Meeting Individual Needs

Extend After children have created their models, have them draw a sketch of their museum in their Sketchbook Journal. Encourage children to label the parts of the museum including the different exhibits they plan to include.

Quick Studio

Have children build a museum model with blocks. Ask them to name the different forms they use.

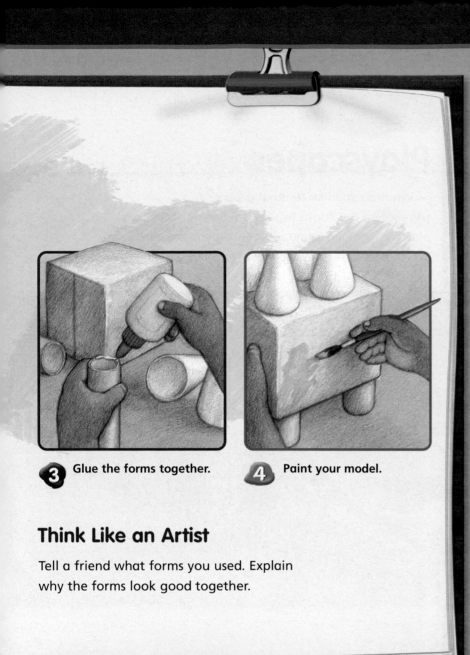

3 Glue the forms together.

4 Paint your model.

Think Like an Artist

Tell a friend what forms you used. Explain why the forms look good together.

 Fine Arts Connection

Theatre Tell children that they will create commercials promoting their museums. Invite them to work in small groups to discuss what information to present and to write their skits. Then have them perform their commercials for the class.

2 Create

Have children read pages 88–89. Then distribute the materials.

- Have children reflect on the brainstorming questions to help them choose from the available forms.
- Remind children to place the larger shapes on the bottom to create a solid base for their museums.
- Demonstrate how to attach forms together with glue. Identify this as a necessary skill for producing models.
- Ask children to think about the feelings created by the forms and colors they chose for their models. Ask: **Do the forms and colors you chose make your museum seem like a happy place to visit? Why or why not?**

Technique Tip To help the forms stick together, mix a few drops of glue into the paint.

3 Close

Use the *Think Like an Artist* feature to have children define reasons why they preferred some forms over others. (Possible responses: cylinders, cones, and cubes; I like the cylinders because they look like columns, and the cones add great detail.)

Ongoing Assessment

If . . . children's forms are not sticking together,

then . . . suggest that they connect them at a point with more surface.

See page 54 from **Unit-by-Unit Resources** for a rubric to assess this studio.

Lesson 2

At a Glance

Objectives

- Identify and describe forms in playscapes.
- Respond to and make judgments about artworks.

Materials

- Sketchbook Journal

Vocabulary

playscape, design

NVAS (K–4) #2 Using knowledge of structures and functions

NVAS (K–4) #5 Reflecting upon and assessing the characteristics and merits of their work and the work of others

NVAS (K–4) #6 Making connections between visual arts and other disciplines

➊ Introduce

Have volunteers pantomime playing in the park. Ask children to describe objects that they enjoy playing on. Invite volunteers to identify the variations between the play equipment in the park and the school playground.

Tell them that when they are playing at the park, they are often playing on a playscape, a combination of the words *playground* and *landscape.* It is a play area that includes the natural environment. Playscape architects design playscapes by planning and arranging forms. Identify this as another job in the world of art. Ask children what forms an architect might use for a playscape. (Possible responses: cylinders and cubes)

- **What are some other jobs in art that would help create a playscape?** (a landscaper, a builder)

Playscapes

What do you like to do at a park? A **playscape** has forms to play on. Look at the playscape below. Name some forms you see. Which part looks like the most fun? Why?

90

🎨 Art Background

Playscapes Many playscape architects observe children at play or ask for children's help before planning a new playscape. This has resulted in effective playscapes that are designed to stimulate imagination and develop muscles. Playscapes often are wheelchair accessible, and many have different areas for school-aged children and for toddlers.

ESL Notes

Point out the playscape on page 90 and talk about the different forms used to build it. As you point out each form, name it: **This is a cone.** Have children repeat after you. Continue until you have named all the forms in the photograph.

Architects **design** playscapes. They begin with models. Architects make sure the playscape is safe and fun. Sometimes they ask children for help.

Look at the drawing. What forms would you add?

Art in My World

Where is your favorite playscape? Draw a picture of it.

91

2 Teach

Have children read pages 90–91 and identify the forms they see. Ask:

- **What does this playscape resemble?** (a fire truck)
- **Which areas of this playscape look the most fun?** (Possible response: The slide looks like fun because children are smiling.)
- **What forms do you see in this playscape?** (Possible response: The wheels look like cylinders.)
- **What questions do you think architects ask themselves as they design playscapes?** (Possible responses: How much room do I have? What objects will be safe and fun to use? What colors should I use?)
- **What would you change about this playscape? Why?** (Answers will vary.)

Art in My World Have children compare the playscape they drew with the one pictured on page 90. Have them consider how the forms are similar and different.

3 Close

After children have finished their drawings, have them discuss the areas that are the most fun.

Assessment Have children work with a partner to point out forms in their playscapes.

 Curriculum Connection

Physical Education Have volunteers take turns pantomiming physical activities that can take place in a playscape. Encourage them to name one or more safety rules for the activity. For example, a child who demonstrates using a slide might mention that only one person should go down the slide at a time. Children may also enjoy working in groups to pantomime cooperative activities (such as taking turns) in a playscape.

Studio 2

At a Glance

Objectives

- Demonstrate how to use forms to make a playscape model.
- Evaluate original artworks by self and peers.

Materials

- construction paper in various colors, cardboard
- tacky glue or craft glue, scissors ⚠, tape
- bendable materials such as pipe cleaners, aluminum foil, or chenille sticks
- clothespins or paper clips (optional)
- Rubric 3 from **Unit-by-Unit Resources**

NVAS (K–4) #1 Understanding and applying media, techniques, and processes

NVAS (K–4) #3 Choosing and evaluating a range of subject matter, symbols, and ideas

NVAS (K–4) #5 Reflecting upon and assessing the characteristics and merits of their work and the work of others

①Introduce

Review forms with children. Have them describe any forms they have seen on playscapes. Ask:

- **What forms will you make?**
- **What will you be able to do on, in, or around the forms?**
- **What shapes will you use to make the forms?**

Quick Studio

Have children make forms by cutting, folding, and rolling paper. Then have them tape their shapes together.

Make a Playscape Model

Be a playscape architect. Make forms for a playscape.

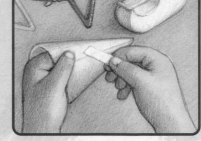

1 Cut and tear shapes. Bend and fold them.

2 Tape and glue them to make forms.

Technique Tip

To make a spiral, cut out a circle. Then start cutting on the outside edge. Cut around and around until you reach the middle.

92

🏃 Meeting Individual Needs

Reteach Have children choose their favorite form and make two or more of these for one area of a playscape. Children can work in groups to combine their completed forms into a model.

Extend Have children work in small groups to discuss a model for the best school in the world. Have groups share the forms they would use in a model for their school.

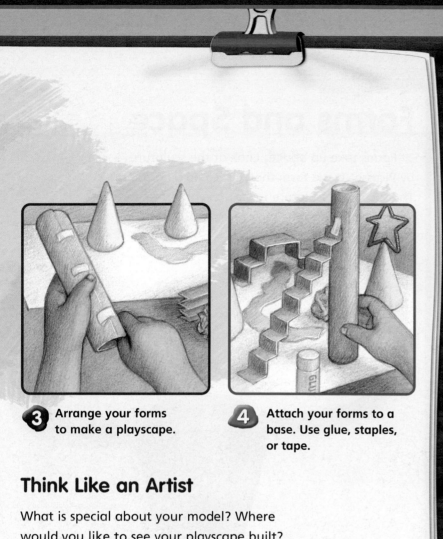

3 Arrange your forms to make a playscape.

4 Attach your forms to a base. Use glue, staples, or tape.

Think Like an Artist

What is special about your model? Where would you like to see your playscape built?

 Fine Arts Connection

Music Bring in various musical instruments or provide children pictures of a number of different instruments. Talk about the various forms of the instruments. Ask:

• **What form is a drum?** (cylinder)
• **What form is an upright piano?** (cube)

Continue in this manner until each child has a chance to identify an instrument's form. Give children an opportunity to play different instruments while singing familiar songs.

2 Create

Have children read pages 92–93. Then distribute the materials.

• Demonstrate how to roll half circles into cones and roll strips of paper to make cylinders.
• Pinch the papers together with clothespins or paper clips while the glue dries.
• Have children think about how they use a playscape as they arrange their forms. Ask: **Do you have something children can climb? Can lots of children play at one time?**
• As children attach each form to the base, remind them to count to ten to give the glue time to dry.

Technique Tip A spiral has a spring-like shape. Suggest children use a spiral to represent a slide or stairs.

3 Close

Have children reflect on their artwork by answering the *Think Like an Artist* questions. (Possible response: I like how I used cones as play places. I'd like to see my playscape built at a school.) Ask children to name the necessary skills for making their playscape model.

Ongoing Assessment

If . . . children are having trouble bending and folding shapes to make forms,

then . . . suggest they make their shapes larger.

See page 54 from **Unit-by-Unit Resources** for a rubric to assess this studio.

Lesson 3

At a Glance

Objectives

- Identify and describe space in artworks.
- Describe, analyze, interpret, and judge artworks.

Materials

- **Fine Art Transparency**
- Sketchbook Journal

Vocabulary

space, positive space, negative space

NVAS (K–4) #2 Using knowledge of structures and functions

NVAS (K–4) #5 Reflecting upon and assessing the characteristics and merits of their work and the work of others

NVAS (K–4) #6 Making connections between visual arts and other disciplines

❶ Introduce

Hold up your hand with your fingers together. Tell children that your hand is a form, something you can go around, and it takes up space. Explain that your hand is an example of positive space, or the space that a form occupies.

Spread your fingers. With your other hand, point out the negative space between your fingers and around your hand. Negative space is the space around a form.

Point out some forms in the classroom. Have children identify the positive space and negative space in each.

Lesson 3

Forms and Space

Forms take up **space.** Look at the sculpture by Picasso. It is a form that you could go around. The space the sculpture takes up is **positive space.** What animal does the sculpture show?

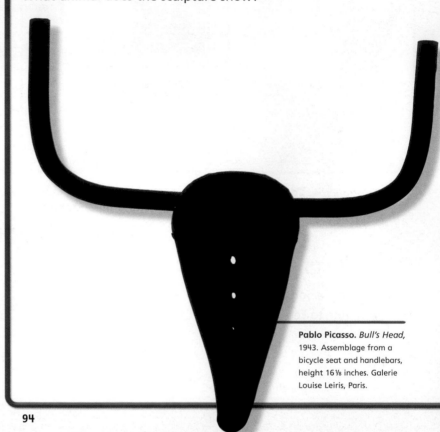

Pablo Picasso. *Bull's Head,* 1943. Assemblage from a bicycle seat and handlebars, height 16⅛ inches. Galerie Louise Leiris, Paris.

94

 Art Background

Bull's Head This artwork was made by Pablo Picasso (1881–1973) with an old bicycle seat and a pair of handlebars that the artist found. Picasso liked to think that the artwork would be recycled back into bicycle parts at some point.

Bird in Space Constantin Brancusi (1876–1957) created this brass sculpture as part of a series from 1923–1940. Its streamlined form suggests a bird in flight.

About the Artist Montana artist Deborah Butterfield (1949–) is best known for her horse sculptures. Her early works were made of mud, sticks, and straw. She wanted to use materials you might find around horses.

These sculptures are made from metal, too. Which sculpture is a bird? How can you tell?

Empty space around forms in an artwork is called **negative space.** Where do you see negative space in the horse sculpture?

Deborah Butterfield. *Woodrow,* 1988. Bronze, 90 by 105 by 74 inches. Walker Art Center, Minneapolis, MN.

Constantin Brancusi. *Bird in Space,* 1940. Bronze. Musée National d'Art Moderne, Centre Georges Pompidou, Paris, France.

Sketchbook Journal

Draw a sculpture made of metal kitchen tools. Use negative space around your artwork.

95

2 Teach

Have children read pages 94–95. Then have them look at *Bull's Head.* Ask:

- **What do you see?** (A bull's head) DESCRIBE
- **What shapes and forms did the artist use?** (a cylinder and a triangular shape) ANALYZE
- **Why did he create it this way?** (Possible response: He wanted to use only found materials.) INTERPRET
- **How would you change it?** (Possible response: I'd add screws for eyes.) JUDGE

Ask similar questions about Brancusi's and Butterfield's sculptures.

Sketchbook Journal Before children begin drawing, have them brainstorm a list of the kitchen tools they could use for their sculptures.

3 Close

After children have completed their sketches, have them point to the negative space around their sculptures.

Assessment Have partners use objects to explain positive and negative space to one another.

Curriculum Connection

Science Explain to children that air surrounds a form. Tell children they will do an experiment to see if air can take up space. Crumple a sheet of paper and place it in the bottom of a glass. Then turn over the glass and quickly place it straight down into a bowl of water. Remove the glass and take out the paper. Explain that the glass was full of air, which protected the paper from getting wet.

Notes

Invite a volunteer to pose like a statue. Point around the child's body. Say: **This is negative space.** Have children repeat after you. Continue using other volunteers to show positive space.

Studio 3

At a Glance

Objectives

- Express ideas by showing space assemblage.
- Demonstrate how to use a variety of art materials to make an assemblage.
- Evaluate original artworks by self and peers.

Materials

- small, lightweight found metal objects ⚠
- tempera paints, paintbrushes, palettes
- white glue, modeling clay, rolling pin (optional)
- Rubric 3 from **Unit-by-Unit Resources**

Vocabulary

assemblage

NVAS (K–4) #1 Understanding and applying media, techniques, and processes

NVAS (K–4) #3 Choosing and evaluating a range of subject matter, symbols, and ideas

NVAS (K–4) #5 Reflecting upon and assessing the characteristics and merits of their work and the work of others

① Introduce

Review forms and space with children. Tell them that they will make an *assemblage,* or sculpture made of various objects. Have children brainstorm ideas about their assemblage. Ask:

- **What objects will you use?**
- **Where will the negative space be in your artwork?**
- **What do you want people to think when they see your assemblage?**

Studio 3

Make a Junk Sculpture

Even "junk" can become art. Make an **assemblage** by putting old metal objects together.

① Gather small metal objects.

② Add a little glue to your paint. Then paint some of the objects.

Technique Tip

Before painting, make the parts more interesting. You can bend and twist paper clips. Or curl wire by wrapping it around a pencil.

👥👥 Meeting Individual Needs

Reteach For those children who are having a hard time deciding how to create their assemblage, give them fewer objects to work with. After they have used three items, they can choose other objects, one at a time.

Extend Challenge children to create an assemblage using specific forms or shapes. For instance, have children use only cylinder-shaped objects.

Quick Studio

Group children to create an assemblage. Then have them draw the assemblage in their Sketchbook Journal.

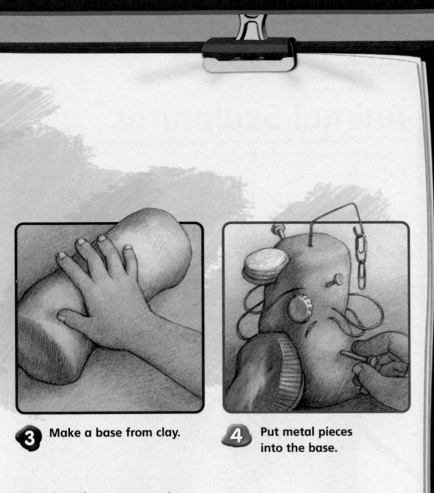

3 Make a base from clay.

4 Put metal pieces into the base.

Think Like an Artist

Turn the base to view all sides. Tell if your assemblage shows an abstract idea or a design that looks real.

Fine Arts Connection

Dance Invite children to create "assemblages" through dance. Divide children into small groups. Play some music. Have one child demonstrate a first movement. Have the next child copy that movement and add a new one.

Continue in this fashion, having each child create and add to the previous movements. Invite volunteers to perform their dances.

2 Create

Have children look at the pictures and read the directions on pages 96–97. Then distribute the materials.

- You may want to provide children with a list of objects to bring from home.
- Have children add paint to a large object and attach smaller items to it.
- Demonstrate how to shape a clay base by using the palms of your hands.
- Remind children to make sure that they have arranged their forms so that the artwork expresses their ideas and feelings.

Technique Tip Children can use their twisted shapes to represent body parts or interesting designs on their assemblages.

3 Close

Have children reflect on their work by responding to *Think Like an Artist* feature. (Possible response: It is an animal and it is realistic.) Continue by asking children to explain how they made an artwork that was abstract or real.

Ongoing Assessment

If . . . children's objects are not sticking in their bases,

then . . . they will need to make the clay bases thicker.

See page 54 from **Unit-by-Unit Resources** for a rubric to assess this studio.

Look and Compare

Look and Compare

At a Glance

Objectives

- Compare and contrast two artworks that show animals.
- Respond to and make judgments about artworks.

Materials

- Art Prints 9, 10, 11
- Fine Art Transparency
- Sketchbook Journal

NVAS (K–4) #4 Understanding the visual arts in relation to history and cultures

NVAS (K–4) #5 Reflecting upon and assessing the characteristics and merits of their work and the work of others

Explore

Display **Art Print 9,** *Baboon.* Help children recall the artwork by Felipe Archuleta from page 84. As children look at the two artworks on pages 98 and 99, ask them to predict which one was created by Archuleta and give reasons for their answers. (*Tiger;* They both show wild animals with jagged teeth.)

Discuss

Read pages 98 and 99. Ask children to name the subject of each artwork. (tiger, polar bear) Help them to identify variations in the subjects using their senses. Ask: **How does the fur of each animal feel? What sounds does each animal make? How are their colors different?** (Accept all reasonable responses.) Explain that artists sometimes need to ask themselves these kinds of questions when creating artworks. Then ask: **What skills did these artists need?** (Possible response: Know how to work with wood and carving tools)

Animal Sculptures

Look at the tiger and the polar bear.
Both sculptures were cut from wood.
Point to the positive space in each.
Where do you see negative space?

Felipe Archuleta. *Tiger,* 1977.
Carved and painted cottonwood, sawdust, and marbles, 35½ by 62¾ by 19½ inches. Smithsonian American Art Museum, Washington, D.C.

98

 Art Background

Tiger During most of his career, Felipe Archuleta created wooden sculptures of various animals, including pigs, cats, giraffes, and cougars, taking inspiration from children's books and magazine pictures. The stride of this tiger illustrates the way in which Archuleta was capable of translating the animal's movements into three-dimensional forms.

Polar Bear *Polar Bear* is an example of folk art, a style of art in which the artists are self-taught. It was created by Isaac Smith (1944–). This carving is abstract and has naturalistic coloring.

Isaac Smith. *Polar Bear,*
1994. Painted wood, plaster,
22 by 49 by 22 inches. Collection
of Dr. Kurt Gitter and Alice Rae Yelen.

Look at the face on each
animal. The faces show
expressions. Are the expressions
alike or different? Tell how
they make you feel.

Sketchbook Journal

Which sculpture
would you like to
have in front of your
school? Write a
sentence to tell why.

99

 Reading Strategy

Compare and Contrast Help children understand that
comparing and contrasting two artworks can help them
to better understand the artworks. By comparing *Tiger* to
Baboon, children were able to determine that these
sculptures were made by the same artist.

Display **Art Print 9,** *Baboon,* **Art Print 10,** *Tiger,* and **Art
Print 11,** *Polar Bear* to create an exhibit of Archuleta's and
Smith's artworks. Find books that also show more of their
artworks and display them. Have children identify ideas
about the exhibition by discussing the similarities and
differences of the artworks. Model by saying: **Archuleta
and Smith both create animal sculptures, however
Archuleta's sculptures appear more realistic.**

Apply

Draw a Venn diagram like the one below on the
chalkboard. Explain that this graphic organizer
will help them to see how the two artworks are
alike and different.

To fill in the diagram, suggest that children first
compare the artworks by seeing how they are
alike. Fill in the middle section as children offer
ideas.

Guide them to look for differences, by suggesting
that they focus on forms and space, the animals'
expressions, stance, and so on.

Animal Sculptures

Tiger

form is thinner
and more erect

less negative
space between
the tiger's legs

the tiger looks
realistic

animals carved
from wood

both animals are
showing their
teeth

Polar Bear

form is rounded
and plump

more negative
space

the polar bear
looks abstract

Close

Ask children what they learned about animal
sculptures. (Possible response: Animals can be
made to look funny or serious.)

Sketchbook Journal Have children complete the
Sketchbook Journal activity. As they choose a
sculpture, ask them to consider its form and space
first.

Lesson 4

At a Glance

Objectives

- Identify and describe toys as art.
- Describe, analyze, interpret, and judge artworks.

Materials

- **Fine Art Transparency**
- wooden toy or sculpture
- Sketchbook Journal

Vocabulary

carved

NVAS (K–4) #4 Understanding the visual arts in relation to history and cultures

NVAS (K–4) #5 Reflecting upon and assessing the characteristics and merits of their work and the work of others

NVAS (K–4) #6 Making connections between visual arts and other disciplines

Introduce

Have children brainstorm one or more of their favorite toys. Ask them to describe its color, form, and texture. Then discuss the materials from which these toys are made.

Pass an example of a wooden toy or sculpture around the class so children can look at the wood more closely. Have children look at the toys on pages 100 and 101 and point to the one made of wood. Explain that wooden toys are often made by *carving* away from a block of wood. This is called the *subtractive method.*

Some artists use the *additive method* to create toys. Just as Yaawaisan used to create his *Toy Helicopter,* artists start with a material and add on until it is finished.

Fun Sculptures

This toy looks like fun. The artist made it by putting together forms cut from foam flip-flop sandals.

Saarenald T. S. Yaawaisan.
Toy Helicopter. Recycled flip-flop sandals. Museum of International Folk Art, Santa Fe, NM. Photo by John Bigelow Taylor.

100

Art Background

Toy Helicopter This toy was created by a Liberian toymaker, Saarenald T.S. Yaawaisan. This helicopter is made from cast-off flip-flop sandals and rubber bands.

Horse Toy This brightly painted artwork, created by an unknown artist from Bangladesh, stands just 10 inches tall. It is one in a collection focusing on the traditional arts of Turkey.

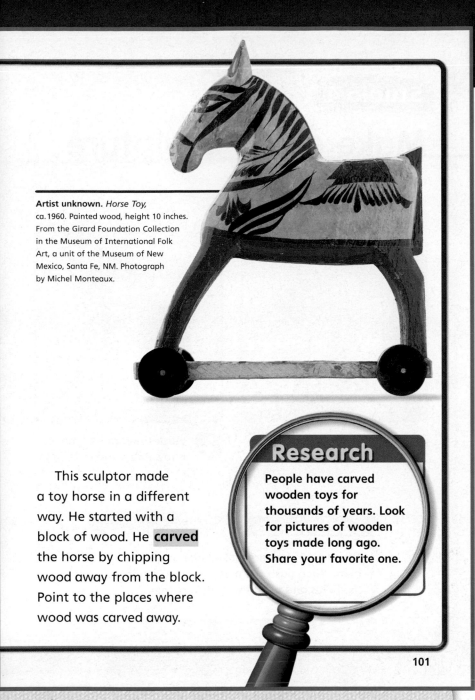

Artist unknown. *Horse Toy,* ca.1960. Painted wood, height 10 inches. From the Girard Foundation Collection in the Museum of International Folk Art, a unit of the Museum of New Mexico, Santa Fe, NM. Photograph by Michel Monteaux.

This sculptor made a toy horse in a different way. He started with a block of wood. He **carved** the horse by chipping wood away from the block. Point to the places where wood was carved away.

Research

People have carved wooden toys for thousands of years. Look for pictures of wooden toys made long ago. Share your favorite one.

101

② Teach

Have children look at the artworks and read pages 100–101. Then have children focus on *Horse Toy.* Ask:

- **How was this artwork made?** (Wood was carved and painted.) DESCRIBE
- **How is space used?** (There is negative space under the horse but not between its legs.) ANALYZE
- **Why did the artist create the horse this way?** (Possible response: to give it an interesting form) INTERPRET
- **Would you like to play with this toy? Explain.** (Possible response: Yes; I like that it has wheels to move around.) JUDGE

Then ask children similar questions about *Toy Helicopter* on page 100.

Research Help children find pictures and information about other wooden toys. Ask them to describe how the toys were made and used.

③ Close

Have children share a picture of their favorite toy with the class. Ask them to tell how they think it was made.

Visual Culture Have children compare toys made with modern technology with toys made long ago.

Curriculum Connection

Social Studies Explain to children that today toys are generally made from plastic and produced in factories. Long ago, however, children played with and made toys from whatever was at hand: newspapers, scrap wood, corncobs, pebbles, twigs, and so on. Have them sketch an idea for a toy using natural objects in their Sketchbook Journal.

 Notes

Show children an example of a carved wooden toy. Pass it around so all children can explore it. Then say: **This is a wooden toy.** Have children repeat after you. Show children other toys. Ask them whether the toys are wooden or not.

Studio 4

At a Glance

Objectives

- Demonstrate how to use a variety of art materials to make a sculpture.
- Evaluate original artworks by self and peers.

Materials

- meat trays ⚠
- pencils, scissors ⚠, glue, tape, pipe cleaners ⚠
- found art objects, such as string, paper clips, toothpicks ⚠, and foam packing peanuts
- Rubric 3 from **Unit-by-Unit Resources**

NVAS (K–4) #1 Understanding and applying media, techniques, and processes

NVAS (K–4) #3 Choosing and evaluating a range of subject matter, symbols, and ideas

NVAS (K–4) #5 Reflecting upon and assessing the characteristics and merits of their work and the work of others

❶ Introduce

Review sculptures with children. Remind children that some artists create sculptures by carving away material and other artists create scuptures by adding on, just like they will. Have children brainstorm ideas for their sculptures. Ask:

- **What forms will you use?**
- **Will your sculpture be realistic or abstract?**
- **What additional objects or materials will you use?**

Make a Fun Sculpture

Collect art tools and materials.
Use them to make a fun sculpture.

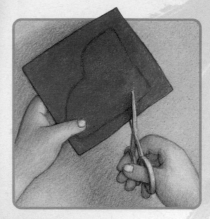

1 Cut foam into different forms.

2 Stack the forms to make a toy. Ask a friend to help.

Technique Tip

To use pipe cleaners, poke holes in the foam. Then push the pipe cleaner through the holes and twist the ends together.

102

🏃 Meeting Individual Needs

Inclusion A child who has difficulties with fine motor skills may have trouble cutting the foam. Provide a variety of precut forms and shapes for the child to use for this studio.

Quick Studio

Have children draw a sculpture using forms they have learned about in this unit.

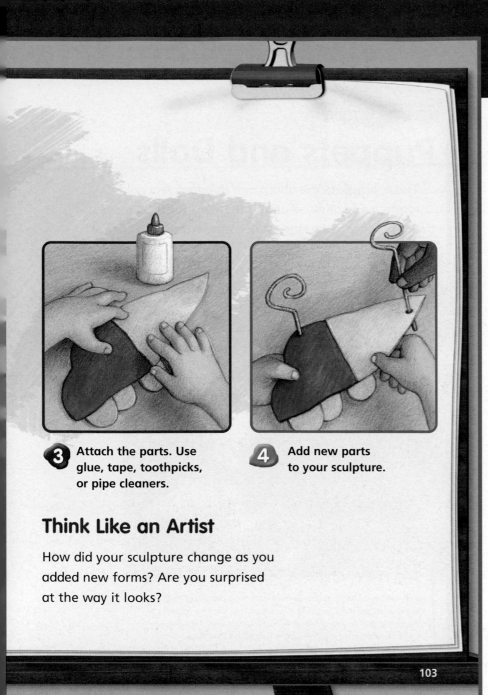

③ Attach the parts. Use glue, tape, toothpicks, or pipe cleaners.

④ Add new parts to your sculpture.

Think Like an Artist

How did your sculpture change as you added new forms? Are you surprised at the way it looks?

Fine Arts Connection

Dance Explain to children that when they are performing creative movement patterns or dances, they are using space, just like sculptures. Play "Freeze Dance" with children. Have them dance or perform movements while listening to music. Then stop the music and have children "freeze" their position. Talk about the positive and negative space they are using. Repeat the activity, stopping the music at different intervals of time.

② Create

Have children look at the pictures and read the directions on pages 102–103. Then distribute materials.

- Remind children that they can cut foam into geometric forms or organic forms.
- Have children finalize their ideas about the type of toy they are trying to make, such as a car or animal.
- Point out that tape will work best if a child wants two forms attached side by side.
- Use new and interesting shapes and forms to add detail.

Technique Tip Model connecting two forms together using pipe cleaners.

③ Close

Have children reflect on their work as they answer the *Think Like an Artist* questions. (Possible response: I planned a dune buggy, but it looked more like an airplane, so I added propellers.) Then have children tell why they like their sculptures.

Ongoing Assessment

If . . . children have a hard time attaching forms together with glue,

then . . . suggest they use tape or pipe cleaners.

See page 54 from **Unit-by-Unit Resources** for a rubric to assess this studio.

Lesson 5

At a Glance

Objectives

- Identify and describe puppets as art.
- Describe, analyze, interpret, and judge artworks.

Materials

- **Fine Art Transparency**
- puppets
- Sketchbook Journal

Vocabulary

puppets, puppeteer, folk art

NVAS (K–4) #2 Using knowledge of structures and functions

NVAS (K–4) #4 Understanding the visual arts in relation to history and cultures

NVAS (K–4) #5 Reflecting upon and assessing the characteristics and merits of their work and the work of others

NVAS (K–4) #6 Making connections between visual arts and other disciplines

① Introduce

Bring to class one or two puppets to share with children. Ask children to describe puppets or puppet shows they have seen. Tell them that puppets and dolls can resemble people or animals.

Explain that the art of using puppets to tell stories is called *puppetry* and it has been around for a long time. The people who move the puppets and tell the stories are called *puppeteers.* A puppeteer is another job in the world of art. Ask children to name other jobs associated with puppetry. (puppet makers)

Explain that many puppets and dolls are *folk art* and reflect the traditions of a particular culture. Ask children to tell about any folk art they have seen or may have at home. Ask: **Did these artworks tell a story? Explain.** (Answers will vary.)

Lesson 5

Puppets and Dolls

These **puppets** are about one hundred years old. They are made of wood and cloth. A **puppeteer** moves the puppets to tell a story. What story would you tell?

Artist unknown. *Marionettes: Sword Fighter and Dancer,* ca.1900. Painted wood and cloth, height 22 inches. From the Girard Foundation Collection in the Museum of International Folk Art, a unit of the Museum of New Mexico, Santa Fe, NM. Photograph by Michel Monteaux.

104

 Art Background

Art and Culture Marionettes are a type of puppet on strings. In the West, puppeteers are usually visible to the audience as they control the puppet above the stage. In parts of India, each puppet is constructed so that its head and body strings are attached to a cloth-covered ring. The ring fits onto the puppeteer's head, and the puppeteer controls the puppet's hands with attached rods.

Art History Although *papier-mâché* is a French term, meaning *chewed paper,* the medium was used in the Far East for centuries before its first use in France, probably during the sixteenth century. At the peak of its popularity in the nineteenth century, papier-mâché was used to create boxes, jewelry, sculptures, and even furniture.

This doll is an example of **folk art**. Folk artists learn about art from other artists. Folk art often shows something about the artist's culture.

How are the clothes on this doll different from other dolls you have seen?

Artist unknown. *Burma Doll*, ca. 1960. Painted papier-mâché, height 10 inches. From the Girard Foundation Collection in the Museum of International Folk Art, a unit of the Museum of New Mexico, Santa Fe, NM. Photograph by Michel Monteaux.

Sketchbook Journal

Draw a puppet. Draw clothes to help people in the future see what your culture is like.

105

② Teach

Have children read pages 104 and 105. Have them look at *Burma Doll*. Ask:

- **How would you describe this doll?** (small head and body; large arms and legs; hair sticks up; painted face; bright colors) DESCRIBE
- **How is it like other dolls you have seen?** (Possible responses: moveable arms and legs; painted face) ANALYZE
- **What mood did the artist want to create? Why?** (Possible response: a humorous feeling using unusual proportions) INTERPRET
- **What do you like best about this doll? Why?** (Possible response: its hair because it adds texture) JUDGE

Now ask similar questions as children look at *Marionettes: Sword Fighter and Dancer*.

Sketchbook Journal Have children think about what they would want someone in the future to know about them from their clothing choices.

③ Close

After children draw their puppets, have them explain the clothing they chose and give reasons for their choices.

Assessment Have children discuss and list objects, other than clothing, that reflect our culture (computers, DVDs, fast food).

 Technology

Make Puppets Have children explore the World Wide Web to find ideas on how to make a variety of puppets. Help them brainstorm different keywords that would help them locate the information they want. Then have children print out an example of a puppet they would like to make.

 Notes

Invite children to play with the puppets you brought to class. Have them "talk" to each other with the puppets for a few minutes. Then say: **This is a puppet.** Have children repeat after you.

Studio 5

At a Glance

Objectives

- Demonstrate how to use a variety of art materials to create a puppet.
- Evaluate original artworks by self and peers.

Materials

- long socks, newspaper, rubber bands, fabric glue, colored paper, yarn, bird seed, fabric pieces
- stapler (optional) ⚠
- Rubric 3 from **Unit-by-Unit Resources**

NVAS (K–4) #1 Understanding and applying media, techniques, and processes

NVAS (K–4) #3 Choosing and evaluating a range of subject matter, symbols, and ideas

NVAS (K–4) #5 Reflecting upon and assessing the characteristics and merits of their work and the work of others

❶ Introduce

Review puppets with children. Have them discuss their experiences with puppets and puppet shows. Then have children brainstorm the kind of puppet they will make for their story. Ask:

- **Will your puppet be a character from a familiar story or a story you create?**
- **Will the puppet be a person or an animal?**
- **What forms will you use to create your puppet?**
- **What will you use for your puppet's hair, eyes, and mouth?**

Studio 5

Make a Sock Puppet

You can make a puppet from a sock.
Use it to tell a story.

1 Make a head. First, stuff the toe of a sock with a wad of newspaper.

2 Then, wrap a rubber band around the wad of newspaper.

Technique Tip

Wrap paper strips around a pencil to make curls. The curls can be used for hair or jewelry.

106

🚶🚶 Meeting Individual Needs

Reteach Provide a selection of precut facial feature shapes made from fabric scraps, colored paper, or felt.

Extend Encourage children to create plays with their puppets. Invite children from other classes to visit your classroom for presentations of the puppet shows.

Quick Studio

Have children make a simple hand puppet using a sock. Provide markers for children to add facial features.

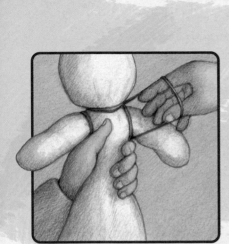

3 **Make arms. Use wads of newspaper and rubber bands.**

4 **Add clothes, hair, and facial details. Use yarn, paper, and other art scraps.**

Think Like an Artist

Artists use puppets to tell stories.
Move your puppet and make it talk.
What story will your puppet tell?

107

Fine Arts Connection

Music Remind children that puppets are used to entertain people. They talk, tell stories, sing, and even dance.

Ask children to listen carefully as you "talk" and "sing" with your puppet. Have them raise their hand if the puppet is talking and raise both hands if the puppet is singing. If possible, present the puppet so that children cannot see your mouth moving.

Continue by organizing children into pairs and having them make their puppets talk and sing.

2 Create

Have children look at the pictures and read pages 106–107. Then distribute materials.

- Demonstrate how to stuff the end of a sock tightly and smooth out any bumps.
- Model how to wrap the rubber band around the puppet's neck to form the head.
- Squeeze and pull on the newspaper and the sock to make the arms longer than the head.
- Encourage children to think of the story they want to tell with their puppet and design their character accordingly.

Technique Tip Show children how to hold one end of a paper strip tightly against a pencil as they wrap the loose end around and around. Have them count to ten before unfurling the strip. Use curls as decorations, mustaches, or antennae.

3 Close

Have children express ideas using their artwork by answering the *Think Like an Artist* question. (Answers will vary.)

Ongoing Assessment

If . . . children have difficulty gluing hair and felt to their puppets,

then . . . suggest that they use just a small amount of glue for each part.

See page 54 from **Unit-by-Unit Resources** for a rubric to assess this studio.

Lesson 6

At a Glance

Objectives

- Identify and describe pottery as art.
- Describe, analyze, interpret, and judge artworks.

Materials

- **Fine Art Transparency**
- Sketchbook Journal

Vocabulary

pottery, clay, kiln

NVAS (K–4) #2 Using knowledge of structures and functions

NVAS (K–4) #4 Understanding the visual arts in relation to history and cultures

NVAS (K–4) #5 Reflecting upon and assessing the characteristics and merits of their work and the work of others

NVAS (K–4) #6 Making connections between visual arts and other disciplines

①Introduce

Have children pantomime eating and drinking. Point out the objects (bowls, plates, glasses, cups) needed to perform these activities.

Then point out that many of these items are made from *pottery.* Explain that pottery is usually made of clay, a powdery substance found in the Earth that becomes pliable when moistened and hardens when baked. Have children share their experiences with clay and pottery.

Lesson 6

Pottery

Some artwork is made to decorate a space. Artists create other artworks to be used. The clay jar below is **pottery.** It is made to decorate and be used.

María and Julian Martínez, San Ildefonso Pueblo. *Jar,* ca. 1937.
Blackware, diameter 9½ inches, height 7¼ inches. The Heard Museum, Phoenix, AZ.

 Art Background

Art and Culture María (1881–1980) and Julian Martínez (1885?–1943) began working together in 1904. María created the pots, and Julian decorated them. Sometime after 1918 the Martínezes started using the black-on-black technique. They baked the red clay pots in a bonfire. After they smothered the flames, the clay turned a shiny black.

About the Artist Mexican folk artist Josefina Aguilar grew up in Oaxaca, Mexico. She learned the craft of making clay sculptures from her mother. Aguilar is known internationally for her work. She is also the subject of *Josefina,* a well-known children's book about her life written by Jeannette Winter.

Josefina Aguilar. *Untitled (Frida Kahlo)*, 2002. Clay, height 28 inches. Private collection. Photograph courtesy CRIZMAC Art and Cultural Education Materials, Inc.

Artists who make pottery are called potters. They work with **clay** from the earth. Potters mold soft, wet clay into a form they like. They bake the forms in an oven called a **kiln.** The pottery gets hard when it is dry. Then the potter paints it.

Sketchbook Journal

Draw a pottery plate. Draw a design or pattern on your plate.

109

② Teach

Have children look at the artworks and read pages 108–109. Focus their attention on Aguilar's pottery. Ask:

- **What do you see?** (a brightly colored woman holding a bird) DESCRIBE
- **What colors and patterns do you see?** (bright blue top with flower pattern; blue scarf; blue skirt with people) ANALYZE
- **What was this artwork used for?** (Possible response: decoration) INTERPRET
- **What do you like best about this artwork?** (Possible response: the bright colors) JUDGE

Now ask similar questions as children look at *Jar*.

Sketchbook Journal As children draw their plates, have them think about the type of pattern or design that will complement its shape.

③ Close

After children have completed their plates, have them discuss the patterns or designs they drew and explain why they chose them.

Visual Culture Have children design plates and cups for an airplane. Then have them discuss why they chose their designs. Ask: **How did the fact that these objects will be used on an airplane affect your design?** (Possible response: I made the plates look like clouds.)

 Curriculum Connection

Social Studies Explain that artists sometimes decorate their artworks with images that are meaningful to them and their culture. Have children draw a pot in their Sketchbook Journals and include a symbol of their community as part of their design.

 Notes

Check children's understanding of the meaning of pottery by showing several examples or photographs of pottery. As you show each item, say: **This is pottery.** Then have children repeat after you.

Studio 6

At a Glance

Objectives

- Demonstrate how to make a pinch pot using clay.
- Evaluate original artworks by self and peers.

Materials

- self-hardening clay
- plastic forks ⚠, pencils, acrylic paint, paintbrushes
- Rubric 3 from **Unit-by-Unit Resources**

NVAS (K–4) #1 Understanding and applying media, techniques, and processes

NVAS (K–4) #3 Choosing and evaluating a range of subject matter, symbols, and ideas

NVAS (K–4) #5 Reflecting upon and assessing the characteristics and merits of their work and the work of others

① Introduce

Review pottery with children. Talk about the many uses of pottery. Have children brainstorm what their pottery will look like and how it will be used. Ask:

- **What form will your pot be? What type of lid will it have?**
- **What designs will you make on your pot?**
- **What color will you paint it?**

Quick Studio

Have children shape modeling clay into a pot. Provide toothpicks for the children to use to add detail.

Make a Pinch Pot

Make a pinch pot with a design.

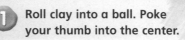

1 Roll clay into a ball. Poke your thumb into the center.

2 Turn and pinch the clay ball until you form a pot.

Technique Tip

You may want to carve patterns of lines and shapes onto the surface of your pot before you paint it.

110

👫👫 Meeting Individual Needs

Reteach Children may need assistance when creating their pot. Model how to begin with a ball of clay, and then use your thumb to create the hole in the center. Explain that the sides of the pot must have the same amount of thickness, or the pot will not form correctly.

Extend Have children work as a group to plan a classroom pottery exhibition in which they will show their completed pinch pots. Help them choose a time for the exhibition, design and create a flyer or banner, and plan where and when they will display their artworks. During the exhibition, encourage children to identify ideas and feelings in artworks by peers.

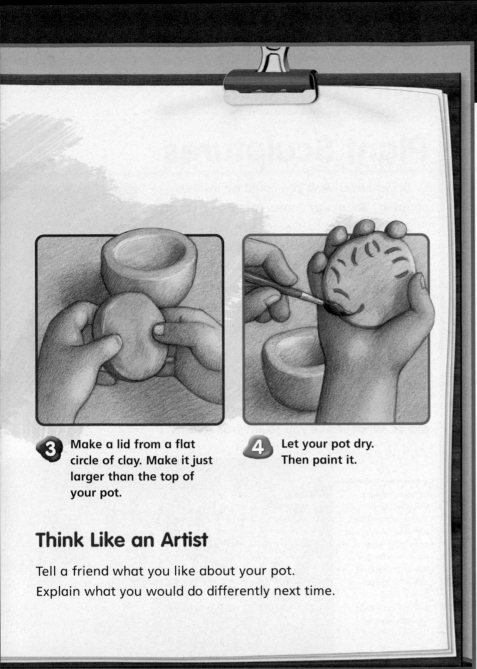

3 Make a lid from a flat circle of clay. Make it just larger than the top of your pot.

4 Let your pot dry. Then paint it.

Think Like an Artist

Tell a friend what you like about your pot.
Explain what you would do differently next time.

 Fine Arts Connection

Theater Tell children that they will create a skit using their pinch pots as a prop. Have children work from the following premise: *A mysterious pot shows up on your doorstep; how did it get there?*

Children can also create a premise of their own. Invite them to work in small groups to compose a skit and present it to the class.

2 Create

Help children read pages 110–111. Then distribute materials. Explain that these pots will not be safe for eating and drinking.

- Suggest that children hold the clay in their non-dominant hand.
- Remind them to be patient and gentle as they press the clay into the pot's shape. Tell them this is an important skill when working with clay.
- Tell them that they can attach a handle to their lids, if they like.
- Remind children to paint with colors and lines that express their ideas about pottery.

Technique Tip Demonstrate how to use a pencil to draw patterns of shapes and lines by pressing gently into the clay.

3 Close

Instruct children to discuss the *Think Like an Artist* prompt to define reasons for preferences in personal artworks. (Possible response: I like the flowers. Next time, I would make a smaller lid.)

Ongoing Assessment

If . . . the walls of children's pots are uneven,

then . . . remind them to apply even pressure with both hands when molding.

See page 54 from **Unit-by-Unit Resources** for a rubric to assess this studio.

Artist at Work

Artist at Work

At a Glance

Objectives

- Read about a career in art.
- Identify the use of art in everyday life.
- Relate art to personal experiences.

Materials

- topiary (optional)

NVAS (K–4) #5 Reflecting upon and assessing the characteristics and merits of their work and the work of others

Explore

Display a small topiary and discuss its form. Explain that topiaries are trees or shrubs that are pruned into interesting shapes. Some people think that they are like sculptures.

Ask children to describe any experiences they have had with topiaries or other plants. Then ask what they would sculpt from plants. (Possible response: animals)

Discuss

Have children read pages 112–113. Ask:

- **Is Mason's topiary garden realistic or abstract?** (realistic)
- **Which figures in the garden can you match to figures in the painting?** (Possible response: I can see the woman with the hat and the umbrella with her daughter.)
- **What skills did Mason need to make his sculpture garden?** (knowledge of plants and gardening; how to tell a story)
- **Do you consider Mason's topiaries sculptures? Explain your answer.** (Possible response: Yes; because he is creating a form out of a plant.)
- **What other jobs combine plants and art?** (Possible response: florist, landscape designer)

Plant Sculptures

Do you ever wish you could go inside a painting? Thanks to James Mason, you can.

In the late 1800s, Georges Seurat painted the artwork below. In the late 1900s, James Mason used the painting as an idea for his own artwork. Mason used metal and plants. He made large sculptures to show people and objects from the painting. He put the sculptures in a park.

James Mason is a sculptor. Most of his sculptures are made from wood, stone, or metal. But he also made sculptures from plants. What would you sculpt from plants?

James Mason

Georges Seurat. *A Sunday on La Grande Jatte–1884*, 1884-1886. Oil on canvas, 83 by 123¼ inches. Holen Birch Bartlett Memorial Collection, 1926. Photograph ©1996, The Art Institute of Chicago. All rights reserved.

112

 Career Research

Have children work in small groups to research other careers with flowers and plants. If possible, invite a local nursery owner, landscape architect, gardener, or other garden professional to talk about his or her career.

James Mason's sculptures add interest to this park.

Which figures in the garden can you match to figures in the painting?

113

Apply

Have children name other careers in which people work with flowers and plants. Display a graphic organizer like the one below. Fill in the chart as children share their ideas. Possible responses are shown below.

Careers	What They Do
gardener	grows and cuts grass, trees, and flowers
florist	sells flowers
landscape designer	creates plans for gardens and outdoor areas

Close

Review the completed graphic organizer. Ask: **What artistic skills are needed in these jobs?** (Possible response: These jobs require a knowledge of the elements of art and the principles of design.)

 Reading Strategy

Summarize and Paraphrase Information Explain to children that good readers often summarize and paraphrase information as they read. As an example, have children read the first paragraph on page 112. Have a volunteer say its meaning in one sentence. Repeat the process for the second and third paragraphs. Then ask:

• **How did breaking up the passage into paragraphs help you to understand its overall meaning?** (Possible response: It is easier to read and understand a little bit at a time.)

Portfolio Project

Portfolio Project

At a Glance

Objectives

- Develop and organize ideas in the environment.
- Demonstrate knowledge about pottery and form.
- Evaluate original artworks by self and peers.

Materials

- aluminum cans with smooth tops
- self-hardening clay, dampened paper towels
- acrylic paints, paintbrushes
- Rubric 3 from **Unit-by-Unit Resources**

NVAS (K–4) #1 Understanding and applying media, techniques, and processes

NVAS (K–4) #3 Choosing and evaluating a range of subject matter, symbols, and ideas

NVAS (K–4) #5 Reflecting upon and assessing the characteristics and merits of their work and the work of others

Make a Thumbprint Pot

Build a pot with balls of clay.
Use your own thumb to decorate it.

1 Roll small balls of clay. Then wrap a can in wet paper towels.

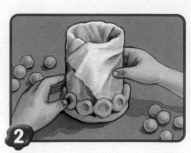

2 Make a flat clay base. Press the balls of clay onto the towels.

3 Remove the can. Carefully peel off the towels.

4 Let your pot dry. Paint it.

114

Plan

Direct children to read page 114. Then ask:

- **What are some things you can store in pots?**
- **How will you use this pot?**

Have children think about the concepts they have learned in this unit about forms and space. Then have them think about what they have learned about pottery. Ask them to brainstorm how they might paint their thumbprint pots. Encourage them to look through their Sketchbook Journals for design ideas.

Quick Project

Have children make a thumbprint plate. Children will roll clay balls and then press them onto wax paper into a plate.

🚶 Meeting Individual Needs

Inclusion Children who are visually impaired should be paired with other children to complete the thumbprint pot. The child who is visually impaired should roll the balls of clay. Their partners will assist them in attaching the balls onto the towels around the can.

114

How did these children make the balls on their pots stay together?

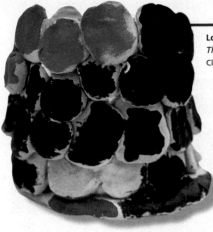

Lauren, Age 7.
Thumbprint Pot.
Clay and tempera paint.

Sophie, Age 7.
Thumbprint Stripes.
Clay and tempera paint.

Share Your Art

1. Tell why it was important that the clay balls touched the bottom and each other.
2. Suggest tips for others who try this project.

115

 Gallery Options

School Display If your school has a glass display case, inquire about using it to display the children's thumbprint pots. Place the pots in the case with a slip of paper beside each, identifying the artist and the title of the artwork.

Create

Gather the materials and guide children through the steps on page 114 to complete the project.

- The balls of clay should be about the size of marbles. Have children wrap several damp paper towels around the can.
- Make sure the pressed clay balls touch each other and the clay meets at the bottom and sides of the can.
- Since the clay will shrink as it dries, have children remove the can by carefully sliding it up and out while the clay is still wet.
- Let the pots dry overnight before children add designs with acrylic paints.

Instruct children to write their names on the bottom of their pots before you store them on a shelf.

Close

Point out the children's art on page 115. Ask:

- **How are these artworks like your own thumbprint pot?** (Possible response: We both made patterns with our thumbprints.)
- **How are they different?** (Possible response: The artist used more than one color.)

Then ask the *Share Your Art* questions on page 115. (Possible responses: to make the pot strong; I would tell them to make the flat clay bottom a little wider than the can's bottom.) Ask children to name some necessary skills an artist should have when working with clay.

See page 54 from **Unit-by-Unit Resources** for a rubric to assess this project.

Unit 3 Review

At a Glance

Objectives

- Relate art terms to the environment.
- Identify form and space in artworks.
- Describe, analyze, interpret, and judge artworks.

Materials

- **Art Print 12**
- **Fine Art Transparency**

NVAS (K–4) #1 Understanding and applying media, techniques, and processes

NVAS (K–4) #2 Using knowledge of structures and functions

NVAS (K–4) #5 Reflecting upon and assessing the characteristics and merits of their work and the work of others

Think About Art

Possible responses:

carve (Point to the artist carving the sculpture.)
positive space (Point to the birds.)
puppeteer (Point to the man making the puppet move.)
puppet (Point to the object that the puppeteer is moving.)
sculptor (Point to the man holding a chainsaw.)
negative space (Point to the sky around the birds.)

Write About Art

Before children write, ask:

- **What types of activities would you want to do on your playscape?** (Possible responses: climb, jump, slide)
- **What kinds of forms will you include in your playscape to do these activities?** (Possible responses: cylinders for slides and tunnels, a sphere for something to jump on, and a cone to climb)

116

Think About Art

Match the pictures with the art words. You may use the pictures more than once.

carve	positive space	puppeteer
puppet	sculptor	negative space

Write About Art

Write about the ideal playscape. Use the names of forms to describe it.

Talk About Art

- Choose an artwork you would like to revise.
- Tell a friend what you would change.

116

 Assessment Options

Options for assessing children appear in the **Unit-by-Unit Resources.**

- Use the **Vocabulary Worksheets** on pages 47–50 for an informal assessment of Unit 3 vocabulary.
- Use the **Unit 3 Test** on pages 55–58 to assess children's mastery of unit vocabulary and concepts.

George Segal. *Walk, Don't Walk,* 1976. Plaster, cement, metal, painted wood, and electric light, 104 by 72 by 72 inches. Collection of Whitney Museum of American Art, New York. ©2003, George Segal/Licensed by VAGA, New York.

Put It All Together

1. Where do you see negative space in this sculpture?
2. Why are the people standing still?
3. What is the purpose of this sculpture?
4. Would you like to talk with these people? Explain.

117

 Art Background

About the Artist George Segal (1924–2000) was born in the Bronx, in New York City. A realist sculptor, Segal is known for his life-sized figures cast in plaster. Many of these artworks display everyday objects or scenarios, such as the sculpture featured on the 1983 cover of *Time* magazine, which shows a man and a woman using computers.

Talk About Art

Prompt children to use words such as *form, design, model, space, positive space,* and *negative space* to describe artworks in their portfolios. Ask children to define reasons as to why they like their artworks.

Model for children how to page through each artwork describing details and what you like about it. Give children an opportunity to identify ideas in each other's portfolios. Organize them into pairs, reminding them to be respectful of each other.

Put It All Together

Use the questions on page 117 to evaluate the artwork. Possible responses follow.

1. There is negative space between the people's legs and all around the people and the traffic light. DESCRIBE
2. They are waiting for the sign to change so they can cross the street. ANALYZE
3. The artist may have wanted to share his ideas and feelings about everyday life in a busy city. INTERPRET
4. No, because they have straight faces and are not smiling. They look too busy to talk. JUDGE

Unit 4 Overview

Artists express how they feel and what they are thinking through their artworks. This process is called creative expression. In this unit, children will learn about the different methods artists use to express themselves, and they will try to discover the artists' true feelings and ideas by viewing their artworks.

	Unit Opener, p. 118	Lesson 1, p. 120 Art and Music Studio 1, p. 122 Make a Slab Instrument	Lesson 2, p. 124 Balance Studio 2, p. 126 Make a Coil Object	Lesson 3, p. 128 Rhythm as Expression Studio 3, p. 130 Make a Shadow Dancer	Look and Compare, p. 132 Movement in Artworks
Artworks	**Édouard Manet.** *The Fifer,* 1866.	**Artist unknown.** *Tang Dynasty Sheng Player, Dancer, and Panpipe Player,* 7th century.	**Artist unknown.** *Smiling Figurine,* ca. A.D. 6th to 9th century.	**Edgar Degas.** *The Star (Dancer on Stage),* 1878.	**Édouard Manet.** *Monet Painting in His Floating Studio,* 1874. **Winslow Homer.** *Breezing Up,* 1873-1876.
Vocabulary	creative expression	clay, slab, ceramic	balance, symmetrical balance, asymmetrical balance, radial balance	movement, rhythm, motion	
Materials	• Art Print 13 • Fine Art Transparency • Instructional Prints	• **Fine Art Transparency** • tape player • Sketchbook Journal • ceramic clay • dowels or rolling pins • plastic knives ⚠, water containers, pencils	• **Fine Art Transparency** • pictures of objects showing different types of balance • Sketchbook Journal • modeling clay • plastic forks ⚠, pencils, sticks	• **Fine Art Transparency** • Sketchbook Journal • brown or black construction paper • white or yellow construction paper • scissors ⚠, white chalk, glue	• **Art Print 13, 14, 15** • **Fine Art Transparency** • Sketchbook Journal
Connections	**Home Connection** invite parents to the classroom **Bookshelf** *Discovering Great Artists: Hands-On Art for Children in the Styles of the Great Masters* by MaryAnn F. Kohl, Bright Ring Publishers, 1997	**Curriculum Connection** Social Studies: instruments of the past, present, and future **ESL Notes** **Fine Arts Connection** Music: Sing or play an instrument **Meeting Individual Needs** Inclusion	**Curriculum Connection** Science: types of balance in butterflies **ESL Notes** **Fine Arts Connection** Theatre: demonstrate types of balance by making a hat **Meeting Individual Needs** Reteach	**Curriculum Connection** Physical Education: forms of exercise **ESL Notes** **Fine Arts Connection** Theatre: make shadow puppets **Meeting Individual Needs** Reteach, Extend	**Reading Strategy** Compare and contrast
Assessment Opportunities		Visual Culture Rubric 4 from **Unit-by-Unit Resources** Ongoing Assessment	Informal Assessment Rubric 4 from **Unit-by-Unit Resources** Ongoing Assessment	Informal Assessment Rubric 4 from **Unit-by-Unit Resources** Ongoing Assessment	

Lesson 4, p. 134 **Unity and Variety** **Studio 4, p. 136** Show Unity and Variety	Lesson 5 p. 138 **Proportion** **Studio 5, p. 140** Draw Proportion	Lesson 6, p. 142 **Symbols** **Studio 6, p. 144** Make a Mosaic	**Artist at Work, p. 146** Window Displays	**Portfolio Project, p. 148** Make Symbol Prints	**Unit Review, p. 150**
Elizabeth Lewis Scott. *Kitty Cat's Ball*, 2002.	**Rosa Bonheur.** *Plowing in the Nivernais (Labourage Nivernais)*, 1849.	**Artist unknown.** *Double-Headed Serpent*, 15th century.	**Maribeth Koutrakos.** *Baseball Locker Room*, 1995.		**Auguste Rodin.** *The Thinker*, 1880.
unity, variety	proportion, faraway, close up	symbol, mosaic			
• **Fine Art Transparency** • water-based markers or crayons • Sketchbook Journal	• **Fine Art Transparency** • Sketchbook Journal	• **Fine Art Transparency** • Sketchbook Journal	Fine Art Transparency	• pencils, scissors ⚠ • tagboard, newsprint • water-based printer's ink, clean meat trays ⚠, brayers	• **Art Print 16** • **Fine Art Transparency**
• a small bag of materials (one per child): 1 clothespin, 3 paper clips, cardboard base, 2 pipe cleaners ⚠, 1 paper towel roll, other found art materials such as paper scraps or buttons • glue • masking tape (optional)	• chairs (for a large space), or small objects with simple shapes such as boxes, balls, and so on (for a small space) • pencils, sheets of drawing paper • watercolors, paintbrushes, palettes, water cups	• construction paper, drawing paper • markers, glue sticks			
Technology Make a class book **ESL Notes**	**Curriculum Connection** Math: proportion in math **ESL Notes**	**Curriculum Connection** Social Studies: create a national symbol **ESL Notes**	**Career Research** Window display designers **Reading Strategy** Draw conclusions	**Gallery Options** Create a digital gallery **Meeting Individual Needs** Extend	
Fine Arts Connection Music: unity and variety in music **Meeting Individual Needs** Reteach, Extend	**Fine Arts Connection** Theatre: create a scene **Meeting Individual Needs** Reteach	**Fine Arts Connection** Dance: expressing emotion through movement **Meeting Individual Needs** Inclusion			
Visual Culture Rubric 4 from **Unit-by-Unit Resources** Ongoing Assessment	Informal Assessment Rubric 4 from **Unit-by-Unit Resources** Ongoing Assessment	Visual Culture Rubric 4 from **Unit-by-Unit Resources** Ongoing Assessment		Rubric 4 from **Unit-by-Unit Resources**	**Unit-by-Unit Resources** Vocabulary Worksheets, pp. 65–68 Unit 4 Test, pp. 73–76

At a Glance

Objectives

- Identify principles of design in artworks.
- Respond to and make judgments about artworks.
- Relate art to personal experiences.

Materials

- **Art Print 13**
- **Fine Art Transparency**

Vocabulary

creative expression

NVAS (K–4) #4 Understanding the visual arts in relation to history and cultures

NVAS (K–4) #5 Reflecting upon and assessing the characteristics and merits of their work and the work of others

Introduce the Unit

Ask a volunteer to read the title of Unit 4. Tell children that they will learn many ways that artists express themselves.

Explain to children that artists use *creative expression* to make artworks. By using creative expression, artists tell what they are thinking, or how they feel about different subjects. Ask: **What is important to you? How will you express it in an artwork?** (Possible responses: I love to play sports; I will paint a picture of me playing soccer.)

Have children look through the unit and choose an artwork that they think best expresses an artist's creativity. Then have them explain what they think the artist may have wanted to say about the subject of their artwork. Ask: **How did the artist express his or her feelings and ideas?** (Answers will vary.)

Édouard Manet. *The Fifer,* 1866. Oil on canvas, 63 ½ by 38 ¼ inches. Musée d'Orsay, Paris.

118

 Art Background

The Fifer Édouard Manet painted *The Fifer* in flat, bright colors against a plain background. His style was greatly influenced by many Spanish painters such as Diego Velázquez. A contemporary of his remarked that the painting looked like a playing card. Manet's choices of style and flat colors also suggest Japanese prints, which greatly influenced French painting in the second half of the nineteenth century.

 Home Connection

Invite parents to the classroom to share creative pursuits they enjoy, such as singing, dancing, listening to music, painting, drawing, and playing an instrument.

Creative Expression

Creative expression is about sharing ideas and feelings. Some artists express themselves by talking. Some write or sing.

Visual artists express themselves through media. Some draw. Some paint or sculpt.

Look at *The Fifer*. What do you think this artist was trying to express?

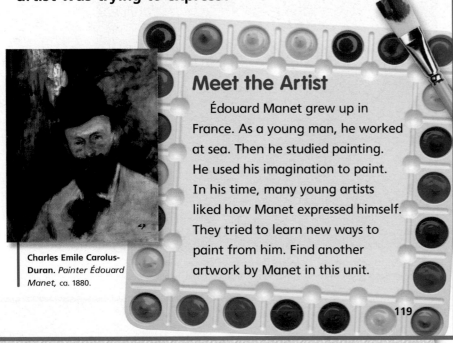

Charles Emile Carolus-Duran. *Painter Édouard Manet,* ca. 1880.

Meet the Artist

Édouard Manet grew up in France. As a young man, he worked at sea. Then he studied painting. He used his imagination to paint. In his time, many young artists liked how Manet expressed himself. They tried to learn new ways to paint from him. Find another artwork by Manet in this unit.

119

Bookshelf

Discovering Great Artists: Hands-On Art for Children in the Styles of the Great Masters
by MaryAnn F. Kohl
Bright Ring Publishers, 1997

This book will provide many activities for children to explore their own creative expression. Children will be able to read information about many great artists as well as try their hand at artworks that are similar to these artists' styles.

Discuss Unit Concepts

Have children read page 119 and look at *The Fifer*. Explain that a fife is a small flute and a fifer is a person who plays it. Have children describe the expression on the fifer's face. (Some may think that he looks intense because he is concentrating on playing his instrument.) Encourage children to discuss the color, texture, and the use of space in the painting.

As you introduce each element of art and principle of design in Unit 4, you may wish to display the **Instructional Prints.** A print is provided for each element and principle.

In addition, **Art Prints 13–16** and **Transparencies** are available for fine art in the unit.

Meet the Artist

Édouard Manet French painter Édouard Manet (1832–1883) was born into an affluent family. Even though he did not follow in his father's footsteps to become a judge, his family supported him as an artist. Manet was known to often give financial support to his artist friends when they were struggling.

Manet is considered an Impressionist painter, even though he never exhibited with them. Unlike the Impressionists, he preferred to paint in his studio rather than outside.

Lesson 1

At a Glance

Objectives

- Identify and describe different kinds of art.
- Describe, analyze, interpret, and judge artworks.

Materials

- **Fine Art Transparency**
- tape player
- Sketchbook Journal

Vocabulary

clay, slab, ceramic

NVAS (K–4) #2 Using knowledge of structures and functions

NVAS (K–4) #4 Understanding the visual arts in relation to history and cultures

NVAS (K–4) #5 Reflecting upon and assessing the characteristics and merits of their work and the work of others

NVAS (K–4) #6 Making connections between visual arts and other disciplines

➊ Introduce

Play some music on a tape player. Invite children to move to the sounds of the music. Explain that music and dancing are forms of art.

Explain that whenever people express their opinions or feelings through art, then they are artists. Tell children that there are many types of artists: visual artists (sculpture, painting), performing artists (dance, film, theatre), and literary artists (books, magazines, poetry).

Next, have children focus their attention on the whistle. Explain that it is made of *clay*, a substance found in the earth that can be shaped when moistened and then baked to form a sculpture. This type of artwork is called *ceramic*. Ask children to name ceramic objects that they see and use everyday. (plates, mugs, sculptures, planters) Encourage children to use their senses to identify how the objects vary in textures and form.

120

Lesson 1

Art and Music

There are many kinds of art. Music is art. Dancing and poetry are art. Storytelling is art too. What do these sculptures show? How do you think the artist made them?

Artists unknown. *Tang Dynasty Sheng Player, Dancer, and Panpipe Player,* 7th century. Clay. Royal Ontario Museum, Toronto.

120

 Art Background

Art and Culture These sculptures were created during the Tang dynasty in China (A.D. 618–907) The Tang Dynasty represented a time of prosperity. Many of the artworks at this time showed examples of luxurious lifestyles. The artworks often showed figures of court officials, dancers, foreigners, and animals.

Art History *Aztec Dancing Whistle* was created by an unknown Aztec artist. The Aztecs were highly developed in engineering, architecture, art, mathematics, and astronomy. Their advanced civilization flourished from the twelfth through the fifteenth and sixteenth centuries.

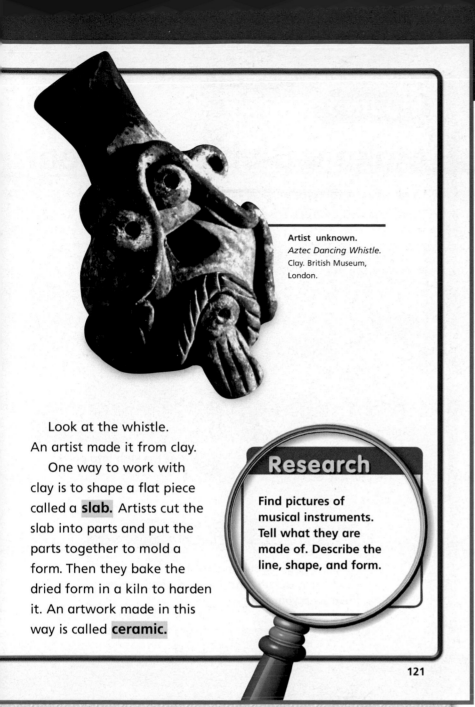

Artist unknown.
Aztec Dancing Whistle.
Clay. British Museum,
London.

Look at the whistle.
An artist made it from clay.
One way to work with
clay is to shape a flat piece
called a **slab.** Artists cut the
slab into parts and put the
parts together to mold a
form. Then they bake the
dried form in a kiln to harden
it. An artwork made in this
way is called **ceramic.**

Research

Find pictures of
musical instruments.
Tell what they are
made of. Describe the
line, shape, and form.

121

 Curriculum Connection

Social Studies Remind children that the clay whistle was
made a long time ago when people made their instruments
out of natural products. Make a list of instruments that
people used in the past. Then have children list instruments
used today. Last, have children make inferences as to how
instruments will change in the future.

 Notes

Check children's understanding of different types of
artists by role-playing. Pretend that you are a ballet
dancer, then say: **I am a dancer.** Have children repeat after
you as they act like dancers. Continue by acting like other
artists, such as a musician, a storyteller, or a writer.

② Teach

Have children read pages 120 and 121. Then focus
their attention on *Aztec Dancing Whistle* and ask:

- **How would you describe this artwork?**
  (Possible response: It is a clay whistle that has
  lots of shapes and lines.) DESCRIBE
- **Do you think this is an old instrument or a new
  instrument? Why?** (Possible response: It is an
  old instrument because I have never seen a
  whistle like this one.) ANALYZE
- **What do you think the artist wanted you to
  know about this whistle?** (Possible response:
  That this is an important whistle.) INTERPRET
- **What do you like best about this artwork?**
  (Possible response: I like the circles and the
  curved lines.) JUDGE

Ask similar questions about the *Tang Dynasty
Sheng Player, Dancer, and Panpipe Player.*

Research Help children to perform online and
library research. Encourage them to identify
variations in the subjects by focusing on different
types of instruments, including stringed,
percussion, and wind instruments.

③ Close

After children have performed their research, have
them write about an instrument using the prompts
on page 121.

Visual Culture Explain to children that many car
designers first design cars in clay. Invite them to
make their own car designs in clay.

Studio 1

At a Glance

Objectives

- Demonstrate how to form a clay slab when creating a clay instrument.
- Evaluate original artworks by self and peers.

Materials

- ceramic clay
- dowels or rolling pins
- plastic knives ⚠, water containers, pencils
- Rubric 4 from **Unit-by-Unit Resources**

NVAS (K–4) #1 Understanding and applying media, techniques, and processes

NVAS (K–4) #3 Choosing and evaluating a range of subject matter, symbols, and ideas

NVAS (K–4) #5 Reflecting upon and assessing the characteristics and merits of their work and the work of others

❶ Introduce

Discuss the musical instrument children read about on page 121. Have children brainstorm ideas for instruments they would like to create. Ask:

- **What instrument is important to you? Tell why.**
- **What instrument will you make?**
- **What shapes and forms will you use?**
- **How will you use lines in your design?**

Make a Slab Instrument

Think of your favorite musical instrument. Then follow the directions to mold it from clay.

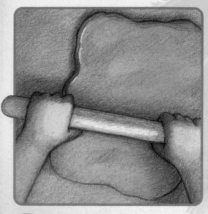
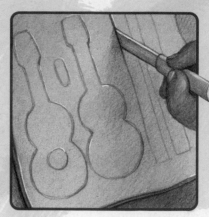

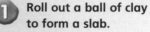 **1** Roll out a ball of clay to form a slab.

2 Cut the slab into parts.

Technique Tip

Join pieces that you have cut from the slab. Pinch them together at the seams and smooth them with your fingers.

122

🚶🚶 Meeting Individual Needs

Inclusion For children who are hearing-impaired, model the steps in the studio with a piece of clay. You may wish to place your hand over the child's hand to guide him or her in pushing, pulling, and rolling the clay.

Quick Studio

Provide modeling clay for children to create simple instruments, such as a flute.

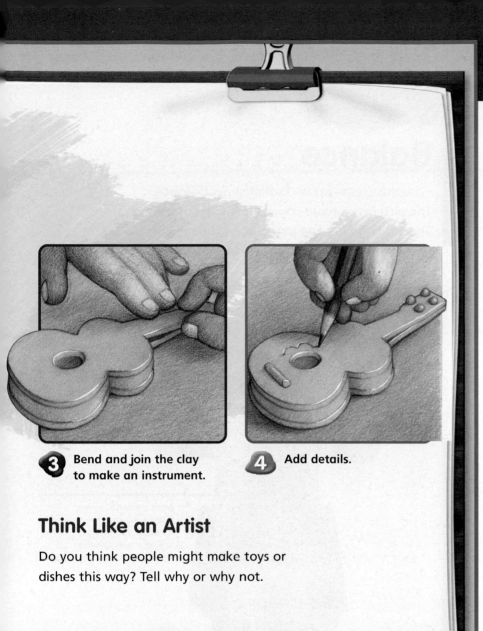

3 Bend and join the clay to make an instrument.

4 Add details.

Think Like an Artist

Do you think people might make toys or dishes this way? Tell why or why not.

123

Fine Arts Connection

Music Sing a version of "If You're Happy and You Know It," suggesting different instruments, such as the clay whistle on page 121. For example:

If you're happy and you know it, blow your whistle. (toot, toot)
If you're happy and you know it, blow your whistle, (toot, toot)
If you're happy and you know it, blow your whistle then you'll show it,
If you're happy and you know it, blow your whistle, (toot, toot)

Provide children with classroom instruments so they can play along.

② Create

Have children read pages 122 and 123 and look at the pictures. Then distribute the materials.

- Model how to use the rolling pin to roll out a slab of clay between two dowels.
- Guide children to make both the front and back side of their instrument.
- Remind children to gently press and then smooth the edges of the clay pieces together. Tell children that this is a necessary skill for producing modeled forms.
- Finally, have them add details using a pencil or plastic knife that express their feelings about this instrument.

Technique Tip Tell children to apply a wet sponge to their clay to help smooth out the seams.

③ Close

Have children identify the skills necessary to create an instrument from clay. Then have them answer the *Think Like an Artist* question. (Possible response: Yes, because clay could be found in nature.)

Ongoing Assessment

If . . . children have difficulty adding details,

then . . . make sure the utensil they are using is free of excess clay.

See page 72 from **Unit-by-Unit Resources** for a rubric to assess this studio.

Lesson 2

At a Glance

Objectives

- Identify and describe balance in artworks.
- Describe, analyze, interpret, and judge artworks.

Materials

- **Fine Art Transparency**
- pictures of objects showing different types of balance
- Sketchbook Journal

Vocabulary

balance, symmetrical balance, asymmetrical balance, radial balance

NVAS (K–4) #2 Using knowledge of structures and functions

NVAS (K–4) #4 Understanding the visual arts in relation to history and cultures

NVAS (K–4) #5 Reflecting upon and assessing the characteristics and merits of their work and the work of others

NVAS (K–4) #6 Making connections between visual arts and other disciplines

❶ Introduce

Show children a picture of an object that shows symmetrical balance, such as an apple. Draw a line through the middle of the object and explain that it shows *symmetrical balance* because both sides are about the same. Show children a picture of the Statue of Liberty and explain that it shows *asymmetrical balance,* or two sides that are not identical. Last, show children an example of an object with *radial balance,* such as a wagon wheel. Explain that this term describes objects with regular shapes that spread out equally from the center.

Tell children that balance is a principle of design. Gather objects that demonstrate balance. Have children identify the variations in objects, noting whether they have symmetrical, asymmetrical, or radial balance.

124

Lesson 2

Balance

Artists create artworks that show **balance.** The pictures on these pages show types of balance. The *Smiling Figurine* looks about the same on both sides. It shows **symmetrical balance.**

Artist unknown. *Smiling Figurine*, ca. A.D. 6th to 9th century. Limestone, approximately 19 ¾ by 12 ¾ by 4 ½ inches. Museum of Anthropology at Xalapa, University of Veracruz, Mexico.

124

 Art Background

Smiling Figurine This sculpture, along with others, was discovered in southern Mexico, in the state of Veracruz near Tierra Blanca. Archaeologists believe that the figures are related to the gods of dance, music, and vegetation.

Inlay of a king or deity This artwork was created in Egypt during the early Ptolemaic Period (305–200 B.C.). It includes the upper torso, neck, and head of a king or deity who is wearing what appears to be a crown of Lower Egypt. The torso indicates that the right arm was raised, perhaps making an offering.

Artworks with **asymmetrical balance** have two different sides. Each side has a special part. Notice the tall hat and long nose on the king.

The pinwheel has **radial balance.** The lines and shapes move equally out from the center.

Art in My World

Go outside. Find objects from nature that show each kind of balance. Draw the objects. Label them.

125

2 Teach

Have children read pages 124–125. Then look at the *Smiling Figurine.* Ask:

- **What lines do you see?** (zigzag, horizontal, curved) DESCRIBE
- **Why did the artist make the head large?** (Possible response: to emphasize the figure's happy expression) ANALYZE
- **What do you think the artist wanted to express?** (Possible response: the feeling of joy and laughter) INTERPRET
- **What do you like best about this sculpture?** (Possible response: the figure's expression) JUDGE

Ask similar questions of *Inlay of a king or deity.* Then have children discuss how individuals are depicted in artworks by comparing *Smiling Figurine* with *Inlay of a king or deity.* Suggest that they focus on balance, expression, and emphasis in each artwork.

Art in My World After children have found objects in nature that have balance, have them sort them according to whether they have symmetrical, asymmetrical, or radial balance.

3 Close

Invite children to talk about the different types of balance that they were able to find.

Assessment Give each child a magazine picture of one large object. Have children describe the type of balance the object has.

Curriculum Connection

Science Organize children into pairs and have them research butterflies. Explain to them that there is a great variety of butterflies. Some have wing designs that show symmetrical balance and others have wing designs that show asymmetrical balance. Tell them to choose one type of butterfly, describe the balance its wing design shows, and then share their findings with the class.

Notes

Model how to fold a geometric shape in half. Indicate that both sides of the shape are about the same and then say: **This is symmetrical.** Have children repeat after you. Continue using several other shapes to show different kinds of balance.

Studio 2

At a Glance

Objectives

- Express ideas by showing balance in an original artwork.
- Demonstrate how to use clay to make a coil object.
- Evaluate original artworks by self and peers.

Materials

- modeling clay
- plastic forks ⚠, pencils, sticks
- Rubric 4 from **Unit-by-Unit Resources**

NVAS (K–4) #1 Understanding and applying media, techniques, and processes

NVAS (K–4) #3 Choosing and evaluating a range of subject matter, symbols, and ideas

❶ Introduce

Review balance with children. Then have children brainstorm what type of balance they would like to use on their coil object. Ask:

- **What type of form will you make?**
- **Will it have symmetrical, asymmetrical, or radial balance?**
- **What type of details will you add to your artwork?**

Make a Coil Object

Create a clay object that shows symmetrical, asymmetrical, or radial balance.

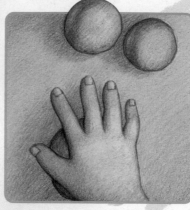
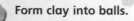
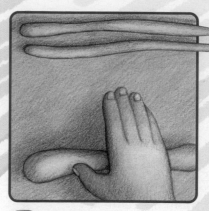

1 Form clay into balls.

2 Use your palms to roll each ball into a coil.

Technique Tip

To form a coil, begin with your palm in the center. Is one side thicker than the other? If so, move your hand to the thicker part and roll there to thin it out.

126

🧑‍🤝‍🧑 Meeting Individual Needs

Reteach Children will have more success in creating a balanced artwork if each of the coils is the same, or very close, in size. Encourage children to make one coil to use as their example of the thickness they need. Every time they make a new coil, they will be able to measure it against the example.

Quick Studio

Have children make a pinch pot out of a ball of clay. Ask children to use a toothpick to create a design with balance on the pot.

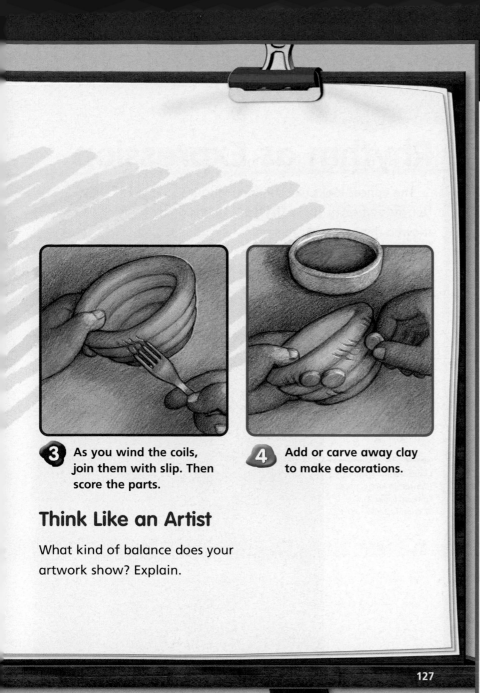

③ As you wind the coils, join them with slip. Then score the parts.

④ Add or carve away clay to make decorations.

Think Like an Artist

What kind of balance does your artwork show? Explain.

127

Fine Arts Connection

Theatre Provide children with long strips of colored construction paper, glue, and scissors. Model how to make a hatband by cutting a strip of construction paper and stapling it so that it fits around a child's head.

Tell children to attach pieces of construction paper to the band to demonstrate symmetrical, asymmetrical, or radial balance. After children have created their hats, invite them to work in small groups to prepare a skit for the class.

② Create

Have children read pages 126–127. Then distribute materials.

- Remind children to use their palms to turn and press the clay into balls.
- Model rolling the coils into an even thickness.
- Make slip by placing a few small pieces of clay and water in a container and let it dissolve into a thick, creamlike mixture.
- Tell children that the forms and lines used to make ceramic pottery often express feelings about different subjects. For instance, say: **Rainbows make me happy, so I am going to decorate my pot with rainbows.** Have children express their feelings using a variety of forms and lines in their design.

Technique Tip If the coil starts to crack while rolling, tell children to wet their hands. Explain that this is a necessary skill to remember when working with clay.

③ Close

Have children answer the *Think Like an Artist* question. (Possible response: My bowl has radial balance because the coils go out from the center.) Continue by asking children to define the reason why they like their coil object.

Ongoing Assessment

If . . . children's coils become too thin while rolling them,

then . . . tell them to just add more clay to the thin area and to keep rolling it.

See page 72 from **Unit-by-Unit Resources** for a rubric to assess this studio.

Lesson 3

At a Glance

Objectives

- Identify and describe rhythm in artworks.
- Describe, analyze, interpret, and judge artworks.

Materials

- **Fine Art Transparency**
- Sketchbook Journal

Vocabulary

movement, rhythm, motion

NVAS (K–4) #2 Using knowledge of structures and functions

NVAS (K–4) #5 Reflecting upon and assessing the characteristics and merits of their work and the work of others

NVAS (K–4) #6 Making connections between visual arts and other disciplines

❶ Introduce

Ask children to tell about a dance performance they have seen. Invite them to show how a dancer moves.

Explain that *movement* or *motion* is shown in artworks when artists create *rhythm*. Rhythm is a principle of design. It is achieved by repeated colors, lines, shapes, or textures. Lead children to say that rhythm is seen in the repeated lines and colors of the caterpillar's body on page 129. Ask children to name any other examples of rhythm that they see in their environment.

Rhythm as Expression

The dancer looks like she is moving. Her **movements** show **rhythm.** Degas often showed rhythm as expression.

Edgar Degas. *The Star (Dancer on Stage),* 1878. Pastel on paper, 23 5/8 x 17 3/8 inches. Musée d'Orsay, Paris.

128

Art Background

About the Artist French painter Edgar Degas (1834–1917) painted his subjects from unusual viewpoints, capturing simple gestures. Although his images include a variety of people involved in daily activities, Degas is perhaps best known for his paintings of ballerinas.

ESL Notes

Lead children through various movements—running, jumping, walking, or crawling. After you model each movement, say: **This is movement. We are running.** Then on a command, such as "Freeze!," have children stop moving and observe the positions of their arms and legs. Continue by performing other movements and having children repeat the sentences after you.

Repeated lines often create a feeling of **motion.** Which picture on this page shows fast movement?

Artists create rhythm to show movement. Look for rhythm in repeated colors, lines, shapes, or forms. Rhythm is a principle of design.

Sketchbook Journal

Look in a mirror.
Watch yourself move.
Then draw yourself
in motion.

129

Curriculum Connection

Physical Education Explain to children that the ballerina in the painting is dancing, which is a form of exercise. Tell children that people should exercise to help strengthen their heart, lungs, and muscular system.

Have children name other types of exercise that help keep their bodies healthy, such as walking, running, swimming, and playing soccer. Invite children to play one of these games outdoors or in a large indoor area.

② Teach

Have children read pages 128–129. Then focus children's attention on *The Star (Dancer on Stage).* Ask:

- **What do you see?** (a ballerina dancing) DESCRIBE
- **How is movement expressed?** (Possible response: through patches of color and the upturned and wavy lines of the dancer) ANALYZE
- **What did the artist want us to know about dancers?** (Possible response: They are beautiful and graceful and they express themselves through movement.) INTERPRET
- **To whom would you like to show this painting? Why?** (Possible response: I would like to show this painting to my sister because she is a dancer.) JUDGE

Have children compare the individuals in the artworks on pages 128–129. Model by saying: **Both of these individuals are showing movement. The man on the bike seems to be moving faster.**

Sketchbook Journal Tell children to use repeated lines to show motion when creating their self-portraits.

③ Close

After children complete their sketches, have them identify rhythm in their artwork.

Assessment Have children point to the lines and patterns they used to create movement in their artworks.

Studio 3

At a Glance

Objectives

- Express ideas by showing rhythm and movement in an original artwork.
- Demonstrate how to make a shadow.
- Evaluate original artworks by self and peers.

Materials

- brown or black construction paper
- white or yellow construction paper
- scissors ⚠, white chalk, glue
- Rubric 4 from **Unit-by-Unit Resources**

NVAS (K–4) #1 Understanding and applying media, techniques, and processes

NVAS (K–4) #3 Choosing and evaluating a range of subject matter, symbols, and ideas

NVAS (K–4) #5 Reflecting upon and assessing the characteristics and merits of their work and the work of others

❶ Introduce

Review how artists show rhythm and movement in artworks. Then have children brainstorm how to create rhythm and movement in their shadow dancer. Ask:

- **What kind of dancer will you create?**
- **What type of movement will you show?**
- **What color, lines, shapes, or forms will you use to show rhythm?**

Quick Studio

Cut out a person from a magazine. Outline it with chalk on black paper and cut it out. Glue them together to create a shadow.

Make a Shadow Dancer

Follow these directions to create an artwork that shows rhythm and movement.

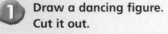

1 Draw a dancing figure. Cut it out.

2 Turn the figure over. Draw over it with white chalk.

Technique Tip

Lay the chalk on its side. Start in the center of your figure and move the chalk outward in every direction.

130

👥 Meeting Individual Needs

Reteach Have children cut and decorate organic shapes from light-colored construction paper. Then ask them to make shadows by outlining these shapes on darker paper and cutting them out. Show children how to position the shadows behind the shapes. Have children glue both cutouts to a sheet of construction paper.

Extend Have children work outdoors on a sunny day to observe and sketch simple objects and their shadows.

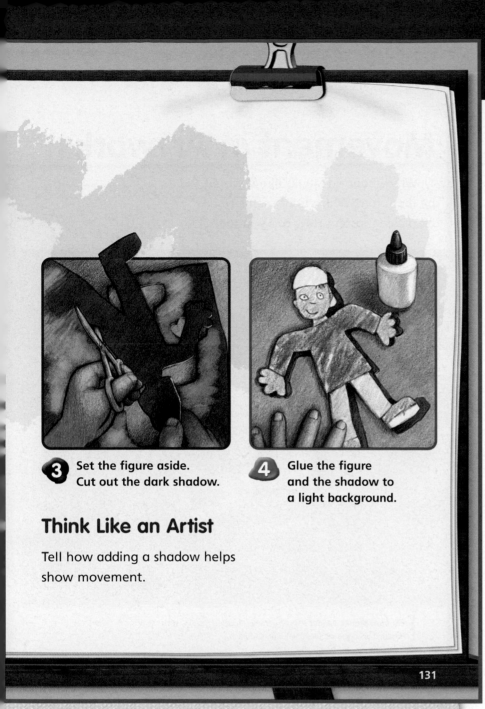

3 Set the figure aside. Cut out the dark shadow.

4 Glue the figure and the shadow to a light background.

Think Like an Artist

Tell how adding a shadow helps show movement.

131

 Fine Arts Connection

Theater Make shadow puppets with children. In a dark room, focus a flashlight on a bare wall. Use your fingers and hands to make different animal shapes in front of the flashlight. These animal shapes will be illuminated onto the wall as a shadow. Invite children to make the animal sounds associated with each animal shape. Then encourage volunteers to make their own animal shapes. Children may want to retell a familiar story using their shadow puppets.

❷ Create

Have children look at the pictures and read the directions on pages 130–131. Then distribute materials.

- Tell children that they can express their feelings about their favorite dance by including a variety of lines, colors and shapes.
- Remind children to be careful not to move their figures when they draw their outlines.
- Ask children to take their time cutting out the figures so the edges are smooth.
- Encourage children to experiment with different arrangements before gluing the figures onto their background.

Technique Tip Remind children to place their dancing figure face down on the black paper before they move the chalk outward over their figure.

❸ Close

Have children discuss the *Think Like an Artist* prompt. (Possible response: The shadow makes the dancer seem like he or she is coming off the page.) Encourage children to define reasons why they like their artwork.

Ongoing Assessment

If . . . children's placement of the shadow and dancer do not create a unified image,

then . . . suggest that they experiment with different arrangements.

See page 72 from **Unit-by-Unit Resources** for a rubric to assess this studio.

Look and Compare

Look and Compare

At a Glance

Objectives

- Compare and contrast two artworks that show movement.
- Respond to and make judgments about artworks.

Materials

- **Art Prints 13, 14, 15**
- **Fine Art Transparency**
- **Sketchbook Journal**

NVAS (K–4) #5 Reflecting upon and assessing the characteristics and merits of their work and the work of others

Explore

Display **Art Print 13,** *The Fifer.* Help children recall this artwork by Édouard Manet from page 118. As children examine the two artworks on pages 132 and 133, ask them to predict which one was also created by Manet and give reasons for their answers. (*Monet Painting in His Floating Studio;* each pays special attention to light.)

Discuss

After children read pages 132 and 133, have them look at the patterns and lines each artist used to show movement. Explain that the curved lines in *Breezing Up* show that the winds are strong and that the boat is moving quickly. By contrast, the two people in Manet's covered boat are in calm water. The repeated pattern of ripples in the water represent a light breeze.

Help children identify the man and woman in Manet's painting as the artist and his wife. Ask: **What story does this painting tell?** (Answers will vary.) Then have children tell the story in *Breezing Up.*

Movement in Artworks

Which boat ride looks like it would be more fun? Which boat seems to be moving faster? How can you tell?

Édouard Manet. *Monet Painting in His Floating Studio,* 1874. Bayerische Staatsgemaldesammlungen, Munich.

132

 Art Background

Monet Painting in His Floating Studio This painting by Édouard Manet (1832–1883) depicts artist Claude Monet painting outdoors, a technique favored by the Impressionists. During 1874, Manet painted with fellow artists Monet and Renoir at Argenteuil, a city near Paris.

Breezing Up This painting by Winslow Homer (1836–1910) is also known as *A Fair Wind.* There is evidence that Homer struggled with how to compose this painting. Before he finished the artwork, Homer added and deleted three sailboats on the right and a small boy near the mast.

Winslow Homer. *Breezing Up*, 1873–1876.
Oil on canvas, 24⅛ by 38⅛ inches. National
Gallery of Art, Washington, D.C.

Talk more about what you
see in these artworks. Do you
think the artists were trying
to express the same ideas
about movement? Why or
why not?

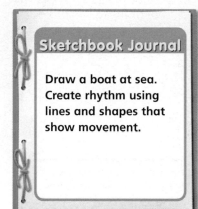

Sketchbook Journal

Draw a boat at sea.
Create rhythm using
lines and shapes that
show movement.

133

Apply

Display a Venn diagram like the one below on the
chalkboard. Tell children that this graphic organizer
is a good way to show how two artworks are the
same and different.

To fill in the diagram, suggest that children first
compare the artworks, looking for ways they are
alike. Fill in the middle section as children suggest
ideas.

Guide children as they look for differences by
suggesting that they focus on how movement is
represented through the use of lines, shapes, and
patterns. Possible responses are shown in blue.

Boat Paintings

Manet

repeated pattern
of ripples represent
calm water

drifting smoke
shows a light
breeze

calm scene

both show
boat scenes

both show
people

Homer

curved lines show
movement and
high waves

billowing sails
show winds are
strong

busy, active
scene

Close

Ask children to describe what they learned about
showing movement from these two artists.
(Possible response: Curved lines can represent
movement; small repeated patterns can represent
a calm scene.)

Sketchbook Journal As children complete their
drawing, remind them that the boat, as well as the
water, can show movement.

 Reading Strategy

Compare and Contrast Explain to children that good
readers often compare and contrast information to better
understand what they are reading. Point out that they
can also use comparing and contrasting to better
understand artworks. Use **Art Print 3,** *The Boating Party,*
and **Art Print 14,** *Monet Painting in His Floating Studio,* to
compare ways families are depicted in artworks. Model by
saying: **In both of these artworks, the families are happy.
They are enjoying spending time with each other.** Have
children list other ways these artworks about families are
similar or different.

Lesson 4

At a Glance

Objectives

- Identify and describe unity and variety in artworks.
- Describe, analyze, interpret, and judge artworks.

Materials

- **Fine Art Transparency**
- water-based markers or crayons
- Sketchbook Journal

Vocabulary

unity, variety

NVAS (K–4) #2 Using knowledge of structures and functions

NVAS (K–4) #5 Reflecting upon and assessing the characteristics and merits of their work and the work of others

NVAS (K–4) #6 Making connections between visual arts and other disciplines

❶ Introduce

Ask children to help you put together a simple puzzle. Once the puzzle is complete, explain that this is an example of *unity*; all of the pieces fit together to form the picture. Then point out that each puzzle piece looks different. Explain that this represents *variety*. Artists use unity and variety to create artworks. They want many interesting parts, but, they want all the parts to work together to make a whole.

Tell children that there are many objects and subjects that express unity and variety, such as the United States flag. It shows variety by including lines and stars; it shows unity because they all work together. Then ask: **What are other objects or subjects that express unity and variety? How?** As children point out each object or subject, lead them to discuss how each varies in some way, yet they each show unity.

Lesson 4

Unity and Variety

The artworks on these pages are alike, but they are different too. Name one way they are the same. What is one way they are different?

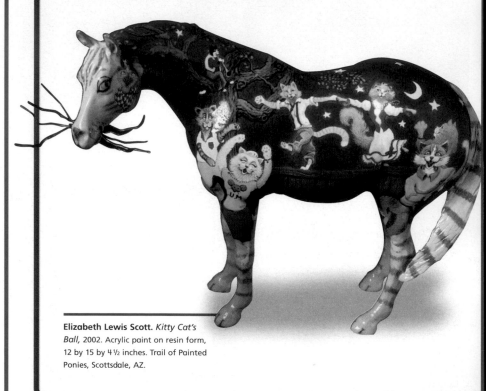

Elizabeth Lewis Scott. *Kitty Cat's Ball,* 2002. Acrylic paint on resin form, 12 by 15 by 4½ inches. Trail of Painted Ponies, Scottsdale, AZ.

134

 Art Background

Art and Culture The first Trail of Painted Ponies was a statewide exhibition that took place in New Mexico in the fall of 2001. This exhibition featured 120 ponies painted by both famous and emerging artists. The three ponies on these pages were included in the exhibition.

 Notes

Have children build with blocks of different shapes and colors. Say: **These blocks show variety and unity.** Have children repeat after you. Explain that the blocks show variety because they are different colors and shapes. Then tell them that the blocks show unity because the parts work together to create a whole.

Joel Nakamura. *Thunderbird Suite,* 2001. Acrylic paint on resin form, 5 by 7 by 2½ feet. Trail of Painted Ponies, Scottsdale, AZ.

Bill Rabbit. *Earth, Wind, and Fire,* 2003. Acrylic paint on resin form, 7 by 9 by 2½ feet. Trail of Painted Ponies, Scottsdale, AZ.

An artwork has **unity** when all the parts seem to go together.

Each horse shows unity. All of the parts work together to make a whole.

Look at all the lines, shapes, and colors. They show **variety.** They have parts that make them different.

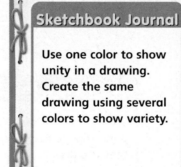

Sketchbook Journal

Use one color to show unity in a drawing. Create the same drawing using several colors to show variety.

135

Technology

Make a Class Book Tell children that the horses on pages 134 and 135 were just three examples of more than 120 horses that were featured in an art exhibit. The show had a variety of horses, yet all of the horses exhibited together showed unity.

Explain to children that they are going to make a class book on the computer. Have each child create a document at the keyboard explaining how they would design their own horse for the show. After they proofread and correct errors, have children print out their story. Next, have them draw a picture of their horse. After all children have written their stories, compile all the pages into a book to show unity.

② Teach

Have children read pages 134–135 and focus on *Kitty Cat's Ball.* Ask:

- **What do you see?** (a horse painted with cats dressed up at a party) DESCRIBE
- **How does this artwork show variety?** (The horse is painted with a variety of colors and lines.) ANALYZE
- **What do you think the artist wanted people to know from looking at the artwork?** (Possible response: that she enjoys cats and dancing) INTERPRET
- **What would you change about this artwork?** (Possible response: I would add other animals.) JUDGE

Sketchbook Journal Remind children that variety can also be expressed through the repeated use of lines and shapes.

③ Close

Have children share their drawings with a classmate and discuss how they expressed variety. Encourage children to take turns identifying ideas in their peer's artwork.

Visual Culture If your school has flowerbeds on the grounds, take children outside to view the plantings there. Talk about the unity and variety of the flowerbeds.

Studio 4

At a Glance

Objectives

- Express ideas by showing unity and variety in an original artwork.
- Evaluate original artworks by self and peers.

Materials

- a small bag of materials (one per child): 1 clothespin, 3 paper clips, cardboard base, 2 pipe cleaners ⚠, 1 paper towel roll, other found art materials such as paper scraps or buttons
- glue
- masking tape (optional)
- Rubric 4 from **Unit-by-Unit Resources**

NVAS (K–4) #1 Understanding and applying media, techniques, and processes

①Introduce

Review unity and variety with children. Then have children brainstorm how they will use these principles of design in their artwork. Ask:

- **What materials will you use?**
- **How will your artwork show unity?**
- **How will it show variety?**

Quick Studio

Have children fold a sheet of paper into four sections. Draw a shape in each box using one color. Add other colors for variety.

136

Studio 4

Show Unity and Variety

Follow these directions. Make a design that shows both unity and variety.

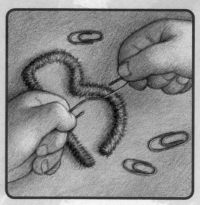

1 Think about ways to put the materials together.

2 Bend the paperclips and pipe cleaners into different shapes.

Technique Tip

Some materials are glued together. Use paperclips to help keep them joined until they are dry.

136

👥 Meeting Individual Needs

Reteach For children who need help organizing their artwork, suggest they first group similar items in piles around their work area. For example, show them how to keep all paper clips in one pile, buttons in another, and pipe cleaners in another. Remind them to keep the piles separate as they work so they can easily find objects they want to include in their artwork.

Extend Explain to children that people who work in fields of design, such as car designers, fashion designers, and furniture designers, work with the concepts of unity and variety all the time. Have children find a photograph of a car, a piece of furniture, or an article of clothing. Then have them write how the item exhibits both unity and variety.

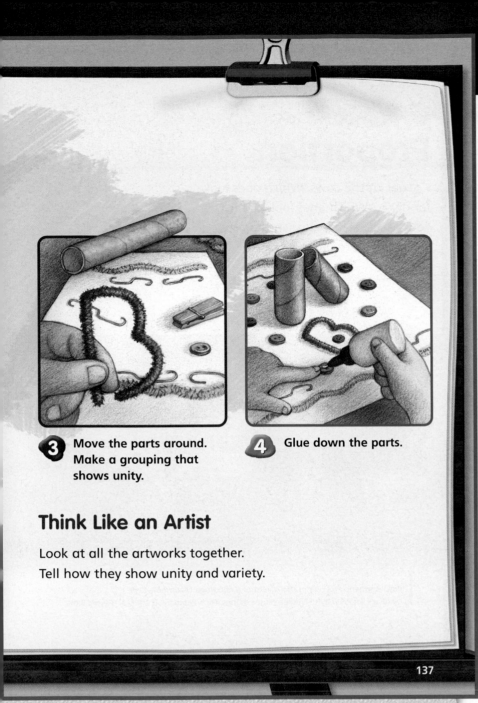

3 Move the parts around. Make a grouping that shows unity.

4 Glue down the parts.

Think Like an Artist

Look at all the artworks together. Tell how they show unity and variety.

137

 Fine Arts Connection

Music Sing "Row, Row, Row Your Boat" with children. Sing it as a group until everyone knows the words and the music. Then divide the class in half and teach the children to sing the song as a round. Do this several times until they are comfortable singing in this way. Invite children to discuss how singing as one group expressed unity and singing in a round expressed variety.

② Create

Have children read the directions on pages 136–137. Then distribute the materials.

- Have children sort the contents by form, size, or color. Then have them think about the ideas they want to express.
- Suggest to children that they use pipe cleaners or paper clips to create a variety of lines. Model how to bend them into curved and zigzag lines.
- Tell children that balance can create unity in their artworks. Remind them to arrange their selected materials to show symmetrical or radial balance.
- Caution children against using too much glue on the items.

Technique Tip Masking tape can also be used instead of paper clips when joining two items together.

③ Close

Ask children to respond to the *Think Like an Artist* feature. (Possible response: The artworks show unity because they are all arrangements of found art materials. They show variety because there are different lines, forms, and colors.)

Ongoing Assessment

If . . . children have difficulty gluing the pieces onto the base,

then . . . suggest they apply a small amount of glue first. Then hold the piece down and count to ten before releasing it.

See page 72 from **Unit-by-Unit Resources** for a rubric to assess this studio.

Lesson 5

At a Glance

Objectives

- Identify and describe proportion in artworks.
- Describe, analyze, interpret, and judge artworks.

Materials

- **Fine Art Transparency**
- **Sketchbook Journal**

Vocabulary

proportion, faraway, close up

NVAS (K–4) #5 Reflecting upon and assessing the characteristics and merits of their work and the work of others

NVAS (K–4) #6 Making connections between visual arts and other disciplines

❶ Introduce

Take children outside or to a very large indoor room. Ask them to name faraway objects. Then have them indicate how big the object appears to them using their thumb and index finger. For instance, say: **Yes, that tree is far away. We know that trees are very big, but from here, it looks about two inches tall.** Then have children discuss the size of close up objects.

Explain to children that artists think about *proportion,* or the size of an object relating to their placement, when they create artworks. If an artist creates an artwork that shows a faraway landscape, then the trees and bushes are shown small. On the other hand, if an artist creates a still life of close up objects, then the size of the still-life objects are large. Ask: **Would you prefer to create an artwork of faraway objects or of close up objects? Why?** (I would create an artwork with far away objects. I would like to show a view of the beach and the ocean.)

Proportion

Look at the cows. Which ones look far away? Which ones look closer to you? Measure the cows in the artwork. Which ones are bigger?

Rosa Bonheur. *Plowing in the Nivernais (Labourage Nivernais),* 1849.
Oil on canvas, 53½ by 104 inches. Musée d'Orsay, Paris. Photograph © R.M.N.-Gérard Blot.

 **Art Background**

About the Artist Born in Bordeaux, France, Rosa Bonheur (1822–1899) learned to paint from her father, a landscape painter. Determined to make her artwork accurate, Bonheur studied animals' anatomy.

About the Artist Russian-born painter Marc Chagall's (1887–1985) artwork expressed a gift for fantasy and folklore. Some of his best-known artworks reside in public buildings in Paris and Jerusalem, including twelve stained-glass windows he created that symbolize the twelve tribes of Israel.

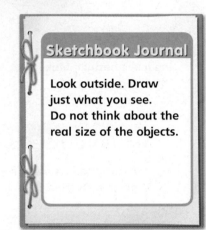

Marc Chagall.
The Spring (Le Printemps),
1977. Oil on canvas, 36¼
by 28¾ inches. Christie's
Images, London.

Proportion is the size of an object compared to other objects. **Faraway** objects look small. Objects that are **close up** look large.

Look at the artwork on this page. Chickens are small, but this chicken looks big. Is it close or far away? The horse looks small. Where is the horse?

Sketchbook Journal

Look outside. Draw just what you see. Do not think about the real size of the objects.

139

2 Teach

Have children read pages 138–139 and look at Bonheur's painting. Guide them to notice that the cows in the back of the line look far away. The cows in front look closer and bigger. Ask:

- **What do you see in this painting?** (cows plowing a field) DESCRIBE
- **Where does your eye go first? Why?** (to the larger animals in front; they look closer) ANALYZE
- **Why do you think the artist showed this scene?** (Possible response: She wanted to show a realistic portrayal of animals plowing a field.) INTERPRET
- **What do you like about this painting?** (Possible response: The animals look real.) JUDGE

Ask similar questions about *The Spring (Le Printemps).*

Sketchbook Journal Remind children that faraway objects look small and should be drawn near the top of the paper. Close up objects look large and should appear at the bottom.

3 Close

After children complete their sketches, have them discuss with a partner what they like about their drawings.

Assessment Have children create a two-column chart to record classroom objects that are far away and those that are close up.

Curriculum Connection

Math Have children look at page 138 again. Remind them that when artists use proportion in their artworks, the close up objects are large and the faraway objects are small. Ask a volunteer to measure the length of the cows in the painting. Write the number of inches each cow measures on the board. Help children determine the difference in size.

 Notes

Focus children's attention on Chagall's painting on page 139. Invite a volunteer to point to a close up object in the painting. Then have children repeat the term *close up.* Continue by having children point to the people who are far away.

Studio 5

At a Glance

Objectives

- Express ideas by showing proportion in an original artwork.
- Demonstrate how to draw items in correct proportion.
- Evaluate original artworks by self and peers.

Materials

- chairs (for a large space) or small objects with simple shapes such as boxes, balls, and so on. (for a small space)
- pencils, sheets of drawing paper
- watercolors, paintbrushes, palettes, water cups
- Rubric 4 from **Unit-by-Unit Resources**

NVAS (K–4) #1 Understanding and applying media, techniques, and processes

NVAS (K–4) #5 Reflecting upon and assessing the characteristics and merits of their work and the work of others

Draw Proportion

Draw objects. Make them bigger or smaller to show how close or far away they are.

1. Draw the closest objects near the bottom. Make them big.

2. Draw objects that are a little farther away. Make them smaller.

Technique Tip

Nearby objects may seem to cover faraway objects. Overlap them in your drawing.

140

① Introduce

Review proportion with children. Remind them that objects that are far away are smaller and objects that are close up are larger. Ask:

- **What will you draw close up?**
- **What will be far away?**
- **What lines and colors will you use in your drawing?**

👫👫 Meeting Individual Needs

Reteach Have children first visualize the size that their objects should appear on their paper. Then have them fold their papers in half. Remind children to draw the close up objects in a larger size near the bottom of the page and the faraway objects in a smaller size near the top of the page.

Quick Studio

Have children draw six round balls of different colors. Show some close up and some far away. Add details to show variety.

140

3 Draw objects that are farthest away. Make them smallest and near the top.

4 Paint your picture.

Think Like an Artist

Tell why you drew some objects larger.
Tell why some are smaller.

 Fine Arts Connection

Theatre Divide children into small groups and provide each group with a large sheet of butcher paper and some markers. Have the groups create a scene for a familiar story on the sheets of paper.

Remind groups to use what they learned about how to make objects appear close or far away. Then have them present a skit of their story that would incorporate this scene.

2 Create

Have children read the directions on pages 140–141. Then distribute the materials.

- Tell children to imagine their sheet of paper divided into three equal parts. In the first part, at the bottom of the page, have them draw the closest objects.
- In the next part, or middle area, have them draw objects that are a little smaller.
- In the final part at the top of the paper, have them draw the remaining objects.
- Remind children to express their feelings through their use of colors and lines.

Technique Tip Tell children that if they use overlap, then parts of the faraway object may not be seen. The close up object will cover part of the faraway object.

3 Close

Have children identify skills necessary for drawing by responding to the *Think Like an Artist*. (Possible response: I drew the first chair larger because it is close up. I drew the others smaller because they are far away.)

Ongoing Assessment

If . . . children want sharper lines,

then . . . tell them to use less water on their paintbrush. A wetter brush creates fuzzier lines.

See page 72 from **Unit-by-Unit Resources** for a rubric to assess this studio.

Lesson 6

At a Glance

Objectives

- Identify and describe symbols in artworks.
- Describe, analyze, interpret, and judge artworks.

Materials

- **Fine Art Transparency**
- Sketchbook Journal

Vocabulary

symbol, mosaic

NVAS (K–4) #2 Using knowledge of structures and functions

NVAS (K–4) #4 Understanding the visual arts in relation to history and cultures

NVAS (K–4) #6 Making connections between visual arts and other disciplines

① Introduce

Display or point to the United States flag. Have children brainstorm what they think of when they see the flag, and write their responses on the board in an idea web.

Then tell children that the flag is a *symbol* for our country. A symbol is something that stands for or represents an object or subject. Ask children to identify the colors of the flag. Have children share other symbols for our country that they may know (the bald eagle, Liberty Bell, Uncle Sam). Ask them to identify colors, lines, forms, and textures in each symbol they name.

Symbols

This artwork was made in Mexico more than 500 years ago. A two-headed snake was a special **symbol** there. It stood for rebirth and renewal.

The serpent is a **mosaic.** Small bits of stone were placed side by side and set in cement.

Artist unknown. *Double-Headed Serpent,* 15th century. Turquoise mosaic, 17 ½ inches. © The British Museum, London.

142

 Art Background

Double-Headed Serpent This serpent, which was probably created in the fifteenth century by an Aztec artist, is carved from wood and covered with small pieces of turquoise. Serpents were important icons in many religions; the Aztecs associated the serpent with several gods.

Born Around the Campfires of Our Past This mosaic by Texas artist Robert T. Ritter appears as a mural on the floor of the Bob Bullock Texas State History Museum in Austin. The scene, which is forty feet in diameter and uses forty-seven colors, has a campfire in the center and includes figures and icons from Texas history.

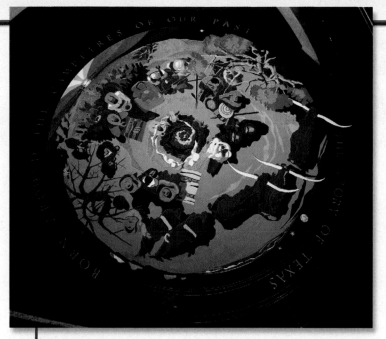

Robert T. Ritter. *Born Around the Campfires of Our Past,* 2001. Terrazo mosaic, diameter 40 feet. Floor of the Bob Bullock Texas History Museum, Austin, TX.

Mosaics can also be made of colored glass, paper, and other objects.

Recently, an artist made the mosaic above. It is on the floor of a museum. It tells a story about the history of Texas. What symbols do you see in this mosaic? What do they stand for?

Sketchbook Journal

Our country has many symbols. Draw your favorite United States symbol as a mosaic. Write what it means to you.

143

2 Teach

Have children read pages 142–143 and look at the artworks. Explain that a *mosaic* can be made from small pieces of many different kinds of materials, including stone, glass, tile, paper, and other objects. These small pieces are called *tesserae*. Focus their attention on *Double-Headed Serpent.* Ask:

- **What do you see?** (a two-headed serpent)
  DESCRIBE
- **Why do you think this animal stands for strength?** (Possible responses: It looks strong.)
  ANALYZE
- **Why did the artist create this animal with two heads?** (Possible response: Having two heads makes it appear wise.) INTERPRET
- **What do you like about this artwork?** (Possible response: I like the materials the artist used.)
  JUDGE

Ask similar questions about *Born Around the Campfires of Our Past.* Guide children to notice the symbols that are from the state of Texas. (the long-horned cattle, Davy Crockett) Explain that the mosaic is viewed from above, or a bird's-eye view.

Sketchbook Journal Have children think about places or books where they may have seen these symbols.

3 Close

Have children share their symbols and give the reasons behind their choices.

Visual Culture Explain that logos are symbols advertisers use to promote products. Discuss common logos, such as for fast-food restaurants.

 Curriculum Connection

Social Studies Explain to children that in 1787, Congress officially adopted the bald eagle as the national symbol of the United States.

Have children pretend that the United States is changing its national symbol. Ask children to draw and write about another symbol they think the United States should adopt and explain why.

 Notes

Discuss international symbols, or common symbols used all over the world, with children. For example, show them a heart and say: **This heart is a symbol for love.** Encourage children to talk about symbols they have seen.

Studio 6

At a Glance

Objectives

- Express ideas by creating a symbol in an original artwork.
- Demonstrate how to make a mosaic using a variety of art materials.
- Evaluate original artworks by self and peers.

Materials

- construction paper, drawing paper
- markers, glue sticks
- Rubric 4 from **Unit-by-Unit Resources**

NVAS (K–4) #1 Understanding and applying media, techniques, and processes

NVAS (K–4) #3 Choosing and evaluating a range of subject matter, symbols, and ideas

NVAS (K–4) #5 Reflecting upon and assessing the characteristics and merits of their work and the work of others

❶ Introduce

Have children review symbols and mosaics. Then tell them to brainstorm symbols that they can use to represent their community. Ask:

- **What colors will you use in your mosaic?**
- **What symbols will you use to represent your community?**
- **How will you express ideas and feelings in your artwork using colors, forms, and lines?**

Quick Studio

Have children draw a symbol for their school. Use circles created from a paper punch to fill in the symbol.

Make a Mosaic

Make a mosaic. Show symbols that stand for your community long ago.

❶ Tear paper into small pieces.

❷ Draw a shape. Draw three symbols inside it.

Technique Tip

Leave a tiny space between each piece of paper that you use to cover the shapes and the symbols.

🚶🚶🚶 Meeting Individual Needs

Inclusion Provide visually-impaired children with mosaic pieces with unusual textures and high-contrast colors. Have them work with a partner to complete their mosaics if necessary.

3 Cover an area with glue. Place paper pieces over the area.

4 Cover the shape and symbols with paper pieces.

Think Like an Artist

Show your mosaic to others. Tell them how your symbols support your ideas.

 Fine Arts Connection

Dance Explain to children that a dance, like symbols, can represent feelings or ideas. For instance, dancers will move slowly and deliberately to express sorrow or unhappiness.

Brainstorm other emotions that a dancer can express. Then play some music and have children show movements to express feelings such as happiness, sorrow, excitement, and so on.

2 Create

Have children read the directions on pages 144–145. Then distribute the materials.

- Guide children to notice that tearing shapes will create edges that add texture to the artwork.
- Explain to children that that they can draw symbols that express ideas or feelings about their community.
- Tell children to use glue sparingly.
- Remind children not to overlap the paper pieces and to leave spaces between them.

Technique Tip Remind children that when they begin from the center and work out, they can fill in the space more easily.

3 Close

Have children respond to the *Think Like an Artist* feature to share ideas about their artwork. (Possible response: My mosaic helped make my symbols stand out.)

Ongoing Assessment

If . . . children have difficulty thinking of symbols,

then . . . suggest ideas and have children determine a symbol that represents them.

See page 72 from **Unit-by-Unit Resources** for a rubric to assess this studio.

Artist at Work

Artist at Work

At a Glance

Objectives

• Read about a career in art.
• Identify the use of art in everyday life.
• Relate art to personal experiences.

Materials

• **Fine Art Transparency**

NVAS (K–4) #5 Reflecting upon and assessing the characteristics and merits of their work and the work of others

NVAS (K–4) #6 Making connections between visual arts and other disciplines

Explore

Ask children to describe any window displays they have enjoyed seeing. Explain that window designers create these displays. Tell them that window design is another kind of job for artists.

Tell them that window display designers use props and other materials to make objects from the store exciting to view. You may want to point out that window display designers need to change their designs often to make way for new items. They may also change them seasonally and to celebrate different holidays.

Discuss

Have children read pages 146–147. Ask:

• **How does the artist use unity to make people react to her windows?** (Possible response: All of the parts of the display work together. They are unified by color and theme.)
• **Where are some places that window display designers work?** (Possible responses: malls, small and large stores, museums)
• **What skills does Koutrakos need to make her artwork?** (Possible responses: visual sense, creativity, color and composition)

Window Displays

Good window displays do not just happen. Designers like Maribeth Koutrakos create them.

Koutrakos was inspired by her mother. The family moved often. Her mother decorated every home they lived in.

Koutrakos works to create the same feeling of beauty with her displays. She talks with the store manager. Then she draws ideas and plans what materials to use. She can use almost any object. Once, she used peanuts!

The goal is to catch people's eye. She knows she has done well when people stop and say, *"Wow!"*

Maribeth Koutrakos

146

 Career Research

Take a field trip to a local mall or downtown area and observe store windows. Have children draw a sketch in their Sketchbook Journals of a window display they would like to create for their favorite store. Alternatively, invite a window display designer from the community to speak to the class.

Maribeth Koutrakos. *Baseball Locker Room,* 1995.
Window display, approximately 14 by 17 feet.

Maribeth Koutrakos turns things
we all use into window displays.

147

Apply

Explain to children that stores and businesses
have many ways to advertise their products.
Brainstorm a list of other ways stores advertise.
Possible responses are shown below.

Advertising Products

1. window displays
2. clothes on mannequins
3. table displays
4. feature items close
   to the cash register
5. posters with sale items

Close

Review the completed graphic organizer and ask:
**How are these different ways of advertising
similar to what the artist does? How are they
different?** (Possible responses: They all are ways
to make the store products stand out. Window
displays are often more detailed and exciting to
look at than other ways to advertise.)

 Reading Strategy

Draw Conclusions Explain to children that often when
they read a passage, they can draw conclusions, or
determine the outcome by noting the details. For
instance, point out that Maribeth Koutrakos was inspired
by her mother. They often moved, yet her mother
decorated every home. Ask: **What conclusion can you
draw about Koutrakos's mother's influence?** (She learned
about decorating from her mother. This possibly led her
to a career in window display designing.)

Have children read on to see if they can draw conclusions
about why Koutrakos would draw sketches before she
actually creates the window display. (She wants to make
sure she and the store manager like it before she begins.)

Portfolio Project

Portfolio Project

At a Glance

Objectives

- Develop and organize ideas from the environment.
- Demonstrate knowledge about symbols and prints.
- Evaluate original artworks by self and peers.

Materials

- pencils, scissors ⒮
- tagboard, newsprint
- water-based printer's ink, clean meat trays ⒮, brayers
- Rubric 4 from **Unit-by-Unit Resources**

NVAS (K–4) #1 Understanding and applying media, techniques, and processes

NVAS (K–4) #3 Choosing and evaluating a range of subject matter, symbols, and ideas

NVAS (K–4) #5 Reflecting upon and assessing the characteristics and merits of their work and the work of others

Make Symbol Prints

Think of symbols for the seasons, traffic signs, or feelings. Make stencil prints of them.

1 Draw a symbol on tagboard. Cut it out to make a stencil.

2 Roll a brayer in ink. Roll the inked brayer over the stencil.

3 Turn the stencil over. Rub the surface. Then pull the print.

4 Repeat. As you work, think about how to show unity and variety.

148

Plan

Direct children to read page 148. Then ask:

- **What are some seasons, traffic signs, and feelings?**
- **What are their symbols?**
- **How can you use colors and lines to express ideas and feelings in your artwork?**

Have children think about other symbols they may know. Suggest that they look in their Sketchbook Journals for additional symbols.

Quick Project

Have children create stencils of symbols from index cards. Have them combine the prints to show unity.

👪👪 Meeting Individual Needs

Extend Invite children to make a secret message using pictures and words. First have them think about their message. Then have them think about the parts of the message that could be replaced with pictures and still convey meaning, such as a gold coin or treasure chest representing money. Have partners exchange messages and guess their meanings.

What symbols did these children use in their stencil prints?

Ashley, Age 7. *Heartbeats.*
Tempera on construction
paper.

Ashley Nicole, Age 8.
Star. Tempera on
construction paper.

Share Your Art

1. What is your print about? Why did you choose that symbol?
2. Explain how you showed unity and variety.

149

Gallery Options

Create a Digital Gallery Have children create their own digital gallery using software. Have them scan their artworks. Then they can import them into another software program as part of a slide show. Present the slide show to another class or to a group of parents at an open house. During the presentation, have each child identify the skills necessary for producing their prints.

Create

Gather the materials and guide children through the steps on page 148 to complete the project.

- Before children begin cutting, have them pinch the center of the symbol and cut a nick to give them a place to begin cutting.
- Have children hold the stencil with one hand and roll the brayer with the other hand.
- Have children pull the newsprint paper very carefully off of the stencil. Identify this as a necessary skill to know when making prints.
- Suggest that children rotate their symbol's position in different directions to show variety.

While children are waiting for their prints to dry, have them put away materials and clean the brayers.

Close

Point out that the artworks on page 149 are from the portfolios of other second-graders. Ask:

- **What are the symbols?** (hearts and stars) **What do they represent?** (hearts, love; stars, night's sky)
- **How did they show unity and variety?** (Both artworks use the same symbol throughout, showing unity. Both artworks show the symbols in different colors on different-colored backgrounds, showing variety.)

Then have children answer the *Share Your Art* questions. (Possible response: I chose a heart. It is a symbol for love. I arranged the symbol so that the whole artwork is balanced and looks complete. It also shows variety because I used different colors.)

See page 72 in the **Unit–by–Unit Resources** for a rubric to assess this project.

Unit 4 Review

At a Glance

Objectives

- Relate art terms to the environment.
- Identify symbol, balance, rhythm, unity, variety, and movement in artworks.
- Describe, analyze, interpret, and judge an artwork.

Materials

- Art Print 16
- Fine Art Transparency

NVAS (K–4) #1 Understanding and applying media, techniques, and processes

NVAS (K–4) #2 Using knowledge of structures and functions

NVAS (K–4) #5 Reflecting upon and assessing the characteristics and merits of their work and the work of others

Think About Art

Responses include:

radial balance (Point to the mosaic.)
movement (Point to the athlete.)
unity (Point to the quilt.)
mosaic (Point to the mosaic.)
rhythm (Point to the athlete.)
variety (Point to the quilt.)

Write About Art

Before children write, ask:

- **What do you like to play and do? What symbol could you use?** (Possible response: play soccer; a soccer ball)
- **What is important to you?** (Possible response: my family)

Think About Art

Match the pictures with the art words.

| radial balance | movement | unity |
| mosaic | rhythm | variety |

Write About Art

Draw a symbol to express an idea about yourself. Write about why you chose the symbol.

Talk About Art

- Choose an artwork from your portfolio.
- What kind of balance does the artwork show?
- Tell a friend. Explain how you know.

Assessment Options

Options for assessing children appear in the **Unit-by-Unit Resources.**

- Use the **Vocabulary Worksheets** on pages 65–68 for an informal assessment of Unit 4 vocabulary.
- Use the **Unit 4 Test** on pages 73–76 to assess children's mastery of unit vocabulary and concepts.

Auguste Rodin. *The Thinker,* 1880. Bronze, approximately 72 by 39 ⅕ by 58 inches. © Rodin Museum, Paris. Photograph ©1995 AKG London/Justus Göpel.

Put It All Together

1. What type of balance does this sculpture have?
2. What idea do you think the artist is expressing?
3. Do you think this sculpture has unity? Explain.
4. Where might be a good place to set this sculpture? Why?

151

Talk About Art

Tell children that they are going to create an exhibit using their artworks. Have them choose their favorite artwork to display. Model how to identify ideas in exhibitions by peers by saying: **I like how both of these mosaics show variety and unity.**

Invite another class to attend the exhibition. Pair each child with a guest. Ask him or her to identify ideas in each of the artworks. Prompt children to use words such as *symmetrical, asymmetrical,* or *radial balance.*

Put It All Together

Use the questions on page 151 to evaluate the artwork. Possible responses follow.

1. This sculpture has asymmetrical balance. Both sides are not the same. DESCRIBE
2. Thinking is hard work. ANALYZE
3. Yes. The figure on this sculpture is one complete person. INTERPRET
4. It might go near a school because a school is a place where people think and solve problems. JUDGE

 Art Background

About the Artist After working as a sculptor's assistant, French artist Auguste Rodin (1840–1917) traveled to Italy in 1875. There he saw the sculptures of Michelangelo and became inspired to create *The Age of Bronze,* which was exhibited in Paris in 1877. The sculpture was so realistic that some critics doubted it had been created without plaster casts of a live model. In 1880 the French government commissioned Rodin to create a set of immense doors for a museum. From his work on these doors evolved some of Rodin's best work. *The Thinker* is one of those.

Unit 5 Overview

In this unit children will learn about how artists create works of various sizes. From very small to very large, they will study artworks of all sizes. Children will also experiment with making their own artworks of various sizes.

	Unit Opener, p. 152	Lesson 1, p. 154 **Large Sculptures** Studio 1, p. 156 **Make a Sculpture Garden**	Lesson 2, p. 158 **Artists Paint Murals** Studio 2, p. 160 **Make a Mural**	Lesson 3, p. 162 **Small Symbols** Studio 3, p. 164 **Design a Stamp**	Look and Compare, p. 166 **Large and Small Artworks**
Artworks	 **Alexander Calder.** *Little Spider,* ca. 1940.	 **Lark Grey Dimond-Cates.** *Dr. Seuss and the Cat in the Hat,* [date not available].	 **Artist unknown.** *Firehouse Door,* [date not available].	 **McRay Magleby.** *First Flight • Wright Brothers •,* 1903, 2003.	 **Alexander Calder.** *Cheval Rouge (Red Horse),* 1974. **Alexander Calder.** *Pin,* ca. 1940.
Vocabulary		public sculptures	mural, realistic, imaginary	postage stamps, symbol	
Materials	• Art Print 17 • Fine Art Transparency • Instructional Prints	• **Fine Art Transparency** • Sketchbook Journal • modeling clay • found objects for creating texture, such as toothpicks ⚠, plastic forks ⚠, straws, buttons, shells, and opened paper clips ⚠ • cardboard, sheets of construction paper, glue • crayons, water-based markers	• **Fine Art Transparency** • Sketchbook Journal • newspaper, butcher paper or large pieces of cardboard, construction paper • tempera paint, large and small paintbrushes • scissors ⚠, glue	• **Fine Art Transparency** • Sketchbook Journal • 3-by-4 inch index cards, paper and tissue scraps • scissors ⚠, colored pencils, glue • pinking shears or scissors that cut zigzag, curvy, or wavy lines (optional) ⚠	• **Art Prints 17, 18, 19** • **Fine Art Transparency** • Sketchbook Journal
Connections	**Home Connection** Search for small and large artworks in your community with a family member. **Bookshelf** *The Life and Work of . . . Alexander Calder* by Adam R. Schaefer, Heinemann Library, 2003	**Curriculum Connection** Social Studies: community artworks **ESL Notes** **Fine Arts Connection** Theatre: sculpture skit **Meeting Individual Needs** Reteach, Extend	**Curriculum Connection** Health: mural about health **ESL Notes** **Fine Arts Connection** Dance: murals and dance groups **Meeting Individual Needs** Reteach, Extend	**Curriculum Connection** Math: money **ESL Notes** **Fine Arts Connection** Music: musical symbols **Meeting Individual Needs** Inclusion	**Reading Strategy** Drawing conclusions
Assessment Opportunities		Informal Assessment Rubric 5 from **Unit-by-Unit Resources** Ongoing Assessment	Visual Culture Rubric 5 from **Unit-by-Unit Resources** Ongoing Assessment	Informal Assessment Rubric 5 from **Unit-by-Unit Resources** Ongoing Assessment	

Lesson 4, p. 168 **Emphasis in Jewelry** Studio 4, p. 170 **Make Tradebeads**	Lesson 5 p. 172 **Artists Design Books** Studio 5, p. 174 **Make a Zigzag Book**	Lesson 6, p. 176 **Artists Make Miniatures** Studio 6, p. 178 **Make a Surprise Egg**	Artist at Work, p. 180 **Puppets**	Portfolio Project, p. 182 **Make a Foil Relief**	Unit Review, p. 184
Artist unknown, Moroccan. *Berber Necklace,* [date not available].	The Grouchy Ladybug Eric Carle **Eric Carle.** Cover of *The Grouchy Ladybug,* 1977.	**Carl Fabergé.** *The Gatchina Palace Egg,* 1901.			**Christo and Jeanne-Claude.** *Running Fence, Sonoma and Marin Counties, California,* 1972–1976.
jewelry, pendant, emphasis	book designer, computer art	miniature			
• **Fine Art Transparency** • Sketchbook Journal • self-hardening clay • wooden matchsticks with ends already burned, sharp pencils ⚠ • acrylic paint, small paintbrushes • stringing materials such as ribbon, macramé, leather, cloth cord, or fishing line	• **Fine Art Transparency** • Sketchbook Journal • 4-by-36-inch strips of colored butcher paper, 1 per child • 4-inch square tagboard templates, 1 per child • scissors ⚠, glue sticks, crayons	• **Fine Art Transparency** • Sketchbook Journal • plastic eggs or small cardboard boxes • found art objects, such as beads, buttons, foil, paper, and fabric scraps • sheets of drawing paper, pencils, glue, scissors ⚠, cotton or paper towels • modeling clay	• **Fine Art Transparency** • puppet (optional) • ballet	• 10-by-10-inch posterboard squares, 2 per child • small cardboard scraps • scissors ⚠, glue, heavy-duty foil, pencil eraser	• **Art Print 20** • **Fine Art Transparency**
Curriculum Connection Social Studies: use tradebeads **ESL Notes** **Fine Arts Connection** Music: make music shakers **Meeting Individual Needs** Reteach, Extend	**Technology** Create covers for a book **ESL Notes** **Fine Arts Connection** Theatre: create scenery and props **Meeting Individual Needs** Reteach	**Curriculum Connection** Science: animal habitats **ESL Notes** **Fine Arts Connection** Dance: animal dances **Meeting Individual Needs** Inclusion	**Career Research** Puppeteers **Reading Strategy** Sequencing	**Gallery Options** Jewelry exhibition **Meeting Individual Needs** Extend	
Visual Culture Rubric 5 from **Unit-by-Unit Resources** Ongoing Assessment	Informal Assessment Rubric 5 from **Unit-by-Unit Resources** Ongoing Assessment	Visual Culture Rubric 5 from **Unit-by-Unit Resources** Ongoing Assessment		Rubric 5 from **Unit-by-Unit Resources**	**Unit-by-Unit Resources** Vocabulary Worksheets, pp. 83–86 Unit 5 Test, pp. 91–94

Unit 5

Objectives

- Identify principles of design in artworks.
- Relate art to personal experiences.
- Respond to and make judgments about artworks.

Materials

- **Art Print 17**
- **Fine Art Transparency**

NVAS (K–4) #5 Reflecting upon and assessing the characteristics and merits of their work and the work of others

Introduce the Unit

Play Eye Spy with children. Choose a large object in the class and describe its size, form, and color. Say, for instance, **I spy an object that is large. It is the form of a rectangular prism and it is brown.** (a book shelf) Continue by having children spy objects and then identify its size, form, and color.

Ask a volunteer to read the title of Unit 5. Explain to children that just as the many objects in their classroom are different sizes, art also comes in all sizes. Have children give examples of both large and small artworks that they have seen. Then ask: **Where might you find a large artwork?** (a park, zoo, city hall, post office) **A small artwork?** (library, post office, art museum, school)

Have children look through the unit and briefly discuss the types of artworks they will learn about. Invite them to share their favorites. As a class, discuss whether children prefer the larger or smaller artworks.

Alexander Calder. *Little Spider,* ca. 1940. Painted sheet metal and wire, 55 by 50 inches. National Gallery of Art, gift of Mr. and Mrs. Klaus G. Perls (1996.120.18). © 2000 Estate of Alexander Calder/Artists Rights Society (ARS), New York.

152

 Art Background

Little Spider This artwork is one of Alexander Calder's free-moving sculptures. Calder was fascinated by movement, and he wanted to incorporate it into his sculptures. He realized that he could make balanced, graceful mobiles that moved with just a finger's touch or small current of air.

 Home Connection

Have children take a walk around the neighborhood or town with a family member and search for large artworks such as murals, sculptures, and so on. Then have them search for small artworks, such as postage stamps or photographs. Ask them to share their discoveries with the class.

Art of All Sizes

Artworks come in all sizes. Some are big and some are small. Some artworks are about the same size as their subjects, but most are not.

The artwork on page 152 is called *Little Spider.* But this spider is not so little! It is about four feet tall and five feet long.

Meet the Artist

Alexander Calder studied to be an engineer. Then he went to art school. One of his first sculptures was a tiny circus. Calder went on to make artworks of all sizes. His huge sculptures can be found in cities all over the world. Find another sculpture by Calder in this unit.

153

Bookshelf

The Life and Work of . . . Alexander Calder
by Adam R. Schaefer
Heinemann Library, 2003

Children will enjoy reading about and looking at the life and artworks of twentieth-century American sculptor Alexander Calder. This book is part of a series about artists that includes books about Diego Rivera and Grandma Moses.

Discuss Unit Concepts

Have children read page 153 and look at the mobile by Alexander Calder. Ask: **Does this look like a spider? Explain.** (Yes, it has lots of legs and many "feet.")

Explain to children that artists like to create artworks in different sizes. Some artworks are very large, like *Little Spider.* Other artworks are very small, such as postage stamps. Tell children that in this unit they will see artworks of all sizes.

As you review each element of art and principle of design in Unit 5, you may wish to display the **Instructional Prints.** A print is provided for each element and principle.

In addition, **Art Prints 17–20** and **Transparencies** are available for fine art in the unit.

Meet the Artist

Alexander Calder (1898–1976) was born in Philadelphia to a family of successful artists. He initially studied engineering but soon changed his focus to painting and sculpture.

Calder is most widely known for being one of the first to create artworks that had movement. He also made jewelry and theatre sets.

Lesson 1

At a Glance

Objectives

- Identify and describe large sculptures.
- Describe, analyze, interpret, and judge artworks.

Materials

- **Fine Art Transparency**
- Sketchbook Journal

Vocabulary

public sculptures

NVAS (K–4) #2 Using knowledge of structures and functions

NVAS (K–4) #5 Reflecting upon and assessing the characteristics and merits of their work and the work of others

NVAS (K–4) #6 Making connections between visual arts and other disciplines

❶ Introduce

Explain to children that public places are places where all people are welcome, such as the library or post office. Tell them that many public places have sculptures on display.

Explain that these are examples of *public sculptures,* because they were created and placed so that everyone can enjoy them. Spend several minutes brainstorming public sculptures in your community.

The subject of many public sculptures relate to the people and the community from which they are located. Ask: **What objects or subjects would you like to see in the form of a public sculpture? Why?** Have children discuss how their objects or subjects vary. Model by saying, **Both Tara and Ben want to see their favorite sport as a public sculpture. However, Tara likes basketball and Ben likes soccer.**

Lesson 1

Large Sculptures

This large sculpture shows characters created by Dr. Seuss. It is an outdoor sculpture. Which characters do you see?

Lark Grey Dimond-Cates. *Dr. Seuss and the Cat in the Hat,* at the Dr. Seuss National Memorial Sculpture Garden, Springfield, MA.

154

Art Background

Dr. Seuss National Memorial Sculpture Garden This sculpture garden is in Springfield, Massachusetts, the birthplace of Theodor Seuss Geisel, or Dr. Seuss. It features five bronze sculptures, including Dr. Seuss and some of his favorite characters. Sculptor Lark Grey Dimond-Cates, Geisel's stepdaughter, created the artworks for the garden.

About the Artists Pop artist Claes Oldenburg (1929–) was born in Sweden. In 1977, he married Coosje van Bruggen (1942–), a former museum curator and his partner on a number of projects. Together they have created more than 40 large-scale projects, which have been placed in public places in Europe, Asia, and the United States.

Claes Oldenburg and Coosje van Bruggen. (Detail) *Bicyclette Ensevelié (Buried Bicycle),* 1990.

These artworks are called **public sculptures.** They are large so that many people can enjoy them at the same time.

You may see public sculptures in parks or in other busy places. They often show familiar objects. What does the sculpture on this page show?

Art in My World

Think about a public sculpture that is in your community. Draw it. Tell what it is. Tell where you saw it.

155

 Curriculum Connection

Social Studies Remind children that public sculptures often depict an important person, place, or time. Brainstorm different public sculptures located in parks or at public buildings, preferably in their own communities.

Pair children and have them research information regarding a public sculpture that the class brainstormed. Have pairs share their information with the class.

 Notes

Take a walk with children around the school. As you pass by different artworks, describe their sizes. Say: **This mural is a large artwork.** Encourage children to repeat after you.

② Teach

Have children read pages 154–155. Focus their attention on page 154. Point out that Dr. Seuss is seated next to the Cat in the Hat. Ask:

- **What is the subject of this artwork?** (Possible response: Dr. Seuss with one of his characters) DESCRIBE
- **What process did the artist use?** (She made sculptures out of bronze.) ANALYZE
- **Why do you think the artist sculpted these figures together?** (Possible response: The Cat in the Hat is one of Dr. Seuss's best-known characters.) INTERPRET
- **What would you change about this sculpture?** (Possible response: I would not change this sculpture because I like the Cat in the Hat, too.) JUDGE

Then have children look at the *Bicyclette Ensevelié* and ask similar questions.

Art in My World Provide pictures or newspaper clippings of several public sculptures in your community or elsewhere.

③ Close

After children have completed their drawings, have them write why they like this public sculpture.

Assessment Have children share their drawings with a partner.

Studio 1

At a Glance

Objectives

- Demonstrate the use of clay to create a sculpture.
- Evaluate original artworks by self and peers.

Materials

- modeling clay
- found objects for creating texture, such as toothpicks ⚠, plastic forks ⚠, straws, buttons, shells, and opened paper clips ⚠
- cardboard, sheets of construction paper, glue
- crayons, water-based markers
- Rubric 5 from **Unit-by-Unit Resources**

NVAS (K–4) #1 Understanding and applying media, technique, and processes

NVAS (K–4) #5 Reflecting upon and assessing the characteristics and merits of their work and the work of others

❶ Introduce

Review sculptures with children. Tell them that they will make a sculpture garden, showing characters from a favorite book. Ask:

- **What is your favorite story?**
- **Who are your favorite characters?**
- **How will you portray these characters?**

Explain to children that they will be able to express feelings about their favorite book by using a variety of colors, forms, and lines.

Make a Sculpture Garden

Work with a group to make a sculpture garden. Show your favorite story characters.

❶ Make book characters from modeling clay.

❷ Add texture and detail to your sculpture.

Technique Tip

To join clay pieces, press and blend them together with your fingers.

156

🧒🧒🧒 Meeting Individual Needs

Reteach Help children brainstorm favorite story characters by paging through a few classroom books. Remind children that they can look at the illustrations to help them recall details of their characters.

Extend Have children write their own stories using the same characters that they created in their sculpture garden. The new stories can be sequels to their favorite stories, or they could be totally different from the original stories.

Quick Studio

Name a familiar story, such as *The Three Pigs.* Have children create one of the characters from the story.

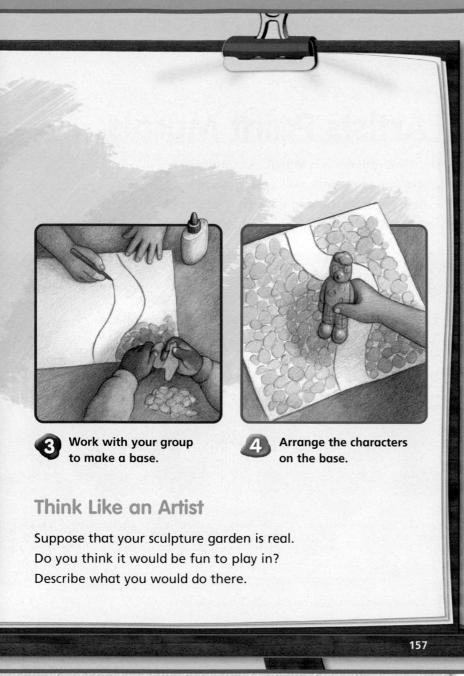

3 Work with your group to make a base.

4 Arrange the characters on the base.

Think Like an Artist

Suppose that your sculpture garden is real.
Do you think it would be fun to play in?
Describe what you would do there.

157

 Fine Arts Connection

Theatre Discuss with the class the concept of improvisational theatre. Then have children brainstorm ideas for a short one-act play that involves a sculpture and your school grounds. For example, children could act out what happens when your school raises money for a new sculpture for its front lawn. Then divide the class into groups and give them some time to brainstorm ideas. Have each group take turns acting out its version of the play for the other children.

2 Create

Have children read the directions on pages 156–157. Then distribute materials.

- Have children pat, press, or roll the clay to resemble the body of the book character.
- Remind children to use lines to show facial features.
- Have children decorate their bases to look like a grassy park using torn paper or a sandy park using sand.
- Encourage children to arrange their clay forms into positions that the entire group is pleased with.

Technique Tip Remind children to hold their sculptures with one hand and use their other thumb to smooth and blend the clay pieces. Tell them that this is an important skill to remember when working with clay.

3 Close

Have children answer the *Think Like an Artist* question on page 157. (Possible response: Yes; There are familiar characters to climb on and play around.) Have children to define other reasons as to why they like their sculpture garden.

Ongoing Assessment

If . . . children's characters do not stand,

then . . . have them add more clay to thicken the legs.

See page 90 from **Unit-by-Unit Resources** for a rubric to assess this studio.

Lesson 2

At a Glance

Objectives

- Identify and describe murals created in realistic and imaginary styles.
- Describe, analyze, interpret, and judge artworks.

Materials

- **Fine Art Transparency**
- **Sketchbook Journal**

Vocabulary

mural, realistic, imaginary

NVAS (K–4) #2 Using knowledge of structures and functions

NVAS (K–4) #5 Reflecting upon and assessing the characteristics and merits of their work and the work of others

Introduce

Provide children with chalk to create a large drawing, either on a classroom chalkboard or outside on the sidewalk. Encourage children to fill the entire space from top to bottom.

Explain to children that some artists enjoy creating paintings and drawings on large areas, such as walls, ceilings, or doors. These artworks are called *murals*.

Murals are created using both realistic and imaginary styles. Artists who prefer to paint subjects that look real have a realistic style. Artists who paint subjects that do not look real have an imaginary style. Have children discuss the style they prefer.

Artists Paint Murals

This artwork is a **mural.** A mural is a large painting on a wall, ceiling, fence, floor, or door. This mural is called *Firehouse Door.* What do you think is behind the door?

Artist unknown. *Firehouse Door,* West Village, New York, NY.

158

 Art Background

Art History The word *mural* is derived from the Latin word *muralis,* which means "wall." The earliest examples of mural art (30,000–10,000 B.C.) are the cave paintings discovered at Altamira, Spain, and at Ardeche Valley, France. These paintings were created with fingers, hands, or brushes and yellow, red, and brown earth pigments. They often show pictures of animals.

ESL Notes

Check children's understanding of the word *mural* by showing a picture of a mural. Indicate how large the mural is by showing where it was created, whether on a wall or ceiling. Say the word **mural** and then have children repeat the word after you.

Murals like *Firehouse Door* show a **realistic** style. They show scenes that look real. Some murals show scenes that are not real. They have an **imaginary** style. Many murals tell stories.

The children on this page are creating a mural. Does their mural show a realistic or imaginary style? What story might it be telling?

Sketchbook Journal

Draw the main parts of a mural that you would like to create. Tell where you would paint the mural.

159

 Curriculum Connection

Health Explain to children that artists often use murals to express their feelings about different topics. For instance, the mural pictured on page 158 shows brave firefighters ready for action.

Have children think of health issues they would like to depict in a mural, such as the importance of good dental health, of healthy foods and exercise, or of washing their hands to keep germs away.

As a class, have them vote on the topic about which they would like to express feelings, and have them create a class mural using a variety of colors and lines. Cover a door or wall with paper and then have children create drawings to add to the mural.

② Teach

Have children read pages 158–159 and examine the artwork. Ask:

- **What do you see?** (a fire engine and four firefighters who look ready to fight a fire)
  DESCRIBE
- **What process did the artist use to create the mural?** (The artist painted the scene on the door.) ANALYZE
- **What is this mural about?** (This mural celebrates firefighters' hard work for 200 years.)
  INTERPRET
- **What impact does it have on you?** (Possible response: The bright colors and the pictures of the firefighters make me feel patriotic.) JUDGE

Sketchbook Journal Explain to children that murals often have stories behind them. Say, for example, *Firehouse Door* **tells the story of hard-working firefighters.** Invite them to share the stories behind the mural they would like to create.

③ Close

After children have completed their sketches, invite them to discuss how the size of a mural affects the artwork.

Visual Culture Have children design a mural for their school. Ask: **What would it say?**

Studio 2

At a Glance

Objectives

- Express ideas by creating a mural.
- Demonstrate how to use a variety of materials to create a mural.
- Evaluate original artworks by self and peers.

Materials

- newspaper, butcher paper or large pieces of cardboard, construction paper
- tempera paint, large and small paintbrushes
- scissors ⚠, glue
- Rubric 5 from **Unit-by-Unit Resources**

NVAS (K–4) #1 Understanding and applying media, techniques, and processes

NVAS (K–4) #3 Choosing and evaluating a range of subject matter, symbols, and ideas

NVAS (K–4) #5 Reflecting upon and assessing the characteristics and merits of their work and the work of others

❶ Introduce

Review murals with children. Have them share murals they have seen before. Then have children brainstorm ideas for their murals. Ask:

- **What ideas will you express in your mural?**
- **What will you draw on your mural?**
- **Will it show a realistic or an imaginary style?**
- **What colors, lines, and textures will you use?**

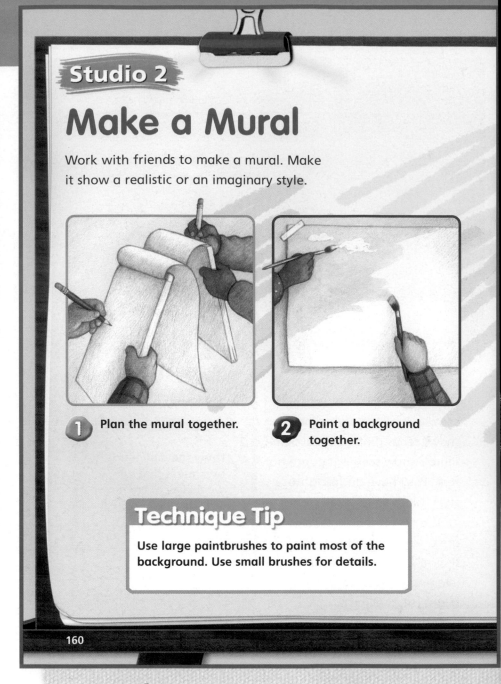

Studio 2

Make a Mural

Work with friends to make a mural. Make it show a realistic or an imaginary style.

1 Plan the mural together.

2 Paint a background together.

Technique Tip

Use large paintbrushes to paint most of the background. Use small brushes for details.

160

Quick Studio

Organize children into groups of five. Have them use crayons and markers to create their murals.

 Meeting Individual Needs

Reteach For children having difficulty planning an idea for a mural, suggest that they create a mural about school. Talk about different parts of the school they could feature, such as the playground, cafeteria, or the library. Once children name a place, then help them brainstorm objects in that setting.

Extend Remind children to plan for a foreground, middle ground, and background for their murals. A large artwork, such as a mural, should have the largest objects in the front, medium-sized objects in the middle, and the smallest objects in the back.

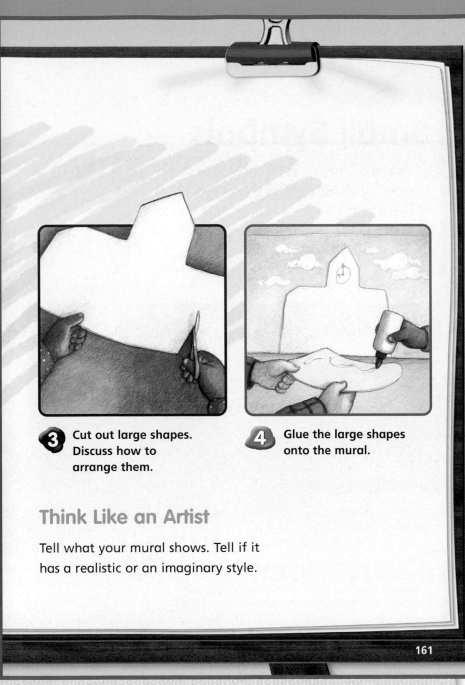

3 Cut out large shapes. Discuss how to arrange them.

4 Glue the large shapes onto the mural.

Think Like an Artist

Tell what your mural shows. Tell if it has a realistic or an imaginary style.

161

 Fine Arts Connection

Dance Remind children that a mural is a large artwork that is a created by organizing many smaller artworks of people, animals, places, and objects together. Tell them this can occur in dance as well.

Show children pictures of people performing folk or country line dances. Lead children to conclude that even though these dances are done by many individual people, they look best when there is a large group of people performing the same movements.

Teach children a simple rhythmic sequence. First have them practice individually, and then have them perform as a class.

❷ Create

Have children read pages 160–161 and look at the pictures. Then provide each group with a large sheet of butcher paper.

- Have children plan which ideas they would like to express in their mural. Then have them list the places, people, and objects they would like to show.
- Encourage children to paint a foreground, middle ground, and a background. Identify this as a necessary skill for producing paintings or murals.
- Have children cut out buildings, people, or objects from paper.
- After children are sure the paint is dry, remind them to find the best arrangement before gluing.

Technique Tip Explain to children that the large brushes will help produce thick strokes, while the small brushes produce thin strokes.

❸ Close

Have children reflect on the *Think Like an Artist* prompt on page 161. (Possible response: Our mural shows our downtown. It is in a realistic style.) Then ask children to identify what skills were necessary to produce their mural.

Ongoing Assessment

If . . . children have difficulty painting details,

then . . . suggest that they use markers to draw details.

See page 90 from **Unit-by-Unit Resources** for a rubric to assess this studio.

Lesson 3

At a Glance

Objectives

- Identify and describe symbols.
- Describe, analyze, interpret, and judge artworks.

Materials

- **Fine Art Transparency**
- Sketchbook Journal

Vocabulary

postage stamps, symbol

NVAS (K–4) #4 Understanding the visual arts in relation to history and cultures

NVAS (K–4) #5 Reflecting upon and assessing the characteristics and merits of their work and the work of others

NVAS (K–4) #6 Making connections between visual arts and other disciplines

❶ Introduce

Invite children to share what they know about postage stamps. Have them discuss the subjects or objects on interesting stamps they have seen before.

Explain to children that postage stamps are small artworks that are often small prints of larger artworks. The artworks on postage stamps also are symbols. For instance, the stamps on pages 162 and 163 all symbolize different topics. (The airplane symbolizes flight; the person with the medal symbolizes the Special Olympics; and the heart and bright colors symbolize love.) Prompt: **Name other subjects that would make good postage stamp artworks.** Invite children to discuss how their ideas are similar or different.

Small Symbols

The next time you get a letter, look at the stamp on it. **Postage stamps** are tiny prints of larger artworks. Some stamps have designs of events in our country's history.

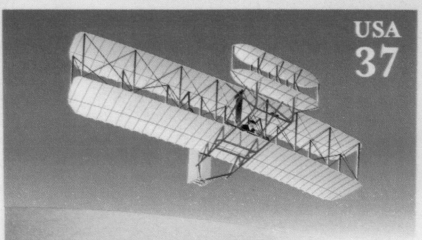

FIRST FLIGHT · WRIGHT BROTHERS · 1903
2003

McRay Magleby. *First Flight • Wright Brothers • 1903,* 2003. Computer-generated design for a U.S. postage stamp. © 2003 USPS.

162

🎨 Art Background

First Flight postage stamp This stamp marks the 100th anniversary of the Wright Brothers' first flight near Kitty Hawk, North Carolina, in 1903.

Special Olympics postage stamp This 2003 stamp was designed to bring attention to Special Olympics' training and athletic competition programs for people with mental disability.

Love postage stamp The first Love stamp, which was issued in 1973 and cost eight cents, was created by Pop artist Robert Indiana. Love stamps have also featured swans, flowers, animals, and cherubs.

Lance Hidy. *Special Olympics,* 2003. Computer-generated design for a U.S. postage stamp. © 2003 USPS.

Michael Osborne. *LOVE,* 2002. Computer-generated design for a U.S. postage stamp. © 2003 USPS.

The postage stamps on this page have something in common. Each one has a **symbol** on it. The symbol stands for a real object or an idea. Point to the heart on the second stamp. The heart stands for love. What symbols do you see on the other stamp? What might the symbols stand for?

Art in My World

Collect postage stamps. Tell a story about your favorite tiny artwork.

163

② Teach

Have children read pages 162–163. Ask:

- **How are these stamps similar?** (Possible response: not much detail; words are at the bottom; lots of negative space; clean images)
- **How are they different?** (Possible response: different subject matters and colors; the *Love* stamp uses its letters as part of its design)
- **Which stamp do you like the best? Why?** (Possible response: *First Flight,* because I like airplanes)
- **If you designed a stamp, who or what would you put on it?** (Possible response: a book because I love reading)

Art in My World Encourage children to look at postage stamps on mail delivered to their homes. Have them choose one to share with the class.

③ Close

After children have created their stories, encourage them to share them with the class.

Assessment Have children talk about what the pictures on their stamps symbolize.

 Curriculum Connection

Math Display a variety of postage stamps with different costs. Have each child choose one stamp to work with and locate its cost.

Provide children with plastic coins. Challenge them to create different combinations of coins equal to the same amount on the postage stamp of their choice. Point out to children that to find the correct combination, they will need to add and subtract coins using the math symbols + and −.

 Notes

Provide examples of stamps. Talk about the pictures and/or symbols on each stamp. After discussing several examples, have children name their favorite stamp.

Studio 3

At a Glance

Objectives

• Demonstrate how to design a postage stamp.
• Evaluate original artworks by self and peers.

Materials

• 3-by-4-inch index cards, paper and tissue scraps
• scissors ⚠, colored pencils, glue
• pinking shears or scissors that cut zigzag, curvy, or wavy lines (optional) ⚠
• Rubric 5 from **Unit-by-Unit Resources**

NVAS (K–4) #3 Choosing and evaluating a range of subject matter, symbols, and ideas

NVAS (K–4) #5 Reflecting upon and assessing the characteristics and merits of their work and the work of others

1 Introduce

Review symbols with children. Then, have children brainstorm ideas for their postage stamps. Ask:

• **What subject will you represent?**
• **What object, person, or place will you use to represent your subject?**
• **What colors will you use?**

Quick Studio
Have children sketch ideas for a postage stamp in their Sketchbook Journals.

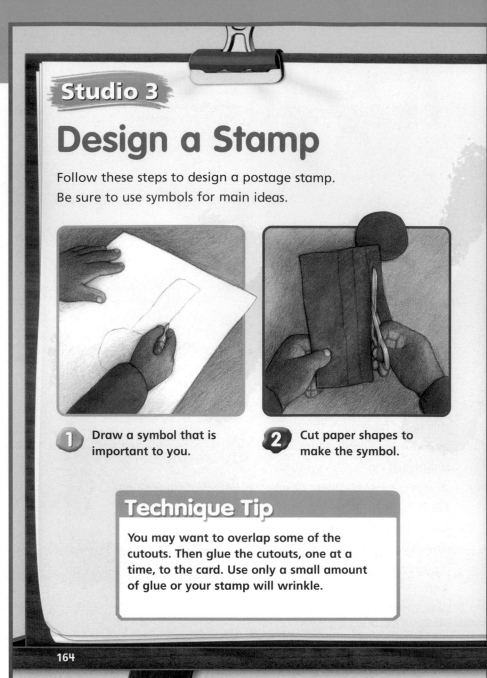

Design a Stamp

Follow these steps to design a postage stamp. Be sure to use symbols for main ideas.

1 Draw a symbol that is important to you.

2 Cut paper shapes to make the symbol.

Technique Tip

You may want to overlap some of the cutouts. Then glue the cutouts, one at a time, to the card. Use only a small amount of glue or your stamp will wrinkle.

164

Meeting Individual Needs

Inclusion A child who does not have strong, fine motor skills may find it difficult to make a small artwork. Provide larger paper for children to create their postage stamp designs.

③ Arrange and then glue the cutouts on the card.

④ Cut around the edges to make it look like a stamp.

Think Like an Artist

Tell a story about your stamp.
Explain what the symbol stands for.

 Fine Arts Connection

Music Explain to children that just as there are different symbols on postage stamps, there are many different symbols in music. For instance, there are symbols that indicate how loud or soft music should be played or sung:

f *forte* means loud

p *piano* means soft

Draw the *forte* symbol and the *piano* symbol on index cards. Sing familiar songs with children. Alternate holding up the *forte* and *piano* symbols as you sing each song, and have children raise or lower their voices accordingly.

② Create

Have children read pages 164–165 and look at the pictures. Then distribute materials.

- You may want to help children prepare by brainstorming some common symbols by having them discuss the subject or ideas they want to express.
- Remind children that simple geometric shapes are easier to cut than intricate ones.
- Remind them to use glue sparingly.
- Show children how to make scalloped borders with the scissors.

Technique Tip Explain that overlapping the shapes can also create depth in artwork.

③ Close

Have children reflect on the *Think Like an Artist* prompt on page 165. (Possible response: My stamp has a medal on it. It is a symbol for bravery, victory, or accomplishment.)

Also have children define reasons as to why they like their artwork. Create your own stamp and model how to define reasons for preference. Say, for example, **I like my stamp because it expresses my ideas on flowers and the overlapping shapes look good.**

Ongoing Assessment

If . . . children are having difficulty making edges appear perforated,

then . . . suggest that they use pinking shears or scissors that zigzag.

See page 90 from **Unit-by-Unit Resources** for a rubric to assess this studio.

Look and Compare

Look and Compare

At a Glance

Objectives

• Compare and contrast two artworks by the same artist.

• Respond to and make judgments about artworks.

Materials

• **Art Prints 17, 18, 19**
• **Fine Art Transparency**
• Sketchbook Journal

NVAS (K–4) #4 Understanding the visual arts in relation to history and cultures

NVAS (K–4) #5 Reflecting upon and assessing the characteristics and merits of their work and the work of others

Explore

Display **Art Print 17,** *Little Spider.* Help children recall this artwork by Alexander Calder from page 152. Then have children look at the two artworks on pages 166 and 167. Explain that these were also created by Calder. Have children discuss how the artworks are similar. (Possible response: strong use of pattern and line; constructed of metal)

Discuss

Have children read pages 166–167. Point out that both of these artworks show an imaginary style because neither looks like its real object. Instead, Calder relies on a strong use of straight and curved lines with regular patterns to suggest form.

Then, discuss the stories behind each of the artworks. Remind children that artists often create artworks to express their ideas. For instance, *Pin* was made by Calder as a gift. It resembles an hourglass and may stand for the concept of time. Have them talk about possible stories behind *Cheval Rouge (Red Horse).*

Large and Small Artworks

Alexander Calder. *Cheval Rouge (Red Horse),* 1974. Sheet metal and paint, approximately 16 by 19 by 19 feet. Private collection.

Alexander Calder made both of these artworks. One is large and one is very small. What is the subject of each artwork? What do you think each symbol stands for?

 Art Background

Cheval Rouge (Red Horse) This outdoor artwork, which resembles a horse, reflects Calder's assertion, "I want to make things that are fun to look at, that have no propaganda value whatsoever." Calder worked with skilled technicians and metal workers at a foundry in Tours, France, to create this artwork.

Pin Alexander Calder produced about 1,500 original pieces of jewelry in his lifetime. He never intended them to be mass-produced and often gave them to family members and friends. Jewelry, such as *Pin*, usually involved bending and twisting brass, gold, or silver wire.

Alexander Calder.
Pin, ca. 1940. Silver,
gold, steel wire, and
glass fragments, 6 15/16
by 4 15/16 by 7/8 inches.
Private collection.

Did Calder use a realistic or an imaginary style? Explain.

Look at the lines in both artworks. Point to the straight lines. What other kinds of lines do you see?

Which is your favorite artwork? Why?

Art in My World

You could wear the artwork on this page. Draw an artwork that you have seen someone wear.

167

 Reading Strategy

Drawing Conclusions Explain to children that good readers often interpret, or draw conclusions, while reading. Direct children to read pages 166 and 167 again. Have children draw conclusions about what other Calder artworks would look like. (They would be abstract, they would have thick, curved lines, and they would be all different sizes.) Then have children look at a portfolio, or a book, of Calder's artworks to determine if their conclusions are correct.

Model how to identify ideas about the portfolio of Calder's artworks: **Calder's artworks are all different sizes. They are also abstract designs.** Then ask children to identify other ideas about Calder's portfolio.

Apply

Draw a Venn diagram like the one below on the chalkboard. Tell children that this graphic organizer is a good way to see how the two artworks are the same and different.

To fill in the diagram, suggest that children first compare the artworks to find out how they are alike. Fill in the middle section as children offer ideas.

Then guide children to notice how they are different. Possible responses are shown in blue.

Calder's Artworks

Cheval Rouge	Similarities	*Pin*
large-scale sculpture	created by the same artist	small jewelry item
painted red	straight and curved lines create patterns	uses stones
resembles an animal	triangular shapes	resembles an hourglass
public sculpture	imaginary style	personal item

Close

Ask children to imagine that *Pin* is a model for a large-scale sculpture. Have them describe how Calder could change it. (Possible response: He could place it on a base and create the same surface on its back side.)

Art in My World Suggest that children create an original design for a piece of jewelry or wearable art.

Lesson 4

At a Glance

Objectives

- Identify and describe emphasis in jewelry.
- Describe, analyze, interpret, and judge artworks.

Materials

- **Fine Art Transparency**
- Sketchbook Journal

Vocabulary

jewelry, pendant, emphasis

NVAS (K–4) #2 Using knowledge of structures and functions

NVAS (K–4) #4 Understanding the visual arts in relation to history and cultures

NVAS (K–4) #5 Reflecting upon and assessing the characteristics and merits of their work and the work of others

NVAS (K–4) #6 Making connections between visual arts and other disciplines

① Introduce

Display a play or real necklace with a pendant. Point out that the pendant is the most important part of the necklace. When artists lend importance to certain parts of an artwork, they create emphasis. Artists use emphasis to draw the viewer's attention.

Show children pictures of other jewelry samples that show emphasis. Ask children to point to the emphasis in each photograph. Ask: **How would you create emphasis in a piece of jewelry?**

Lesson 4

Emphasis in Jewelry

Jewelry is art that is small enough to wear. Look at the **pendant** that is hanging from this necklace of tradebeads. It is small, but it gets your attention!

Artist unknown, Moroccan. *Berber Necklace.* Beads, metalwork, and inlaid precious stones. Photograph © Francesco Venturi/CORBIS.

168

 Art Background

Art and Culture People in many cultures have traded beads in exchange for goods and services. They have been made from a variety of materials, including clay, glass, shells, wood, metal, bone, ivory, seeds, and nuts.

Art History The term *pre-Columbian art* refers to art that was created in the Americas before the arrival of Columbus in 1492.

 Notes

Provide pictures or examples of different types of jewelry. Say: **This is a bracelet.** Have children repeat. Encourage them to name any jewelry that they may be wearing.

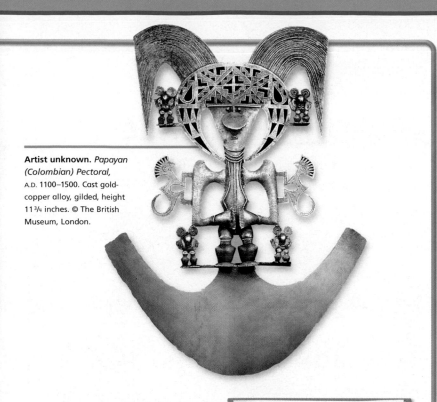

Artist unknown. *Papayan (Colombian) Pectoral,* A.D. 1100–1500. Cast gold-copper alloy, gilded, height 11 ¾ inches. © The British Museum, London.

Artists often give importance, or **emphasis,** to one part of an artwork. They use color, size, shape, or placement to make you look.

The pendant on this page is very old. Someone wore it long ago as part of a necklace. Point to the part that shows emphasis.

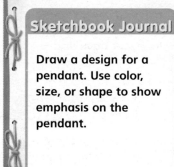

Sketchbook Journal

Draw a design for a pendant. Use color, size, or shape to show emphasis on the pendant.

169

② Teach

Have children read pages 168–169 and look at *Papayan (Columbian) Pectoral.* Ask:

- **What do you see in this artwork?** (a figure with an elaborate headdress) DESCRIBE
- **Why do you think this pendant was worn?** (Possible response: It was a decorative item.) ANALYZE
- **Why do you think the artist created it this way?** (Possible response: to demonstrate his or her mastery of casting) INTERPRET
- **What do you like best about this artwork?** (Possible response: The shapes and the lines make it look like it was worn on special occasions.) JUDGE

Sketchbook Journal Children may want to use meaningful symbols as part of their designs.

③ Close

Have children share their pendants and discuss how they created emphasis on their pendant.

Visual Culture Invite children to look at magazines for jewelry designs. Have them think about the forms, colors, and patterns that show emphasis.

 Curriculum Connection

Social Studies Explain to children that in other countries, tradebeads are used, like money, in exchange for goods that people need. In a corner of the classroom, set up a class store where children may "buy" school supplies, such as pencils, erasers, and paper.

Give each child a number of beads—perhaps twenty—to trade for goods at the store. Allow each child time in the store to make trades with the store owner. Have children take turns being the owner so each can have an experience on both sides of a trade.

Studio 4

At a Glance

Objectives

- Express ideas by showing emphasis in an original artwork.
- Demonstrate how to create tradebeads from clay.
- Evaluate original artworks by self and peers.

Materials

- self-hardening clay
- wooden matchsticks with ends already burned, sharp pencils ⚠
- acrylic paint, small paintbrushes
- stringing materials such as ribbon, macramé, leather, cloth cord, or fishing line
- Rubric 5 from **Unit-by-Unit Resources**

NVAS (K–4) #1 Understanding and applying media, techniques, and processes

NVAS (K–4) #5 Reflecting upon and assessing the characteristics and merits of their work and the work of others

Studio 4

Make Tradebeads

Make beads to trade with friends. Use them to make a necklace with a pendant.

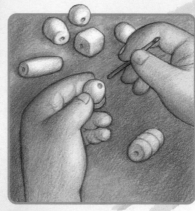

1 Make small clay forms. Make a hole in each form. Let them dry.

2 Paint patterns with lines and shapes. Trade the dried beads.

Technique Tip

Do not make the holes in your beads and pendant too small. The holes will shrink as they dry.

① Introduce

Review tradebeads with children. Have children brainstorm design ideas for their beads. Explain to children that they will express their ideas using a variety of colors, forms, and lines. Ask:

- **Which forms will you use?**
- **How will your lines, shapes, and colors look together?**
- **Which patterns will you create?**

Quick Studio

Provide different colored modeling clay for children to make beads and a pendant. Have children use a toothpick to apply designs.

🧍🧍🧍 Meeting Individual Needs

Reteach For children having trouble deciding on a form for their beads, encourage them to use simple forms, such as spheres and cylinders. Remind them to choose a size for their beads that would be easy to paint detail on.

Extend As children are creating their tradebeads, encourage them to plan a pattern. For instance, they should make three different forms, so they can make an ABC pattern.

3 Cut a pendant from clay. Poke a hole in it and let it dry. Paint it.

4 String the beads and your pendant to make a necklace.

Think Like an Artist

Did you like trading the beads? Explain. Tell which beads on your necklace show emphasis.

171

Fine Arts Connection

Music Remind children that tradebeads were made from a variety of materials, including shells and seeds. Tell children that they will make shakers, a type of instrument, using some of these materials.

Bring in a variety of cans and jars. Have children fill the containers with small materials, such as seeds and beans, to create sound. Ask children to listen to the different sounds created by different materials.

② Create

Have children look at the pictures and read the directions on pages 170–171. Then distribute materials.

- Have children roll each small piece of clay into a sphere. Then it will be easier to shape them into other forms, if desired.
- After beads are completely dry, have children use small paintbrushes to apply paint in a variety of lines. Small paintbrushes will help create thinner lines. Identify this as a necessary skill in producing paintings.
- Have children cut organic shapes for their pendants.
- Encourage children to place their beads onto their necklaces in a pattern.

Technique Tip Remind children to make the holes extra wide. The clay will shrink after it dries.

③ Close

First have children identify the skills necessary for painting their tradebeads. Then have children answer the *Think Like an Artist* feature. (Answers will vary.)

Ongoing Assessment

If . . . children's beads are sticking to one another,

then . . . have them wait longer for the paint to dry.

See page 90 from **Unit-by-Unit Resources** for a rubric to assess this studio.

Lesson 5

At a Glance

Objectives

- Identify and describe the bookmaking process.
- Describe, analyze, interpret, and judge artworks.

Materials

- **Fine Art Transparency**
- Sketchbook Journal

Vocabulary

book designer, computer art

NVAS (K–4) #2 Using knowledge of structures and functions

NVAS (K–4) #5 Reflecting upon and assessing the characteristics and merits of their work and the work of others

NVAS (K–4) #6 Making connections between visual arts and other disciplines

❶ Introduce

Have children look through a variety of classroom storybooks and textbooks. Help them to evaluate the design layouts by asking whether they like the way art is placed on the pages. Ask them to identify the emphasis on the book cover. Model by pointing out the emphasis on the cover of *The Grouchy Ladybug* (the ladybug). Then ask children to look at the classroom storybooks and textbooks again. Have them identify the emphasis on each cover.

Then have children consider the size of the title and whether the type style is easy to read. Explain that book designers use computers and computer art when creating books. Point out that computer artists can easily change designs on the pages, such as size and placement of words. Tell children that book design is another job in art.

Artists Design Books

Look at all the lines, colors, and shapes on this book cover! A **book designer** planned how the cover and each page of the book would look.

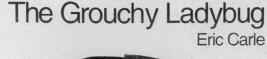

Eric Carle. Cover of *The Grouchy Ladybug*, by Eric Carle, 1977. Harper Collins Publishers.

172

 Art Background

Computer Artists Visual artists, engineers, and book designers are just a few people who use computer-generated art. With computers, they can "paint" a picture directly onto a screen. A computer can also produce, change, and move colors, shapes, and patterns quickly and repeatedly. Computer art can also be sent electronically.

 Notes

Tell children that a book designer is a person who organizes the text and the illustrations of a book. Show children a book and point out and name various parts with which a book designer works, such as the cover, title, and illustrations. Then have children point out and name examples of these parts in other books.

Book designers often use computers to design books. They choose a style for the letters and words. They choose pictures and decide how to fill the space on the pages.

Some book designers use **computer art.** They use computer software to create artworks. What other tools do they need?

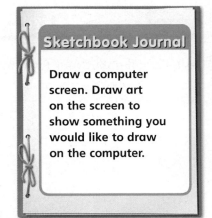

Sketchbook Journal

Draw a computer screen. Draw art on the screen to show something you would like to draw on the computer.

ART TOOLS

173

Create Covers for a Book Invite children to make a new cover for one of their favorite books using a word-processing program. Have them experiment using various fonts and type sizes to make the title. Then have them print it out. Continue by having them illustrate the title using crayons or markers.

② Teach

Have children read pages 172–173 and look at the illustrations. Ask:

- **What is the emphasis of this cover?** (the ladybug)
- **Do you think the art and title work well together? Why or why not?** (Possible response: No, I think the title is too small.)
- **Would you like to read this book if you saw its cover?** (Possible response: Yes, because I'd like to know why the ladybug is so grouchy.)
- **What would you change about this cover?** (Possible response: I would make the ladybug's face a lighter color so I could see its frown better.)

Sketchbook Journal As preparation, brainstorm items that a computer artist would create (CD covers, Internet sites, book jackets, etc.).

③ Close

Encourage children to share the computer art they created.

Assessment Organize children into pairs. Have them talk about book designers and their responsibilities.

Studio 5

At a Glance

Objectives

- Demonstrate how to make a zigzag book.
- Evaluate original artworks by self and peers.

Materials

- 4-by-36-inch strips of colored butcher paper, 1 per child
- 4-inch square tagboard templates, 1 per child
- scissors ⚠, glue sticks, crayons
- Rubric 5 from **Unit-by-Unit Resources**

NVAS (K–4) #1 Understanding and applying media, techniques, and processes

NVAS (K–4) #3 Choosing and evaluating a range of subject matter, symbols, and ideas

❶ Introduce

Review book layout and design with children. Have them share their thoughts about their favorite books. Then, have children brainstorm ideas for their zigzag book. Ask:

- **What school subject will you use?**
- **What will you draw on the front and back covers?**
- **What will you draw on the pages inside your book?**

Make a Zigzag Book

Design pages about your favorite school subject or activity to make a zigzag book.

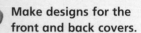

① Make designs for the front and back covers.

② Fold a long paper to make the book pages.

Technique Tip

Use a template to mark where your folds should be. Fold the paper on the marks. Fold it like a big fan.

174

Meeting Individual Needs

Reteach You may need to give individual attention to children who are unable to fold their paper into the accordion style. First, model how to mark where each fold should be. Then demonstrate how to make that fold. Next, show children how to reinforce the crease by rubbing over the fold a second time.

Quick Studio

Have children fold their paper to make a four-page book about their favorite subject.

③ Draw a design for each book page.

④ Glue the folded paper to the front and back covers.

Think Like an Artist

Tell how you might use a computer to design your book.

175

 Fine Arts Connection

Theatre Tell children that a good place to look for scenery ideas for a play would be the book in which the story appeared. Ask children to choose a book that they would like to role-play. Encourage them to create scenery and props based on the illustrations of the story.

Invite another class to watch the performance. Ask the audience to guess what story the role-play was based on by looking at the scenery and the props.

② Create

Have children read pages 174–175 and look at the pictures. Then distribute the materials.

- Encourage them to create their cover using a variety of colors, shapes, and lines.
- Have children draw lines at 4-inch intervals on their butcher paper. Then have them fold the paper along the lines, accordion-style.
- Remind children that as they draw, they should vary the pressure on their pencil or crayons to create different ranges of color and intensity. Identify this as a skill in producing drawings.
- Have children make sure the folds of the accordion are positioned together before gluing.

Technique Tip Instruct children to use one hand to hold the template in place and the other to mark the paper.

③ Close

First have children identify how they produced their drawings in their zigzag book. Then have children answer the *Think Like an Artist* feature on page 175. (Possible response: I would choose the style for the words and letters.)

Ongoing Assessment

If . . . children have trouble deciding what to draw in their books,

then . . . have them think of the most recent lesson in their favorite subject.

See page 90 from **Unit-by-Unit Resources** for a rubric to assess this studio.

Lesson 6

At a Glance

Objectives

- Identify and describe miniature art.
- Describe, analyze, interpret, and judge artworks.

Materials

- **Fine Art Transparency**
- Sketchbook Journal

Vocabulary

miniature

NVAS (K–4) #2 Using knowledge of structures and functions

NVAS (K–4) #4 Understanding the visual arts in relation to history and cultures

NVAS (K–4) #5 Reflecting upon and assessing the characteristics and merits of their work and the work of others

NVAS (K–4) #6 Making connections between visual arts and other disciplines

Introduce

Share toy furniture from a dollhouse, or small toy cars. Explain to children that these toys are small renditions, or models, of the actual items. Further explain that tiny models of actual items are called *miniatures*.

Tell children that some artists like to create miniatures. Even though they are tiny artworks, they often involve great detail. Artists use emphasis so the audience will first look at specific parts of their artwork. Ask: **Where is the emphasis on *The Gatchina Palace Egg?*** (the palace)

Artists Make Miniatures

You can hold this fancy egg in your hand. But look inside. Surprise! When you open the egg, a tiny palace appears. It is a model of a real palace in Russia. A tiny model is called a **miniature.**

Carl Fabergé. *The Gatchina Palace Egg,* 1901. Enamel, gold, seed pearls, diamonds (at each extremity), 5 by 3 inches. The Walters Art Gallery, Baltimore, MD.

176

Art Background

The Gatchina Palace Egg This artwork by Carl Fabergé (1846–1920) was presented by Czar Nicholas II (1868–1918) to his mother on Easter Day in 1901. When opened, the egg reveals a miniature replica of the Gatchina Palace that includes cannons, a flag, some landscaping, and even a statue of a previous Russian emperor, Paul I.

ESL Notes

Show children a dollhouse chair or table. Then point to a chair or table in the classroom. Point again to the dollhouse chair or table and say the word *miniature.* Have children repeat.

Gatchina Palace

Look at the design on the outside of the egg. The lines in the design lead your eye to the palace.

Now look at the picture of the real palace. Where did the architect show emphasis?

Art Fact

In the 1800s, the Russian czar, or emperor, gave a Fabergé egg to his wife. The empress loved it! She got a new one every year.

177

Curriculum Connection

Science Talk with children about large animals that have roamed the Earth in the past, such as dinosaurs, or large animals that live on Earth today, such as elephants or whales. Have children do research on the Internet to learn more about one of these large animals.

Then have children create shoebox dioramas, or miniature models, of each animal's habitat based on their research.

❷ Teach

Have children read pages 176–177 and look at *The Gatchina Palace Egg*. Tell children that this artwork also shows a construction. A construction is a human-made structure, like the Gatchina Palace. Then ask:

- **What do you see?** (a construction; a gold palace inside of a decorated egg) DESCRIBE
- **What do you notice first? Why?** (I notice the palace first. The lines on the egg seem to be pointing at the palace in the center.) ANALYZE
- **Why do you think the artist created this artwork in this way?** (Possible response: He wanted to create a beautiful yet realistic artwork full of miniature details.) INTERPRET
- **What is your favorite part of this artwork?** (Answers will vary.) JUDGE

Art Fact Have children research other Fabergé egg designs on the Internet and print them out.

❸ Close

Invite children to share their research about Fabergé eggs with the class.

Visual Culture Have children explore dollhouses. Have them design and draw their own furniture to place inside the dollhouse.

Studio 6

At a Glance

Objectives

- Express ideas by using emphasis in an original artwork.
- Demonstrate the use of clay when creating miniature art.
- Evaluate original artworks by self and peers.

Materials

- plastic eggs or small cardboard boxes
- found art objects, such as beads, buttons, foil, paper, and fabric scraps
- sheets of drawing paper, pencils, glue, scissors ⚠, cotton or paper towels
- modeling clay
- Rubric 5 from **Unit-by-Unit Resources**

NVAS (K–4) #1 Understanding and applying media, techniques, and processes

NVAS (K–4) #3 Choosing and evaluating a range of subject matter, symbols, and ideas

NVAS (K–4) #5 Reflecting upon and assessing the characteristics and merits of their work and the work of others

---

Studio 6

Make a Surprise Egg

Decorate an egg that will hide a clay surprise.

1 Draw an egg shape. Show a surprise in the egg.

2 Decorate a plastic egg. Glue objects to the outside.

Technique Tip

Work slowly. Let the glue dry before adding each new object to the egg.

178

❶ Introduce

Review and discuss miniatures with children. Tell children they will decorate an egg and put a miniature surprise inside. Then have children brainstorm ideas for their artworks. Ask:

- **What surprise will you put inside?**
- **What will you use to decorate your egg?**
- **What colors, shapes, and lines will you use to create emphasis?**

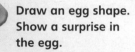

Quick Studio

Invite children to draw and color a miniature version of their school or library. Have them place it inside a plastic egg.

👪👪 Meeting Individual Needs

Inclusion Children who are visually impaired will enjoy creating the surprise but may need assistance to secure it to the inside of the plastic egg. They can decorate the outside of the egg using a variety of found art objects with tactile texture, such as beads, buttons, and ribbons.

3 Fill the bottom of your egg so the surprise will stand out.

4 Use clay to make a tiny surprise. Place the surprise in your egg and close it.

Think Like an Artist

Surprise a friend by opening your egg. Tell how the design on the outside of your egg gives emphasis to the surprise inside.

179

 Fine Arts Connection

Dance Have children think about the types of movements associated with large animals, such as the way a dinosaur or rhinoceros might walk. What kinds of movement does a large bird make, such as an eagle? Next, ask them to think about the kinds of movements made by smaller animals, such as a fluttery hummingbird or skittering mouse.

Play some instrumental music for children, preferably pieces with differing tempos and moods. Have children take turns demonstrating large animal movements and small animal movements with the music.

❷ Create

Have children read pages 178–179 and look at the pictures. Then distribute the materials. If plastic eggs are unavailable, then use very small boxes, such as those used for jewelry.

- Have children draw a person, place, or object that they would like to be their surprise.
- Remind children to use a variety of lines, shapes, and textures to express their ideas.
- Have children fill the bottom half of their eggs with cotton.
- Have children refer to their sketches to determine what form they will create to be the surprise.

Technique Tip To attach objects to the egg, have children spread a thin layer of glue on the item and hold it in place on the egg for a count of ten.

❸ Close

Create your own surprise egg and work with a volunteer to model identifying ideas in artworks by peers. Then have children reflect on their artworks by completing the *Think Like an Artist* feature. (Answers will vary.)

Ongoing Assessment

If . . . children's surprises do not stand out when the egg is opened,

then . . . have them add more cotton to the bottom of the eggs.

See page 90 from **Unit-by-Unit Resources** for a rubric to assess this studio.

Artist at Work

Artist at Work

At a Glance

Objectives

- Read about a career in art.
- Identify the use of art in everyday life.
- Relate art to personal experiences.

Materials

- puppet (optional)

NVAS (K–4) #5 Reflecting upon and assessing the characteristics and merits of their work and the work of others

NVAS (K–4) #6 Making connections between visual arts and other disciplines

Explore

Display a puppet and move its arms and legs. Ask children to share their experiences with puppets or puppet shows that they have seen in their everyday life. You may also want to discuss the wide variety of puppets, including shadow puppets, marionettes, and hand puppets.

Discuss

Have children read pages 180–181. Talk about the photograph and question on page 181. (Possible response: through her puppets) Tell children that a puppeteer is another job in art. Then ask:

- **How are Zhang's puppets different from those you have seen before?** (Possible response: They are bigger.)
- **What skills does a puppeteer need?** (craft skills, such as carving, painting, and sewing, for constructing puppets, and acting, singing, and writing)
- **What other jobs are necessary to create a puppet show?** (Possible response: People who make puppets and puppet stages.)

Puppets

When Hua Hua Zhang was a child, she liked to sing and dance. Then she went to the Arts Academy in Beijing. There she learned a new way to share her ideas. She learned to use puppets!

Being a puppeteer can be hard work. Zhang writes her own stories. She makes puppets to share the stories. Then she rehearses until everything is just right.

Hua Hua Zhang

Materials Hua Hua Zhang uses in her art.

180

 Career Research

To help children better understand the career of puppetry, invite a puppeteer to the class to discuss his or her career, or take children to a local puppet show and arrange for a puppeteer to talk with them afterward.

How does Hua Hua Zhang share her ideas?

Hua Hua Zhang loves her job. Every day is different. She gets to travel to new places. She gets to meet new people. Her art makes her happy. She likes using her art to make others happy too.

181

Apply

Tell children to imagine that they are a director of a movie that will feature puppets. Have children write an advertisement looking for a puppeteer to work in the movie.

Use the chart below to help children organize their ideas. Possible answers are shown below.

Close

Invite volunteers to share their help-wanted ads with classmates. Then ask: **Would you like to be a puppeteer? Why?** (Possible response: Yes, because I like telling stories and making people happy.)

 Reading Strategy

Sequencing Tell children that to better understand a story or passage, it helps to sequence, or list, important things in order. Reread pages 180 and 181 and then ask children to list the steps Hua Hua Zhang takes to create her puppet show. Children may want to illustrate each step after the list is completed.

Preparing for a Puppet Show
1. Write the story.
2. Make the puppets.
3. Practice putting the show together.

Portfolio Project

Portfolio Project

At a Glance

Objectives

- Develop and organize ideas from the environment.
- Demonstrate knowledge about emphasis.
- Evaluate original artworks by self and others.

Materials

- 10-by-10-inch posterboard squares, 2 per child
- small cardboard scraps
- scissors ⚠, glue, heavy-duty foil, pencil eraser
- Rubric 5 from **Unit-by-Unit Resources**

NVAS (K–4) #1 Understanding and applying media, techniques, and processes

NVAS (K–4) #3 Choosing and evaluating a range of subject matter, symbols, and ideas

NVAS (K–4) #5 Reflecting upon and assessing the characteristics and merits of their work and the work of others

Plan

Direct children to read page 182. Then ask:

- **What shape will you cut out?**
- **How will you show emphasis?**

Have children think about the shapes and lines they will create. Ask them to brainstorm what they might like to show in their foil relief art. Then suggest that they look through their Sketchbook Journals for ideas.

Quick Project

Provide precut shapes and torn scraps for children to make their foil relief designs.

Make a Foil Relief

A relief design stands out from its background. Make a large foil relief design. Let it be a plan for small jewelry.

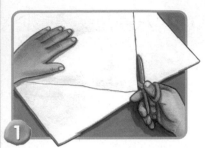

1 Cut out a large simple shape.

2 Glue scraps to your shape.

3 Glue your shape onto a cardboard square.

4 Cover the square with foil. Press it with your fingers to make the shapes and scraps stand out.

182

🚶🚶🚶🚶 Meeting Individual Needs

Extend Explain to children that the foil relief will show different textures as well. Encourage them to add paper of different thickness, as well as textured papers, to their shapes.

Look at some foil relief jewelry designs other children made.

Cole, Age 7. *Foil Shapes*.
Cardboard and foil.

Adriana, Age 7. *Heart Design*.
Cardboard and foil.

Share Your Art

1. Who would wear your jewelry?
   Why would they like it?
2. Where did you show emphasis?

183

Gallery Options

Jewelry Exhibition Have children place their foil relief artworks on tables. Arrange the artworks as a store would to create display tables. Invite children from another class to look at the foil relief displays.

Pair children with a guest to identify ideas in the exhibition. Encourage them to point out the emphasis in each artwork. Model by saying, **This exhibit includes many interesting foil reliefs. Each artist used different shapes and lines.**

Create

Gather the materials and guide children through the steps on page 182 to complete the project:

- Explain to children that posterboard is thicker than construction paper. Tell them to hold onto the posterboard tightly with one hand and cut with the other hand.
- Children may want to tear scraps to add texture to their designs.
- Remind children to place glue on the back of their large shapes and then affix the shapes to the cardboard squares.
- Starting from the center, tell children to press down gently so that the foil does not tear. Explain to children that this is an important skill when producing prints or reliefs.

Have children bring their foil relief jewelry designs to you to store one at a time. Explain to them that foil will wrinkle very easily.

Close

Point out the children's art on page 183. Ask:

- **Which design would you like to create jewelry from? Why?** (I would like a necklace made from Adrianna's designs because she used a flower.)
- **Where is the emphasis in these artworks?** (The emphasis is on large organic shapes in both artworks.)

Have children identify how to produce their foil relief. Then use the *Share Your Art* questions on page 183 to help children explain reasons for preferences in their own artworks. (Answers will vary.)

See page 90 from **Unit-by-Unit Resources** for a rubric to assess this project.

Unit 5 Review

At a Glance

Objectives

- Relate art terms to the environment.
- Identify realism and emphasis in artworks.
- Describe, analyze, interpret, and judge an artwork.

Materials

- Art Print 20
- Fine Art Transparency

NVAS (K–4) #1 Understanding and applying media, techniques, and processes

NVAS (K–4) #2 Using knowledge of structures and functions

NVAS (K–4) #5 Reflecting upon and assessing the characteristics and merits of their work and the work of others

Think About Art

Responses:

realistic (Point to horse statue.)
pendant (Point to the pendant on the necklace.)
mural (Point to the mural.)
jewelry (Point to necklace.)
public sculpture (Point to horse statue.)
symbol (Point to a symbol on the mural.)

Write About Art

Before children write, ask:

- **Where did you see this stamp?** (Possible response: my sister's stamp collection)
- **What is the emphasis on the stamp?** (Answers will vary.)

Think About Art

Match the art words with the pictures.

realistic	pendant	mural
jewelry	public sculpture	symbol

Write About Art

Write a description of an interesting stamp that you have seen. Describe its size, shape, color, and design. Tell what the design stands for.

Talk About Art

- Choose an artwork of yours that you could use as a book illustration.
- Think like a book designer. Describe the page where the artwork would appear.

184

Assessment Options

Options for assessing children appear in the **Unit-by-Unit Resources.**

- Use the **Vocabulary Worksheets** on pages 83–86 for an informal assessment of Unit 5 vocabulary.
- Use the **Unit 5 Test** on pages 91–94 to assess children's mastery of unit vocabulary and concepts.

Christo and Jeanne-Claude. *Running Fence, Sonoma and Marin Counties, California,*
1972–1976. Woven nylon fabric, stretched between steel poles, supported by steel cables,
18 feet by 24½ miles. © 1976 Christo. Photograph by Jeanne-Claude.

Put It All Together

1. Is this public sculpture a miniature or
   a large artwork? How can you tell?
2. Where is the emphasis in this sculpture?
3. Do you think this sculpture is a symbol
   of something? What?
4. Do you think *Running Fence* is a good
   title? Why or why not?

185

 Art Background

Running Fence On September 9, 1976, Christo (1935–)
and Jeanne-Claude (1935–) unveiled this large-scale
artwork. This 18-1/2-foot-high fence was more than
20 miles long. It stretched from Cotati, California, to the
Pacific Ocean. This artwork was created with the same
fabric that is used to make automobile safety airbags.

Talk About Art

Encourage children to choose an artwork they
like. Ask them to give reasons for their
preferences. Prompt them to use words such as
realistic, imaginary, and *emphasis* to describe it.

Continue talking about book illustrations by
creating a classroom exhibition of books by
famous illustrators. Display several of the class'
favorite picture books. Then have children identify
ideas about the exhibition. Model by saying: **I like
how the illustrators used a variety of ways to
create emphasis.**

Put It All Together

Use the questions on page 185 to help children
evaluate the artwork. Possible responses follow.

1. It is a public sculpture. I can see the landscape
   around the sculpture. **DESCRIBE**
2. The artists create emphasis by showing a high
   contrast in colors between the sculpture and the
   landscape. **ANALYZE**
3. It symbolizes freedom because it seems to be
   moving freely across a large space. **INTERPRET**
4. Yes, the artwork looks like a fence. **JUDGE**

Unit 6 Overview

There are many different types of artworks. They range from paintings to sculptures to quilts. In this unit, children will learn about the different ways to create art. They will also create their own artworks using the elements of art and the principles of design.

	Unit Opener, p. 186	Lesson 1, p. 188 Weaving Studio 1, p. 190 Weave Paper	Lesson 2, p. 192 More Fun with Sculpture Studio 2, p. 194 Make a Wire Sculpture	Lesson 3, p. 196 Celebrate with Art Studio 3, p. 198 Make a Headdress	Look and Compare, p. 200 Media in Artworks
Artworks	David Bates. *The Whittler,* 1983.	Artist unknown, Inupiat culture. *Birch Basket,* date unknown.	Alexander Calder. *Finny Fish,* ca. 1948.	Artist unknown, Equadoran. *Corpus Christi Festival Headdress,* ca. 1900–1950.	David Bates. *Feeding the Dogs,* 1986. William Wegman. *Cinderella,* 1992.
Vocabulary		weaving, fabric, loom	medium, media, style	headdress, artifact	
Materials	• **Art Print 21** • **Fine Art Transparency** • **Instructional Prints**	• **Fine Art Transparency** • Sketchbook Journal • 8-inch squares of wallpaper or construction paper; wallpaper scraps or colored construction paper cut into 1-inch by 18-inch strips • scissors ⚠, glue	• **Fine Art Transparency** • Sketchbook Journal • pencils, sheets of drawing paper • lengths of colored, plastic-coated wire available in craft shops and hardware stores • found objects for shaping the wire, such as blocks, dowels of varying thickness, and hard rubber balls • modeling clay	• **Fine Art Transparency** • Sketchbook Journal • brown paper grocery sacks, 1 per child; construction paper in various colors • pencil, scissors ⚠, glue, stapler ⚠ • crayons or oil pastels • found art materials, such as feathers, photos, foil, fiber, shiny buttons, and fabric scraps	• **Art Prints 21, 22, 23** • **Fine Art Transparency** • Sketchbook Journal
Connections	**Home Connection** objects with interesting designs at home **Bookshelf** *Pieces: A Year in Poems and Quilts* by Anna Grossnickle Hines, Harper Trophy, 2003	**Curriculum Connection** Science: observing spun fibers **ESL Notes** **Fine Arts Connection** Dance: opposites in movement **Meeting Individual Needs** Reteach, Extend	**Curriculum Connection** Math: graph with preferred media **ESL Notes** **Fine Arts Connection** Music: sing with movements **Meeting Individual Needs** Inclusion	**Curriculum Connection** Social Studies: distinctive costumes in cultures **ESL Notes** **Fine Arts Connection** Dance: dance with headdresses **Meeting Individual Needs** Inclusion	**Reading Strategy** Identifying details
Assessment Opportunities		Informal Assessment Rubric 6 from **Unit-by-Unit Resources** Ongoing Assessment	Informal Assessment Rubric 6 from **Unit-by-Unit Resources** Ongoing Assessment	Informal Assessment Rubric 6 from **Unit-by-Unit Resources** Ongoing Assessment	

Lesson 4, p. 202 **Masks for Expression** Studio 4, p. 204 **Make a Sack Mask**	Lesson 5 p. 206 **Community Art** Studio 5, p. 208 **Make an Art Train**	Lesson 6, p. 210 **Artists Make Quilts** Studio 6, p. 212 **Make a Class Quilt**	Artist at Work, p. 214 **Jewelry**	Portfolio Project, p. 216 **Make a Woven Bookmark**	Unit Review, p. 218
  Artist unknown, Eskimo (Yupik). *Mask: Bear Spirit*, late 19th century.	 **Colleena Hake and Phillip Estrada.** *The Doll Car*, 1994.	 **Artist unknown.** *Sampler Block Quilt*, 1905.	 **Mario Chaves.** *Past, Present, and Future; Grecian Sea; Pearl Island*, 2002.		 **Artist unknown,** Cameroon. *Large Dance Headdress*, 19th century.
mask	art car, theme	quilt, quilt blocks			
• **Fine Art Transparency** • Sketchbook Journal • brown paper grocery sacks, 1 per child; construction paper in various colors • scissors ⚠, water-based markers, glue	• **Fine Art Transparency** • Sketchbook Journal • milk cartons or shoeboxes, 1 per child • packing peanuts or blocks • tempera paints, paintbrushes • construction paper in light colors • scissors ⚠, glue • found art materials, such as yarn, sequins, foil, paper clips, wire ⚠, and buttons	• **Fine Art Transparency** • quilt (optional) • Sketchbook Journal • paper squares in a uniform size, 1 per child; colored construction paper • crayons or water-based markers • scissors ⚠, glue	• piece of jewelry such as a necklace or bracelet (optional)	• yarn in various colors, cut to 12-inch by 18-inch lengths • plastic drinking straws, 5 per child • various decorative objects, such as beads, small bells, shells, and feathers	• **Art Print 24** • **Fine Art Transparency**
Technology Create and print a mask **ESL Notes** **Fine Arts Connection** Theater: role-play feelings **Meeting Individual Needs** Reteach, Extend	**Curriculum Connection** Physical Education: bodies in motion **ESL Notes** **Fine Arts Connection** Music: songs about trains **Meeting Individual Needs** Reteach	**Curriculum Connection** Social Studies: liberty and freedom in a quilt **ESL Notes** **Fine Arts Connection** Theater: quilt skit **Meeting Individual Needs** Extend	**Career Research** People who work with jewelry **Reading Strategy** Sequencing	**Meeting Individual Needs** Reteach **Gallery Options** Connect with literature	
Informal Assessment Rubric 6 from **Unit-by-Unit Resources** Ongoing Assessment	Visual Culture Rubric 6 from **Unit-by-Unit Resources** Ongoing Assessment	Informal Assessment Rubric 6 from **Unit-by-Unit Resources** Ongoing Assessment		Rubric 6 from **Unit-by-Unit Resources**	**Unit-by-Unit Resources** Vocabulary Worksheets, pp. 101–104 Unit 6 Test, pp. 109–112

Unit 6

At a Glance

Objectives

- Identify cultural expression in artworks.
- Relate art to personal experiences.
- Respond to and make judgments about artworks.

Materials

- Art Print 21
- Fine Art Transparency

NVAS (K–4) #5 Reflecting upon and assessing the characteristics and merits of their work and the work of others

Introduce the Unit

Ask a volunteer to read the title of Unit 6. Display several examples of children's artworks. Talk about the variety of artworks they have created. Tell children that in this unit they will learn about other types of artworks, such as weavings and quilts. Have children page through the unit to look at examples of these types of artworks. Have them identify variations between their own artworks and the ones they see in this unit.

Tell children that in this unit they will also learn about a variety of other materials that artists use, such as wood, fabric, and found objects. Ask: **What are some unusual materials that you might like to use to create art?**

David Bates. *The Whittler,* 1983. Oil on canvas, 96 by 78 inches. Jack S. Blanton Museum of Art, The University of Texas at Austin, Michener Collection Acquisition Fund, 1983. ©David Bates. Photograph by George Holmes.

186

 Art Background

The Whittler In this painting, David Bates shows a man sitting on a porch carving while his dog rests contentedly nearby. The happy, relaxed expression on the man's face and the uncarved sticks on the floor announce the man's enjoyment of his craft. This painting is one of many in which Bates presents colorful portraits of ordinary people engaged in simple daily acts.

 Home Connection

Have children look around their homes or communities for objects with interesting designs, such as a piece of furniture or a quilt. Encourage children to share sketches of their discoveries with the class.

Types of Artworks

You have seen many types of artworks in this book. It is filled with paintings, sculptures, prints, and more. Look at the artwork on page 186. What type of artwork is it?

Artists use different materials to make their artworks. What materials do you think were used for *The Whittler?* What materials have you used to make art?

Meet the Artist

David Bates was born in Texas in 1952. His first works were paintings, such as *The Whittler.* Now Bates is a sculptor who works with wood, wire, and other materials. Bates says his artworks tell stories. What story do you think *The Whittler* tells? Find another artwork by Bates in this unit.

187

 Bookshelf

Pieces: A Year in Poems and Quilts
by Anna Grossnickle Hines
HarperTrophy, 2003

Children will delight in reading these poems about the seasons accompanied by photographs of quilts by the author. Each of the 19 quilts is unique and paired with an original poem. The book ends with a discussion about how the quilts were made.

Discuss Unit Concepts

Have children read page 187 and look at *The Whittler.* Explain that a *whittler* is a person who whittles, or carves, wooden sticks. Ask children to name this type of artwork (painting) and describe the materials used to make it. (oil paint, paintbrush, canvas) Have children identify the ideas in *The Whittler.* Then ask: **Why do you think the man is smiling?** (He seems to enjoy whittling.) **How would you describe the dog's expression?** (happy, contented)

As you review each element of art and principle of design in Unit 6, you may wish to display the **Instructional Prints.** A print is provided for each element and principle.

In addition, **Art Prints 21–24** and **Transparencies** are available for fine art in the unit.

Meet the Artist

David Bates (1952–) After studying art in college, David Bates spent a year in New York City in the independent study program at the Whitney Museum of American Art. He returned to Texas to find his style and study art history. After a 1982 trip to Grassy Lake, a wildlife preserve in Arkansas, Bates began to paint his own personal experiences, focusing on people and animals. Although Bates now prefers sculpture, he continues to get inspiration from the same subjects.

Lesson 1

Lesson 1

At a Glance

Objectives

- Identify and describe ways of weaving.
- Describe, analyze, interpret, and judge artworks.

Materials

- **Fine Art Transparency**
- Sketchbook Journal

Vocabulary

weaving, fabric, loom

NVAS (K–4) #2 Using knowledge of structures and functions

NVAS (K–4) #4 Understanding the visual arts in relation to history and cultures

NVAS (K–4) #5 Reflecting upon and assessing the characteristics and merits of their work and the work of others

NVAS (K–4) #6 Making connections between visual arts and other disciplines

① Introduce

Display an example of a woven object such as a basket or textile. Demonstrate with your finger how the materials are woven together. Describe the colors, textures, and any patterns. Say, for example, **This basket is (brown and yellow). It has a (bumpy) texture. It also has a repeating pattern of brown and yellow diamond shapes.** Then ask children to share their own experiences weaving paper, fabric, or other materials.

Invite children to look for examples of woven objects or *fabric* in the classroom. (For example, point out weaving in children's clothing.) Ask them to identify colors, shapes, and patterns in the weavings. Explain that yarn, thread, cords, and ropes can all be used for weaving on a tool called a *loom*.

Weaving

This basket is useful art. It can hold many things. The artist made the basket by **weaving.** The artist wove stiff strips of birch bark over and under each other to bind them. Weaving gives the basket texture and pattern.

Artist unknown, Inupiat culture. *Birch Basket.* Woven birch. Private collection.

 **Art Background**

Art History Baskets are made from a variety of materials, including wood and unspun fibers. Archeologists have found the oldest known baskets in El Faiyum, Egypt. Tests have shown that these baskets are between 10,000 and 12,000 years old. Interestingly enough, basket weaving is one of the few types of art that have not yet been mechanized. All baskets are still made by hand.

Art History Saltillo serapes originated in the town of Saltillo in northern Mexico. These textiles, woven during the eighteenth and nineteenth centuries, were mainly used by horsemen, which accounts for their size. They are characterized by a central serrated diamond design.

Artist unknown, Mexican. *Serape*, mid-19th century. Wool weft, cotton warp, silk, metallic thread, natural dyes. Fred Harvey Collection of the International Folk Art Foundation at the Museum of International Folk Art, Santa Fe, NM.

This artwork is called a serape. A serape is a soft blanket made of **fabric,** or cloth. The artist made the fabric by weaving thread or yarn. The artist used a **loom.** A loom is a weaving tool. It helps artists hold threads in place as they work. How are the two woven artworks alike? How are they different?

Sketchbook Journal

Draw a woven basket. Then draw something special you would keep inside the basket.

189

 Curriculum Connection

Science Gather some examples of spun fibers (twine, yarn, thread), grasses, and plant parts (reed, willow, pine needles, corn husks). Have groups of three or four children examine them. As children observe and feel the samples, have them think of woven items they may make out of each one. Point out that the hard grasses must be soaked in warm water in order to weave into items such as baskets.

 Notes

Display a picture of a woven cloth or basket. Model the weaving movements as you say the following: **over, under, over, under.** Have the children act out the movements and say the position words along with you.

② Teach

Have children read pages 188–189. Point out that the artworks are both woven and use natural colors, yet they have different textures. The basket is stiff, and the serape is soft. They are also made of different materials. Then direct children's attention to *Serape.* Ask:

- **What do you see?** (a serape with a diamond pattern in the center and a border) DESCRIBE
- **How does the weaver use color?** (Possible response: to create pattern and depth) ANALYZE
- **Why do you think the weaver chose to create it this way?** (Possible responses: The weaver is following a weaving tradition. The colors go well together.) INTERPRET
- **What do you like about this serape?** (Possible response: I like the diamond shape in the middle.) JUDGE

Now ask similar questions as children look at *Birch Basket*.

Sketchbook Journal Encourage children to think about the materials they would use to make their baskets and then create their sketches accordingly.

③ Close

Have children discuss the item they placed in their baskets and explain why they chose it.

Assessment Pair children and have them identify the colors, patterns, and lines on their baskets and explain their choices.

Studio 1

At a Glance

Objectives

- Express ideas by weaving paper.
- Evaluate original artworks by self and peers.

Materials

- 8-inch squares of wallpaper or construction paper; wallpaper scraps or colored construction paper cut into 1-inch by 18-inch strips
- scissors ⚠, glue
- Rubric 6 from **Unit-by-Unit Resources**

NVAS (K–4) #1 Understanding and applying media, technique, and processes

NVAS (K–4) #3 Choosing and evaluating a range of subject matter, symbols, and ideas

NVAS (K–4) #5 Reflecting upon and assessing the characteristics and merits of their work and the work of others

①Introduce

Review weaving with children. Model the movement that weavers follow: over, under, over, under. Ask children to join in. Then have children brainstorm ideas about weaving patterns. Ask:

- **What colors will you weave?**
- **What patterns will you create?**
- **How could you use your paper artwork? Will it be a wall hanging or a background for another artwork?**

Quick Studio
Give each child two sheets of construction paper, each a different color to make a weaving.

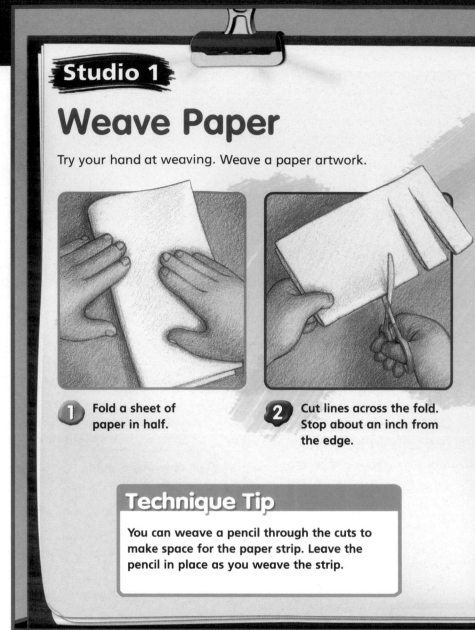

Studio 1
Weave Paper

Try your hand at weaving. Weave a paper artwork.

1 Fold a sheet of paper in half.

2 Cut lines across the fold. Stop about an inch from the edge.

Technique Tip

You can weave a pencil through the cuts to make space for the paper strip. Leave the pencil in place as you weave the strip.

190

👪 Meeting Individual Needs

Reteach To help children with Step 2, provide a template so children can mark where to begin cutting each line.

Extend Supply found objects such as buttons, yarn, raffia, foil, and other materials for children to use to decorate their weaving strips. Then have them use the decorated strips to weave their artwork.

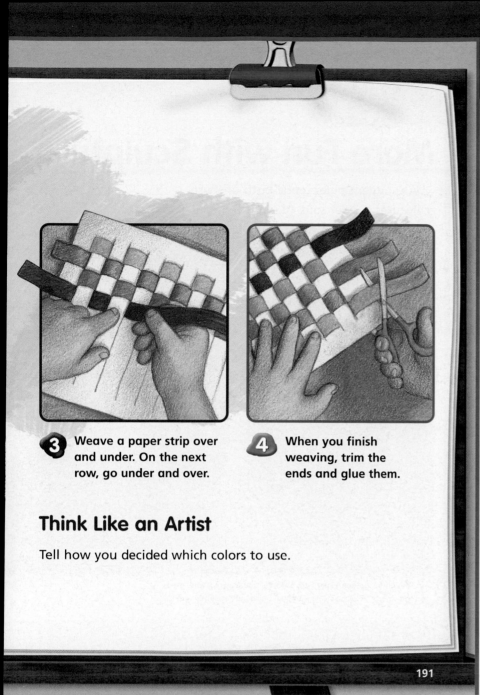

3 Weave a paper strip over and under. On the next row, go under and over.

4 When you finish weaving, trim the ends and glue them.

Think Like an Artist

Tell how you decided which colors to use.

191

Fine Arts Connection

Dance Tell children that when weaving, many artists work up/down and then over/under. Organize children into groups. Have each group create movements based on different "opposites," such as those used in weaving (up/down; over/under; right/left). Play music and have each group share their movements for their respective opposites.

You may want to tell children about the Maypole celebration. Explain that children weave ribbons around a large pole in celebration of spring. Tell them that children use the same weaving movements that they used above.

2 Create

Have children look at the pictures and read the directions on pages 190–191. Remind children to choose colors that express their ideas. Then distribute materials.

- Demonstrate holding the paper firmly with one hand and using the other hand to fold it over until the edges meet.
- Remind children to space their cuts evenly and to make them as straight as possible.
- As children complete weaving each strip, remind them to make sure each strip is tight against the previous strip. Tell children that this is an important skill for weaving.
- Remind children to use glue sparingly to secure the ends of the strips.

Technique Tip Invite volunteers who have mastered the technique to help others.

3 Close

Ask children to identify the skills they needed to create their weaving. Then have them explain the *Think Like an Artist* prompt on page 191. (Possible response: I chose my favorite colors, and they look good together.)

Ongoing Assessment

If . . . children's weavings look uneven,

then . . . they may have cut their lines unevenly. Let them start over using a template to help mark consistent size strips.

See page 108 from **Unit-by-Unit Resources** for a rubric to assess this studio.

Lesson 2

At a Glance

Objectives

- Identify and describe sculptures that show an artist's style and medium.
- Describe, analyze, interpret, and judge artworks.

Materials

- **Fine Art Transparency**
- Sketchbook Journal

Vocabulary

medium, media, style

NVAS (K–4) #2 Using knowledge of structures and functions

NVAS (K–4) #5 Reflecting upon and assessing the characteristics and merits of their work and the work of others

NVAS (K–4) #6 Making connections between visual arts and other disciplines

Introduce

Discuss two child-made artworks from the class. Have children talk about the similarities and the differences of their use of colors, textures, and line. Explain to them that even though both children were given the same assignment, their artworks looked different. Tell children that the artworks are different because each child, or artist, has his or her own style, or special way of creating artworks. Ask: **When you create artworks, which elements of art do you most consider—color, texture, line, or shape? Describe your style.**

Have children examine the artworks on pages 192–193. Explain to children that the artist's style is often characterized by the medium, or material that they use in their artworks. Ask children to name the media used in Calder's artworks.

More Fun with Sculpture

Alexander Calder made both of these sculptures. Calder said, "I want to make things that are fun to look at." What makes these sculptures fun to look at?

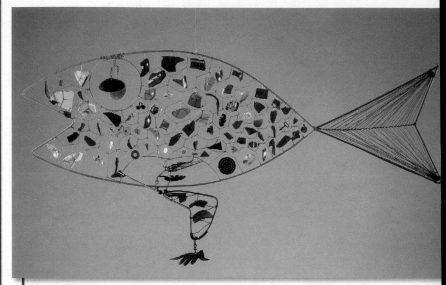

Alexander Calder. *Finny Fish*, 1948. Painted steel rod, wire, glass, and objects, 26 by 60 inches. National Gallery of Art, Washington, D.C.

192

Art Background

About the Artist American artist Alexander Calder (1898–1976) was one of the first artists to create mobiles. He was fascinated by the idea of sculptures that allowed for movement. In Calder's later years, he created large-scale commissioned works. *El Sol Rojo* was his largest sculpture, standing 80 feet high.

ESL Notes

Point to *Finny Fish* on page 192. Check children's understanding of the word *media*. Tell children that this sculpture was made out of different media, or materials. Say the word **media** and have children repeat. Continue by pointing to the media Calder used to make this sculpture (wire, glass, paint, and objects).

Alexander Calder. *Big Bird*, 1937.
Sheet metal, bolts, and paint, 88 by
50 by 59 inches . Private collection.

A material that an artist
uses is called a **medium.**
More than one medium is
called **media.** These artworks
were made from different
media. The fish was made
from wire and glass. The bird
was made from sheet metal.

Calder had his own **style.**
Style is an artist's special way
of making art. How would
you describe it?

Art Fact

Calder could find
materials for making
sculptures anywhere.
At dinner one night,
he sculpted a chicken
from bread and a
hairpin.

193

Curriculum Connection

Math Have children fill in a class graph indicating which
media they prefer to work with. On the vertical axis, write
each child's name. On the horizontal axis, create several
columns naming media they have used in class, such as
crayons, markers, paint, clay, or oil pastels. After each
child has filled in the graph with their choice, discuss the
results. Ask: **What is the favorite medium in our class?**
Which is the least favorite medium?

❷ Teach

Have children read pages 192–193. Focus their
attention on *Finny Fish.* Ask:

- **What shapes do you see?** (rectangles, ovals,
  triangles, circles, organic shapes) DESCRIBE
- **Why do you think Calder used a combination of
  organic and geometric shapes?** (Possible
  response: to create variety within the artwork)
  ANALYZE
- **Why do you think Calder titled his artwork
  *Finny Fish?*** (Possible response: It is the shape of
  a fish.) INTERPRET
- **What part of this artwork do you find most
  interesting?** (I like the lines in the fish's tail.)
  JUDGE

Now ask children similar questions as they look at
Big Bird.

Art Fact Provide a portfolio, or book with several
examples of Calder's artworks, for children to
explore. Point out the various media Calder used
to create his artworks. Ask children to identify
ideas they have about Calder's portfolio. Model
by saying, **Calder's portfolio has many different
types of artworks, such as sculptures, public
sculptures, and jewelry. He uses a variety of
media.**

❸ Close

After children explore Calder's portfolio, have
them talk about the media he used.

Assessment Have children choose an artwork in
the unit and take turns giving clues about its style
and medium until their classmates guess it.

Studio 2

At a Glance

Objectives

- Express ideas by making a wire sculpture.
- Demonstrate bending, twisting, and curling wire to create an artwork.
- Evaluate original artworks by self and peers.

Materials

- pencils, sheets of drawing paper
- lengths of colored, plastic-coated wire ⚠ available in craft shops and hardware stores
- found objects for shaping the wire, such as blocks, dowels of varying thickness, and hard rubber balls
- modeling clay
- Rubric 6 from **Unit-by-Unit Resources**

NVAS (K–4) #1 Understanding and applying media, techniques, and processes

NVAS (K–4) #3 Choosing and evaluating a range of subject matter, symbols, and ideas

NVAS (K–4) #5 Reflecting upon and assessing the characteristics and merits of their work and the work of others

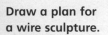
Make a Wire Sculpture

Follow these steps to make a sculpture with wire.

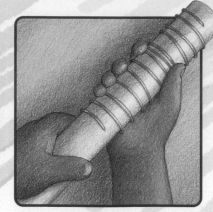

1 Draw a plan for a wire sculpture.

2 Get some wire. Bend it, twist it, and curl it.

Technique Tip

One way to shape wire is to bend it or curl it around a block or a pencil. Press the wire against the object. Then slide the object out.

194

①Introduce

Review wire sculptures with children. Have children brainstorm how to express ideas in their wire sculptures. Ask:

- **What kinds of lines will you use?**
- **What colors will you use?**
- **What techniques will you use to create interesting lines?**

🏃🏃🏃 Meeting Individual Needs

Inclusion For children who lack fine motor skills, provide them with large dowel sticks to help bend and curl their wire. These larger sticks are easier to handle than pencils or other smaller shapes.

Quick Studio

Pair children. Have each pair twirl and bend wires into shapes. Have children arrange their wires and place them into a base.

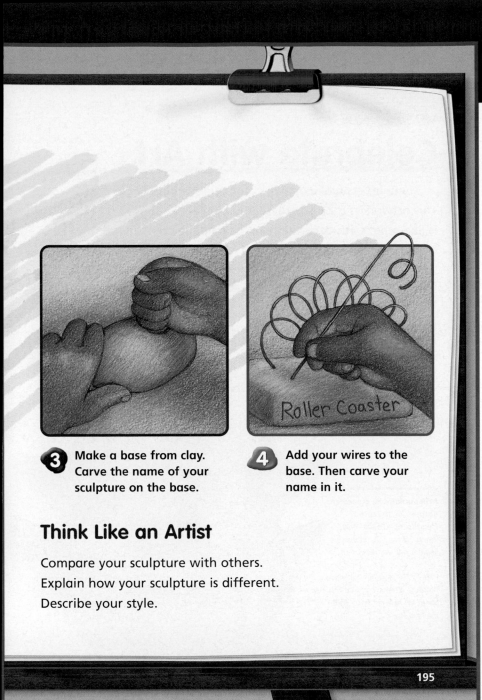

3 Make a base from clay. Carve the name of your sculpture on the base.

4 Add your wires to the base. Then carve your name in it.

Think Like an Artist

Compare your sculpture with others.
Explain how your sculpture is different.
Describe your style.

195

See page 108 from **Unit-by-Unit Resources** for a rubric to assess this studio.

 Fine Arts Connection

Music Sing the following song to the tune of "Row, Row, Row, Your Boat." Create movements that show how you are manipulating wire.

Bend, bend, bend your wire,
Bend it just like this,
Bend, bend, bend your wire,
Until it looks like this.

Have children sing and perform the movements with you. Continue by changing the word *bend* to other ways the wire can move (twist, curl, straighten). You may want to have children make up their own songs about wire. Tell them to create a song based on the tune of a familiar nursery rhyme or song.

2 Create

Have children look at the pictures and read the directions on pages 194–195. Remind children that they can express ideas in their artwork by using a variety of colors, forms, and lines. Then distribute materials.

- Before children draw their plan, model different ways the wire can be manipulated into different lines.
- Explain to children that the size of the pencil or dowel stick is going to be the same size as the curl the wire will make around it.
- Tell children to create a clay form that would best support their sculpture.
- Remind children that they may want to use symmetrical or radial balance to create unity in their sculptures.

Technique Tip Demonstrate how a tighter coil creates a tighter spring than a loosely coiled wire.

3 Close

Have children define their reasons why they like their sculpture by responding to the *Think Like an Artist* prompt on page 195. (Answers will vary.)

Ongoing Assessment

If . . . children's wires do not stand up in the clay,

then . . . suggest that they work the clay with their fingers around the point where the wires are inserted.

See page 108 from **Unit-by-Unit Resources** for a rubric to assess this studio.

Lesson 3

At a Glance

Objectives

- Identify and describe artworks used in festivals and celebrations.
- Describe, analyze, interpret, and judge artworks.

Materials

- **Fine Art Transparency**
- Sketchbook Journal

Vocabulary

headdress, artifacts

NVAS (K–4) #2 Using knowledge of structures and functions

NVAS (K–4) #4 Understanding the visual arts in relation to history and cultures

NVAS (K–4) #5 Reflecting upon and assessing the characteristics and merits of their work and the work of others

NVAS (K–4) #6 Making connections between visual arts and other disciplines

❶ Introduce

Explain to children that people all over the world enjoy celebrations. Explain that in some cultures, people wear a special headdress during celebrations.

Point out that a birthday crown and a wedding tiara are special headdresses with which they may be familiar. Have children discuss variations between these hats and those on pages 196 and 197.

Lead children into determining the emphasis of each headdress. Remind children that the first object to catch their eye is the emphasis of the artwork. Point out that the emphasis of the *Corpus Christi Festival Headdress* is the large oval reliquary at the top of the headdress.

Explain that these headdresses were worn many years ago. Tell children that these headdresses, as well as any other object that was used long ago, is called an artifact. Ask children to share their experiences with artifacts, either from their homes or those they have seen in museums.

Celebrate with Art

Some artists make artworks for celebrations. This artwork is a **headdress.** A headdress is like a hat with decorations. When might a person wear this headdress?

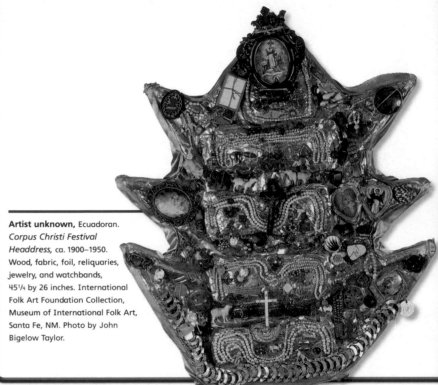

Artist unknown, Ecuadoran. *Corpus Christi Festival Headdress,* ca. 1900–1950. Wood, fabric, foil, reliquaries, jewelry, and watchbands, 45¼ by 26 inches. International Folk Art Foundation Collection, Museum of International Folk Art, Santa Fe, NM. Photo by John Bigelow Taylor.

196

Art Background

Art and Culture The *Corpus Christi Headdress* was created by an unknown Ecuadoran artist for use in an annual festival. The Corpus Christi festival falls in June each year. Ecuador is one of the many countries in the world that celebrate Corpus Christi, however, each place celebrates based on the traditions of the area. In Ecuador, most often the celebration includes costumes, music, and dancing.

Art and Culture *Epa Headdress* is one of many headdresses made for the annual Epa festival, a Yoruban celebration of the male deity Epa. Epa was once a wood carver. This festival is a time to celebrate the social roles of their town: its chiefs, farmers, warriors, hunters, priests, and women. A big attraction of the festival is when male dancers appear wearing these elaborate headdresses.

Bamgboye. *Epa Headdress*, 1920. Carved polychrome wood, height 55 inches. Collection of The Newark Museum, Newark, NJ.

Headdresses have special meanings. The Yoruba people in Africa used this headdress in a festival many years ago. It celebrated the roles of the people.

Objects people used long ago are called **artifacts.** They were made to be used. Over time, people have come to see them as art.

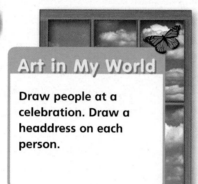

Art in My World

Draw people at a celebration. Draw a headdress on each person.

197

2 Teach

Have children read pages 196–197 and look at *Epa Headdress*. Ask:

- **What do you see in this artifact?** (a head with people and a horse above) DESCRIBE
- **Where is the emphasis in this headdress? Why?** (the horse; It is the largest figure, signifying its importance.) ANALYZE
- **What do you think the artist wanted people to know by looking at this artwork?** (that everyone in their town or community depend on one another) INTERPRET
- **Which carvings are most interesting to you? Why?** (I like the horse because it stands out the most.) JUDGE

Now ask similar questions as children look at *Corpus Christi Headdress*.

Art in My World Have children consider whether the headdress should look the same or different for each person at the celebration.

3 Close

After children complete their sketches, have them write a short paragraph that describes the celebration.

Assessment Ask children to identify the colors, textures, and patterns used in their headdresses. Then have them describe why each celebrant is wearing a particular headdress.

Curriculum Connection

Social Studies Remind children that many cultures around the world are known for distinctive costumes worn for celebrations and festivals. Have them bring in photographs of costumes worn by their family members and friends or have them find examples in books. Ask them to explain ways the costumes are similar to or different from the headdresses on pages 196–197.

 Notes

Point to the headdress on page 196, say the word **headdress,** and have children repeat. Talk about both headdresses on pages 196 and 197. Invite volunteers to point to the one they like the most and say why.

Studio 3

At a Glance

Objectives

- Express feelings by making a headdress.
- Demonstrate knowledge of line, shape, and color.
- Evaluate original artworks by self and peers.

Materials

- brown paper grocery sacks, 1 per child; construction paper in various colors
- pencil, scissors ⚠, glue, stapler ⚠
- crayons or oil pastels
- found art materials, such as feathers, photos, foil, fiber, shiny buttons, and fabric scraps
- Rubric 6 from **Unit-by-Unit Resources**

NVAS (K–4) #1 Understanding and applying media, techniques, and processes

NVAS (K–4) #3 Choosing and evaluating a range of subject matter, symbols, and ideas

NVAS (K–4) #5 Reflecting upon and assessing the characteristics and merits of their work and the work of others

① Introduce

Review headdresses with children. Remind children that headdresses are generally used during celebrations. Have them brainstorm ideas of how they will express their feelings in their headdresses. Ask:

- **What lines, shapes, and colors will you use?**
- **Where will your headdress be worn?**
- **Who will wear your headdress? Explain.**

Quick Studio

Have each child cut a two-inch strip of construction paper to create a headband. Have them decorate their bands.

Studio 3

Make a Headdress

Celebrate! Make and wear a special headdress.

1 Draw and cut out two large U-shapes. Make them the same size.

2 Decorate the cutouts with different types of lines.

Technique Tip

Staple one side of the headdress. Then hold it on your head while your teacher staples the other side to make it fit.

198

🚶 Meeting Individual Needs

Inclusion For children who have a difficult time focusing, organize the materials at different stations in the room. Have found objects at one table, crayons and markers at another table, and the stapler on yet another. As children finish using materials at each table, they can go to the next.

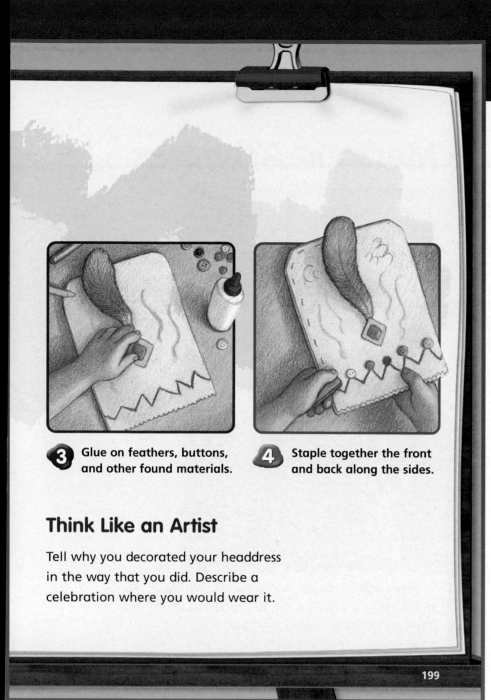

3 Glue on feathers, buttons, and other found materials.

4 Staple together the front and back along the sides.

Think Like an Artist

Tell why you decorated your headdress in the way that you did. Describe a celebration where you would wear it.

 Fine Arts Connection

Dance Organize children into groups according to the type of headdresses they created. For instance, all children who created headdresses for birthday celebrations will work together, and all children who created headdresses for the Fourth of July will work together.

Then ask small groups to create an original dance that celebrates their special occasion. Invite them to wear their headdresses as they perform their dances. You may want to provide appropriate music or have children use classroom instruments to create music.

2 Create

Have children look at the pictures and read the directions on pages 198–199. Then distribute materials.

- Cut both the front and the back of the bag together so the large U-shapes are exactly the same size.
- Tell them to use both the sides and tips of the crayons or oil pastels for thick and thin lines. Remind children to use a variety of colors and lines to express their feelings.
- Have children decide where they want to place emphasis and choose their materials accordingly.
- Model correct use of the stapler before children use it.

Technique Tip Remind children to staple close to the edge of the crown to ensure correct fit.

3 Close

Have children read and discuss *Think Like an Artist* on page 199. (They should give reasons for choosing the designs on their headdresses and then associate the design with a type of celebration.) In addition, have children explain reasons as to why they like their headdresses.

Ongoing Assessment

If . . . children's headdresses do not fit,

then . . . . suggest that they remove the staples and staple again, closer to the edge of the paper.

See page 108 from **Unit-by-Unit Resources** for a rubric to assess this studio.

Look and Compare

Look and Compare

At a Glance

Objectives

- Compare and contrast two artworks created with different media.
- Respond to and make judgments about artworks.

Materials

- **Art Prints 21, 22, 23**
- **Fine Art Transparency**
- Sketchbook Journal

NVAS (K–4) #4 Understanding the visual arts in relation to history and cultures

NVAS (K–4) #5 Reflecting upon and assessing the characteristics and merits of their work and the work of others

Explore

Display **Art Print 21,** *The Whittler.* Help children recall the artwork by David Bates from page 186. Then invite children to look at the artworks on pages 200 and 201. Ask children to predict which artwork was also created by Bates and give reasons for their answer. (Possible response: *Feeding the Dogs;* both artworks show a man smiling with a dog.) Then have children compare the two individuals in these paintings. Model by saying: **These two individuals look similar. They both have long arms and are smiling.**

Discuss

After children read pages 200–201, have them discuss the media each artist used and their different styles (Bates uses paint; Wegman uses photography). Point out that Bates's painting is an example of folk art with a realistic subject. By contrast, Wegman's photograph features an imaginary subject. Then talk about the story that each artwork represents.

Media in Artworks

David Bates. *Feeding the Dogs,* 1986. Oil on canvas. 90^{1}/$_{16}$ by 67 inches. Collection of Phoenix Art Museum, Phoenix, AZ. Museum purchase.

What animal do you see in these artworks? The subjects are similar, but the artists used different media and have different styles.

200

 Art Background

Feeding the Dogs David Bates (1952–) often creates scenes in his artwork from memory. In *Feeding the Dogs,* Bates shows a smiling man encircled by numerous dogs. There is little depth or dimension, only the man's pleasure with this simple task.

Cinderella American photographer William Wegman (1943–) is known for his books featuring his photogenic Weimaraner dogs, such as *Little Red Riding Hood* and *Mother Goose.* His first children's book, *Cinderella,* was published in 1992. He named his first dog Man Ray after a Surrealist photographer and painter. Man Ray was the subject of 12 years of photographs.

William Wegman.
Cinderella, 1992.
Unique Polacolor ER
photograph, 20 by 24
inches. © William
Wegman. From the
book *Cinderella,*
Hyperion Books for
Children, New York,
1993.

What medium did each artist use? How does the media change the way the subjects look? Which artwork shows more details? Tell what you think the artists were trying to say.

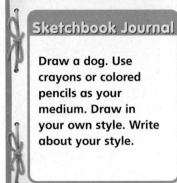

Sketchbook Journal

Draw a dog. Use crayons or colored pencils as your medium. Draw in your own style. Write about your style.

201

 Reading Strategy

Identifying Details Explain to children that good readers use strategies like identifying details to help them understand what they have read. Have children reread pages 200 and 201. Point out that the author uses the word *similar* to make comparisons and words like *different* and *change* to illustrate contrast. Ask: **What does the author want you to compare?** (subjects) **and contrast?** (media, styles, subjects, details, artists' messages)

Apply

Draw a Venn diagram like the one below on the chalkboard. Tell children that this graphic organizer is a good way to show how two artworks are the same and different.

To fill in the diagram, suggest that children first compare the artworks, looking for ways that they are alike. Fill in the middle section as children suggest ideas.

Guide children as they look for differences by suggesting that they focus on the media and the subjects. Possible responses are shown in blue:

Dog Artworks

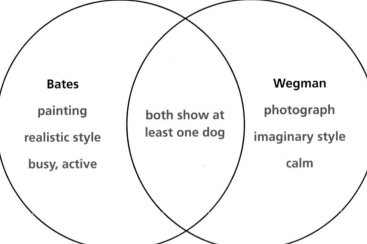

Bates

painting

realistic style

busy, active

both show at least one dog

Wegman

photograph

imaginary style

calm

Close

Ask children to share what they learned about animals in art. (Possible response: They do not have to be realistic. They can look funny too.)

Sketchbook Journal Suggest that children draw a dog that they know, either their pet or the pet of a family member or friend.

Lesson 4

At a Glance

Objectives

- Identify and describe masks as a form of expression.
- Describe, analyze, interpret, and judge artworks.

Materials

- **Fine Art Transparency**
- Sketchbook Journal

Vocabulary

mask

NVAS (K–4) #2 Using knowledge of structures and functions

NVAS (K–4) #4 Understanding the visual arts in relation to history and cultures

NVAS (K–4) #5 Reflecting upon and assessing the characteristics and merits of their work and the work of others

NVAS (K–4) #6 Making connections between visual arts and other disciplines

❶ Introduce

Ask children to share experiences when they have worn a mask, such as at a party or in a play. Have children describe the colors, lines, and texture of the masks. Ask: **How did the mask help you to feel different?**

Then have children discuss masks they have seen in movies or in real life. You may also want to point out that elaborate theatrical makeup (such as in *Cats* or *The Lion King*) can also be a sort of mask because it helps the performer better portray a character.

Explain to children that masks are often created in various cultures to use during a festival or special occasion. Even though these masks were created for special purposes, people soon recognized them as artworks.

Masks for Expression

Have you ever worn a **mask** during a celebration? A mask hides your face and lets you express an idea. This mask shows a bear. What idea do you think the mask expresses?

Artist unknown, Eskimo (Yupik). *Mask: Bear Spirit,* late 19th century. Wood, paint, fiber, gut cord. Dallas Museum of Art, Dallas, TX. Gift of Elizabeth H. Penn. 1976.49.

202

Art Background

Art and Culture The Yupik people of Alaska created masks that were used in dances and ceremonies during the long Alaskan winters to honor the spirits. The meaning of each mask was specific to each carver and the story he or she wished to tell.

Art and Culture This artwork depicts Chalchihuitlicue, the Aztec goddess known as "Jade Skirt" or "Lady Precious Green." To the Aztecs, she was a symbol of youthful beauty and ruled over the waters of the Earth.

Artist unknown, Aztec. *Mask Representing Chalchihuitlicue, "Lady Precious Green."* Wood inlaid with shell and turquoise. Museo Preistorico ed Etnografico Luigi Pigorini, Rome, Italy.

The mask on this page shows an Aztec goddess. It was made in Mexico.

Both masks were made in different places and long ago. Today, artists from all over the world make masks that express ideas about their culture.

Sketchbook Journal

Draw animal faces that you think might make good masks. What ideas do the masks express? List your ideas.

203

Have children read pages 202 and 203 and look at the artworks. Focus their attention on *Mask: Bear Spirit.* Point out the pattern in this artwork. (the repeating round lines) Remind children that artists create pattern by repeating lines and shapes. Ask:

- **What pattern do you see?** (thin, regular, and repeating round lines; vertical, regular thin lines; circles and half-circles) DESCRIBE
- **What is the relationship between round and straight shapes and lines?** (They intersect throughout.) ANALYZE
- **Why do you think the artist created it this way?** (It looks like a cage and makes the bear look more fierce.) INTERPRET
- **How would you feel if you wore this mask?** (powerful, fierce) JUDGE

Now ask similar questions about *Mask Representing Chalchihuitlicue, "Lady Precious Green."*

Sketchbook Journal Have children brainstorm animals that make them feel happy, and those that make them feel afraid. Tell them to choose an animal based on the feeling they want to express.

③ Close

After children complete their sketches, have them share their masks and discuss the feelings they wanted to evoke.

Assessment Ask children to describe when and where they would use their mask.

Technology

Create and Print a Mask Discuss with children the types of events they celebrate each year. Ask them to think about a celebration for which they might wear a mask. Ask them to think about what their masks would look like.

Have children create their masks in a computer art program. Remind them to add details that will tell viewers what they are celebrating. Then have them "paint" their masks on the screen before printing them. Add a string loop to each mask so children can wear them in the classroom.

 Notes

Show children a mask and say: **This is a mask.** Then have children repeat after you. Encourage children to discuss times they have seen or worn a mask.

Studio 4

Studio 4

At a Glance

Objectives

- Express feelings by creating a sack mask.
- Evaluate original artworks by self and peers.

Materials

- brown paper grocery sacks, 1 per child; construction paper in various colors
- scissors ⚠, water-based markers, glue
- Rubric 6 from **Unit-by-Unit Resources**

NVAS (K–4) **#1** Understanding and applying media, techniques, and processes

NVAS (K–4) **#5** Reflecting upon and assessing the characteristics and merits of their work and the work of others

❶ Introduce

Review masks with children. Have children brainstorm ideas that will help them express feelings in their sack masks. Ask:

- **What type of mask will you make? Will it show a real person, an animal, or an imaginary creature?**
- **What lines, shapes, and colors will you use?**
- **How will you use paper to create interesting textures?**

Make a Sack Mask

Make a special mask to express yourself.

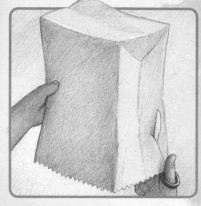 

❶ Cut shoulder curves in the sides of a sack.

❷ Try on the sack. Ask a friend to mark the eyes.

Technique Tip

Be very careful when marking the eyeholes. Press gently and draw circles around the eyes.

👥 Meeting Individual Needs

Reteach For those children who are having difficulty thinking of ideas for their mask, encourage them to think of previous masks they have worn or seen. Children may also get inspiration by thinking of their pets or favorite animals.

Extend For those children who typically finish early, invite them to continue working on the back of their mask. Supply more paper for children to add more details, such as hair or fur.

Quick Studio

Provide small paper sacks to create sack puppets. Have children cut eye holes and add detail with crayons and markers.

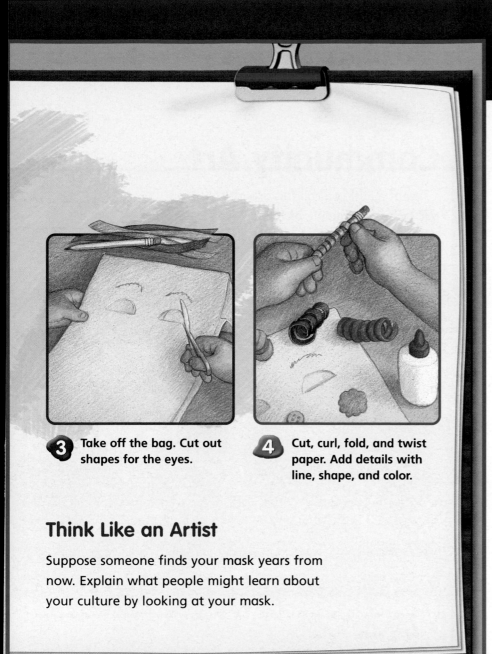

③ Take off the bag. Cut out shapes for the eyes.

④ Cut, curl, fold, and twist paper. Add details with line, shape, and color.

Think Like an Artist

Suppose someone finds your mask years from now. Explain what people might learn about your culture by looking at your mask.

205

 Fine Arts Connection

Theatre Remind children that masks often express different feelings and ideas. Tell children that they are going to create a role-play based on the feelings that their masks express. For instance, if a child created a mask of an imaginary creature from outer space, then he or she should act like that character.

Invite another class to watch the children perform. Ask children from the other class to guess whom each mask represents, whether it is an animal, a person, or an imaginary creature.

② Create

Have children read the directions on pages 204–205. Then distribute materials.

- Provide templates for children to measure exactly how wide to cut the shoulder holes.
- Suggest that children consider marking places for noses and mouths also.
- To make the cutting easier, have children pinch the eye circles and make a cut in the middle of each first.
- Remind children to create design and detail that express their emotion.

Technique Tip Suggest to children that they use a crayon or marker when creating the eye holes on their friend's mask. Pencils are often too light to see on a paper bag.

③ Close

Create your own sack mask and model how to define reasons for your preferences by saying statements such as **I was able to show a fierce expression with diagonal lines for the eyes** and **The fur texture looks real.** Have children define the reasons they are satisfied with their masks. Then have them answer *Think Like an Artist.* (Answers will vary.)

Ongoing Assessment

If . . . children find that the eye holes are too high,

then . . . tell them to make their shoulder holes a little higher to help drop the mask lower onto their face.

See page 108 from **Unit-by-Unit Resources** for a rubric to assess this studio.

Lesson 5

At a Glance

Objectives

- Identify and describe artworks in the community.
- Describe, analyze, interpret, and judge artworks.

Materials

- **Fine Art Transparency**
- Sketchbook Journal

Vocabulary

art car, theme

NVAS (K–4) #2 Using knowledge of structures and functions

NVAS (K–4) #5 Reflecting upon and assessing the characteristics and merits of their work and the work of others

NVAS (K–4) #6 Making connections between visual arts and other disciplines

①Introduce

Have children name some of the artworks they have seen in their community (buildings, sculptures, gardens, etc.). Encourage them to describe these artworks by their color, form, or pattern. Tell children that people all over the world create artworks that express how they feel. Some of these artworks reflect artists' communities and where they live. Ask: **What type of artwork would you like to see in your favorite park? your school?**

Often artworks that reflect an artist's community have a theme, or meaning. Artists choose from a wide range of themes, such as love, friendship, teamwork, and patriotism.

Lesson 5

Community Art

What might you call this artwork? This is an example of folk art. Each year Houston, Texas, has an art car parade. What kinds of fun artworks are in your community?

Colleena Hake and Phillip Estrada. *The Doll Car,* 1994. Automobile with plastic dolls and mixed media.

206

Art Background

The Doll Car Performance artist Colleena Hake (1966–) got the idea for an art car after attending Houston's art car parade. Later she and her husband, artist Phillip Estrada (1961–), created their own art car using old dolls and decorating them with found objects, vintage clothes, and old jewelry. Gods and goddesses, along with portraits of the artists' children, are painted on the ceiling of the car.

We the Youth In 1987, American Pop artist Keith Haring (1958–1990) painted this mural on a building in Philadelphia, Pennsylvania, along with local school children, to celebrate the bicentennial of the U.S. Constitution.

Keith Haring. *We the Youth*, 1987. Mural, approximately 100 by 30 feet (at tallest point). Philadelphia, PA.

This mural is a large artwork. It was painted on a wall in a community in Pennsylvania. The mural has a **theme.** A theme is a big idea, such as love or beauty. Artists express ideas about themes in different ways. What do you think is the theme of this mural?

Sketchbook Journal

Go outdoors with your class. Draw a street near your school. Draw a plan for a mural to be placed near the street.

207

 Curriculum Connection

Physical Education Explain to children that Keith Haring's mural shows bodies in motion. As a class, discuss some of the ways they keep their bodies healthy through exercise.

Have children sketch ideas for a mural in the Sketchbook Journal. Ask them to include different exercises and activities they enjoy playing with their friends.

 Notes

Tell children that the theme of the art car on page 206 is the love of dolls. Then ask them to identify the theme of the mural on page 207. (children)

2 Teach

Have children read pages 206 and 207. Lead children to look at the mural *We the Youth.* Identify the rhythm in the artwork. (the pattern of the bodies and the lines) Remind children that rhythm is repeated lines and shapes that show movement. Ask:

- **What shapes and lines do you see?** (the rounded and curved lines of the bodies) DESCRIBE
- **How does the artist show movement and rhythm?** (He used repeated lines around the bodies.) ANALYZE
- **What do you think the artist wanted people to know about this artwork?** (that young people are active) INTERPRET
- **What is your favorite part of the artwork?** (Possible response: I like the different positions of each of the bodies.) JUDGE

Now ask children similar questions as they look at *The Doll Car.*

Sketchbook Journal Encourage children to consider the theme they will represent in their artworks.

3 Close

After children complete their sketches, have them write a sentence explaining the theme and why they chose to represent it in their artwork.

Visual Culture Have children discuss how artworks in a community can shape its personality.

Studio 5

At a Glance

Objectives

- Express ideas by creating an art train.
- Evaluate original artworks by self and peers.

Materials

- milk cartons or shoeboxes, 1 per child
- packing peanuts or blocks
- tempera paints, paintbrushes
- construction paper in light colors
- scissors ⚠, glue
- found art materials, such as yarn, sequins, foil, paper clips, wire ⚠, and buttons
- Rubric 6 from **Unit-by-Unit Resources**

NVAS (K–4) #1 Understanding and applying media, techniques, and processes

NVAS (K–4) #3 Choosing and evaluating a range of subject matter, symbols, and ideas

NVAS (K–4) #5 Reflecting upon and assessing the characteristics and merits of their work and the work of others

1 Introduce

Review art cars with children. Discuss other examples of art in community places. Have children brainstorm ideas for their art trains. Ask:

- **What theme or subject will you use?**
- **What lines, shapes, and colors will you use?**
- **What found objects will you put on your train?**

Quick Studio

Have children use small milk cartons to complete this studio. Have them paint on day one, and add details on the next.

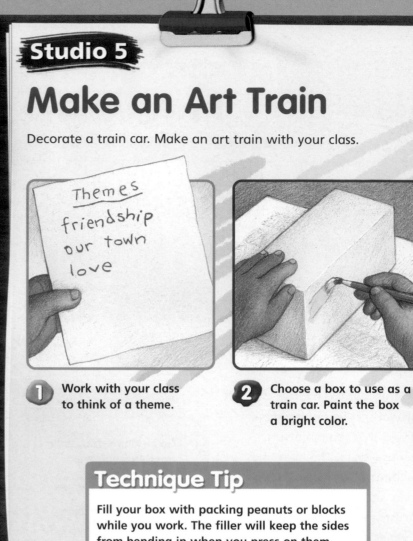

Studio 5

Make an Art Train

Decorate a train car. Make an art train with your class.

Themes
friendship
our town
love

1 Work with your class to think of a theme.

2 Choose a box to use as a train car. Paint the box a bright color.

Technique Tip

Fill your box with packing peanuts or blocks while you work. The filler will keep the sides from bending in when you press on them.

208

👪👪 Meeting Individual Needs

Reteach Help children brainstorm what a real train car may have on it. For instance, a train car that is holding passengers has windows and a door; a train car holding goods, may have only a door. Then have them create their train car accordingly.

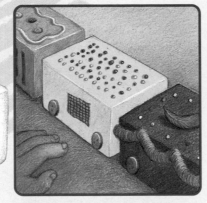
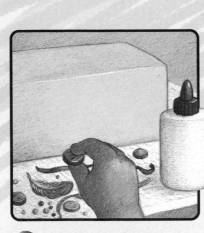

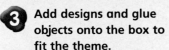 **Add designs and glue objects onto the box to fit the theme.**

4 Put the cars together to make a model, or small copy, of a train.

Think Like an Artist

Tell how your decorations fit the theme. Talk about each artist's part in making the model.

 Fine Arts Connection

Music Tell children that trains have been very important in U.S. history. Explain that there were many songs written about trains and the railroad, such as "I've Been Working on the Railroad." Find the lyrics to this song on the Internet or in a children's book and teach the words to the children. They can either sing along as they work on their train cars, or you can have them hold their train cars as they sing and pantomime blowing the whistle and the horn.

② Create

Have children look at the pictures and read the directions on pages 208–209. Then distribute materials.

- Remind children to explore their ideas about the important events, people, and places in their community as possible themes.
- Have children write their names on the inside of their boxes.
- Allow paint to dry overnight. Remind children to keep in mind their theme as they create their designs.
- Finally, have children identify the best arrangements for their train cars.

Technique Tip Explain to children that the packing peanuts will also help your box maintain its shape. The weight of the paint and the found objects may make the box fall.

③ Close

Have children discuss reasons why they like their art trains. Then have them respond to the *Think Like an Artist* prompt on page 209. (Possible response: I made a heart that shows our theme of love.)

Ongoing Assessment

If . . . children are having difficulty gluing objects to the shoebox,

then . . . suggest they hold them down firmly and count to ten before lifting up.

See page 108 from **Unit-by-Unit Resources** for a rubric to assess this studio.

Lesson 6

At a Glance

Objectives

- Identify and describe quilts as artworks.
- Describe, analyze, interpret, and judge artworks.

Materials

- **Fine Art Transparency**
- quilt (optional)
- Sketchbook Journal

Vocabulary

quilt, quilt blocks

NVAS (K–4) #2 Using knowledge of structures and functions

NVAS (K–4) #4 Understanding the visual arts in relation to history and cultures

NVAS (K–4) #5 Reflecting upon and assessing the characteristics and merits of their work and the work of others

NVAS (K–4) #6 Making connections between visual arts and other disciplines

❶ Introduce

Show children a quilt, or a photograph of a quilt. Point out that a quilt is usually made by sewing blocks, or patches of fabric, together in a meaningful way. Invite children to tell about quilts they have seen including any special images or patterns. Then discuss common items that are quilted, such as pillows, bedspreads, clothing, and so on.

Explain to children that artists who create quilts are also called fiber artists. Fiber artists often have a theme in their quilts. They express their feelings or thoughts through the way they create their artwork.

Artists Make Quilts

A **quilt** is made of several layers of fabric. The top layer has fabric **quilt blocks** that are sewn together. Some quilts cover beds. Others hang on walls.

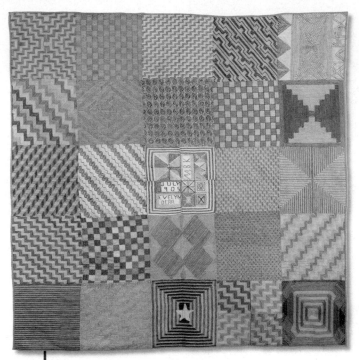

Artist unknown. *Sampler Block Quilt,* 1905.
Smithsonian American Art Museum, Washington, D.C.

210

 Art Background

Art History The quilting technique of stitching to hold a layer of padding between two fabric layers was used in clothing in ancient China and Egypt for warmth as well as for decoration. More recently, people, especially women, throughout the world have created quilts for bed covers.

About the Artist American fiber artist and collagist Katherine Westphal (1919–) was born in Los Angeles, California. After completing a master's degree in painting, she traveled to Mexico, where she met muralists David Alfaro Siqueiros and Diego Rivera. In her hand-printed textiles, she uses techniques from India, Iran, Indonesia, Japan, and Africa.

Katherine Westphal.
Unveiling of the Statue of Liberty (After Edward Moran), 1964. Batiked, quilted, and embroidered fabric, 92¾ by 66½ inches. Smithsonian American Art Museum, Washington, D.C.

Some quilts have a theme. A quilt's theme might come from fabric scraps that were cut from special clothing or material. Or, a quilt might show a theme in its design. What theme does this quilt show? Hint: look at the symbol in the center.

Research

Find other symbols of the United States or your community. Plan how you would show them in quilt blocks.

211

2 Teach

Have children read pages 210–211. Then have them look at the quilt on page 211. Ask:

- **What do you see?** (the Statue of Liberty) DESCRIBE
- **How did the artist show unity and variety in this quilt?** (The artist included a variety of shapes and colors that fit together.) ANALYZE
- **Why did the artist create it this way?** (Possible response: The colorful quilt symbolizes the diversity of the United States.) INTERPRET
- **What is the most interesting part?** (I like the cityscape at the bottom.) JUDGE

Now ask children similar questions about *Sampler Block Quilt.* Discuss with them how many quilt blocks they see (25) and which they find most interesting. (Possible response: I like the block with the star pattern.)

Research Suggest children perform research on the Internet or by looking in their social studies textbooks.

3 Close

Have children share their plans for their quilt blocks and discuss why they chose a particular symbol.

Assessment As children discuss their symbols, check children's understanding of how to create a theme within a quilt's design.

 Curriculum Connection

Social Studies Explain to children that the theme of Westphal's quilt is liberty and freedom and features the Statue of Liberty. Have children draw an idea for a quilt in their Sketchbook Journal. Encourage them to emphasize liberty and freedom by using U.S. symbols, such as the U.S. flag, Uncle Sam, or the bald eagle.

 Notes

Bring to class items used to make a quilt. Hold up each item and say its name, asking children to repeat after you. For example, hold up a needle and say **needle.** Ask children to repeat. Continue saying the name of each item, such as **fabric, thread, scraps, material,** and **quilt,** and ask children to repeat after you say each word.

Studio 6

At a Glance

Objectives

- Express ideas by making a class quilt.
- Demonstrate knowledge of themes to create an original artwork.
- Evaluate original artworks by self and peers.

Materials

- paper squares in a uniform size, 1 per child; colored construction paper
- crayons or water-based markers
- scissors ⚠, glue
- Rubric 6 from **Unit-by-Unit Resources**

NVAS (K–4) #1 Understanding and applying media, techniques, and processes

NVAS (K–4) #3 Choosing and evaluating a range of subject matter, symbols, and ideas

❶ Introduce

Review quilts with children. Have them brainstorm ideas that they would like to express in their quilts. Ask:

- **What theme will you show in your quilt?**
- **What colors, shapes, and lines will you use?**
- **Will you create a symbol or a scene?**

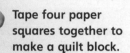

Make a Class Quilt

Work with your classmates to choose a theme for a class quilt. Make the quilt together.

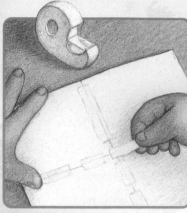 

1 Tape four paper squares together to make a quilt block.

2 Draw symbols or a scene to fit the theme.

Technique Tip

You can draw four pictures, one in each small square. Or, you can draw one large picture across the entire quilt block.

212

🏃 Meeting Individual Needs

Extend Encourage children to create a border for their class quilt with construction paper. Remind them to decorate their border with crayons or markers, using a variety of colors, shapes, and lines.

Quick Studio

Provide each child with a block. Have them draw symbols or a scene to fill each quilt block. Create a quilt by placing all of the quilt blocks together.

3 Fill in the shapes with color.

4 Attach your block to the bulletin board with the others.

Think Like an Artist

Tell why the different quilt blocks work well together.

213

Fine Arts Connection

Theater Have children work in small groups to create a short skit in which their class quilt is the scenery of their play. Remind children to keep the theme in mind as they plan the story or ideas they want to present. Remind children that each child should have a speaking part.

② Create

Have children look at the pictures and read the directions on pages 212–213. Then distribute materials.

- Have children choose squares and tape them together on the back side. Make sure they do not overlap.
- Remind children to draw thin lines using the tip of their pencil. Thicker lines can be created by using the side of the tip. Identify this as an important skill for producing drawings.
- Encourage children to incorporate texture into their coloring.
- When the quilt is together, have the class suggest a title based on the ideas they wanted to express.

Technique Tip Remind children that if they decide to draw one object, then it still should fill the entire space of the quilt block.

③ Close

Ask children to identify how they produced their drawing on the quilt block forms. Then have children respond to the *Think Like an Artist* prompt on page 213. (Possible response: They have a common theme.)

Ongoing Assessment

If . . . children cannot decide on a theme,

then . . . suggest a school-related theme.

See page 108 from **Unit-by-Unit Resources** for a rubric to assess this studio.

Artist at Work

Artist at Work

At a Glance

Objectives

• Read about a career in art.
• Identify the use of art in everyday life.
• Relate art to personal experiences.

Materials

• **Fine Art Transparency**
• piece of jewelry such as a necklace or bracelet (optional)

NVAS (K–4) #5 Reflecting upon and assessing the characteristics and merits of their work and the work of others

NVAS (K–4) #6 Making connections between visual arts and other disciplines

Explore

Display a piece of jewelry, such as a necklace or bracelet, and ask children to describe its shape and form. Then ask children to share any experiences they have had with making jewelry or watching it being made. Explain to children that many artists create jewelry. It is one of the many jobs in the world of art.

Discuss

Have children read pages 214–215. Ask:

• **What makes Chavez's jewelry unique?** (Possible response: He uses unusual materials, such as a gold coin.)
• **How would you describe Chavez's style?** (Possible response: He uses simple lines and geometric shapes.)
• **Think about having a career working with jewelry. What would you find most interesting?** (Possible response: making beautiful things that people enjoy)

Jewelry

Mario Chavez chose his life's work when he was only fourteen years old. That is when he took his first jewelry class. Later he learned more by working for skilled jewelry makers.

Chavez creates jewelry that makes him happy. First, he draws a design. Then, he melts gold and silver. He shapes the metals and adds stones, such as diamonds or sapphires. Sometimes he uses strange objects instead. He has even used old coins and bones!

Mario Chavez creates art that you can wear.

 Career Research

Have small groups conduct research to find out more about careers with jewelry. If possible, invite someone who creates jewelry to talk to the class. Have children prepare questions based on the research they completed.

You may want to take children on a field trip to a community marketplace or festival. Local jewelry artists often bring their jewelry to sell it and demonstrate how they make it. Have children look for the wide range of materials used by jewelry artists.

Mario Chavez. *Past, Present, and Future; Grecian Sea; Pearl Island;* 2002. 22K gold and diamonds; 18 and 22K gold, Ancient Greek coin, and blue Australian opal; platinum and 22K gold, diamond, and South Sea pearl. Photograph © Alison Watson.

Chavez has fun with his work and hopes that his customers will enjoy his jewelry so much that they hand it down to their children. Chavez wants his artworks to last a long time.

215

Apply

Tell children they are going to create their own jewelry. Ask children to think about their style and medium. Then, based on the information on pages 214–215, ask them to list the steps in making a piece of jewelry. Display the following graphic organizer to help children organize their ideas. Possible responses are shown below.

Making Jewelry

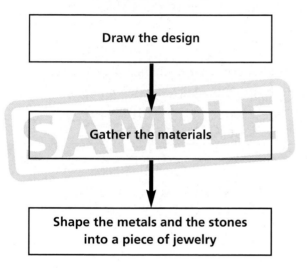

Draw the design

↓

Gather the materials

↓

Shape the metals and the stones into a piece of jewelry

Close

Invite volunteers to talk about the type of jewelry they would like to make. Encourage them to talk about the order of events involved in creating each piece of jewelry.

Reading Strategy

Sequencing Tell children that readers better understand a passage if they sequence the events that happened. Ask children to read pages 214 and 215 again. Have them identify and list each event that happened in Chavez's life before he became a jewelry designer. For example, point out that Chavez knew at a young age that he wanted to make jewelry. Ask: **What happened next?** Continue this process until children have identified and sequenced the major events in the passage.

Portfolio Project

Portfolio Project

At a Glance

Objectives

- Develop and organize ideas from the environment.
- Demonstrate knowledge about weaving using mixed media.
- Evaluate original artworks by self and peers.

Materials

- yarn in various colors, cut to 12-inch by 18-inch lengths
- plastic drinking straws, 5 per child
- various decorative objects, such as beads, small bells, shells, and feathers
- Rubric 6 from **Unit-by-Unit Resources**

NVAS (K–4) #1 Understanding and applying media, techniques, and processes

NVAS (K–4) #3 Choosing and evaluating a range of subject matter, symbols, and ideas

NVAS (K–4) #5 Reflecting upon and assessing the characteristics and merits of their work and the work of others

---

Make a Woven Bookmark

Make a special artwork that is useful. Weave a bookmark.

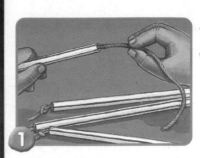
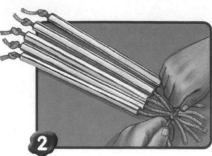

Push five strips of yarn through five drinking straws. Tie a knot in one end of each yarn strip.

Tie the other ends of the yarn strips together.

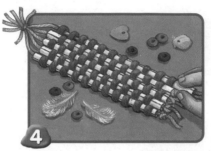

Weave over and under the straws. Weave back and forth. Do it again and again.

Cut the small knots. Pull out the straws. Tie the loose ends. Then add beads or other decorations.

216

Plan

Direct children to read page 216. Then ask:

- **What color yarns will you use?**
- **What decorations will you use?**
- **How will you use line and pattern in your bookmarks?**

Ask children to think about the patterns and lines they might like to show in their woven bookmarks. Then have them look at the artworks on pages 188–189 and point out how the **artists wove the materials together.** Suggest that children look through their Sketchbook Journals for other examples of interesting lines and patterns.

Quick Project

Cut yarn into 2-foot lengths. Tie nine strands together at one end and **braid the strands in groups of three.** Knot the end.

🧍🧍🧍🧍 Meeting Individual Needs

Reteach You may want to have partners help each other hold the straws while the first few rows of yarn are woven around them. Some children may find it easier to weave if they first loop the big knot created in Step 2 around an object such as a doorknob or other support.

How would you describe the patterns in these woven bookmarks by other children?

Chandler, Age 7.
Smiley Bookmark.
Yarn, sequins,
and beads.

Carissa, Age 8.
Flag Bookmark.
Yarn, sequins,
and beads.

Share Your Art

1. Explain how to weave.
2. Describe a problem you had.
   Tell how you solved it.

217

 Gallery Options

Connect with Literature Have the children write their name and the title for their woven bookmarks on slips of white paper. Then display them in the library. You might coordinate with the librarian to add books to the display or create a reading theme for the presentation.

Create

Gather the materials and guide children through the steps on page 216.

- Have children place tape on one end of the yarn to make it easier to thread through the straw.
- Have children ask a partner to hold the straws while they tie the knot.
- As children finish each row, make sure that they push it tight against the previous row.
- Make sure children have woven to the bottom of the straws. If not, they can tie on another length of yarn and continue.

Have children who master the technique help the children who are having difficulty.

Close

Point out the children's art on page 217. These artworks are from other second graders. Model how to identify ideas in peers' artworks. Say, for example, **Carissa created a pattern using lines and shapes.** Ask children to identify ideas. Ask:

- **What colors and patterns do you see?** (Possible responses: purple, blue, and red; shades of blue; pattern of lines; pattern of beads)
- **What do you like about these bookmarks?** (Answers will vary.)

Have children express reasons for preferences in their own artwork. Then use the *Share Your Art* prompts on page 217. (Possible responses: Go over and under the straws. It was hard to thread the straws, but I dropped the end through the top.)

See page 108 from **Unit-by-Unit Resources** for a rubric to assess this project.

Unit 6 Review

At a Glance

Objectives

- Relate art terms to the environment.
- Identify media, themes, and styles in artworks.
- Describe, analyze, interpret, and judge an artwork.

Materials

- **Art Print 24**
- **Fine Art Transparency**

NVAS (K–4) #1 Understanding and applying media, techniques, and processes

NVAS (K–4) #2 Using knowledge of structures and functions

NVAS (K–4) #5 Reflecting upon and assessing the characteristics and merits of their work and the work of others

Think About Art

Responses:

art car (Point to the model of the art car.)
fabric (Point to the quilt.)
model (Point to the model of the art car.)
artifact (Point to the mask.)
mask (Point to the mask.)
quilt (Point to the quilt.)

Write About Art

Before children write, ask:

- **Would you create an object to use or to look at?** (Possible response: a basket to use)
- **What do you want people to know from looking at your artwork?** (Possible response: I like red and green.)

Unit Review

 ### Think About Art

Match each word to a picture.

| art car | fabric | model |
| artifact | mask | quilt |

Artist unknown.
*Pende Mbuyu
Initiation Mask.*

 ### Write About Art

Think about all the art projects that you have made. Then write a plan for a new project that you would enjoy making. Tell what media and style you would use. Tell the theme.

 ### Talk About Art

- Tell about the kind of artist you want to be.
- What media do you most enjoy working with?
- What themes will your artworks express?

218

 Assessment Options

Options for assessing children appear in the **Unit-by-Unit Resources.**

- Use the **Vocabulary Worksheets** on pages 101–104 for an informal assessment of Unit 6 vocabulary.
- Use the **Unit 6 Test** on pages 109–112 to assess children's mastery of unit vocabulary and concepts.

Put It All Together

1. What materials did the artist use?
2. How does the headdress show balance?
3. Why do you think the artist made the headdress?
4. Where and when might you wear this headdress?

219

Talk About Art

Pair children to share each other's portfolios. Prompt children to use words such as *weaving, headdress, artifact, mask, art car,* and *quilt block* to discuss the artworks. Ask children to identify ideas about their partner's portfolio. Model by saying, **I like how Mark uses different lines and shapes to create patterns in his artworks.**

Put It All Together

Use the questions on page 219 to evaluate the artwork. Possible responses are below:

1. The artist used wood.
2. The sculpture is nearly identical on each side of the line of symmetry that extends from the forehead to the nose.
3. It was probably made for a special ceremony or celebration.
4. I would wear the headdress in a celebration.

 Art Background

Large Dance Headdress This headdress is from Cameroon, a country on the western coast of Africa. Cameroonian carvings were generally created by men and are characterized by their bold and expressive techniques and often show skillfully applied beadwork.

Line

straight

curved

zigzag

thin

thick

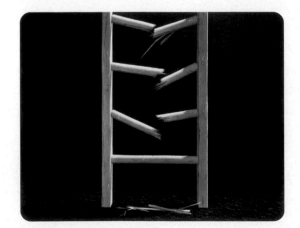

broken

Color

cool

warm

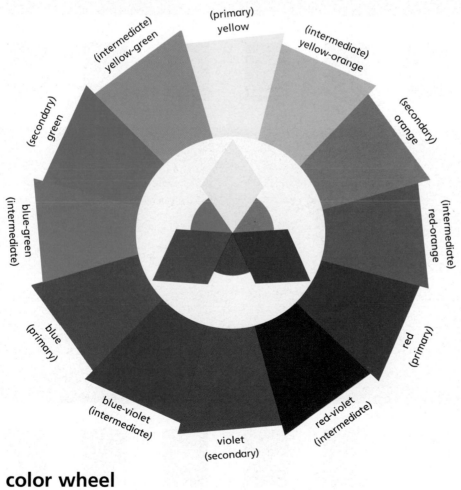

(intermediate)
yellow-green

(primary)
yellow

(intermediate)
yellow-orange

(secondary)
green

(secondary)
orange

blue-green
(intermediate)

(intermediate)
red-orange

blue
(primary)

red
(primary)

blue-violet
(intermediate)

red-violet
(intermediate)

violet
(secondary)

color wheel

Value

Shape

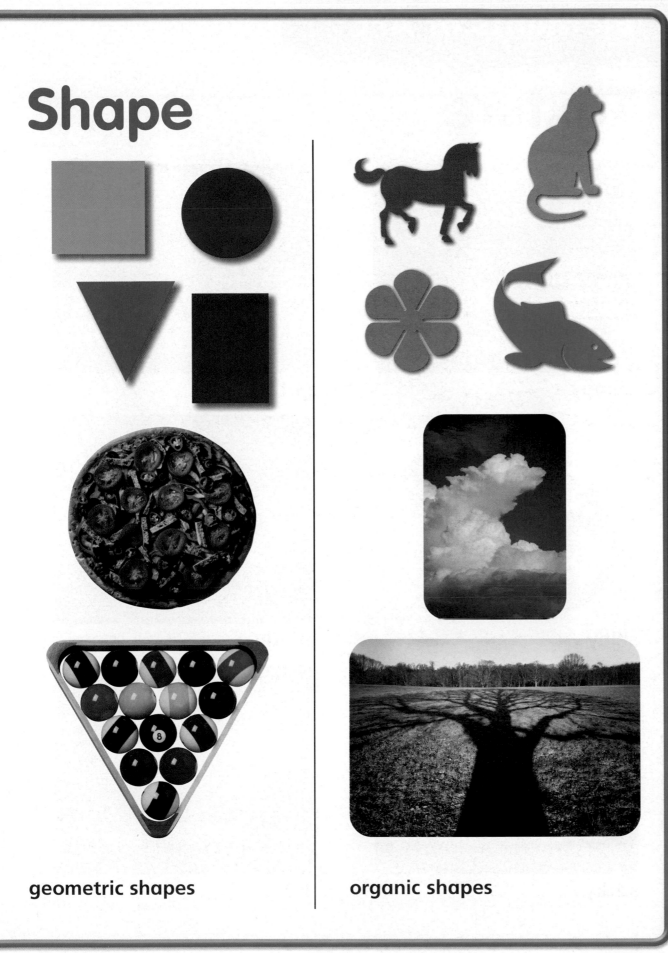

geometric shapes   organic shapes

Texture

bumpy

soft

shiny

prickly

sticky

fluffy

224

Form

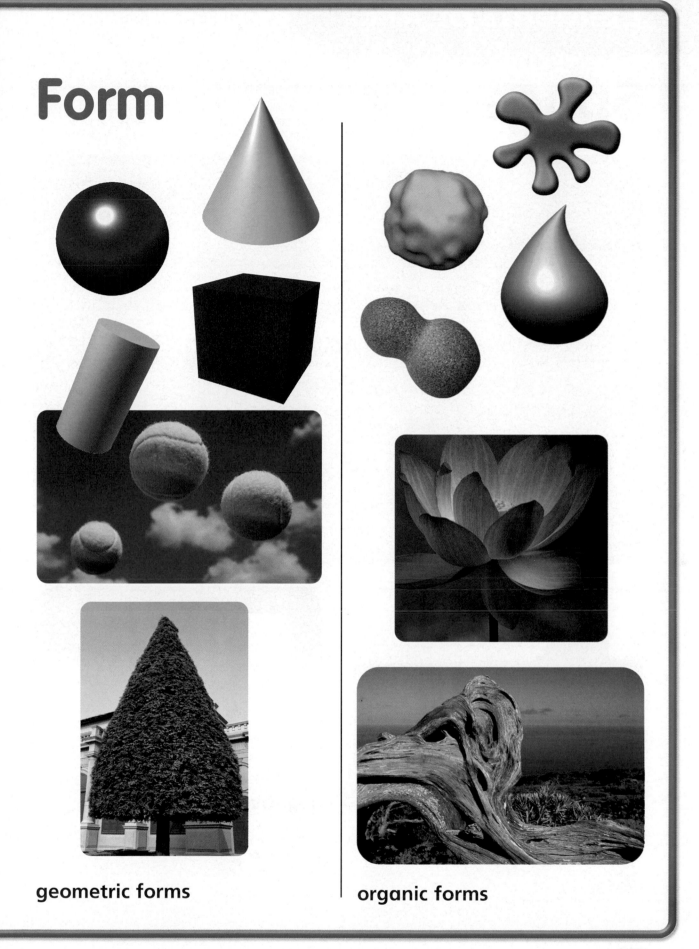

geometric forms

organic forms

Space

positive space

negative space

226

Principles of Design

Unity

227

Variety

228

Emphasis

Principles of Design

Balance

Proportion

231

Pattern

232

Rhythm

Think Safety

Read these safety rules. Be sure to follow these rules when you create artworks.

1. Keep art materials away from your mouth.

2. Keep art materials away from your eyes.

3. Do not breathe chalk dust or art sprays.

4. Look for the word *nontoxic* on labels. This means the materials are safe to use.

5. Always use safety scissors. Take care with all sharp objects.

6. Use only unused meat trays and egg cartons.

7. Wash your hands when you finish an artwork.

8. Get help from your teacher if you have a problem.

Can you think of more ways to be safe?

234

List of Artists

Unknown Artists

Artists

List of Artists

237

Picture Glossary

A

abstract
page 61

architecture
page 86

art car
page 206

Colleena Hake and Phillip Estrada.
The Doll Car, 1994.

artifact
page 197

Artist unknown. *Acoma Polychrome Jar, ca.* 1900.

asymmetrical balance
page 125

Artist unknown. *Inlay of a king or deity. ca. 305–200 B.C.*

B

balance
page 124

book designer
page 172

clay
page 109

C

carve
page 101

ceramic
page 121

close up
page 139

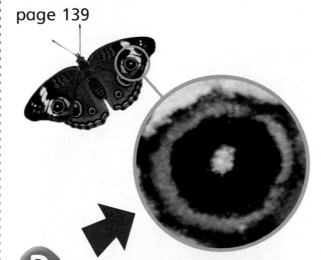

D

design
page 91

E

emphasis
page 169

239

expression
page 66

form
page 87

F

fabric
page 189

H

headdress
page 196

faraway
page 139

I

imaginary
page 159

Still from the animated feature *Monsters, Inc.*

intermediate colors
page 37

lines
page 18

J

jewelry
page 168

Artist unknown. *Berber Necklace.*

loom
page 189

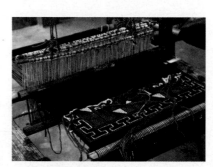

K

kiln
page 109

M

mask
page 202

Artist unknown. *Mask Representing Chalchihuitlicue.*

L

landscape
page 74

medium
page 193

241

miniature
page 176

model
page 209

mood
page 40

mosaic
page 142

Artist unknown. *Double-Headed Serpent.*
A.D. 15th century.

motion
page 129

movement
page 128

mural
page 158

N

negative space
page 95

O

overlap
page 75

P

pattern
page 52

pendant
page 168

playscape
page 90

portrait
page 66

Leonardo da Vinci. *Mona Lisa,* 1503-1506.

positive space
page 94

pottery
page 108

primary colors
page 36

243

prints
page 53

proportion
page 139

public sculpture
page 155

Alexander Calder. *Red Horse*, 1974.

puppet
page 104

puppeteer
page 104

Q

quilt
page 210

Artist unknown. *Sampler Block Quilt*, 1905.

quilt block
page 210

R

radial balance
page 125

realistic
page 60

Rosa Bonheur. *The King of the Desert*, 19th century.

rhythm
page 128

S

sculpture
page 85

Edgar Degas. *The Little Fourteen-Year-Old Dancer*, 19th–20th century (executed ca. 1880; cast in 1922).

self-portrait
page 67

Mary Cassatt. *Self-Portrait*, ca. 1880.

shade
page 71

shapes
page 22

slab
page 121

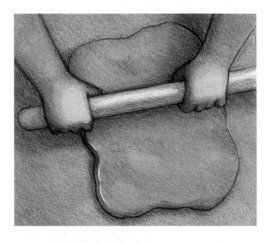

space
page 94

stencil print
page 57

still life
page 70

style
page 56

Franz Marc. *The Tiger*, 1913.

subject
page 60

symbol
page 142

symmetrical balance
page 124

Artist unknown. *Smiling Figurine,* ca. A.D. 6th–9th century.

 T

tactile texture
page 27

texture
page 26

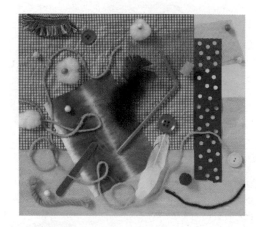

theme
page 207

tint
page 71

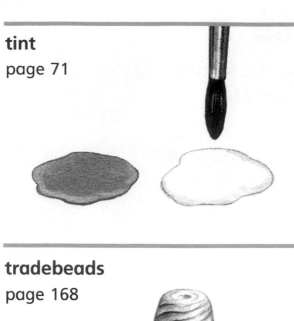

tradebeads
page 168

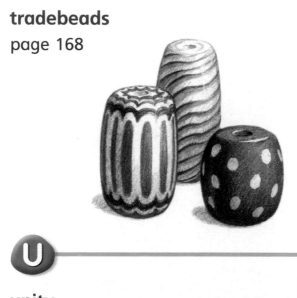

U

unity
page 135

Bill Rabbit. *Earth, Wind, and Fire*, 2003.

Joel Nakamura. *Thunderbird Suite*, 2001.

V

variety
page 135

visual texture
page 32

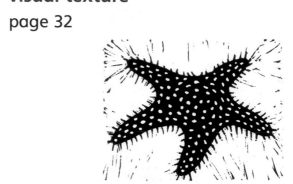

W

warm colors
page 41

Index

Index

Acknowledgments

ILLUSTRATIONS

13, 15 Ron Berg; 20-21, 24-25, 28-29, 34-35, 38-39, 42-43, 53-55, 58-59, 62-63, 68-69, 72-73, 75-77, 87-89, 91-93, 96-97, 102-103, 106-107, 110-111, 122-123, 126-127, 130-131, 136-137, 140-141, 144-145, 156-157, 160-161, 164-165, 168, 170-171, 174-175, 178-179, 190-191, 194-195, 198-199, 204-205, 208-209, 212-213, 239, 244, 246, 248, 246 Renee Graef; 46, 80, 114, 148, 182, 216 Linda Hill Griffith; 239, 245, 248 Anni Matsick; 241-242, 247 Meredith Johnson.

PHOTOGRAPHS

Every effort has been made to secure permission and provide appropriate credit for photographic material. The publisher deeply regrets any omission and pledges to correct errors called to its attention in subsequent editions.

Unless otherwise acknowledged, all photographs are the property of Scott Foresman, a division of Pearson Education.

Photo locators denoted as follows: Top (T), Center (C), Bottom (B), Left (L), Right (R), Background (Bkgd).

Cover: (TR) "Spirit War Pony" by Tavlos/The Trail of Painted Ponies.

Front Matter

iv © 2005 Artists Rights Society (ARS), NY/Art Resource, NY; 1 © West Baffin Eskimo Co-operative Ltd./Dorset Fine Arts; 2 Réunion des Musées Nationaux/Art Resource, NY; 3 National Gallery of Art, Washington, D.C. Gift of the W. L. and May T. Mellon Foundation. Photograph by Bob Grove/Image © 2003 Board of Trustees, National Gallery of Art, Washington D.C.; 4 © Roy King/SuperStock; 5 Smithsonian American Art Museum, Washington, D.C./Art Resource, NY; 6 Rainbow Educational Concepts; 7 (TL) Art Resource, NY, (TR) © Henry Moore Foundation/Scala/Art Resource, NY, (B) © Malcah Zeldis/Art Resource, NY; 10 Lysiane Gauthier/© Musée des Beaux-Arts de Bordeaux; 14 Réunion des Musées Nationaux/Art Resource, NY.

Units 1–6

16 *Children Playing on the Beach*, Ailsa Mellon Bruce Collection, Image © 2003 Board of Trustees/National Gallery of Art, Washington D.C.; 17 (BL) Mary Cassatt. *Self-Portrait*, c. 1880. Watercolor on paper, 13 by 9 5/8 inches (33 by 24.4 cm.). The National Portrait Gallery, Smithsonian Institution. © Art Resource, NY, (R) © C Squared Studios/Getty Images; 18 © Historical Picture Archive/Corbis; 22 © 2005 Artists Rights Society (ARS), NY/VG Bild-Kunst, Bonn./Art Resource, NY; 23 Collection of Roberta Arenson; 26 Art Resource, NY; 27 (TC) Digital Stock, (TR) Corbis, (CR) Getty Images, (CL) © Michael and Patricia Fogden/Corbis; 30 © 2005 Artists Rights Society (ARS), NY/Art Resource, NY; 31 National Gallery of Art, Washington, D.C./SuperStock; 32 Sotheby's; 33 Winifred Wisniewski/Frank Lane Pictures/Corbis; 36 Hirshhorn Museum and Sculpture Garden; 40 © Janet Fish/Licensed by VAGA, New York, NY/Abudefduf Inc.; 41 © MedRes/Getty Images; 44 (BR) © Diane Chrenko Becker, (BR) Getty Images; 45 (T, B) © Diane Chrenko Becker; 48 (L, C, R) Getty Images; 49 © 2005 Successio Miro/Artist Rights Society (ARS), NY/Art Resource, NY; 50 © 2005 Artists Rights Society (ARS), NY/Art Resource, NY; 51 © Bettmann/Corbis; 52 © West Baffin Eskimo Co-operative Ltd./Dorset Fine Arts; 56 © West Baffin Eskimo Co-operative Ltd./Dorset Fine Arts; 57 Courtesy Pena Studio; 60 *Red Squirrel*, Woodner Collection, Image © 2003 Board of Trustees/National Gallery of Art, Washington D.C.; 61 Staedtische Galerie Im Lenbachhaus, Munich; 64 © Estate of Fernand Léger/Artists Rights Society (ARS), NY/Digital image © The Museum of Modern Art/Licensed by Scala/Art Resource, NY; 65 Art Resource, NY; 66 Smithsonian American Art Museum, Washington, D.C./Art Resource, NY; 67 Estate of Alice Neel/Courtesy Robert Miller Gallery, NY; 70 Musée d'Orsay, Paris/SuperStock; 71 © 2005 Artists Rights Society (ARS), NY/VG Bild-Kunst, Bon/Hamburg Kunsthalle/Fotowerkstadt; 74 Kunstmuseum, Bale, Germany/SuperStock; 78 Corbis; 79 *Vanishing Point*, 1999; photo montage on wood, 42" x 60"/©Keba Armand Konte; 82 (L) © Jose Luis Pelaez, Inc./Corbis, (C) © Lee Canfield/SuperStock, (R) SuperStock; 83 Photo by David Heald/© The Solomon R. Guggenheim Foundation, NY; 84 Art Resource, NY; 85 © Davis Mather, Santa Fe, NM; 86 (C) © Phillip Koblentz/Worldtravelimages, (B) © Richard Cummins/Corbis; 90 © David Young-Wolff/PhotoEdit; 94 © 2005 Estate of Pablo Picasso/Artists Rights Society (ARS), NY/Réunion des Musées Nationaux/Art Resource, NY; 95 (BL) © 2005 Artist Rights Society (ARS), NY/ADAGP, Paris/Bridgeman Art Library, (TR) © ART on FILE/Corbis; 98 Smithsonian American Art Museum, Washington, D.C./Art Resource, NY; 99 Collection of Dr. Kurt Gitter and Alice Rae Yelen; 100 Photo by John Bigelow Taylor/Museum of International Folk Art, Santa Fe, NM; 101 Museum of International Folk Art, Santa Fe, NM; 104 Photo by Michel Monteaux/International Folk Art Collections at the Museum of International Folk Art, Santa Fe, NM; 105 International Folk Art Collections at the Museum of International Folk Art, Santa Fe, NM; 108 Heard Museum; 109 Crizmac; 112 (B) The Art Institute of Chicago, (TR) © James Mason/Photo courtesy of the Columbus Cultural Art Center; 113 Photo courtesy of the Columbus Cultural Art Center; 116 (L) © Lon C. Diehn/PhotoEdit, (C) © Omni Photo/Index Stock Imagery, (R) © Dale O'Dell/Corbis; 117 © 2005 The George and Helen Segal Foundation/Licensed by VAGA, NY/Whitney Museum of American Art, NY; 118 Art Resource, NY; 119 (BR) © W. Cody/Corbis, (BL) © Erich Lessing/Art Resource, NY; 120 © Royal Ontario Museum/Corbis; 121 Werner Forman/Art Resource, NY; 124 Universidad Veracruzana; 125 Charles Edwin Wilbour Fund, 49.61.1-4/Brooklyn Museum of Art; 125 © Peter Dazeley/Getty Images; 128 Musée d'Orsay, Paris/SuperStock; 129 © Paul A. Souders/Corbis, Getty Images; 132 © World Films Enterprise/Corbis; 133 National Gallery of Art, Washington, D.C. Gift of the W. L. and May T. Mellon Foundation. Photograph by Bob Grove/Image © 2003 Board of Trustees, National Gallery of Art, Washington D.C.; 134 The Trail of Painted Ponies; 135 (TR, TL) The Trail of Painted Ponies; 138 Photograph © R.M.N.-Gérard Blot/Art Resource, NY; 139 © 2004 Artists Rights Society (ARS), NY/ADAGP, Paris/Christie's Images/SuperStock; 142 © The Trustees of The British Museum; 143 The Bob Bullock Texas State History Museum; 146 Maribeth Koutrakos; 147 Maribeth Koutrakos; 150 (L) © Phil Schermeister/Corbis, (C) Corbis, (R) © Lisa Berkshire/Illustration Works, Inc./Getty Images; 151 © Rodin Museum, Paris. Photograph © 1995/AKG London Ltd.; 152 © 2005 Estate of Alexander Calder/Artists Rights Society (ARS), NY/Gift of Mr. and Mrs. Klaus G. Perls/Image © 2003 Board of Trustees, National Gallery of Art, Washington D.C.; 153 (BR) © Hulton-Deutsch Collection/Corbis, © The Studio Dog/Getty Images, Getty Images, © ThinkStock/SuperStock; 154 Springfield Library & Museums; 155 © Claes Oldenburg & Coosje van Bruggen/Art on File/Corbis; 158 © Roy King/SuperStock; 159 © Jeffry W. Myers/Corbis; 162 *The Wright Brothers* and related rights ™/© of the Wright Family Fund, used under license. Represented by The Roger Richman Agency, Inc./©United States Postal Service. Used with permission. Written authorization from the Postal Service is required to use, reproduce, post, transmit, distribute, or publicly display these images; 163 (C) *Love*, 2002/© United States Postal Service. Used with permission. All rights reserved. Written authorization from the Postal Service is required to use, reproduce, post, transmit, distribute, or publicly display these images. (T) *Special Olympics*, 2003/© United States Postal Service. Used with permission. All rights reserved. Written authorization from the Postal Service is required to use, reproduce, post, transmit, distribute, or publicly display these images; 166 © 2004 Estate of Alexander Calder/Artists Rights Society (ARS), NY/Art Resource, NY; 167 ©2004 Estate of Alexander Calder/Artists Rights Society (ARS), NY/Art Resource, NY; 168 © Francesco Venturi/Kea Publishing Service/Corbis; 169 © The Trustees of The British Museum; 172 Harper Collins Children's Publishers; 176 The Walters Art Museum, Baltimore; 177 © Roger-Viollet/Getty Images; 180 (TR) © Andrew B. Duvall III, (BR) © David H. Wells/Corbis; 181 Richard Termine; 184 (L) SuperStock, (C) © Lindsay Hebberd/Corbis, (R) © Archivo Iconografico, S.A./Corbis; 185 © 1976 Christo.

251

Acknowledgments

Photograph by Jeanne-Claude; 186 © David Bates. Photograph by George Holmes/Jack S. Blanton Museum of Art; 187 (B) Weinberg Clark Photography, (BL) Photograph by Lee Clockman/David Bates; 188 © Pat O'Hara/Corbis; 189 Fred Harvey Collection of the International Folk Art Foundation, Photo by: Blair Clark/Museum of International Folk Art, Santa Fe, NM; 192 Gift of Mr. and Mrs. Klaus G. Perls/Image © 2003 Board of Trustees, National Gallery of Art, Washington D.C.; 193 © 2004 Estate of Alexander Calder/Artists Rights Society (ARS), NY/Art Resource, NY; 196 Photo by John Bigelow Taylor/ Museum of International Folk Art Foundation/Museum of International Folk Art, Santa Fe, NM; 197 The Newark Museum/Art Resource, NY; 200 Museum purchase/Collection of Phoenix Art Museum; 201 *Untitled*, 1991 (from *Cinderella*, Hyperion) Color Poloroid, 24" x 20"/William Wegman; 202 Dallas Museum of Art; 203 © Werner Foreman/Art Resource, NY; 206 Harrod Blank; 207 © The Estate of Keith Haring/Composite Inc.; 210 Smithsonian American Art Museum, Washington, D.C./Art Resource, NY; 211 Smithsonian American Art Museum, Washington, D.C./Art Resource, NY; 214 Alison Watson Photography; 215 Alison Watson Photography; 218 (L) © Jonathan Blair/Corbis, (C) © Bowers Museum of Cultural Art/Corbis; 219 Werner Foreman/Art Resource, NY.

End Matter

220 (TL, TR, CR, BL) Getty Images, (CL, BR) © Corbis; 221 (TL) Getty Images, (TR) © DK Images; 222 (B) © Darrell Gulin/Corbis, (T) © Eric Crichton/Corbis; 223 (CL) © Paul Chauncey/Corbis, (BL, CR) Corbis, (BR) © Pat Doyle/Corbis; 224 (TL) © Robert Yin/Corbis, (TR) © David Frazier/Corbis, (CL) © Peter Dazeley/Corbis, (CR) © Richard Hamilton Smith/Corbis, (BL) © Charles Gold/Corbis, (BR) © Lance Nelson/Corbis; 225 (CL) © Randy Faris/Corbis, (BL) © The Purcell Team/Corbis, (CR) © Lindsey P. Martin/Corbis, (BR) © Nik Wheeler/Corbis; 226 Corbis; 227 © Randy Faris/Corbis; 228 © Bob Krist/Corbis; 229 © Charles & Josette Lenars/Corbis; 230 © Mark Gibson/Corbis; 231 © Tom Bean/Corbis; 232 Corbis; 233 Getty Images; 238 (BR) © Dave Bartruff/Corbis, (TL) © Burnstein Collection/Corbis, (CL) © Alan Schein Photography/Corbis, (BL) Harrod Blank, (TR) Sotheby's, (CR) Charles Edwin Wilbour Fund, 49.61.1-4/Brooklyn Museum of Art; 239 (CR) © Gary W. Carter/Corbis, (CL) © Lon C. Diehn/PhotoEdit, (TL) © Johnny Johnson/Getty Images, (BL) © Royalty-Free/Corbis, (TR) © Omni Photo Communications Inc./Index Stock Imagery; 240 (BR) Everett Collection, Inc., (CR) © R.W. Jones/Corbis, (CL) © ThinkStock/SuperStock, (BL) © Dave G. Houser/Corbis; 241 (CL) © Francesco Venturi/Kea Publishing Service/Corbis, (CR) © Werner Foreman/Art Resource, NY, (CR) © David Samuel Robbins/Corbis; 242 (CR) © David Robinson/Corbis, (TR) © Chris Rogers/Corbis, (BL) © The Trustees of The British Museum, (BR) Corbis, (TL) © Werner H. Müller/Corbis; 243 (TL) Corbis, (TR) © Gianni Dagli Orti/Corbis, (BL) © Alan Schein Photography/Corbis, (CL) © Elio Ciol/Corbis; 244 (BL) © 2004 Estate of Alexander Calder/Artists Rights Society (ARS), NY/Art Resource, NY, (BR) Smithsonian American Art Museum, Washington, D.C./Art Resource, NY, (CR) © Omni Photo/Index Stock Imagery, (TR) © Eric Meola/Getty Images, (CL) © Dave Bartruff/Corbis; 245 (CR) Mary Cassatt. *Self-Portrait*, c. 1880. Watercolor on paper, 13" by 9 5/8" (33 by 24.4 cm.). The National Portrait Gallery, Smithsonian Institution/©Art Resource, NY, (TR) © Christie's Images/SuperStock, (CL) Sotheby's, (TL) Corbis; 246 (BL) Corbis, (CR) © David Young-Wolff/PhotoEdit, (BR) Staedtische Galerie Im Lenbachhaus, Munich, (TR) © Stapleton Collection/Corbis; 247 (CL) Corbis, (BR) © Phil Schermeister/Corbis, (BL) Universidad Veracruzana, (TR) © Zeva Oelbaum/Corbis; 248 (CR) Corbis, (BL) The Trail of Painted Ponies, (CR) © Martha Paulos/Getty Images.

TE Units 1-6

16A (TL) *Children Playing on the Beach*, Ailsa Mellon Bruce Collection, Image © 2003 Board of Trustees/National Gallery of Art, Washington, (TL) © Historical Picture Archive/Corbis, (TC) Art Resource, (TR) © 2005 Artists Rights Society (ARS), NY/Art Resource, NY, (TR) National Gallery of Art, Washington, D.C./SuperStock; 16B (TL) Sotheby's, (TL) Hirshhorn Museum and Sculpture Garden, (TC) © Janet Fish/Licensed by VAGA, New York, NY/Abudefduf Inc., (TC) © Diane Chrenko Becker, © 2005 Successió Miró/Artist Rights Society (ARS), NY/(TR) © 1996 Art Resource, NY; 50A (TL) Art Resource, NY, (TC) © West Baffin Eskimo Cooperative Ltd./Dorset Fine Arts, (TR) *Red Squirrel*, Woodner Collection, Image © 2003 Board of Trustees/National Gallery of Art, Washington, D.C., (TR) © Estate of Fernand Léger/Artists Rights Society (ARS), NY/Digital image © The Museum of Modern Art/Licensed by Scala/Art Resource, NY, (TR) Art Resource, NY; 50B (TL) Smithsonian American Art Museum, Washington, D.C./Art Resource, NY, (TL) Musée d'Orsay, Paris/SuperStock, (TC) Kunstmuseum, Bale, Germany/SuperStock, (TC) *Vanishing Point*, 1999; photo montage on wood, 42" x 60", © Keba Armand Konte, (TR) photo by David Heald/©The Solomon R. Guggenheim Foundation, New York; 83A (TL) Art Resource, NY, (TL) © Phillip Koblentz/World Travel Images, (TR) Réunion des Musées Nationaux/Art Resource, NY, (TR) Smithsonian American Art Museum, Washington, D.C./Art Resource, NY, (CR) Collection of Dr. Kurt Gitter and Alice Rae Yelen; 83B (TL) Photo by John Bigelow Taylor/Museum of International Folk Art, Santa Fe, NM, (TL) Photo by Michel Monteaux/International Folk Art Collections at the Museum of International Folk Art, Santa Fe, NM, (TC) Heard Museum, (TC) Photo courtesy of the Columbus Cultural Art Center, (TR) © 2005 The George and Helen Segal Foundation/Licensed by VAGA, NY/ Whitney Museum of American Art, New York; 118A (TL) Art Resource, NY, (TL) © Royal Ontario Museum/Corbis, (TC) Universidad Veracruzana, (TR) Musée d'Orsay, Paris/SuperStock, (TR) © World Films Enterprise/Corbis, (TR) National Gallery of Art, Washington, D.C. Gift of the W. L. and May T. Mellon Foundation. Photograph by Bob Grove, © 1998 Board of Trustees, National Gallery of Art, Washington, D.C./Image © 2003 Board of Trustees, National Gallery of Art, Washington, D.C.; 118B (TL) © R.M.N.-Gérard Blot./Art Resource, NY, (TL) The Trail of Painted Ponies, (TC) © The Trustees of The British Museum, (TC) Maribeth Koutrakos, (TR) © Rodin Museum, Paris/Photo © 1995 AKG London Ltd.; 152A (TL) © 2005 Estate of Alexander Calder/Artists Rights Society (ARS), NY/Gift of Mr. and Mrs. Klaus G. Perls/Image © 2003 Board of Trustees, National Gallery of Art, Washington, D.C., (TL) Springfield Library & Museums, (TC) © Roy King/SuperStock, (TR) © 2004 Estate of Alexander Calder / Artists Rights Society (ARS), NY /Art Resource, NY; 152B (TL) © Francesco Venturi/Kea Publishing Service/Corbis, (TL) Harper Collins Children's Publishers, (TC) The Walters Art Museum, Baltimore, (TR) © 1976 Christo/Photograph by Jeanne-Claude; 186A (TL) © David Bates. Photograph by George Holmes/Jack S. Blanton Museum of Art, (TL) © Pat O'Hara/Corbis, (TC) Gift of Mr. and Mrs. Klaus G. Perls/Image © 2003 Board of Trustees, National Gallery of Art, Washington, D.C., (TR) Photo by John Bigelow Taylor/ Museum of International Folk Art Foundation/Museum of International Folk Art, Santa Fe, NM, (TR) Museum purchase/Collection of Phoenix Art Museum, (TR) *Untitled*, 1991 (from Cinderella, Hyperion) Color Polaroid, 24"x20"/William Wegman; 186B (TL) Dallas Museum of Art, (TL) Harrod Blank, (TC) Smithsonian American Art Museum, Washington, DC/Art Resource, NY, (TC) Alison Watson Photography, (TR) © Werner Foreman/Art Resource, NY.

252

Teacher Resources

Art Connections

	Strands/Themes/Concepts	Fine Art Images	Studios/Projects
Social Studies	History	*Self-Portrait*, U1 p. 17 *The Gatchina Palace Egg*, U5 p. 176	
	Geography	*London Bridge*, U1 p. 30 *Children's Museum of Houston*, U3 p. 86 *Plowing in the Nivernais (Labourage Nivernais)*, U4 p. 138 *Running Fence, Sonoma and Marin Counties, California*, U5 p. 185	
	Economics	*The Construction Workers*, U2 p. 50	
	Government	*First Flight • Wright Brothers • 1903*, U5 p. 162	
	Citizenship	*Unveiling of the Statue of Liberty (After Edward Moran)*, U6 p. 211	
	Culture	*The Return of the Sun*, U2 p. 52 *Young Owl Takes a Ride*, U2 p. 56 *Vanishing Point*, U2 p. 79 *Jar*, U3 p. 108 *Inlay of a king or deity*, U4 p. 125 *Papayan (Colombian) Pectoral*, U5 p. 169 *Birch Basket*, U6 p. 188 *Serape*, U6 p. 189 *Corpus Christi Festival Headdress*, U6 p. 196 *Epa Headdress*, U6 p. 197 *Mask: Bear Spirit*, U6 p. 202 *Large Dance Headdress*, U6 p. 219	U3 Studio 6 p. 110 U6 Studio 1 p. 190 U6 Studio 3 p. 198 U6 Studio 4 p. 204
	Science, Technology, and Society	*Toy Helicopter*, U3 p. 100 *The Doll Car*, U6 p. 206	
Science	Life Science	*Cat and Bird*, U1 p. 22 *Rhinoceros*, U1 p. 26 *Young Owl Takes a Ride*, U2 p. 56 *Virgin Forest*, U2 p. 74 *Yellow Cow*, U2 p. 83 *Baboon*, U3 p. 84 *Bird in Space*, U3 p. 95 *Tiger*, U3 p. 98 *Polar Bear*, U3 p. 99 *Horse Toy*, U3 p. 101 *The Grouchy Ladybug*, U5 p. 172 *Finny Fish*, U6 p. 192 *Mask: Bear Spirit*, U6 p. 202	U1 Studio 2 p. 24 U1 Studio 6 p. 42 U2 Studio 1 p. 54 U2 Studio 2 p. 58 U2 Studio 3 p. 62
	Earth Science	*The Great Wave Off Kanagawa*, U1 p. 18	U2 Portfolio Project p. 80
	Physical Science	Photograph of Cyclist, U4 p. 129	
	Space and Technology	*Toy Helicopter*, U3 p. 100	
Reading	Myself and Others	*Self-Portrait*, U1 p. 17 *Jonathan and Lorraine*, U1 p. 40	U1 Portfolio Project p. 46 U2 Studio 4 p. 68

	Strands/Themes/Concepts	Fine Art Images	Studios/Projects
	Myself and Others (continued)	*Woman with Three Hairs Surrounded by Birds in the Night*, U1 p. 49 *Sarah Greenberg*, U2 p. 67 *Feeding the Dogs*, U6 p. 200 *We the Youth*, U6 p. 207	
	The World Around Us	*Children Playing on the Beach*, U1 p. 16 *The Great Wave Off Kanagawa*, U1 p. 18 *London Bridge*, U1 p. 30 *The Boating Party*, U1 p. 31 *Unveiling of the Statue of Liberty (After Edward Moran)*, U6 p. 211	U1 Studio 1 p. 20 U1 Studio 6 p. 42 U1 Portfolio Project p. 46 U2 Studio 6 p. 76 U3 Studio 2 p. 92 U5 Studio 1 p. 156
	Learning and Working	*The Construction Workers*, U2 p. 50 *Firehouse Door*, U5 p. 158	
	Traditions	*Middle Billy Goat Gruff*, U1 p. 23 *Born Around the Campfires of Our Past*, U4 p. 143 *Serape*, U6 p. 189 *Corpus Christi Festival Headdress*, U6 p. 196 *Epa Headdress*, U6 p. 197 *Mask: Bear Spirit*, U6 p. 202 *Mask Representing Chalchihuitlicue "Lady Precious Green,"* U6 p. 203 *Sampler Block Quilt*, U6 p. 210 *Unveiling of the Statue of Liberty (After Edward Moran)*, U6 p. 211 *Large Dance Headdress*, U6 p. 219	U6 Studio 1 p. 190 U6 Studio 3 p. 198 U6 Studio 4 p. 204 U6 Studio 6 p. 212
	Journeys in Time and Space	*Born Around the Campfires of Our Past*, U4 p. 143 *First Flight • Wright Brothers • 1903*, U5 p. 162	
	Creativity	*Dr. Seuss and the Cat in the Hat*, U5 p. 154 *The Whittler*, U6 p. 186	
Fine Arts	**Music**	*Three Musicians*, U2 p. 64 *Three Musicians*, U2 p. 65 *The Fifer*, U4 p. 118 *Tang Dynasty Sheng Player, Dancer, and Panpipe Player*, U4 p. 120 *Aztec Dancing Whistle*, U4 p. 121	U4 Studio 1 p. 122
	Theatre	*The Star (Dancer on Stage)*, U4 p. 128	
	Dance	*Marionettes: Sword Fighter and Dancer*, U3 p. 104 *The Star (Dancer on Stage)*, U4 p. 128	
Elements of Art	**Line**	*Children Playing on the Beach*, U1 p. 16 *The Great Wave Off Kanagawa*, U1 p. 18 *London Bridge*, U1 p. 30 *The Boating Party*, U1 p. 31	U1 Studio 1 p. 20 U1 Studio 6 p. 42 U1 Portfolio Project p. 46

Art Connections

Strands/Themes/Concepts	Fine Art Images	Studios/Projects
Line (continued)	*The Construction Workers*, U2 p. 50 *Virgin Forest*, U2 p. 74 *Tiger*, U3 p. 98 *Running Fence, Sonoma and Marin Counties, California*, U5 p. 185 *The Whittler*, U6 p. 186 *Finny Fish*, U6 p. 192 *We the Youth*, U6 p. 207	
Shape	*Cat and Bird*, U1 p. 22 *Middle Billy Goat Gruff*, U1 p. 23 *Woman with Three Hairs Surrounded by Birds in the Night*, U1 p. 49 *The Construction Workers*, U2 p. 50 *The Return of the Sun*, U2 p. 52 *Bull's Head*, U3 p. 94 *Little Spider*, U5 p. 152 *Pin*, U5 p. 167 *Finny Fish*, U6 p. 192 *We the Youth*, U6 p. 207	U1 Studio 2 p. 24 U1 Portfolio Project p. 46 U2 Studio 2 p. 58 U2 Studio 6 p. 76 U2 Portfolio Project p. 80 U3 Studio 2 p. 92 U4 Studio 3 p. 130 U4 Portfolio Project p. 148 U5 Portfolio Project p. 182
Form	*Baboon*, U3 p. 84 *Children's Museum of Houston*, U3 p. 86 *Woodrow*, U3 p. 95 *Bird in Space*, U3 p. 95 *Tang Dynasty Sheng Player, Dancer, and Panpipe Player*, U4 p. 120 *Aztec Dancing Whistle*, U4 p. 121 *The Thinker*, U4 p. 151 *Little Spider*, U5 p. 152 *Bicyclette, Ensevelié*, U5 p. 155 *Cheval Rouge (Red Horse)*, U5 p. 166 *The Gatchina Palace Egg*, U5 p. 176 *Birch Basket*, U6 p. 188 *Finny Fish*, U6 p. 192 *Big Bird*, U6 p. 193	U3 Studio 1 p. 88 U3 Studio 2 p. 92 U3 Studio 3 p. 96 U3 Studio 4 p. 102 U3 Studio 5 p. 106 U3 Studio 6 p. 110 U3 Portfolio Project p. 114 U4 Studio 1 p. 122 U4 Studio 2 p. 126 U5 Studio 1 p. 156 U5 Studio 4 p. 170 U6 Studio 2 p. 194 U6 Studio 4 p. 204 U6 Studio 5 p. 208
Space	*Plowing in the Nivernais (Labourage Nivernais)*, U4 p. 138 *The Spring (Le Printemps)*, U4 p. 139	
Value		U2 Studio 5 p. 72 U2 Portfolio Project p. 80
Color	*Children Playing on the Beach*, U1 p. 16 *Conception Synchromy*, U1 p. 36 *Jonathan and Lorraine*, U1 p. 40 *Mr. Bubbles*, U1 p. 45 *Fire and Ice*, U1 p. 45 *Woman with Three Hairs Surrounded by Birds in the Night*, U1 p. 49 *Sarah Greenberg*, U2 p. 67 *Yellow Cow*, U2 p. 83 *Cheval Rouge (Red Horse)*, U5 p. 166	U1 Studio 5 p. 38 U1 Studio 6 p. 42 U1 Portfolio Project p. 46 U2 Studio 5 p. 72 U6 Portfolio Project p. 216

Strands/Themes/Concepts	Fine Art Images	Studios/Projects

Texture	*Rhinoceros*, U1 p. 26
	London Bridge, U1 p. 30
	The Boating Party, U1 p. 31
	The King of the Desert, U1 p. 32
	Young Owl Takes a Ride, U2 p. 56
	Red Squirrel, U2 p. 60
	Big Elk, a Famous Warrior, U2 p. 66
	Baboon, U3 p. 84
	*Running Fence, Sonoma and Marin
	   Counties, California*, U5 p. 185
	*Mask Representing Chalchihuitlicue
	   "Lady Precious Green,"* U6 p. 203
	Large Dance Headdress, U6 p. 219
		U1 Studio 3 p. 28
		U1 Studio 4 p. 34
		U6 Portfolio Project p. 216

Principles of Design — **Balance**	*Cat and Bird*, U1 p. 22
	Smiling Figurine, U4 p. 124
	Inlay of a king or deity, U4 p. 125
	Breezing Up, U4 p. 133
	Double-Headed Serpent, U4 p. 142
	Firehouse Door, U5 p. 158
	*Papayan (Colombian)
	   Pectoral*, U5 p. 169
	The Grouchy Ladybug, U5 p. 172
	Serape, U6 p. 189
	Mask: Bear Spirit, U6 p. 202
	*Mask Representing Chalchihuitlicue
	   "Lady Precious Green,"* U6 p. 203
		U4 Studio 2 p. 126

Emphasis	*The King of the Desert*, U1 p. 32
	Jonathan and Lorraine, U1 p. 40
	The Whittler, U6 p. 186
	Serape, U6 p. 189
	Feeding the Dogs, U6 p. 200
	Cinderella, U6 p. 201
	Mask: Bear Spirit, U6 p. 202
	*Unveiling of the Statue of Liberty
	   (After Edward Moran)*, U6 p. 211
	*Past, Present, and Future; Grecian Sea;
	   Pearl Island*, U6 p. 215	

Proportion	*Plowing in the Nivernais (Labourage Nivernais)*, U4 p. 138 *The Spring (Le Printemps)*, U4 p. 139 *Feeding the Dogs*, U6 p. 200	U4 Studio 5 p. 140
Pattern	*London Bridge*, U1 p. 30 *Birch Basket*, U6 p. 188 *Serape*, U6 p. 189 *Sampler Block Quilt*, U6 p. 210	U6 Studio 1 p. 190 U6 Studio 6 p. 212 U6 Portfolio Project p. 216

Rhythm	*The Great Wave Off Kanagawa*,
	   U1 p. 18
	The Star (Dancer on Stage), U4 p. 128
	Monet Painting in His Floating Studio,
	   U4 p. 132
	Breezing Up, U4 p. 133
	*Plowing in the Nivernais (Labourage
	   Nivernais)*, U4 p. 138
		U4 Studio 3 p. 130

Art Connections

Strands/Themes/Concepts	Fine Art Images	Studios/Projects
Rhythm (continued)	*Running Fence, Sonoma and Marin Counties, California,* U5 p. 185 *We the Youth,* U6 p. 207	
Unity	*Kitty Cat's Ball,* U4 p. 134 *Thunderbird Suite,* U4 p. 135 *Earth, Wind, and Fire,* U4 p. 135 *Baseball Locker Room,* U4 p. 147 *Sampler Block Quilt,* U6 p. 210	U4 Studio 4 p. 136 U4 Portfolio Project p. 148 U6 Studio 6 p. 212
Variety	*Kitty Cat's Ball,* U4 p. 134 *Thunderbird Suite,* U4 p. 135 *Earth, Wind, and Fire,* U4 p. 135 *Baseball Locker Room,* U4 p. 147 *Corpus Christi Festival Headdress,* U6 p. 196 *Sampler Block Quilt,* U6 p. 210	U4 Studio 4 p. 136 U4 Portfolio Project p. 148 U6 Studio 6 p. 212

Techniques/Media	Fine Art Images	Studios/Projects
Collage	*Middle Billy Goat Gruff,* U1 p. 23 *The Grouchy Ladybug,* U5 p. 172	U1 Studio 2 p. 24 U2 Studio 3 p. 62 U2 Studio 6 p. 76 U4 Studio 4 p. 136 U5 Studio 3 p. 164
Computer Graphics **Computer Generated Art/Design**	*Special Olympics,* U5 p. 163	
Drawing • **Charcoal** • **Crayon** • **Pastel** • **Pen & Ink** • **Pencil**	*Fernand Léger,* U2 p. 51 *The Star (Dancer on Stage),* U4 p. 128	U1 Studio 1 p. 20 U1 Studio 3 p. 28 U2 Studio 4 p. 68 U4 Studio 3 p. 130 U4 Studio 5 p. 140 U6 Studio 6 p. 212
Glass	*Mr. Bubbles,* U1 p. 45 *Fire and Ice,* U1 p. 45	
Metal	*Papayan (Colombian) Pectoral,* U5 p. 169	U5 Portfolio Project p. 182
Mixed Media/ **Multi-Media**	*Cat and Bird,* U1 p. 22 *Pin,* U5 p. 167 *The Gatchina Palace Egg,* U5 p. 176 *Corpus Christi Festival Headdress,* U6 p. 196 *The Doll Car,* U6 p. 206 *Past, Present, and Future; Grecian Sea; Pearl Island,* U6 p. 215	U1 Studio 6 p. 42 U1 Portfolio Project p. 46 U4 Studio 4 p. 136 U5 Studio 6 p. 178 U6 Studio 3 p. 198 U6 Studio 4 p. 204 U6 Studio 5 p. 208
Mosaic	*Double-Headed Serpent,* U4 p. 142 *Born Around the Campfires of Our Past,* U4 p. 143	U4 Studio 6 p. 144
Painting • **Acrylic** • **Oil** • **Watercolor**	*Children Playing on the Beach,* U1 p. 16 *Woman with Three Hairs Surrounded by Birds in the Night,* U1 p. 49 *The Construction Workers,* U2 p. 50 *Red Squirrel,* U2 p. 60	U1 Studio 4 p. 34 U1 Studio 5 p. 38 U2 Studio 5 p. 72 U5 Studio 2 p. 160

Techniques/Media

Techniques/Media	Fine Art Images	Studios/Projects
Painting (continued) • **Acrylic** • **Oil** • **Watercolor**	*Sarah Greenberg*, U2 p. 67 *Blumen in der Nacht (Flowers at Night)*, U2 p. 71 *Yellow Cow*, U2 p. 83 *The Fifer*, U4 p. 118 *The Spring (Le Printemps)*, U4 p. 139 *Firehouse Door*, U5 p. 158 *The Whittler*, U6 p. 186 *Feeding the Dogs*, U6 p. 200 *We the Youth*, U6 p. 207	
Paper		U5 Studio 5 p. 174 U6 Studio 1 p. 190
Photography	*Vanishing Point*, U2 p. 79 *Cinderella*, U6 p. 201	
Printing	*The Great Wave Off Kanagawa*, U1 p. 18 *Rhinoceros*, U1 p. 26 *Young Owl Takes a Ride*, U2 p. 56 *Los Pescados Peña*, U2 p. 57	U2 Studio 1 p. 54 U2 Studio 2 p. 58 U2 Portfolio Project p. 80 U4 Portfolio Project p. 148
Sculpture • **Clay** • **Stone** • **Metal** • **Mixed Media** • **Pottery/Ceramics** • **Industrial Design** • **Furniture** • **Installations**	*Baboon*, U3 p. 84 *Bull's Head*, U3 p. 94 *Woodrow*, U3 p. 95 *Bird in Space*, U3 p. 95 *Tiger*, U3 p. 98 *Polar Bear*, U3 p. 99 *Toy Helicopter*, U3 p. 100 *Horse Toy*, U3 p. 101 *Marionettes: Sword Fighter and Dancer*, U3 p. 104 *Burma Doll*, U3 p. 105 *Jar*, U3 p. 108 *Untitled (Frida Kahlo)*, U3 p. 109 *Tang Dynasty Sheng Player, Dancer, and Panpipe Player*, U4 p. 120 *Aztec Dancing Whistle*, U4 p. 121 *Smiling Figurine*, U4 p. 124 *Earth, Wind, and Fire*, U4 p. 135 *The Thinker*, U4 p. 151 *Bicyclette, Ensevelié*, U5 p. 155 *Cheval Rouge (Red Horse)*, U5 p. 166 *Finny Fish*, U6 p. 192 *Big Bird*, U6 p. 193	U3 Studio 1 p. 88 U3 Studio 2 p. 92 U3 Studio 3 p. 96 U3 Studio 4 p. 102 U3 Studio 5 p. 106 U3 Studio 6 p. 110 U3 Portfolio Project p. 114 U4 Studio 1 p. 122 U4 Studio 2 p. 126 U5 Studio 1 p. 156 U5 Studio 4 p. 170 U6 Studio 2 p. 194 U6 Studio 5 p. 208
Textiles • **cloth** • **yarn** • **clothing** • **costume**	*Birch Basket*, U6 p. 188 *Serape*, U6 p. 189 *Sampler Block Quilt*, U6 p. 210 *Unveiling of the Statue of Liberty (After Edward Moran)*, U6 p. 211	U6 Portfolio Project p. 216
Wood	*Epa Headdress*, U6 p. 197 *Mask: Bear Spirit*, U6 p. 202 *Mask Representing Chalchihuitlicue "Lady Precious Green,"* U6 p. 203 *Large Dance Headdress*, U6 p. 219	

Art Connections

Techniques/Media	Fine Art Images	Studios/Projects
Architecture	*Children's Museum of Houston,* U3 p. 86 *Baseball Locker Room,* U4 p. 147 *The Gatchina Palace Egg,* U5 p. 176 *Running Fence, Sonoma and Marin Counties, California,* U5 p. 185	U3 Studio 1 p. 88 U3 Studio 2 p. 92

Front Matter	Art Prints	Fine Art Transparencies
Start with Art		Transparency 2-7a: *The Janitor Who Paints* Transparency 2-7b: *Study for a Family Group* Transparency 2-7c: *Thanksgiving*
Visit a Museum		Transparency 2-10: *Rabbits Nibbling Carrots*
Make a Sketchbook Journal		Transparency 2-14: *Seven Monkeys*

Unit/Lesson	Art Prints	Fine Art Transparencies
Unit 1 Opener	Art Print 1: *Children Playing on the Beach*	Transparency 2-16: *Children Playing on the Beach* Transparency 2-17: *Self Portrait*
Unit 1, Lesson 1		Transparency 2-18: *The Great Wave Off Kanagawa*
Unit 1, Lesson 2		Transparency 2-22:*Cat and Bird* Transparency 2-23: *Middle Billy Goat Gruff*
Unit 1, Lesson 3		Transparency 2-26: *Rhinoceros*
Look and Compare	Art Print 2: *London Bridge* Art Print 3: *The Boating Party*	Transparency 2-30: *London Bridge* Transparency 2-31:*The Boating Party*
Unit 1, Lesson 4		Transparency 2-32: *The King of the Desert*
Unit 1, Lesson 5		Transparency 2-36: *Conception Synchromy*
Unit 1, Lesson 6		Transparency 2-40: *Jonathan and Lorraine*
Artist at Work		Transparency 2-45a: *Mr. Bubbles* Transparency 2-45b: *Fire and Ice*
Unit 1 Review	Art Print 4: *Woman with Three Hairs Surrounded by Birds in the Night*	Transparency 2-49: *Woman with Three Hairs Surrounded by Birds in the Night*
Unit 2 Opener	Art Print 5: *The Construction Workers*	Transparency 2-50: *The Construction Workers* Transparency 2-51: *Fernand Léger*
Unit 2, Lesson 1		Transparency 2-52: *The Return of the Sun*
Unit 2, Lesson 2		Transparency 2-56: *Young Owl Takes a Ride* Transparency 2-57: *Los Pescados Peña*

Art Prints and Transparencies

Art Prints and Transparencies

Unit/Lesson	Art Prints	Fine Art Transparencies
Unit 2, Lesson 3		Transparency 2-60: *Red Squirrel* Transparency 2-61: *The Tiger*
Look and Compare	Art Print 6: *Three Musicians* Art Print 7: *Three Musicians*	Transparency 2-64: *Three Musicians* Transparency 2-65: *Three Musicians*
Unit 2, Lesson 4		Transparency 2-66: *Big Elk, Famous Warrior* Transparency 2-67: *Sarah Greenberg*
Unit 2, Lesson 5		Transparency 2-70: *Still Life with Basket* Transparency 2-71: *Blumen in der Nacht (Flowers at Night)*
Unit 2, Lesson 6		Transparency 2-74: *Virgin Forest*
Artist at Work		Transparency 2-79: *Vanishing Point*
Unit 2 Review	Art Print 8: *Yellow Cow*	Transparency 2-83: *Yellow Cow*
Unit 3 Opener	Art Print 9: *Baboon*	Transparency 2-84: *Baboon*
Unit 3, Lesson 1		Transparency 2-86: *Children's Museum of Houston*
Unit 3, Lesson 2		
Unit 3, Lesson 3		Transparency 2-94: *Bull's Head* Transparency 2-95a: *Woodrow* Transparency 2-95b: *Bird in Space*
Look and Compare	Art Print 10: *Tiger* Art Print 11: *Polar Bear*	Transparency 2-98: *Tiger* Transparency 2-99: *Polar Bear*
Unit 3, Lesson 4		Transparency 2-100: *Toy Helicopter* Transparency 2-101: *Horse Toy*
Unit 3, Lesson 5		Transparency 2-104: *Marionettes: Sword Fighter and Dancer* Transparency 2-105: *Burma Doll*
Unit 3, Lesson 6		Transparency 2-108: Jar Transparency 2-109: *Untitled*
Artist at Work		Transparency 2-112: *A Sunday on La Grande Jatte—1884*
Unit 3 Review	Art Print 12: *Walk, Don't Walk*	Transparency 2-117: *Walk, Don't Walk*
Unit 4 Opener	Art Print 13: *The Fifer*	Transparency 2-118: *The Fifer* Transparency 2-119: *Painter Édouard Manet*
Unit 4, Lesson 1		Transparency 2-120: *Tang Dynasty Sheng Player, Dancer, and Panpipe Player* Transparency 2-121: *Aztec Dancing Whistle*
Unit 4, Lesson 2		Transparency 2-124: *Smiling Figurine* Transparency 2-125: *Inlay of a king or deity*
Unit 4, Lesson 3		Transparency 2-128: *The Star (Dancer on Stage)*

Art Connections

Unit/Lesson	Art Prints	Fine Art Transparencies
Look and Compare	Art Print 14: *Monet Painting in His Floating Studio* Art Print 15: *Breezing Up*	Transparency 2-132: *Monet Painting in His Floating Studio* Transparency 2-133: *Breezing Up*
Unit 4, Lesson 4		Transparency 2-134: *Kitty Cat's Ball* Transparency 2-135a: *Thunderbird Suite* Transparency 2-135b: *Earth, Wind, and Fire*
Unit 4, Lesson 5		Transparency 2-138: *Plowing in the Nivernais (Labourage Nivernais)* Transparency 2-139: *The Spring (Le Printemps)*
Unit 4, Lesson 6		Transparency 2-142: *Double-Headed Serpent* Transparency 2-143: *Born Around the Campfires of Our Past*
Artist at Work		Transparency 2-147: *Baseball Locker Room*
Unit 4 Review	Art Print 16: *The Thinker*	Transparency 2-151: *The Thinker*
Unit 5 Opener	Art Print 17: *Little Spider*	Transparency 2-152: *Little Spider*
Unit 5, Lesson 1		Transparency 2-154: *Dr. Seuss and the Cat in the Hat* Transparency 2-155: *Bicyclette Enseveli*
Unit 5, Lesson 2		Transparency 2-158: *Firehouse Door*
Unit 5, Lesson 3		
Look and Compare	Art Print 18: *Cheval Rouge (Red Horse)* Art Print 19: *Pin*	Transparency 2-166: *Cheval Rouge (Red Horse)* Transparency 2-167: *Pin*
Unit 5, Lesson 4		Transparency 2-169: *Papayan (Colombian) Pectoral*
Unit 5, Lesson 5		Transparency 2-172: *The Grouchy Ladybug*
Unit 5, Lesson 6		Transparency 2-176: *The Gatchina Palace Egg*
Artist at Work		
Unit 5 Review	Art Print 20: *Running Fence, Sonoma and Marin Counties, California*	Transparency 2-185: *Running Fence, Sonoma and Marin Counties, California*
Unit 6 Opener	Art Print 21: *The Whittler*	Transparency 2-186: *The Whittler*
Unit 6, Lesson 1		Transparency 2-188: *Birch Basket* Transparency 2-189: *Serape*
Unit 6, Lesson 2		Transparency 2-192: *Finny Fish* Transparency 2-193: *Big Bird*

Unit/Lesson	Art Prints	Fine Art Transparencies
Unit 6, Lesson 3		Transparency 2-196: *Corpus Christi Festival Headdress* Transparency 2-197: *Epa Headdress*
Look and Compare	Art Print 22: *Feeding the Dogs* Art Print 23: *Cinderella*	Transparency 2-200: *Feeding the Dogs* Transparency 2-201: *Cinderella*
Unit 6, Lesson 4		Transparency 2-202: *Mask: Bear Spirit* Transparency 2-203: *Mask Representing Chalchihuitlicue "Lady Precious Green"*
Unit 6, Lesson 5		Transparency 2-206: *The Doll Car* Transparency 2-207: *We the Youth*
Unit 6, Lesson 6		Transparency 2-210: *Sampler Block Quilt* Transparency 2-211: *Unveiling of the Statue of Liberty (After Edward Moran)*
Artist at Work		Transparency 2-215: *Past, Present, and Future; Grecian Sea; Pearl Island*
Unit 6 Review	Art Print 24: *Large Dance Headdress*	Transparency 2-219: *Large Dance Headdress*

Technique Handbook

Using Glue

1

Have students cover the work area with newspaper. Remind them to find an arrangement that pleases them before they apply the glue.

2

Demonstrate applying glue near the center of the object. Make available brushes or instruct students to use their fingers to spread glue to the edges. Point out that too much glue causes paper to wrinkle.

3

Instruct students to lay paper over the object and gently rub to make sure that all edges are glued down.

Using Paper

1

Help students notice the texture and color of different kinds of paper. Point out different uses for paper, such as cover stock or tissue paper.

2

Students can cut paper with scissors. They can tear paper. Or they can first fold, then tear. Help students notice how the edges of the paper look.

3

Encourage students to experiment with paper. They can curl paper by wrapping a strip around a pencil, for example. They can also fold or crumple paper.

Drawing with Crayons and Oil Pastels

1

Students can use the tip of a crayon or an oil pastel to make thin lines.

2

Show students how to make thick lines with the side of a crayon or oil pastel. Peel part or all of the paper off, depending on how thick the student wants the line to be. Then have students draw thick lines with the side.

3

Remind students that pressing firmly with a crayon or oil pastel makes a bold or bright color. Pressing lightly yields a softer color. Note that oil pastels break somewhat more easily than crayons do. Caution students about pressing *too* hard.

4

Demonstrate mixing colors by pressing lightly with one color (the lighter color), then going over it lightly with another, darker color. Show how to blend colors by rubbing over them with a tissue.

Using a Paintbrush

1

Tell students to dip only the bristles into the paint. To make a thin line, use the tip of the brush. Use the side for broader lines. Advise students not to push down hard.

2

Remind students to clean their paintbrushes before they switch colors. Make water and paper towels available.

3

Painters should wash each paintbrush with warm, soapy water. After a clear rinse, blot the paintbrush on a paper towel, then place in a can or jar with the bristles up.

Mixing Colors with Tempera Paints

1

Demonstrate for students how to mix secondary colors. For orange, start with yellow and add a dot of red. For green, start with yellow and add a dot of blue. For violet, start with red and add a dot of blue.

2

Tell students that a tint is a lighter value of a color. To mix a tint, start with white. Then add a small amount of color to it. Remind students to add very small amounts of color until they get the tint they want.

3

To mix a shade, or a darker value of a color, have students begin with a color. Then add a small dot of black. Adding small amounts is important when mixing shades.

Making Prints

1

Point out that when students dip an object into paint, then press it on paper, they are making a print.

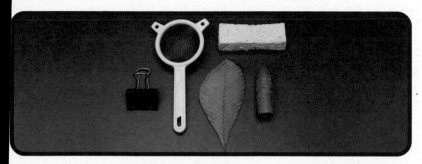

2

Students can also make their own stamps out of cardboard, craft foam, or clean foam plates or meat trays. After students cut a desired shape, attach a twisted piece of masking tape to the back for a handle. Remind students to press the stamp onto their paper firmly, but not to wiggle it.

3

To make a relief print, have students draw a design on a clean foam plate or meat tray. Direct them to roll water-based printer's ink evenly over the design. Have students place a sheet of paper over the inked surface and rub gently. Pull the paper off and see the print.

Making a Collage

1

Have students first decide on an idea. Will their collage show only shape and color? Will it include photographs?

2

Tell students to select shapes, colors, and pictures that go well together. For example, they can choose shapes that are all warm or cool colors. They can also choose pictures that have related subjects.

3

Encourage students to experiment with different arrangements before they begin gluing. Suggest that they cover all parts of the background paper. Remind them to glue one piece at a time.

Technique Handbook

Working with Clay

1

Have students cover the work area with brown paper or canvas. Make available tools for carving, found objects for pressing designs into the clay, and bowls of water. Provide cardboard on which to dry artworks.

2

Show students how to prepare clay by wedging it. Thump the clay down on the work surface. Press into it with the heels of your hands. Tell students to continue turning and pressing until there are no more air bubbles.

3

Demonstrate how to score clay parts, then add slip, or water-thinned clay, and stick the clay parts together.

Sculpting with Clay

1

Have students use a tool to carve shapes from the clay. Students can then join shapes together, or they can press tools or found objects into the clay to show texture.

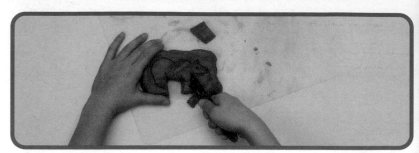

2

To make a clay sculpture by pinching, have students begin with a ball of clay. Tell them to press one thumb into the middle of the ball. Then they should push outward, or pinch the clay between their thumb and their fingers on the outside of the ball.

3

To use the coil method, instruct students to make ropes of clay. Show how to roll a lump of clay on the work surface with flat palms, starting in the middle and working outward as the rope lengthens. Students can coil ropes into forms by stacking them or by cutting and pressing pieces together.

Using Found Objects in an Artwork

1

Students can use found objects in many types of artworks. Tell them to be on the lookout for usable objects that people throw away.

2

Point out that found objects can also be natural objects. Remind students not to pick up anything they cannot identify. Also, students should never use living materials.

3

Students can use found objects in a collage. Have them try different arrangements before gluing.

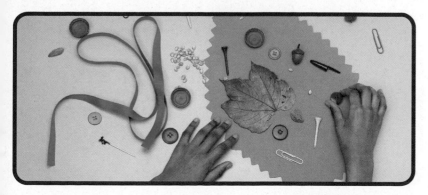

4

Students can build a sculpture out of found objects. The sculpture may stand on its own, or it can be formed on a background.

5

Tell students that most found objects can be used as stamps to make prints. Have students dip the surface of a found object in paint, then press it onto paper.

6

Students can add interest to a sculpture by pressing found objects into the clay to create texture.

Technique Handbook

Weaving

1

Follow these steps to make looms for weaving. Cut squares or rectangles of sturdy cardboard. Keep in mind that the finished product will be roughly the size of the loom. Draw a line half an inch from the top and bottom edge of the loom. Then make a mark every quarter inch or so along the lines. Cut out a little V at each mark to make "teeth" along the top and bottom of the loom. ⚠

2

Now students can create a warp on the loom. Tell them to make a loop in one end of a long piece of yarn and hook it around the first "tooth" at the top of the loom. From there, the yarn goes down and around the first "tooth" at the bottom. Then it comes back up and around the next "tooth" at the top, then down, and so on. Advise students to pull snugly, but not too tightly as they create the warp. Have students continue hooking the yarn until the loom is full. At the last "tooth," students should loop the yarn around an extra time and tie a knot.

3

Now students can begin weaving. They can use their fingers or they may tie yarn through a hole in a narrow craft stick. Demonstrate how to go over and under, over and under, all the way across the warp. As they begin a second row, point out that it will be opposite the previous row—i.e., under and over, under and over. Tell students not to weave too close to the loom's "teeth." They will need to leave enough room to tie knots in the warp threads when they remove the weaving from the loom.

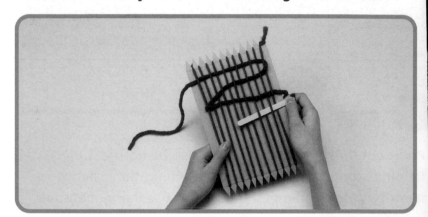

4

Show students how to weave each row at about a 45° angle to the previous row. Then provide plastic forks for students to use as "rakes" to pull each row tight against the others. Weaving at an angle prevents the warp threads from getting pulled in too tightly at the edges. When the weaving is complete, tell students to unhook the warp threads from the ends of the loom. Knot each pair of warp threads together and secure any loose yarn ends on the sides of the weaving.

Making a Mosaic

1

Students can make mosaics out of a number of materials, depending on what you have available. Tell students that the small pieces, or tesserae, can be paper, stones, beads, or shells, for example.

2

Students can draw the shape for their mosaic on a base. The base can be heavy paper, wood, or cardboard. It can also be an item a student wants to design, such as a small box or picture frame.

3

Instruct students to prepare their tesserae. If they are using paper, they must choose colors. Then they can decide whether to cut or tear the pieces. Help students notice the different effects the two methods create. ⚠

4

Tell students to begin gluing tesserae at the center of their mosaic's shape. They should cover a small area with glue and place their tesserae, leaving a small amount of space around each piece. Then, continuing to work outward from the center, students should apply glue in another area, place tesserae, and so on, until the shape is covered.

Technique Handbook

Stitching

1

Show students a large darning needle. Point out that the eye is large enough for thick fibers, such as yarn. WARNING: Even a blunt darning needle is somewhat sharp. Students should not use needles without the help of an adult. ⚠

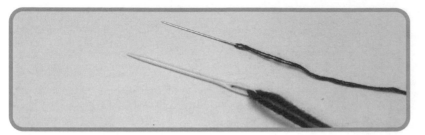

2

Provide darning needles and yarn. Instruct students to dampen their fingers, then pinch the end of the yarn. Push this flattened end of yarn through the eye of the needle, then pull it through. Tie a knot in the end of the yarn. ⚠

3

Have students push the needle through from the back of the fabric and pull until the knot stops the yarn. When students finish stitching, instruct them to push the needle through to the back of the fabric. There, they should make two small stitches right next to each other. Then they should push the needle under these two stitches, knot the yarn, and cut it off. ⚠

Making Armatures

1

An armature provides a basic shape for a mask, a sculpture, or other form. Materials used in an armature depend on the use or form of the final product.

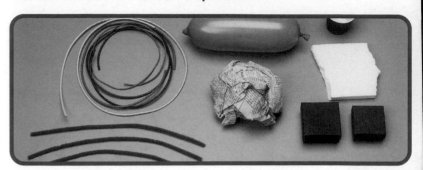

2

Show students how to cut and bend wire or pipe cleaners in whatever shape they desire. ⚠

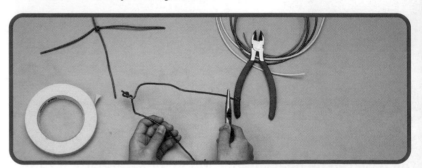

3

To form an armature for a mask or an animal sculpture, begin with an object such as an inflated balloon, a wad of newspaper, a piece of foam, or an empty box. Tell students that they can attach objects with tape or glue. Point out that the entire armature is likely to be covered with another medium such as foil, papier-mâché, or paint.

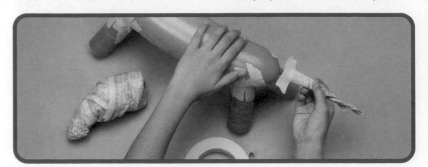

Working with Papier-Mâché

1

Once students build an armature, they can use papier-mâché to complete a mask or sculpture. Have them prepare by tearing newspaper into 1-inch-wide strips.

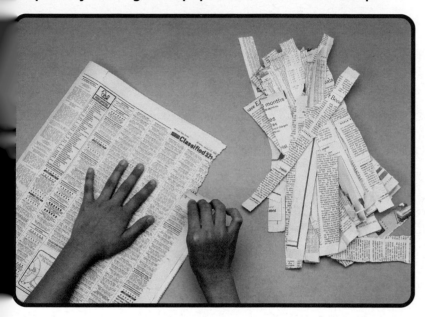

2

When it is time to apply the papier-mâché paste, cover all work areas with plastic or multiple layers of newspaper. You can choose to use wallpaper paste, or you can prepare your own mixture, using equal parts of flour and water. Place the paste in large, open bowls or saucers that students can easily reach.

3

Direct students to soak their newspaper strips in the paste, then apply them over their armature. They should lay the strips in various directions, criss-crossing them to build a smooth surface. Plan on having students apply at least two layers of strips. Allow for drying time between layers as well as after the final layer.

4

Students will enjoy painting their sculptures. You may also wish to make other materials available so students can add details. Yarn, raffia, beads, fabric, and found objects can add interest to sculptures.

List of Artworks

List of Artworks

Seasonal Projects

 **Fall**

Clay Pumpkins

Materials

- pumpkin or pictures of pumpkins
- self-hardening clay
- sculpting tools (paper clips, toothpicks) ⚠
- orange and black paint
- paintbrushes
- fall leaves
- small branches

1. If possible, display a pumpkin. Ask children to describe its color, size, shape, and texture. Talk about how pumpkins grow, how they are used in cooking and baking, and how the seeds can be roasted and eaten as snacks. Then tell children that they will make and paint clay pumpkins.

2. Have each child form a ball of clay into the general shape of a pumpkin. Direct children to add details, such as the stem and the vertical lines of the rind. Have children etch their names into their pumpkin bottoms with sculpting tools.

3. When children have finished their pumpkins, put them in a safe place to dry.

4. Once the clay has dried, have children paint their pumpkins. Some children may wish to paint faces on their pumpkins.

5. Have children then create a tabletop display with fall leaves, branches, and their pumpkins.

Fall Quilt

Materials

- 8" construction paper squares (red, yellow, orange, brown, and green)
- laminating machine or clear contact paper
- hole punch ⚠
- yarn
- crayons
- markers
- scissors ⚠
- construction paper
- fabric scraps
- glue

1. Tell children they will decorate the paper squares with symbols of fall and then "sew" the squares together to make a quilt.

2. Discuss fall events, such as changing leaves, the start of the new school year, Columbus Day, football season, apple harvest, Thanksgiving, and the World Series. Have children provide a list of symbols that represent these changes and events—for example: fall leaves, a school bus, the *Santa Maria,* a football, a basket of apples, Pilgrims, and a baseball.

3. Have children each choose a different symbol from the list and collect a paper square and other materials to construct the symbol. Direct children to cut out shapes from the construction paper and fabric scraps to glue onto the square. They can add details with crayons and markers.

4. Laminate each square or demonstrate how to cover a square with clear contact paper. Offer help as needed.

5. Punch four holes at equal intervals along the sides of the squares and then use yarn to "sew" the squares together to assemble a class quilt. Display the quilt in the classroom, hallway, or cafeteria.

Seasonal Projects

 **Winter**

A Winter Landscape

Materials

- blue construction paper
- pencils
- construction paper scraps
- scissors ⚠
- glue
- newspaper
- art smocks
- white tempera paint
- clean pieces of screening
- toothbrushes

1. Tell children they will make a northern winter landscape, a snowy scene showing outdoor scenery, such as trees, mountains, fields, or lakes.

2. Give each child a sheet of blue construction paper. Have children draw a horizon line to show where sky and land meet. Then have children sketch and cut out land features, such as trees, clouds, and mountains, from construction paper scraps.

3. Tell children to try different arrangements until they find the one they like best and then glue them in place on the blue paper.

4. Cover the work area with newspaper and have children put on an old shirt or smock. To add snow to their landscapes, have children dip a toothbrush in white paint, hold a piece of screening over the landscape, and gently rub the toothbrush across the screen.

5. After the paint dries, display the completed landscapes.

Wintertime Swag

Materials

- grapevines from craft stores or gardens
- wire ⚠
- ribbon or bows
- natural materials (pinecones, evergreen branches, seed pods)
- construction paper
- scissors ⚠
- glitter (optional)
- glue (optional)

1. Tell children they will help to make and decorate a wintertime swag for the classroom door.

2. Have children take turns helping you bend grapevines into a large swag. Use a piece of wire to hold the vines in place. Children can then twist more vines into the swag to make it fuller.

3. To begin, place the swag on a work surface. Have children work together to fasten pinecones, seedpods, and sprigs of evergreen around the swag with wire. For color, they can add small colorful bows. Children may enjoy decorating pinecones and seedpods by dabbing them with glue and sprinkling glitter on them. Hang the swag above the door, letting it drape to one side if it is longer than the width of the door.

4. As different holidays and events approach throughout the winter season, remove the swag and have children make and add construction paper ornaments to replace the natural objects, such as clocks for New Year's Day or hearts for Valentine's Day.

 **Spring**

Windsock

Materials

- scissors ⚠
- cardboard oatmeal containers
- crayons or markers
- glue
- construction paper
- crepe paper
- string
- hole punch ⚠

1. In advance, cut out the top and bottom of an oatmeal container for each child.

2. As a class, discuss the windy weather that often accompanies the arrival of spring in the month of March. Then tell children that they will make windsocks, which are hung outside to determine how hard the wind is blowing.

3. Have children draw spring scenes on construction paper and glue the drawings onto a container, cutting around the top and bottom rims so that the paper covers it.

4. Have children cut four or five long streamers from crepe paper and glue them to the inside bottom rim of the containers.

5. Punch four evenly spaced holes around the top rim of each container. Have children thread string through the holes and double-knot each strand to secure it in place. Help children tie all four strands together at the top.

6. Take children outside on a dry, windy day to hang their windsocks from playground equipment and observe how the wind moves the streamers.

May Flower Bouquet

Materials

- cardboard egg carton cups with holes poked in the bottom of each
- pastel-colored tissue paper circles with holes in the centers (diameters of 2", 3", and 4")
- pipe cleaners ⚠
- florist tape
- scissors ⚠
- construction paper half circles and strips
- tape

1. Tell children that on May 1, children in England give flowers to friends by hanging bouquets on doorknobs. Tell children they will make a May flower bouquet too.

2. To make a flower, have children thread a pipe cleaner up through the bottom hole of the cup and then add two or three tissue paper circles into the center. To keep the papers in place, have children bend the end of the pipe cleaner and then wrap green florist tape around the stem below the cup. Have children make several flowers.

3. To make a hanging basket for the flowers, have children color and shape a construction paper half circle into a cone, tape the seams, and attach a construction paper strip on opposite sides to make a handle. Encourage children to surprise a family member or friend with a May flower bouquet.

Seasonal Projects

 **Summer**

Summertime Fun Frame

Materials

- 8 ½" x 11" drawing paper
- crayons
- precut 9" x 12" poster board frames
- glue
- decorating materials (felt scraps, construction paper scraps, wallpaper and wrapping paper, seashells, seeds, glitter, used postage stamps, dried flowers, dried beans, seeds)
- tape

1. Invite children to tell about the fun activities they hope to enjoy during the summer, such as going to the beach, visiting relatives, camping, learning to swim, or watching fireworks on Independence Day. Have children use crayons to draw a picture of themselves enjoying one of the activities with family or friends.

2. Then tell children they will design and decorate a poster board frame for their drawing. Provide each child with a frame. Have children place decorating materials on their frame to create a pleasing arrangement.

3. Direct children to glue on the materials, adding designs and color with crayons as they wish.

4. When the glue dries, help children tape each corner of the artwork to the back of the frame. Tell children that throughout the summer, they can create new pictures to place in the frame.

Cloud Mural

Materials

- sky blue butcher paper
- gray and white tempera paints
- paintbrushes
- water

1. In advance, line a wall with sky blue butcher paper.

2. Read *Cloudland* by John Burningham or *Cloudy with a Chance of Meatballs* by Judith Barrett with children to spark a discussion about clouds, what they are, what kinds of weather they indicate, and how they change shapes.

3. Take children outside on a day when the clouds are billowy, moving quickly, and changing shapes. If possible, have them lie down on blankets or towels to observe and describe what the clouds look like, such as faces, animals, and objects. Have children describe the movement and variations they see.

4. When you return to the classroom, have children use gray and white paint to make a mural that depicts the clouds they observed. When the mural dries, hang it from the ceiling. Children may also enjoy creating an imaginative adventure story that takes place in the land of clouds or a story about a drop of water as it goes through the water cycle.

Materials

The following lists include suggested materials needed to complete all Studio Activities and Portfolio Projects.

Drawing and Painting Tools

☐ colored chalk (including white, one box per child)

☐ colored pencils (one set per child)

☐ crayons (two sets per child)

☐ markers (one set per child)

☐ oil pastels (one set per child)

☐ paintbrushes (different sizes, at least three per child)

☐ pencils (one box per child)

Paint

☐ acrylic paint (assorted colors, ten pints)

☐ printer's ink (one tube per child)

☐ tempera paint (three pints per child, to include primary and secondary colors)

☐ watercolor paint (one set per child)

Paper Products

☐ butcher paper (one 36" roll)

☐ construction paper (assorted colors, ten packs of 100)

☐ drawing paper (assorted sizes, three reams of 500)

☐ heavy stock paper (one package of 100)

☐ index cards (3" × 5", one package)

☐ manila paper (one pack of 100)

☐ newsprint (one pad of 100)

☐ poster board (two sheets per child)

☐ tag board (assorted sizes, three packs of 100)

☐ tissue paper (assorted colors, one pack)

Clay

☐ ceramic clay (one pound per child)

☐ modeling clay (three pounds per child)

☐ self-hardening clay (two pounds per child)

Materials

Classroom Materials

- [ ] glue stick (one per child)
- [ ] paper clips ⚠ (three boxes)
- [ ] rubber bands (one package)
- [ ] scissors ⚠ (one per child)
- [ ] stapler ⚠ (several per classroom)
- [ ] tape, clear (one roll per child)
- [ ] tape, masking (several rolls per classroom)
- [ ] white bottle glue (two per child)

Specialty and Craft Materials

- [ ] beads, buttons, etc. (large assortment)
- [ ] blocks, wooden (two per child)
- [ ] brayer (one per child)
- [ ] black glue (one bottle per child)
- [ ] craft glue (one bottle per child)
- [ ] craft sticks ⚠ (one package of 500)
- [ ] dowel (one per child)
- [ ] fabric glue (one bottle per child)
- [ ] foam packing peanuts (one bag)
- [ ] meat trays, foam ⚠ (three packages of 50)
- [ ] muffin tin (one per child)
- [ ] palette (one per child)
- [ ] pipe cleaners ⚠ (assorted colors, three packages of 100)
- [ ] ribbon (assorted colors and sizes, several rolls)
- [ ] toothpicks ⚠ (one box)
- [ ] water containers (one per child)
- [ ] yarn (assorted colors and weights, several bundles)

Others

- ☐ aluminum foil, heavy-duty (two rolls)
- ☐ clothespin (one per child)
- ☐ long sock (one per child)
- ☐ mirror, unbreakable ⚠ (one per child)
- ☐ paper towels (three rolls per classroom)
- ☐ plastic-coated wire ⚠ (colored, several spools)
- ☐ plastic egg (one per child)
- ☐ straws (three boxes of 100)
- ☐ tissue (one box)
- ☐ wire screen scraps ⚠ (assortment)
- ☐ wooden matchsticks, headless (one box of 100)

Inexpensive Materials and Sources

- ☐ aluminum cans (child provided)
- ☐ brown paper grocery sacks (grocery stores, child provided)
- ☐ cardboard, sheets (retail and grocery stores, child provided)
- ☐ fabric scraps (tailor services, fabric or decorating stores)
- ☐ milk cartons (child provided)
- ☐ newspaper (child provided)
- ☐ paper towel rolls (child provided)
- ☐ plastic forks and knives ⚠ (restaurants, child provided)
- ☐ sandpaper scraps (student provided, woodworking business)
- ☐ shoebox (child provided)

Optional

- ☐ cardboard box (small, one per child)
- ☐ cotton swabs (one package)
- ☐ pinking shears ⚠ (one per child)
- ☐ rolling pin (one per child)
- ☐ tape, clear (one roll per child)
- ☐ string (one roll)
- ☐ wallpaper (8" squares, one per child)

Books for Teachers

General Reference Books

Arnason, H. H. *History of Modern Art: Painting, Sculpture, Architecture.* 3rd ed. New York: Harry N. Abrams, 1986.

Arnheim, Rudolf. *Visual Thinking.* Berkeley and Los Angeles, California: University of California Press, 1969.

Carpenter, James M. *Visual Art: A Critical Introduction.* New York: Harcourt Brace Jovanovich, 1982.

Gardner, Helen. *Art Through the Ages.* 7th ed. New York: Harcourt Brace Jovanovich, 1986.

Gombrich, E. H. *The Story of Art.* 16th ed. London: Phaidon Press, Ltd., 1995.

Hobbs, Jack A. and Robert L. Duncan. *Arts, Ideas, and Civilization.* 2nd ed. Englewood Cliffs, New Jersey: Prentice Hall, 1992.

Janson, H. W. *History of Art.* 5th ed. New York: Harry N. Abrams, 1995.

Katz, Elizabeth L., Louis E. Lankford, and Jan D. Plank. *Themes and Foundations of Art.* St. Paul, Minnesota: West Publishing Company, 1995.

Silver, Larry. *Art in History.* New York: Abbeville Press, 1993.

Art Education

Armstrong, Carmen L. *Designing Assessment in Art.* National Art Education Association, 1994.

Berk, Ellyn, Jerrold Ross. *A Framework for Multicultural Arts Education.* New York: The National Arts Education Research Center at New York University, 1989.

Berry, Nancy and Susan M. Mayer, eds. *Museum Education: History, Theory, and Practice.* Reston, Virginia: National Art Education Association, 1989.

Blandy, Douglas and Elizabeth Hoffman. "Toward an Art Education of Place," *Studies in Art Education,* 1993.

Chapman, Laura H. *Approaches to Art Education.* New York: Harcourt Brace Jovanovich, 1979.

_____. *Instant Art Instant Culture: The Unspoken Policy for American Schools.* New York: Teachers College Press, 1982.

Cohen, Elaine P. and Ruth S. Gainer. *Art: Another Language for Learning.* New York: Schocken Books, 1984.

Day, Michael and Al Hurwitz. *Children and Their Art.* 5th ed. Harcourt Brace Jovanovich, 1991.

Eisner, Elliot W. *Educating Artistic Vision.* New York: Macmillan Publishing Co., 1972.

_____. "What the Arts Taught Me About Education." *Art Education,* September 1991.

Gardner, H. *Artful Scribbles: The Significance of Children's Drawings.* New York: Basic Books, 1980.

Henry, Carole, ed. *Middle School Art: Issues of Curriculum and Instruction.* Reston, Virginia: The National Art Education Association, 1996.

Hume, Helen D. *A Survival Kit for the Secondary School Art Teacher.* West Nyack, New York. The Center for Applied Research in Education, Inc., 1990.

Hurwitz, Al and Michael Day. *Children and Their Art: Methods for the Elementary School.* 5th ed. New York: Harcourt Brace Jovanovich, 1991.

Lowenfeld, Viktor and Lambert W. Brittain. *Creative and Mental Growth.* 8th ed. New York: Macmillan Publishing Co., 1987.

_____. *Safety in the Artroom.* Reston, Virginia, 1986.

_____. Visual Standards Task Force (Jeanne Rollins, Chair). *National Visual Art Standards.* Reston, Virginia, 1994.

Ocvirk, Otto, et al. *Art Fundamentals, Theory and Practice.* 6th ed. Dubuque, Iowa: William C. Brown, 1990.

Qualley, Charles. *Safety in the Artroom.* Worcester, Massachusetts: Davis Publications, 1986.

Reynolds, Nancy Walkup. *Art Lessons for the Middle School: A DBAE Curriculum.* Portland, Maine: J. Weston Walch Publishers, 1992.

Smith, Peter. "Art and Irrelevance." *Studies in Art Education.* Winter 1995.

Smith, R. A. *Excellence in Art Education: Ideas and Initiatives.* Reston, Virginia: National Art Education Association, 1986.

Sullivan, Graeme. "Art-Based Art Education: Learning That Is Meaningful, Authentic, Critical and Pluralistic," *Studies in Art Education,* September 1993.

Texas Education Agency. *Art Education: Planning for Teaching and Learning.* Austin, TX: TEA, 1989.

Thompson, Christine, ed. *The Visual Arts and Early Childhood Learning.* Reston, VA: National Art Education Association, 1995.

Wolf, D. P. and N. Pistone. *Taking Full Measure: Rethinking Assessment Through the Arts.* New York: The College Board.

Teaching Art History

Baxandall, M. *Patterns of Intention: On the Historical Explanation of Pictures.* New Haven: Yale University Press, 1985.

Bourde, N. and M. D. Garrard. *Feminism and Art History: Questioning the Litany.* New York: Harper & Row, 1982.

Richter, H. *DaDa: Art and Anti-Art.* New York: Norton, 1985.

Art and Multiple Intelligences/ Interdisciplinary Education

Coming to Our Senses: The Significance of the Arts for American Education. New York: American Council for the Arts, 1988.

Gardner, Howard. *Frames of Mind: The Theory of Multiple Intelligences.* New York: Basic Books, Inc., 1983.

Art Criticism and Aesthetics

Arnheim, Rudolph. *Visual Thinking.* Berkeley: University of California Press, 1980.

Barrett, Terry. *Criticizing Art: Understanding the Contemporary.* Mountain View, California: Mayfield Publishing Company, 1994.

Cromer, James. *Criticism: History, Theory and Practice of Art Criticism in Art Education.* Reston, Virginia: National Art Education Association, 1990.

Day, Michael, and Elliot Eisner, et al. *Art History, Art Criticism, and Art Production.* Santa Monica: Rand Corporation, 1984.

Feldman, Edmund B. *Becoming Human Through Art: Aesthetic Experience in the School.* Englewood Cliffs, New Jersey: Prentice-Hall, 1970.

_____. "The Teacher as Model Critic." *Journal of Aesthetic Education,* January 1973.

_____. *Thinking About Art.* Englewood Cliffs, New Jersey: Prentice-Hall, 1985.

_____. *Varieties of Visual Experience.* 4th ed. New York: Harry N. Abrams, 1992.

Hamblen, Karen A. "An Art Criticism Questioning Strategy Within the Framework of Bloom's Taxonomy." *Studies in Art Education,* September 1984.

Lankford, E. L. *Aesthetics: Issues and Inquiry.* Reston, Virginia: National Art Education Association, 1992.

Werhane, P. H. *Philosophical Issues in Art.* Englewood Cliffs, New Jersey: Prentice-Hall, 1984.

Art in Cultural Traditions

Bearden, Romare and Harry Henderson. *A History of African-American Artists from 1792 to the Present.* New York: Pantheon Books, 1993.

Driskell, David C. *Hidden Heritage: Afro-American Art, 1800–1950.* San Francisco: The Art Museum of America, 1985.

_____. *Two Centuries of Black American Art.* New York: Alfred A. Knopf and the Los Angeles County Museum of Art, 1976.

Lee, S. *A History of Far Eastern Art.* New York: Harry N. Abrams, 1982.

Lewis, Samella. *African American Art and Artists.* Berkeley, California: University of California Press, 1990.

_____. *Art: African American.* Los Angeles: Hancraft Studios, 1990.

Rosenak, Chuck and Jan. *Museum of American Folk Art Encyclopedia of Twentieth-Century American Folk Art and Artists.* New York: Abbeville Press, 1991.

Studio Museum in Harlem. *Harlem Renaissance Art of Black America.* New York: Harry N. Abrams, 1987.

Sullivan, Charles, ed. *Children of Promise: African American Literature and Art for Young People.* Bergenfield, New Jersey: Harry N. Abrams, 1994.

Turner, Robyn Montana. *Texas Traditions: The Culture of the Lone Star State.* Boston: Little, Brown, 1996.

Weatherford, Jack. *Native Roots: How the Indians Enriched America.* New York: Fawcett Columbine, 1991.

Young, Bernard, ed. *Art, Culture, and Ethnicity.* Reston, Virginia: National Art Education Association, 1991.

Women and Art

Broude, Norma and Mary D. Garrard, eds. *Feminism and Art History—Questioning the Litany.* New York: Harper & Row, 1982.

Collins, Georgia and Renee Sandell, eds. *Gender Issues in Art Education: Content, Contexts, and Strategies.* Reston, Virginia: National Art Education Association, 1996.

Collins, Georgia and Renee Sandell. *Women, Art, and Education.* Reston, Virginia: National Art Education Association, 1984.

Collins, Jim and Glenn B. Opitz. *Women Artists in America: Eighteenth Century to the Present.* Poughkeepsie, New York: Apollo, 1980.

Bibliography/Additional Resources

Fine, Elsa Honig. *Women & Art: A History of Women Painters and Sculptors from the Renaissance to the 20th Century.* Montclair, New Jersey, and London: Allanheld & Schram: Prior, 1978.

Freedman, Kerry. "Interpreting Gender and Visual Culture in Art Classrooms." *Studies in Art Education,* Spring 1994.

Greer, Germaine. *The Obstacle Race: The Fortunes of Women Painters and Their Work.* New York: Farrar, Straus, & Giroux, 1979.

Harris, Ann Sutherland, and Linda Nochlin. *Women Artists: 1550–1950.* New York: Alfred A. Knopf and the Los Angeles County Museum of Art, 1984.

Hedges, Elaine and Ingrid Wendt, comps. *In Her Own Image, Women Working in the Arts.* Old Westbury, New York: Feminist Press; McGraw-Hill, 1980.

Heller, Reinhold. *Gabriele Münter: The Years of Expressionism 1903–1920.* Munich, Germany and New York, New York: Prestel-Verlag, 1997.

Lerner, Gerda. *The Majority Finds Its Past: Placing Women in History.* New York: Oxford University Press, 1979.

Munro, Eleanor. *Originals: American Women Artists.* New York: Simon & Schuster, 1979.

Nemser, Cindy. *Art Talk: Conversations with Twelve Women Artists.* New York: Scribner, 1975.

Nochlin, Linda. *The Politics of Vision: Essays on Nineteenth-Century Art and Society.* New York: Harper & Row Publishers, 1989.

Petersen, Karen and J. J. Wilson. *Women Artists: Recognition and Reappraisal, From the Early Middle Ages to the Twentieth Century.* New York: Harper Colophon Books and New York University Press, 1976.

Rubinstein, Charlotte Streifer. *American Women Artists: From Early Indian Times to the Present.* Boston: G. K. Hall, 1982.

Slatkin, Wendy. *Women Artists in History: From Antiquity to the 20th Century.* Englewood Cliffs, New Jersey: Prentice-Hall, 1985.

Tufts, Eleanor. *American Women Artists, Past and Present: A Selected Bibliographic Guide (to Works on 500 Selected Artists).* New York: Garland, 1984.

_____. *Our Hidden Heritage: Five Centuries of Women Artists.* New York and London: Paddington Press, 1974.

Art Forms and Techniques

Betti, Claudia and Teel Sale. *Drawing: A Contemporary Approach,* 2nd ed. Orlando, Florida: Holt, Rinehart and Winston, 1986.

Brooke, Sandy. *Hooked on Drawing: Illustrated Lessons & Exercises for Grades 4 and Up.* Englewood Cliffs, New Jersey: Prentice Hall, 1996.

Edwards, Betty. *Drawing on the Artist Within.* New York, New York: Simon & Schuster, Inc., 1986.

Enstice, Wayne and Melody Peters. *Drawing: Space, Form, and Expression.* Englewood Cliffs, New Jersey: Prentice-Hall, 1990.

Hurwitz, Al, Brent Wilson, and Marjorie Wilson. *Teaching Drawing from Art.* Worcester, Massachusetts: Davis Publications, Inc., 1987.

Mayer, Ralph. *The Artist's Handbook of Materials and Techniques.* 5th ed. New York: Viking-Penguin, 1991.

Mills, John. *The Encyclopedia of Sculpture Techniques.* New York: Watson-Guptill, 1990.

Nicolaides, Kimon. *The Natural Way to Draw: A Working Plan for Art Study.* Boston: Houghton Mifflin, 1990.

Patterson, Freeman. *Photography and the Art of Seeing.* San Francisco: Sierra Club Books, 1990.

Ross, John, Tim and Claire Romano. *The Complete Printmaker.* New York: The Free Press/Macmillan, 1990.

Periodicals

American Artist

Art Education

Art in America

Communication Arts

Design for Art Education

Graphic Design

Journal of Aesthetic Education

Journal of Aesthetics and Art Criticism

National Art Education Association News

School Arts

Smithsonian

Studies in Art Education

Books for Students

Davidson, Rosemary. *Take a Look: An Introduction to the Experience of Art.* New York: Viking, 1993.

Epstein, Vivien S. *History of Women Artists for Children.* Denver: V. S. Epstein, 1987.

Flower, Cedric, and Alan Fortney. *Puppets: Methods and Materials.* Worcester, Massachusetts: Davis Publications, 1983.

Franc, Helen M. *An Invitation to See: 125 Paintings from the Museum of Modern Art.* New York: Harry N. Abrams/Museum of Modern Art, 1973.

Gatto, Joseph. *Drawing Media and Techniques.* Worcester, Massachusetts: Davis Publications, 1986.

Greenberg, Jan and Sandra Jordan. *The Painter's Eye.* New York: Delacorte Press, 1991.

Janson, H. W. *History of Art for Young People.* 4th ed. New York: Harry N. Abrams, 1992.

Laybourne, Kit. *The Animation Book: A Complete Guide to Animated Film-Making—From Flip-Books to Sound Cartoons.* New York: Crown Publications, 1988.

Price, Susanna & Tim Stephens. *Click!: Fun with Photography.* New York, New York: Sterling Publishing Company, Inc., 1995.

Storr, Robert. *Chuck Close.* New York: The Museum of Modern Art, 1998.

Turner, Robyn Montana. *Portraits of Women Artists for Children (Rosa Bonheur, Georgia O'Keeffe, Mary Cassatt, Frida Kahlo, Faith Ringgold, Dorothea Lange)* (series). Boston, Massachusetts: Little, Brown, 1991–1994.

Von Oech, Roger. *A Whack on the Side of the Head: How You Can Be More Creative.* New York, New York: Warner Books, 1983.

_____. *A Kick in the Seat of the Pants: Using Your Explorer, Artist, Judge, & Warrior to be More Creative.* New York, New York: Harper & Row Publishers, Inc., 1986.

Zelanski, Paul. *Shaping Space.* Fort Worth, Texas: Holt, Rinehart & Winston, 1987.

Art on the Internet

Web sites often change. The following Web sites are examples of acceptable sources for information. Establish guidelines for your students' safe and responsible use of the Internet.

American Folk Art Museum
http://www.ny.com/museums/museum.of.american.folk.art.html/

Art Access
http://www.artic.edu/artaccess/

Artchive
http://www.artchive.com/core.html/

Artcyclopedia
http://www.artcyclopedia.com/

Art Museum of the Americas
http://www.museum.oas.org/

Art Net
http://www.artnet.com/library/index.asp/

Artlex Art Dictionary
http://www.artlex.com/

ArtsConnectEd
http://artsconnected.org/

Asian Art Museum of San Francisco
http://www.asianart.org/

Ask Art
http://askart.com/

Carnegie Museum of Art
http://www.cmoa.org/

Dallas Museum of Art
http://www.dm-art.org/

Fine Arts Museums of San Francisco
http://www.famsf.org/

Guggenheim Museum
http://www.guggenheim.org/
http://www.guggenheimcollection.org/

J. Paul Getty Museum
http://www.getty.edu/museum/

Metropolitan Museum of Art, New York
http://www.metmuseum.org/

Milwaukee Art Museum
http://www.mam.org/

Museum of Fine Arts, Houston
http://www.mfah.org/

Museum of Latin American Art
http://www.molaa.com/

Museum of Modern Art
http://www.moma.org/

National Gallery of Art
http://www.nga.gov/

National Museum of African Art
Smithsonian/Washington, D. C.
http://www.nmafa.si.edu/

National Museum of Women in the Arts
http://www.nmwa.org/

Smithsonian American Art Museum
http://americanaart.si.edu

Web Museum
http://www.ibiblio.org/wm/

Whitney Museum of American Art
http://www.whitney.org/

Learning Styles

A Student Who Is . . .	Is Likely to Enjoy Art projects that . . .	And May Enjoy Helping Out in the Classroom by . . .
An Interpersonal Learner • interactive • communicative • group-oriented • extroverted	• are group projects • require giving/receiving feedback • require group leaders	• distributing and collecting materials • mediating
An Intrapersonal Learner • individualistic • solitary • self-reflective • introverted	• are individual projects • focus on feelings, dreams, or self • are goal-oriented	• arranging items in storage spaces • assisting the teacher before or after class
A Bodily/Kinesthetic Learner • physically active • hands-on • talkative	• involve motion such as dancing or acting • involve touching various objects, materials, and textures	• running errands • role-playing safety rules • distributing and collecting materials
A Verbal/Linguistic Learner • oriented toward language, words, reading, and writing	• involve spoken or written words • involve storytelling	• reading instructions aloud • labeling storage spaces • creating "rules" posters
A Logical/Mathematical Learner • inquisitive • experimental • oriented toward numbers, patterns, and relationships	• involve patterns, relationships, or symbols • require problem-solving	• arranging or classifying materials • counting materials for distribution • helping solve problems
A Visual/Spatial Learner • imaginative • oriented toward colors and pictures	• involve colors and designs • involve painting, drawing, or sculpture • require active imagination	• creating displays of artworks • designing charts and posters
A Musical/Rhythmic Learner • oriented toward music, rhythmic sounds, and environmental sounds	• involve rhythmic patterns, singing, humming, responding to music, keeping time, or listening for sounds	• thinking of or leading clean-up songs (primary grades) • creating displays about music or musicians
Acquiring English	• require limited word usage • involve terminology from their first language • involve simple name/word games	• creating labels and posters in their first language • creating images or icons for bulletin boards • sharing elements of their culture with other students

Safety

Art should be fun. It should also be safe. Use these guidelines to help ensure the safety of your art classroom and to help teach your students about safety.

⚠ Make your classroom safe.

- Provide water-based materials (markers, paints, clay, etc.).
- Provide nontoxic glue, clay, and other materials.
- Provide safety scissors for young children. Do not use glass containers. Instead, use plastic, polystyrene, or waxed-paper cups or containers.
- Do not provide sharp-edged tools such as knives or razor blades. Students can use plastic knives for cutting clay and toothpicks or paperclips for carving clay. (Remind students to be especially careful with any objects that have sharp points.)
- Keep a well-stocked first-aid kit in the classroom.
- Label and date all materials and chemicals. Store them properly. Keep solvents and powders in containers with lids. If you must store potentially hazardous materials in the classroom, do so in a place where students do *not* have access to them.
- Report unsafe or malfunctioning equipment or facilities to the administration, verbally and in writing.
- Dispose of waste materials properly.
- Clean up spills immediately.

⚠ Read labels.

- Check for age-appropriateness. The Art and Creative Materials Institute (ACMI) labels art materials as approved or certified when they are safe for young children, even if ingested. Look for these round ACMI labels. A product bearing the square "Health Label" is safe only for children over twelve.
- Check products' ventilation requirements. For products that do require ventilation, an open classroom door or one window is probably not adequate.

⚠ Know your students.

- Be aware of students' allergies. Children with allergies to wheat (gluten), for example, may be irritated by the wheat paste used in papier-mâché. Other art materials that may cause allergic reactions include chalk or other dusty substances, water-based clay, and any material that contains petroleum products.
- Use your knowledge of individual student's tendencies to plan art activities that are safe for all students.

A note on toxicity:

Toxic materials can enter the body in a number of ways.

Inhalation Eliminate from your classroom aerosol spray mists or paints, solvents that give off vapors (turpentine, paint thinners, etc.), and gases such as those given off by some kiln fuels. Inhalation of a toxic substance can cause allergic reactions as well as other, more dire or long-lasting conditions.

Ingestion Children frequently taste substances that are visually appealing, even though they know the substances are not edible. In particular, certain colors of paint and ceramic glazes may be tempting for children to taste. Doing so could be fatal. Be aware of the "food appeal" factor any time you offer a material to a child.

Skin contact Allergic reactions and burns may result from skin contact with some art materials, particularly solvents. Even "safe" materials such as powdered tempera paint can cause irritation if rubbed in the eyes, for example. Encourage students to minimize the splashing, spilling, and pouring of liquid or powdered art materials. Provide protective gloves or clothing if necessary.

⚠ Discuss safety.

- Teach students how to care for and safely use art materials, tools, and equipment.
- Post rules where they will be effective. For example, place a "Don't forget to wash up!" sign over the sink.
- Before each art activity, alert students to potential dangers and relevant safety procedures.
- Teach students what to do in an emergency. Practice emergency procedures such as room evacuation regularly.

Teacher Glossary

abstract A style of art that does not show a realistic style. Abstract art usually contains geometric shapes, bold colors, and lines.

abstraction A subject that has been simplified, stylized, or broken down into basic shapes.

actual lines Lines that are real, not imaginary.

altered proportion A technique used by an artist to change the size relationship of shapes in an artwork. See *monumental,* and *miniature.*

alternating rhythm Rhythm created in an artwork by repeating two or more elements on a regular, interchanging basis.

analogous Colors that appear next to each other on the color wheel. Analogous colors have one hue in common. For example, blue, blue-green, and blue-violet all contain blue. Also known as *related colors.*

animation The art of putting together drawings in a sequence. The pictures are recorded onto film. When the film is run at high speed, the pictures appear to be in motion.

applied art Artworks that are functional. Also known as *utilitarian art.*

aqueduct A channel or conduit built for transporting water from a distant source.

arch A semicircular or curved shape in a building. An arch can frame a doorway or it can support a wall or ceiling.

architect An artist who plans buildings and other structures.

architecture The art and science of designing buildings and other structures.

armature A skeletal framework or support for a sculpture.

art historians Those who study art history and cultural traditions that relate to art, such as forms of government, religious beliefs, and social activities.

art media The materials used by artists to create artworks.

Art Nouveau French for "new art," this style of art in the late 1800s and early 1900s, uses exaggerated asymmetrical designs and makes use of undulating forms of all kinds, most notably tendrils, plant stems, flames, waves, and flowing hair.

art teacher A specialist in the field of visual art who teaches and helps students and others understand and participate in the world of visual arts and ideas.

artificial intelligence The ability of a computer or other machine to perform those activities that are normally thought to require intelligence.

artwork Any artistic object or production.

assemblage An additive sculpture often made of recycled objects that assume new meaning within the artwork.

asymmetrical balance A type of balance in which the two sides of an artwork look equally important even though they are not alike. Also known as *informal balance.*

atmospheric perspective A technique used to create the illusion of air and space in an artwork through changes in value. Close-up objects are bright and consist of darker colors; faraway objects consist of muted colors. Also known as *aerial perspective.*

background The part of an artwork that seems the farthest away.

balance The way an artwork is arranged to make different parts seem equally important. Balance is a principle of design.

barrel vault A semi-cylindrical structure made up of successive arches.

Bauhaus design A twentieth-century German school of design and art. This style of art used simplified forms and unadorned functionalism. It was influenced by and derived from techniques and materials used in industrial fabrication and manufacture.

binder A material, such as wax, egg, glue, resin, or oil, that binds together the coloring grains and powder in a pigment.

blending A shading technique that changes the value of a color little by little.

block In printmaking, a piece of flat material, such as wood or metal, with a design on the surface, which is a mirror image of the composition that will appear as a print. The block is used to print the design. (See also *plate.*) In sculpture, a solid material, such as wood or stone, used for carving.

blue screen A technique used in filmmaking to create special effects. The subjects are filmed against a blue screen. Later, the blue screen is replaced by another background.

blueprint A photographic print used to copy the final drawing of a plan for building something.

bronze A metal alloy made of copper and tin and other metals, often used in cast sculpture.

calligraphy Ornamental writing, done mainly with a pen in the West and with a brush in China and Japan.

caricature An artwork that exaggerates the features or aspects of a person or object, usually in a way that is funny.

cartoonist An artist who draws cartoons for newspapers, magazines and other print media.

carving A subtractive method of sculpting requiring the sculptor to cut or chip away pieces from a block of material, such as wood, stone, or other hard material.

casting A sculpting process in which a liquid, such as molten bronze or liquid plaster, is poured into a heat-proof mold to create a three-dimensional form or an impression.

cathedral A church that is the official seat of a bishop.

cell One frame of an animated film that is created by hand. Before digital and computer technology, all cells that comprised a film had to be drawn and painted by hand.

ceramics The art of making objects from clay and hardening them with fire. Also, artworks made by this process.

cityscape Artwork that gives a view of a city.

Classical Style A term applied to an artwork that exhibits the characteristics of ancient Greek and Roman art, such as proportion, balance, and idealized forms and themes.

Claymation An animation process in which clay figurines are manipulated and filmed to produce an image of lifelike movement.

Teacher Glossary

collage A medium in which the artist glues bits of cut or torn paper, photographs, fabric, or other materials to a flat surface.

color The visual quality of objects caused by the amount of light they reflected. Color is an element of art. See *hue.*

color scheme A plan for combining colors in a work of art.

complementary Colors that contrast with one another. Complementary colors are opposite one another on the color wheel.

compositing A process by which combined images are burned or recorded onto a single piece of film by using either photographic or computer equipment.

composition The plan, placement, or arrangement of the elements of art in an artwork. Composition may also refer to any work of art.

Computer Aided Design (CAD) The use of computer programs and systems to design detailed two- or three-dimensional models of physical objects, such as mechanical parts or buildings.

computer arts Artworks created using computer technology as a medium.

conservator A person who works to protect artworks from damage and decay.

contrast The difference between two unlike things, such as a light color and a dark color.

converging lines Actual or implied lines that recede toward an intersecting point in space.

cool colors The family of colors that includes greens, blues, and violets. Cool colors bring to mind cool things, places, and feelings.

costume A style of dress characteristic of a particular country, historical period, or culture. An outfit or disguise worn for certain celebrations, or an outfit in dramatic productions.

creativity A state characterized by originality, imagination, and expression.

cross-hatching A shading technique using lines that cross each other.

curator A person who does research for a museum. Curators recommend artworks for the museum to consider purchasing. They also select artworks for display from the museum's permanent collection.

 D

decorative art Handicrafts that result in beautiful, useful objects. Rug and fabric design, furniture-making, and glassblowing are all decorative arts.

depth The third dimension or the illusion of deep space on a two-dimensional plane.

detail A small part of a larger artwork enlarged for closer viewing. Also, a minute or particularly interesting part of an artwork.

diagonal line A slanted edge or line.

digital technology Technology that converts visual images into binary code through the use of items such as digital cameras, video and audio recorders, or computers.

docent A person who volunteers in an art museum. Docents give information and conduct tours.

earth art A type of art created with natural materials. The completed artwork often becomes a part of the environment in which it was created. Also known as *earth work.*

elements of art The basic parts and symbols of an artwork. The elements of art are line, color, value, shape, texture, form, and space.

emphasis Importance given to certain objects or areas in an artwork. Color, texture, shape, space, and size can be used to create dominance, contrast, or a focal point. Emphasis is a principle of design.

etching A printing process in which a design is drawn into a wax-covered metal plate. The plate is then bathed in acid, which eats the metal on the areas unprotected by the wax. The wax is removed and ink is applied to the etched surface. The plate is then pressed onto a surface to reveal the print. Also, a print made by this process.

exhibition A public display of artworks.

F

fantasy art Art that reflects the imagination.

fashion The prevailing style or custom, as in dress or behavior.

feature Any distinct part of the face, such as the nose, mouth, or eyes.

fiber arts Artworks created from yarn, thread, or cloth. Stitchery and weaving are examples.

fine art Artworks that are created for the sole purpose of being viewed.

focal point The center of interest in a work of art. A way to show emphasis in an artwork in which the artist sets an area or element apart from the others.

foreground The part of an artwork that seems nearest.

form A three-dimensional object, such as a cube or ball. Form is an element of art.

frame One of many pictures in a filmstrip. Also, a decorative border or support for an artwork.

function The purpose or use of an object.

G

geometric form A form such as a sphere, cube, or pyramid whose contours represent a circle, square, and triangle, respectively.

geometric shape A shape that is precise and mathematical. Circles, squares, triangles, ovals, and rectangles are geometric shapes.

gesture A motion of the limbs or body made to express or help express a thought or to emphasize speech.

gesture drawing A drawing technique in which artists move a drawing medium, such as a pencil, quickly and freely over a surface to capture the form and actions of a subject.

glaze A thin layer of transparent paint made of minerals. A glaze can be applied to a piece of pottery, which is then re-fired.

Gothic A word used to describe all medieval art from the middle of the twelfth century to the beginning of the Renaissance.

Teacher Glossary

hardware Computer components, such as monitors, keyboards, CPUs, and modems.

hatching A shading technique using thin parallel lines.

hieroglyphics A system of writing using symbols and pictures.

horizon line The line created in an artwork by the meeting of sky and ground. In linear perspective it also represents the viewer's eye level.

horizontal line In an artwork, a line that runs side-to-side, parallel to the horizon. Horizontal lines appear peaceful and calm.

hue Another word for color.

human form Form of the human body.

implied lines Lines that are not real, but suggested by the placement of other lines, shapes, and colors.

impressionism An art movement and style developed in the late 1800s by a group of French artists. Artists of the Impressionist style drew and painted their impressions of visual reality by showing the effects of light and color on everyday objects.

indoor space The space inside a house or building.

installation An artwork that is assembled for an exhibition and removed when the exhibition is over.

intensity The brightness or dullness of a hue. A hue mixed with its complement is less intense than the pure color.

intermediate color A color that is a mixture of a primary and a secondary color that are next to each other on the color wheel. Blue-green, red-orange, and red-violet are examples of intermediate colors.

landscape architecture The planning and design of outdoor areas.

light source A point of illumination for emphasis, contrast, unity, or dramatic effect in an artwork.

line A thin mark on a surface created by a pen, pencil, brush, or any other tool. Line is an element of art.

linear perspective A technique that makes use of actual and implied lines to create the illusion of depth on a two-dimensional surface. If the lines in an artwork created with this technique are extended, they converge at a point on an imaginary line that represents the eye level of the viewer. This point is called the vanishing point.

lithograph A type of print made by drawing a design on a metal or stone plate using a greasy substance. The plate is washed with water, and then covered with greasy ink that adheres only to the design and not the wet surface of the plate. The plate is then processed onto paper.

loom A frame or machine used to hold yarn, or other fibers, for weaving, usually at right angles to one another.

M

matte painting Scenery, such as a darkened city or a vast ocean, painted on glass or created with a computer as a background to replace the blue screen in a film shot.

medium A material used to create artworks, such as clay or paint. The plural of *medium* is *media.*

Middle Ages The period in European history between the fall of Rome in A.D. 410 to about 1450. Also known as the *Medieval period* and the *Dark Ages.*

middle ground In an artwork, the part between the foreground and the background.

miniature Artworks that are of smaller-than-life proportions.

mixed media Artworks that are created from more than one medium.

modeling A sculpture technique in which a three-dimensional form is manipulated in a soft material, such as clay.

monochromatic A color scheme that uses different values of a single hue by showing tints and shades of that hue.

monumental Artworks that are of larger-than-life proportions.

morphing Transforming an image by computer. Transforming from one shape to another.

motif An element that is repeated often enough to be an important feature of a design.

N

natural form A form of, relating to, or concerning nature.

negative space The empty space around and between forms or shapes in an artwork. See *positive space.*

neutral A word used for black, white, and tints and shades of gray. Some artists use tints and shades of brown as neutrals.

O

oil-based paints Paints made from a mixture of colored pigment and linseed oil.

one-point perspective A form of linear perspective in which all lines appear to meet at a single vanishing point on the horizon.

opaque The quality of not letting light through; the opposite of *transparent.*

Op Art A style of art in which artists create the illusion of movement or other optical illusions. Op Art flourished in the 1950s and 1960s.

optical illusion A visually perceived image that is deceptive or misleading.

organic form A "free-form" that has irregular and uneven edges and may be found in nature, such as an apple, tree, or animal.

organic shape A "free-form" shape that is irregular and uneven, such as the shape of a leaf, flower, or cloud.

outdoor space The space outside of a structure or building; space that is in the open or leading to the open.

overlapping Partly or completely covering one shape or form with another to show space and distance in an artwork.

Teacher Glossary

palette A flat board on which a painter mixes color.

parallel lines Two or more straight lines or edges on the same plane that do not intersect. Parallel lines have the same direction.

pattern Repeated colors, lines, shapes, forms, or textures in an artwork. Pattern is a principle of design. Also, a plan or model to be followed when making something.

pediment In classical architecture, a triangular space at the end of a building, formed by the ends of the sloping roof and the cornice. Also, an ornamental feature having this shape.

permanent installation Art made for a specific space, often outdoors, that is not intended to be moved.

Pharaoh A ruler of ancient Egypt.

photographer A camera artist.

pigment A coloring material made from crushed minerals and plants or chemicals, usually held together with a binder.

pixel The basic unit of the composition of an image on a television screen, computer monitor, or similar display.

placement The act of placing or arranging elements and objects in an artwork.

plaque An ornamental or informative tablet.

plate In printmaking, a piece of flat material, such as wood or metal, with a design on the surface. The plate is used to print the design, which is a mirror image of the composition. See also *block*.

portfolio A portable container used to hold and organize artworks, especially drawings and paintings. Also, the artworks collected in this container.

portrait A work of art created to show a person, animal, or group of people, usually focusing on the face.

pose The way a subject sits or stands while an artist creates a portrait.

positive space Shapes, forms, or lines that stand out from the background in a work of art. See *negative space*.

pottery Objects made of clay, which can be useful and/or decorative.

Pre-Columbian Art Artworks created in the Americas before Christopher Columbus and other Europeans arrived in the area.

primary color A color that cannot be mixed from other colors, but from which other colors are made. The primary colors are red, yellow, and blue.

principles of design Guidelines that artists use to organize the elements in a composition. Unity, variety, emphasis, balance, proportion, pattern, and rhythm are the principles of design.

printmaking The process of transferring an image from an inked surface to another surface to create an artwork.

profile The side view of a subject.

progressive rhythm Rhythm created in an artwork by showing regular changes in a repeated element, such as a series of circles that progressively increase in size from small to large. The changes may also progress from light to dark, or from bottom to top.

proportion The relation of the parts of an artwork to each other and to the whole. Proportion is a principle of design.

Q

quilt A padded bedcover made from two layers of cloth that are sewn together and stuffed. Usually, one or both layers are made from scraps of fabric that have been arranged and stitched together in a colorful design. Also, the process of creating a quilt.

R

radial balance A type of balance in which lines or shapes spread out from a center point.

regular rhythm Rhythm in an artwork created by repeating the same element, such as a shape, without variation.

relief print The technique of printing in which an image raised from a background is inked and printed.

relief sculpture A type of sculpture in which forms project from a background and are meant to be seen from one side.

Renaissance The period between the 1300s and 1600s, during which new ideas and technological advances, as well as renewed interest in the Classical styles of the Romans and Greeks, laid the foundation for modern art and society.

rhythm The repetition of elements, such as lines, shapes, or colors, that creates a feeling of visual motion in an artwork. Rhythm is a principle of design. In music, rhythm refers to the pattern of the notes.

S

scale The size of an object in relation to an ideal or standard size.

scanner A device used to transfer text or graphics into a computer.

sculpture An artwork made by modeling, carving, casting, or joining materials into a three-dimensional form. Clay, wood, stone, and metal are often used to make sculptures.

secondary color A color made by mixing two primary colors. The secondary colors are orange, violet, and green.

shade A color made by adding black to a hue. For example, adding black to green results in dark green. Also, the darkness of a color value. See *value.*

shading A way of showing gradual changes in lightness or darkness in a drawing or painting. Shading helps make a picture look more three-dimensional.

shape A flat, two-dimensional area with height and width, which might have an edge, or outline, around it. Shape is an element of art.

size relationships A technique that alters the proportions of compositions. The three categories are monumental, miniature, and exaggerated.

slip A soft, wet mixture of clay and water that acts as glue to join scored pieces of clay.

Teacher Glossary

software Computer applications used for various functions, such as drawing, editing text, creating graphics, or altering images.

solvent A liquid, such as turpentine or water, used to control the thickness or thinness of paint.

space The open or empty area around, above, between, within, or below objects. Shapes and forms are defined by the empty space surrounding them. Space is an element of art.

still photography The art and science of making a picture with a camera.

stippling A shading technique creating dark values by applying a dot pattern.

stirrup A part of a vessel shaped like an inverted U in which something is held, supported, or fixed.

stitchery A term for artwork created with a needle, thread or yarn, and cloth, such as a quilt.

stop action A technique for filming animated features in which figures are positioned into place, a frame is shot, and the figures are repositioned for the next frame. When played back, the figures appear to move naturally.

storyboard A series of drawings on small cards that represents the visual plan of a video production.

style An artist's individual way of expressing his or her ideas. Also, a technique used by a group of artists in a particular time or culture.

subject What an artwork is about. A person, animal, object, or scene can be the subject of an artwork.

Surrealism A style of art developed during the 1920s that combines realistic images and dream-like ideas. Many Surrealist artworks contain illusions.

symbol A letter, color, sign, or picture that represents words, messages, or ideas, such as thoughts and feelings. For example, a red heart is often used as a symbol for love.

symmetrical balance A type of balance in which both sides of an artwork look the same or almost the same. Also known as *formal balance*.

tactile texture A texture you can feel with your hands, such as rough or smooth. Also known as *actual texture*.

Taoism A principle philosophy and system of religion of China based on the teachings of Lao-tzu in the sixth century B.C. It advocates restoring in the mind and body the Tao, or the source of being, non-being, and change, in the universe.

technique The way an artist uses and applies art media and tools to create a certain type of artwork.

tempera paint A chalky, water-based paint that is thick and opaque. Also known as *poster paint*.

temporary installation A form of installation art that is not meant to be permanently on display.

terra cotta Fired clay with no glaze, usually reddish-brown in color, used for pottery, architectural ornament, and sculpture.

tessellation A pattern of shapes that fit together in a way that leaves no space in between, as in the artworks of M. C. Escher.

textile An artwork made from cloth or fibers, such as yarn.

texture The way something feels to the touch or how it may look. Texture is an element of art.

tint A light value of a color, such as pink, that is created by mixing a hue with white. Also, the lightness of a color value. See *value.*

transparent The quality of letting light pass through; the opposite of *opaque.*

triptych A picture or carving in three panels.

trompe l'oeil (meaning "fool the eye") A type of painting in which various illusionary devices persuade the viewer that he or she is looking at the actual objects represented.

two-point perspective A form of linear perspective in which all lines appear to meet at either of two vanishing points on the horizon.

unity The quality of seeming whole and complete, with all of the parts looking right together. Unity is a principle of design.

urban Of, relating to, or located in a city.

urban environment The circumstances or surroundings in a city.

utilitarian Designed for a specific purpose.

value The lightness or darkness of a color. Tints have a light value. Shades have a dark value. Value is an element of art.

vanishing point In linear perspective, the place on the horizon where parallel lines seem to meet or converge.

variety The use or combination of elements of art, such as line, shape, or color, to provide interest in an artwork. Variety is a principle of design.

vertical line In an artwork, a line that runs up and down, such as a flagpole or a giant redwood tree. Vertical lines appear strong and powerful.

vessel A functional and/or decorative container made from clay used to hold solids or liquids.

video art A medium for creating motion pictures, such as motion picture films or videotaped television programs. An artwork whose medium includes television or film images.

visual texture The way a surface appears through the sense of vision. For example, the surface of a sculpture may appear shiny or dull. Also known as *simulated texture.*

Teacher Glossary

warm colors The family of colors that includes reds, yellows, and oranges. Warm colors bring to mind warm things, places, and feelings.

warp In weaving, the threads attached to the top and bottom of a loom.

water-based paints Water-soluble paints, such as tempera, watercolor, or acrylic, that use different binders and have different qualities.

weaving A process of interlocking thread, yarn, or other fibers to create a fabric, usually on a loom.

Web design Design specializing in the development of a page or site on the World Wide Web for a person, group, or organization.

weft The threads that cross over and under the warp fibers on a loom.

Artistic Perception

Awareness and sensitivity to natural and human-made environments

Concepts

Students progressively learn that their multisensory experiences, such as hearing, touching, moving, and seeing, can help them perceive and identify the visual elements of art as well as the visual principles of design.

Legend

○ Open circles indicate the grade where aspects are introduced.

● Shaded circles indicate the grades where aspects are developed.

			Levels						
	K	1	2	3	4	5	6	7	8
Elements of Art — Line									
Explore and examine line in art	○	●	●	●	●	●	●	●	●
Identify and name types of lines such as curved, straight, thick, thin, fine, broad, dotted, wavy, zigzag, continuous, broken	○	●	●	●	●	●	●	●	●
Use a variety of art media and tools to create line	○	●	●	●	●	●	●	●	●
Recognize horizontal, vertical, and diagonal lines				○	●	●	●	●	●
Recognize actual and implied lines					○	●	●	●	●
Use line to create shape or form	○	●	●	●	●	●	●	●	●
Use line to create pattern and texture	○	●	●	●	●	●	●	●	●
Use line to create movement	○	●	●	●	●	●	●	●	●
Use line to express thoughts and emotions	○	●	●	●	●	●	●	●	●
Name, identify, and use line as an element of art	○	●	●	●	●	●	●	●	●
Color									
Explore and examine color in art	○	●	●	●	●	●	●	●	●
Name and identify warm colors and use them in a composition	○	●	●	●	●	●	●	●	●
Name and identify cool colors and use them in a composition	○	●	●	●	●	●	●	●	●
Name and identify primary and secondary colors	○	●	●	●	●	●	●	●	●
Mix primary colors to make secondary colors	○	●	●	●	●	●	●	●	●
Name and identify intermediate colors				○	●	●	●	●	●
Mix primary colors with secondary colors to make intermediate colors		○	●	●	●	●	●	●	●
Name, identify, and use neutrals such as white, black, gray				○	●	●	●	●	●
Name, identify, and use color schemes: harmonies			○	●	●	●	●	●	●
Recognize properties of color such as hue, value, intensity					○	●	●	●	●
Name, identify, and use color as an element of art	○	●	●	●	●	●	●	●	●

Scope and Sequence

					Levels				
	K	1	2	3	4	5	6	7	8
Value									
Explore and examine value in art		○	●	●	●	●	●	●	●
Recognize value as being the lightness or darkness of a color		○	●	●	●	●	●	●	●
Create color tints	○	●	●	●	●	●	●	●	●
Create color shades	○	●	●	●	●	●	●	●	●
Name, identify, and use value as an element of art		○	●	●	●	●	●	●	●
Shape									
Explore and examine shape in art	○	●	●	●	●	●	●	●	●
Recognize shape as being a two-dimensional flat space enclosed by actual or implied lines	○	●	●	●	●	●	●	●	
Identify organic shapes		○	●	●	●	●	●	●	●
Name and identify geometric shapes	○	●	●	●	●	●	●	●	●
Arrange shapes to create a work of art	○	●	●	●	●	●	●	●	●
Use shape to create pattern and texture	○	●	●	●	●	●	●	●	●
Name, identify, and use shape as an element of art		○	●	●	●	●	●	●	●
Texture									
Explore and examine texture in art	○	●	●	●	●	●	●	●	●
Recognize texture as the look and/or feel of a surface	○	●	●	●	●	●	●	●	●
Name and identify different types of textures	○	●	●	●	●	●	●	●	●
Distinguish between tactile and visual texture		○	●	●	●	●	●	●	●
Create texture in a work of art	○	●	●	●	●	●	●	●	●
Name, identify, and use texture as an element of art		○	●	●	●	●	●	●	●
Form									
Explore and examine form in art	○	●	●	●	●	●	●	●	●
Recognize form as being a three-dimensional object with height, width, and depth	○	●	●	●	●	●	●	●	●
Identify organic forms		○	●	●	●	●	●	●	●
Name and identify geometric forms	○	●	●	●	●	●	●	●	●
Arrange forms to create a work of art	○	●	●	●	●	●	●	●	●
Name, identify, and use form as an element of art	○	●	●	●	●	●	●	●	●

		Levels								
		K	1	2	3	4	5	6	7	8
Space										
Explore and examine space in art		○	●	●	●	●	●	●	●	●
Recognize that space is the actual or visual area within and around shapes and forms: foreground, middle ground, background			○	●	●	●	●	●	●	●
Recognize positive space			○	●	●	●	●	●	●	●
Recognize negative space			○	●	●	●	●	●	●	●
Work with space in a work of art		○	●	●	●	●	●	●	●	●
Name, identify, and use space as an element of art		○	●	●	●	●	●	●	●	●
Principles of Design	**Unity**									
Explore and examine unity in art				○	●	●	●	●	●	●
Recognize that unity in a work of art is a quality that occurs when all its elements and principles are working together				○	●	●	●	●	●	●
Name and identify the elements and/or principles in a work of art that create unity					○	●	●	●	●	●
Understand and use unity as a principle of design				○	●	●	●	●	●	●
	Variety									
Explore and examine variety in art				○	●	●	●	●	●	●
Recognize that variety in a work of art is a change in shape, form, appearance, or detail that creates interest				○	●	●	●	●	●	●
Recognize that unity and variety often work together in design				○	●	●	●	●	●	●
Understand and use variety as a principle of design				○	●	●	●	●	●	●
	Emphasis									
Explore and examine emphasis in art			○	●	●	●	●	●	●	●
Recognize that emphasis implies areas in a work of art that dominate and draw attention to the main idea			○	●	●	●	●	●	●	●
Identify emphasis in works of art			○	●	●	●	●	●	●	●
Understand and use emphasis as a principle of design			○	●	●	●	●	●	●	●

Legend

○ Open circles indicate the grade where aspects are introduced.

● Shaded circles indicate the grades where aspects are developed.

Scope and Sequence

	Levels								
	K	1	2	3	4	5	6	7	8
Balance									
Explore and examine balance in art	○	●	●	●	●	●	●	●	●
Recognize that balance is a way of arranging elements of design to give an artwork a sense of equality in visual weight	○	●	●	●	●	●	●	●	●
Identify symmetrical balance	○	●	●	●	●	●	●	●	●
Identify radial balance			○	●	●	●	●	●	●
Identify asymmetrical balance		○	●	●	●	●	●	●	●
Understand and use balance as a principle of design	○	●	●	●	●	●	●	●	●
Proportion									
Explore and examine proportion in art			○	●	●	●	●	●	●
Recognize that proportion is the size relationship of one part to the whole			○	●	●	●	●	●	●
Recognize that proportion can indicate distance			○	●	●	●	●	●	●
Understand and use proportion as a principle of design			○	●	●	●	●	●	●
Pattern									
Explore and examine pattern in art	○	●	●	●	●	●	●	●	●
Recognize that pattern is an arrangement of lines, shapes, colors, or forms in a regular repetition	○	●	●	●	●	●	●	●	●
Understand and use pattern as a principle of design	○	●	●	●	●	●	●	●	●
Rhythm									
Explore and examine rhythm in art		○	●	●	●	●	●	●	●
Recognize that rhythm is a sense of visual movement achieved by the repetition of one or more elements of art in a work of art			○	●	●	●	●	●	●
Recognize types of rhythm: random, regular, alternating, flowing, progressive							●	●	●
Understand and use rhythm as a principle of design			○	●	●	●	●	●	●

Creative Art Process

Inventive and imaginative expression through art materials and tools

Concepts

Students progressively learn to experiment with art materials in order to understand properties and develop manipulative skills and in order to express individual ideas, thoughts, and feelings in simple media.

	Levels								
	K	1	2	3	4	5	6	7	8
Media and Methods — Drawing									
Express individual ideas, thoughts, and feelings through drawing	○	●	●	●	●	●	●	●	●
Draw with a variety of materials such as pencils, crayons, pastels, chalk, water-based pens	○	●	●	●	●	●	●	●	●
Draw from memory, imagination, or observation	○	●	●	●	●	●	●	●	●
Create an artwork using a variety of drawing materials, such as charcoal, pen and ink							○	●	●
Collage, Mosaic, and Mixed Media									
Express individual ideas, thoughts, and feelings through collage, mosaic, and mixed media	○	●	●	●	●	●	●	●	●
Create a collage using a variety of materials such as paper, found objects, cardboard, string, plastic, fiber	○	●	●	●	●	●	●	●	●
Create a mosaic using a variety of materials such as pieces of tile, construction-paper pieces, small stones		○	●	●	●	●	●	●	●
Create a mixed-media artwork using a variety of materials such as photographs, magazine pictures, paper, yarn, paint, crayons	○	●	●	●	●	●	●	●	●
Painting									
Express individual ideas, thoughts, and feelings through painting	○	●	●	●	●	●	●	●	●
Create an artwork using a variety of painting tools and materials such as tempera or liquid school acrylic, brushes, string, fingers, sponges, found objects, paper	○	●	●	●	●	●	●	●	●
Printmaking									
Express individual ideas, thoughts, and feelings through printmaking	○	●	●	●	●	●	●	●	●
Create an artwork using a variety of printmaking tools and materials such as tempera or liquid school acrylic, brushes, string, fingers, sponges, found objects, paper	○	●	●	●	●	●	●	●	●
Sculpture									
Express individual ideas, thoughts, and feelings through sculpture	○	●	●	●	●	●	●	●	●
Understand the differences between two-dimensional artworks and sculpture	○	●	●	●	●	●	●	●	●
Create an artwork using a variety of sculpture tools and materials for sculpture such as papier-mâché, plaster of Paris, kiln-fired clay	○	●	●	●	●	●	●	●	●
Differentiate between additive and subtractive sculpture			○	●	●	●	●	●	●

Scope and Sequence

	Levels								
	K	1	2	3	4	5	6	7	8
Textiles and Fibers									
Express individual ideas, thoughts, and feelings through textiles or fibers	○	●	●	●	●	●	●	●	●
Identify characteristics of fibers in textiles: heavy, light, smooth, rough, natural, synthetic, tightly woven, loosely woven			○	●	●	●	●	●	●
Create a textile artwork using a variety of fiber tools and materials such as yarn, string, plastic, synthetic fabric, natural fabric	○	●	●	●	●	●	●	●	●
Create a textile artwork using a variety of methods: weaving, knotting, batik, stitchery	○	●	●	●	●	●	●	●	●
Technology and Photographic Imagery									
Express individual ideas, thoughts, and feelings through photographic imagery				○	●	●	●	●	●
Create a photographic artwork using a variety of tools and materials such as sun prints, photograms, photomontages				○	●	●	●	●	●
Understand that photographic imagery can be still or motion		○	●	●	●	●	●	●	●
Understand that photographic imagery can be made with a variety of tools and materials such as still cameras, video cameras, motion picture cameras	○	●	●	●	●	●	●	●	●
Explore and examine a variety of ways that computer technology is used to create works of art	○	●	●	●	●	●	●	●	●
Simple Architectural Structures and Environmental Art									
Express individual ideas, thoughts, and feelings through simple architectural structures and environmental art	○	●	●	●	●	●	●	●	●
Recognize simple architectural structures and environmental art	○	●	●	●	●	●	●	●	●
Construct simple architectural models of structures from a variety of materials such as sticks, rocks, bricks, plastic, wood, boxes, fabric	○	●	●	●	●	●	●	●	●
Differentiate among a variety of architectural styles							○	●	●
Recognize how architectural styles relate to environmental factors: cultural traditions, aesthetic values, climates, geographic locations, types of available materials, landscapes					○	●	●	●	●
Sketchbook and Portfolio — **Keep a sketchbook to:**									
record own artworks	○	●	●	●	●	●	●	●	●
observe and evaluate development of creativity, originality, and individuality in style	○	●	●	●	●	●	●	●	●
Keep a portfolio to:									
organize own artworks	○	●	●	●	●	●	●	●	●
document, observe, and evaluate artistic development	○	●	●	●	●	●	●	●	●
Safety in the Creative Art Process — **Safety**									
Demonstrate a cautious respect for art materials and tools	○	●	●	●	●	●	●	●	●
Demonstrate caring for and cleaning art materials and tools	○	●	●	●	●	●	●	●	●

Art History

Art appreciation through historical and cultural context

Legend

○ Open circles indicate the grade where aspects are introduced.

● Shaded circles indicate the grades where aspects are developed.

Concepts

Students progressively learn and talk about contemporary and past styles and types of artworks, to include cultural origins and functions. They study themes, relative ages of artworks, reasons for creative art, art museums, careers in art, and biographical information about individual artists.

	Levels								
	K	1	2	3	4	5	6	7	8
Artistic Traditions, Past and Present									
Recognize art as a visual record of humankind	○	●	●	●	●	●	●	●	●
Focus on cultural traditions and ethnic heritage in art by recognizing images, symbols, motifs, and themes representing the art of specific cultures, traditions, and schools of artists	○	●	●	●	●	●	●	●	●
Focus on cultural traditions and ethnic heritage in art by recognizing differences among styles of art reflecting cultural tradition and ethnic heritage				○	●	●	●	●	●
Focus on historical time frames in which art was created					○	●	●	●	●
Focus on contextual information about the art of individual artists			○	●	●	●	●	●	●
Art in the Environment and Community									
Focus on the role of art museums in the community	○	●	●	●	●	●	●	●	●
Recognize the function of visual arts in the community			○	●	●	●	●	●	●
Develop an awareness of art and its origins in natural and manufactured environments				○	●	●	●	●	●
Art Careers									
Explore careers in the field of art	○	●	●	●	●	●	●	●	●
Recognize the value of art in a variety of careers	○	●	●	●	●	●	●	●	●

Art Criticism

Aesthetic valuing through initial response and evaluation

Legend

○ Open circles indicate the grade where aspects are introduced.

● Shaded circles indicate the grades where aspects are developed.

Concepts

Students progressively learn about looking at and exploring art—perceiving, analyzing, comparing, contrasting, evaluating, and judging their own and others' artworks. Positive attitudes are reinforced through thoughtful response, as well as through individual and group evaluations.

	Levels								
	K	1	2	3	4	5	6	7	8
Explore and Examine Artworks									
Selections from self and other students	○	●	●	●	●	●	●	●	●
Selections of major artists	○	●	●	●	●	●	●	●	●
Selections from home and community design	○	●	●	●	●	●	●	●	●
Focus on Contextual Clues									
Setting in which art is created				○	●	●	●	●	●
Manner and setting in which art is experienced				○	●	●	●	●	●
Focus on Functions and Purposes of Art	○	●	●	●	●	●	●	●	●
Develop a Knowledge of the Process of Art Criticism									
Discuss initial response to an artwork	○	●	●	●	●	●	●	●	●
Describe sensory qualities and technical aspects of an artwork by identifying elements of art and principles of design				○	●	●	●	●	●
Describe sensory qualities and technical aspects of an artwork by identifying media, techniques, and processes used to create artworks	○	●	●	●	●	●	●	●	●
Analyze an artwork by comparing and contrasting principles of design	○	●	●	●	●	●	●	●	●
Interpret an artist's meaning, mood, and symbolism and other expressive qualities of artwork	○	●	●	●	●	●	●	●	●
Judge an artwork and offer reasons	○	●	●	●	●	●	●	●	●

Index

Index

Chagall, Marc, 139

Chavez, Mario, 214–215

Christo and Jeanne-Claude, 185

Color. *See* Elements of Art

Comparison. *See* Look and Compare

Culture. *See* Art Background: Art and Culture; Visual Culture

Curriculum Connection. *See also* Fine Arts Connection

    Health, 71, 159

    Math, 23, 53, 87, 139, 163, 193

    Physical Education, 19, 91, 129, 207

    Science, 27, 57, 61, 95, 125, 177, 189

    Social Studies, 33, 41, 75, 101, 109, 121, 143, 155, 169, 197, 211

D

Dance. *See* Fine Arts Connection

Degas, Edgar, 128

Derain, André, 30

Describe, 19, 23, 27, 33, 37, 41, 49, 53, 57, 61, 67, 71, 75, 83, 95, 101, 105, 109, 117, 121, 125, 129, 135, 139, 143, 151, 155, 159, 169, 177, 185, 189, 193, 197, 203, 207, 211

Dimond-Cates, Lark Grey, 154

Dolbin, 51

Dürer, Albrecht, 26

E

Elements of Art

    color, 8, 17, 35, 36–37, 38–39, 40–41, 42–43, 44, 47, 51, 52, 56–57, 62–63, 71, 72–73, 129, 135, 169, 172, 191, 205, 208, 213, 221

    form, 8, 86–87, 88–89, 90–91, 92–93, 94–95, 100, 102–103, 109, 121, 129, 225

    line, 8, 12, 17, 18–19, 20–21, 22, 30, 34–35, 47, 51, 52, 69, 110, 125, 129, 135, 167, 170, 172, 177, 198, 205, 220

    shape, 8, 17, 22–23, 24–25, 28–29, 44, 47, 51, 52, 58, 61, 62–63, 69, 75, 92, 110, 121, 125, 129, 135, 136, 161, 164, 169, 170, 172, 178, 182, 198, 205, 213, 223

    space, 8, 69, 94–95, 173, 226

    texture, 8, 26–27, 28–29, 30–31, 32–33, 34–35, 47, 51, 156, 188, 224

    value, 8, 222

Emphasis. *See* Principles of Design

ESL Notes, 8, 14, 18, 23, 26, 32, 36, 40, 52, 57, 61, 67, 71, 74, 86, 90, 95, 101, 105, 109, 121, 125, 128, 134, 139, 143, 155, 158, 163, 168, 172, 176, 189, 192, 197, 203, 207, 211. *See also* Meeting Individual Needs

Estrada, Phillip, 206

Evaluating art. *See* Analyze, Describe, Interpret, Judge

Extend. *See* Meeting Individual Needs: Extend

F

Fabergé, Carl, 176

Fine Arts Connection. *See also* Curriculum Connection

    Dance, 21, 55, 63, 97, 103, 145, 161, 179, 191, 199

    Music, 29, 39, 59, 73, 93, 107, 123, 137, 165, 171, 195, 209

    Theatre, 25, 35, 43, 69, 77, 89, 111, 127, 131, 141, 157, 175, 205, 213

Fish, Janet, 40

Form. *See* Elements of Art

G

Gallery Options

    Digital gallery, 149

    Make your own frame, 81

    Jewelry exhibition, 183

Index

Index

National Visual Arts Standards

Content Standards	Page Numbers
(K–4) #1 Understanding and applying media, techniques, and process	
• Students know the differences between materials, techniques, and processes. • Students describe how different materials, techniques, and processes cause different responses. • Students use different media, techniques, and processes to communicate ideas, experiences, and stories. • Students use art materials and tools in a safe and responsible manner.	8, 9, 12, 13, 14, 15, 20, 21, 24, 25, 28, 29, 34, 35, 38, 39, 42, 43, 46, 47, 48, 49, 54, 55, 58, 59, 62, 63, 68, 69, 72, 73, 76, 77, 80, 81, 82, 83, 88, 89, 92, 93, 96, 97, 102, 103, 106, 107, 110, 111, 114, 115, 116, 117, 122, 123, 126, 127, 130, 131, 136, 137, 140, 141, 144, 145, 148, 149, 150, 151, 156, 157, 160, 161, 164, 165, 170, 171, 174, 175, 178, 179, 182, 183, 184, 185, 190, 191, 194, 195, 198, 199, 204, 205, 208, 209, 212, 213, 216, 217, 218, 219
(K–4) #2 Using knowledge of structures and functions	
• Students know the differences among visual characteristics and purposes of art in order to convey ideas. • Students describe how different expressive features and organizational principles cause different responses. • Students use visual structures and functions of art to communicate ideas.	8, 9, 10, 11, 18, 19, 26, 27, 32, 33, 36, 37, 40, 41, 48, 49, 52, 53, 60, 61, 66, 67, 70, 71, 74, 75, 82, 83, 86, 87, 90, 91, 94, 95, 104, 105, 108, 109, 116, 117, 120, 121, 124, 125, 128, 129, 134, 135, 142, 143, 150, 151, 154, 155, 158, 159, 168, 169, 172, 173, 176, 177, 184, 185, 188, 189, 192, 193, 196, 197, 202, 203, 206, 207, 210, 211, 218, 219
(K–4) #3 Choosing and evaluating a range of subject matter, symbols and ideas	
• Students explore and understand prospective content for works of art. • Students select and use subject matter, symbols, and ideas to communicate meaning.	6, 7, 10, 11, 12, 13, 14, 15, 20, 21, 24, 25, 28, 29, 34, 35, 38, 39, 42, 43, 46, 47, 54, 55, 62, 63, 72, 73, 76, 77, 80, 81, 88, 89, 92, 93, 96, 97, 102, 103, 106, 107, 110, 111, 114, 115, 122, 123, 130, 131, 144, 145, 148, 149, 156, 157, 160, 161, 164, 165, 170, 171, 174, 175, 178, 179, 182, 183, 190, 191, 194, 195, 198, 199, 204, 205, 208, 209, 212, 213, 216, 217

National Visual Arts Standards

Content Standards	Page Numbers
(K–4) #4 Understanding the visual arts in relation to history and cultures	
• Students know that the visual arts have both a history and specific relationships to various cultures. • Students identify specific works of art as belonging to particular cultures, times, and places. • Students demonstrate how history, culture, and the visual arts can influence each other in making and studying works of art.	21, 50, 52, 53, 56, 57, 66, 67, 74, 75, 84, 85, 98, 99, 100, 101, 104, 105, 108, 109, 118, 119, 120, 121, 124, 125, 142, 143, 162, 163, 166, 167, 176, 177, 188, 189, 196, 197, 200, 201, 202, 203, 210, 211
(K–4) #5 Reflecting upon and assessing the characteristics and merits of their work and the work of others	
• Students understand there are various purposes for creating works of visual art. • Students describe how people's experiences influence the development of specific artworks. • Students understand there are different responses to specific artworks.	8, 9, 10, 11, 12, 13, 16, 17, 18, 19, 20, 21, 22, 23, 24, 25, 26, 27, 28, 29, 30, 31, 32, 33, 34, 35, 36, 37, 38, 39, 40, 41, 42, 43, 44, 45, 48, 49, 50, 51, 52, 53, 54, 55, 56, 57, 58, 59, 60, 61, 62, 63, 64, 65, 66, 67, 68, 69, 70, 71, 72, 73, 74, 75, 76, 77, 78, 79, 80, 81, 82, 83, 84, 85, 86, 87, 88, 89, 90, 91, 92, 93, 94, 95, 96, 97, 98, 99, 100, 101, 102, 103, 104, 105, 106, 107, 108, 109, 110, 111, 112, 113, 114, 115, 116, 117, 118, 119, 120, 121, 122, 123, 124, 125, 128, 129, 130, 131, 132, 133, 134, 135, 138, 139, 140, 141, 144, 145, 146, 147, 148, 149, 150, 151, 152, 153, 154, 155, 156, 157, 158, 159, 160, 161, 162, 163, 164, 165, 166, 167, 168, 169, 170, 171, 178, 179, 180, 181, 182, 183, 184, 185, 186, 187, 188, 189, 190, 191, 192, 193, 194, 195, 196, 197, 198, 199, 200, 201, 202, 203, 204, 205, 206, 207, 208, 209, 210, 211, 212, 213, 214, 215, 216, 217, 218, 219
(K–4) #6 Making connections between visual arts and other disciplines	
• Students understand and use similarities and differences between characteristics of the visual arts and other arts disciplines. • Students identify connections between the visual arts and other disciplines in the curriculum.	16, 17, 18, 19, 22, 23, 26, 27, 32, 33, 40, 41, 56, 57, 60, 61, 74, 75, 78, 79, 86, 87, 90, 91, 94, 95, 100, 101, 104, 105, 108, 109, 120, 121, 124, 125, 128, 129, 134, 135, 138, 139, 142, 143, 146, 147, 154, 155, 162, 163, 168, 169, 172, 173, 176, 177, 180, 181, 188, 189, 192, 193, 196, 197, 202, 203, 206, 207, 210, 211, 214, 215

Notes

Notes

Notes